African AND African American Children's AND Adolescent Literature IN THE Classroom

Rochelle Brock and Richard Greggory Johnson III
Executive Editors

Vol. 11

The Black Studies and Critical Thinking series
is part of the Peter Lang Education list.
Every volume is peer reviewed and meets
the highest quality standards for content and production.

PETER LANG
New York • Washington, D.C./Baltimore • Bern
Frankfurt • Berlin • Brussels • Vienna • Oxford

African AND African American Children's AND Adolescent Literature IN THE Classroom

A CRITICAL GUIDE

EDITED BY
Vivian Yenika-Agbaw & Mary Napoli

PETER LANG
New York • Washington, D.C./Baltimore • Bern
Frankfurt • Berlin • Brussels • Vienna • Oxford

Library of Congress Cataloging-in-Publication Data

African and African American children's and adolescent
literature in the classroom: a critical guide / edited by
Vivian Yenika-Agbaw, Mary Napoli.
p. cm. — (Black studies and critical thinking; v. 11)
Includes bibliographical references and index.
1. American literature—African American authors—Study and teaching.
2. Young adult literature, American—Study and teaching.
3. Children's literature, American—Study and teaching.
4. Blacks in literature. I. Yenika-Agbaw, Vivian S. II. Napoli, Mary.
PS153.N5A3375   810.9'928208996073—dc23   2011028971
ISBN 978-1-4331-1196-9 (hardcover)
ISBN 978-1-4331-1195-2 (paperback)
ISSN 1947-5985

Bibliographic information published by **Die Deutsche Nationalbibliothek**.
Die Deutsche Nationalbibliothek lists this publication in the "Deutsche
Nationalbibliografie"; detailed bibliographic data is available
on the Internet at http://dnb.d-nb.de/.

The paper in this book meets the guidelines for permanence and durability
of the Committee on Production Guidelines for Book Longevity
of the Council of Library Resources.

Contents

Acknowledgments   ix

INTRODUCTION: Domestic and International Multiculturalism:
  Children's Literature about Africans and African Americans   xi
  Vivian Yenika-Agbaw & Mary Napoli

SECTION I: BLACK MULTICULTURAL LITERATURE THAT TARGETS PRE-K–3

CHAPTER 1: Fathers Know Best: Traditional Families in Recently Published
  African American Children's Literature for the Early Grades   3
  Ruth McKoy Lowery

CHAPTER 2: Powerful Words: Celebrating Poetry with Young Children   18
  Mary Napoli

CHAPTER 3: Representing Cultural Identity in Children's Literature:
  Black Children in Their Communities   33
  Janet Helmberger

CHAPTER 4: Spirituality and Young Children: Literature
  as a Support for Resilience and Coping   45
  Patricia Crawford

CHAPTER 5: Sharing Culturally Relevant Literature with Preschool
Children and Their Families   59
April Whatley Bedford & Renée Casbergue

SECTION II: BLACK MULTICULTURAL LITERATURE
THAT TARGETS UPPER ELEMENTARY AND MIDDLE GRADES: 4–8

CHAPTER 6: "I Want My Mama!": Young Black Adolescents
Reading through the Grief   75
Shanetia Clark & Kimetta Hairston

CHAPTER 7: African American Female Literacies and the Role
of Double Dutch in the Lives and Literature for Black Girls   90
Rachel Grant

CHAPTER 8: Discrimination and Preadolescence:
Two Readers' Constructions   106
Ann Berger-Knorr

CHAPTER 9: Daring to Dream: Characters in Coretta Scott King
Author Award-Winning Books and Their Pursuits
of the American Dream   122
Linda T. Parsons & Michele D. Castleman

CHAPTER 10: Representing Black Experiences: Engaging Hearts
and Minds with Excellent Nonfiction Literature   139
Barbara Marinak

CHAPTER 11: Riddles as Critical Thinking Tools: A Case of African
Traditional Oral Literature in the Social Studies Classroom   157
Lewis Asimeng-Boahene

SECTION III: BLACK MULTICULTURAL LITERATURE
THAT TARGETS HIGH SCHOOL GRADES: 9–12

CHAPTER 12: Reading "Black" Poverty in Postcolonial Anglophone
Caribbean Young Adult Fiction: Michael Anthony's *The Year in San
Fernando* and Cyril Everard Palmer's *The Cloud with the Silver Lining*   173
Denise Jarrett

CHAPTER 13: Alternative Families in Young Adult Novels:
    Disrupting the Status Quo   191
    Corinna Crafton

CHAPTER 14: Disability in Africana Adolescent Literature   209
    Vivian Yenika-Agbaw

CHAPTER 15: Lessons on Discrimination: Historical Fiction   219
    and the Culture of Struggle
    Lauren Lewis

CHAPTER 16: Keeping Hope Alive: Reading and Discussing
    Adolescent Novels and Modern-Day Miracles   233
    Barbara A. Ward & Deanna Day

CHAPTER 17: The Exoticizing of African American Children
    and of Children of Color: Care Work and Critical Literacy   251
    Tamara Lindsey

    Afterword: Global Literacy: Implications for the Classroom   265
    Mary Napoli & Vivian Yenika-Agbaw

    Appendix: Listing of African American and Small Multicultural   271
    Children's Book Publishers

    Contributors   273

    Index   281

Acknowledgments

This professional contribution would not have been possible without the support of our family, friends, colleagues, administrators, and the interlibrary loan staff at The Pennsylvania State University, who made sure Vivian had access to the relevant professional resources in a timely manner. In addition, a special thanks goes to the library staff at The Pennsylvania State University–Harrisburg for assisting Mary with materials and children's books.

We also wish to thank Dr. Richard Johnson III for his guidance and patience throughout this project, beginning with the proposal. We would like to also thank Dr. Kathy Short, who agreed, despite the short notice, to review the manuscript, as well as thank the editorial team at Peter Lang. A book is nothing without the dedication of the authors; for that reason, we wish to thank all the contributors who worked diligently on their papers to make this project a reality.

A version of "Domestic and International Multiculturalism" has appeared in Write4Children. We are grateful for permission to include it in this book.

We owe a lot of gratitude to our families. [Vivian and Mary]

Special thanks to Ekema, Yenik, Luma, and Joy for their encouragement as always and their unconditional love and support. [Vivian Yenika-Agbaw, PhD]

Finally, a special thank you to my sister, Victoria Yahner, and my parents, Josephine and Patrick Napoli, for their encouragement and unconditional love and support. [Mary Napoli, PhD]

Domestic and International Multiculturalism

Children's Literature about Africans and African Americans

Vivian Yenika-Agbaw & Mary Napoli

Children's literature, as many educators can attest, does make a difference in children's lives, for not only does it entertain, it stretches children's imagination, reminds them of their humanity, and exposes them to other cultures (Norton, 2011; Temple, Martinez, Yokota, & Naylor, 2002; Lynch-Brown & Tomlinson 2005). In addition, Rudine Sims (1982) notes that literature should also serve a social function, helping children develop a sense of self.

With such a high premium placed on children's literature, selecting books to include in one's library collection or literacy curriculum, therefore, requires great care and thought, especially when it involves choosing books that reflect our diverse cultures. This is not necessarily because the books are not there. However, for some reason, despite the availability of appropriate resources such as Violet Harris' (1997) *Using Multiethnic Literature in K–8 Classroom*, which clearly identifies some basic criteria to consider for this purpose, some classroom teachers, like most pre-service teachers we have worked with, remain unsure as to how to select such books. When uncertainty sets in, as Henderson (2005) observes about a former student's experience, some may simply fill the void in their curriculum with classic stories with which they were familiar while growing up. Although this is a good survival strategy because classics are celebrated within our educational and scholarly community for their artistic and aesthetic merit, some contain cultural content that may be problematic. Therefore, the story may be well-written and quite entertaining, but the characters and what they represent may be troubling, especially to young readers who look like these fictional characters.

This strategy of falling back on an old classic tale can be a nightmare to teacher educators, since most of us, like Henderson, take the trouble to expose student teachers to a variety of books about our diverse cultures and to a cross-section of professional resources that would facilitate the process as well. However, when a former student—now a teacher—is still unable to select wisely, it can be frustrating and disturbing as we learn from Henderson's experience. For example, Henderson could not understand how a former student (now a teacher in her own right) would actually think that by including *Little Black Sambo* in her curriculum, she was indeed exposing children to African American culture. Although Henderson eventually helped her figure things out, not many schoolteachers have direct access to professors who are willing to patiently guide them *again* through the process of selecting books; neither do most remain in touch with their professors nor have the resources to take advanced literature courses or workshops where this exposure would occur. The situation can be complicated further when teachers have to decide on the cultural relevance of books to their curriculum identified as international literature and those labeled multicultural. This notwithstanding, we argue that schoolteachers should include both sets of literature in their curriculum, especially as it pertains to black culture. It is the only way they would get a comprehensive understanding of who blacks are, the cultural origins of their traditions, and fate as a people vis-à-vis Eurocentric cultures. We begin by explaining our definitions of international and domestic multiculturalism; then we demonstrate one way teachers can integrate both types of literature in their classrooms as we focus specifically on literature about African and African Americans. We conclude the essay with a general discussion on the advantages of incorporating both types of literature in the K–8 curriculum.

CHILDREN'S LITERATURE:
INTERNATIONAL AND DOMESTIC MULTICULTURALISM

What exactly is international children's literature? To Freeman and Lehman (2001), this type of literature basically is published in countries outside of the United States. Many perceive this literature culturally diverse primarily because it reflects multiple experiences and cultures across the globe. Some educators in the United States, however, are skeptical of this kind of diversity, partly because American society already reflects an array of cultures from racial and ethnic categories through gender and lifestyle considerations (Temple et al., 2002).

In their book *Global Perspectives in Children's Literature*, Freeman and Lehman (2001) not only clarify this issue but also provide pertinent information about international children's literature and its importance to the understanding of our global cultural diversity. To them, education should "foster children's understanding and appreciation for others so they can actively participate as citizens in a global community" (p. 12). One way teachers can promote this kind of understanding, they believe, is through international children's literature. Despite this benefit to the curriculum, many schoolteachers are still not familiar with international children's literature, especially texts that originate from non-Eurocentric traditions.[1] Perhaps this lack of awareness is partly due to the fact that international literature may inadvertently "compete" with multicultural literature—literature many in the United States believe truly reflects our cultural reality as "Americans"—hence this emphasizes what we may refer to as domestic diversity.

Temple et al. (2002) define multicultural literature as "literature that reflects the multitude of cultural groups within the United States" (p. 84). They argue that although they see value in an "inclusive definition, . . . a broad definition dilutes the focus" (p. 84). We understand perfectly what they mean; however, they make it sound as though global diversity and domestic diversity are competing for space within the American school curriculum. This should not be so. Norton (2005), on the other hand, advocates a much more inclusive definition focusing exclusively on ethnicity without necessarily distinguishing global from domestic diversity. From her perspective, the two forms of cultural diversity are interdependent. We find her definition particularly interesting, especially when she makes the connection between the cultures of the old world, as in Africa, and those of the new world, as in America. She remarks that "our journey through the study of African American literature includes both the literature from Africa and from the Americas" and that "African American traditional literature . . . cannot be understood and appreciated without also studying the literature that provides the foundations for it; namely African folklore" (p. 15). Thus, like Freeman and Lehman, she acknowledges a certain interconnectedness among cultures, in this case, between African and African American.

In his article "Multicultural Literature and the Politics of Reaction," Joel Taxel (2003) takes the debate one step further, providing a slightly more complex definition of multicultural literature advanced by Cai and Bishop. For these children's literature scholars, there are three kinds: "World literature, Cross-cultural literature, and Parallel literature" (as quoted by Cai & Bishop, 1994, pp. 65–67, 144). Each of these three can therefore be considered multicultural literature depending on the individual and his or her purpose. Without necessarily rejecting this view, Taxel (2003) simply reminds educators and authors of their social responsibility to all children. This means, despite our lack of consensus as to how the term should be defined, or how the concept should be implemented in practice, we may still be held accountable. And as Cai (2003) adds, we must never lose sight of the fact that books do impact children in ways that many may not realize.

We gather from this debate then that inasmuch as African American literature and literature set in Africa emphasize different cultural experiences in their capacities as multicultural and international literatures, it is still important to read them simultaneously. We believe that regardless of how educators reconfigure the cultural diversity landscape, there will still be an overlap among cultures, especially between African and African American literary traditions (Harris, 1997; Norton, 2005). In this case, literature set in Africa, although considered rightly as international literature, continues to be relevant to our overall understanding of African American culture and people. We are not arguing here that African and African American cultures are one and the same; rather, we are suggesting that to fully understand black experience as a collective whole, it is important to read the international version of its literature vis-à-vis the domestic version. In the closing chapter of their edited book, Henderson and May (2005) share a dialogue they had with Dianne Johnson, a children's literature scholar and children's book author on this topic. Johnson declares that "multiculturalism has to be interpreted in terms of the cultural and linguistic diversity of the limited states and of the world" and that "multicultural children's literature, like any literature, (is) a cultural product that can help people to think about their own humanity as individuals and as members of small and large communities" (Henderson & May, 2005, p. 371). Multicultural literature, therefore, whether from a global or a domestic perspective, remains a cultural product that has tremendous value to the community at large and to the schools. What we as educators should do then is harness the benefits it provides as we seek to understand who we are right now, where we came from, and how we can make our world more accepting of everyone. It is for all these reasons that we advocate for the pairing of books about Africans with books about African Americans, in the classrooms, especially those that explore similar themes or issues.

It is true that there are some cultural differences that exist between Africans and African Americans and that there may be friction among pockets within the groups. When it comes to the school curriculum, however, black culture in general unsettles many educators just as it fascinates some. However, with consistent exposure to high-quality literature, be it international or domestic, this pervasive uneasiness and/or objectification of blackness may slowly dissipate. Thus, although literature set in Africa may not necessarily fall under the domestic category of multicultural literature, we reiterate that it is worthy of the classroom teacher's attention. Teachers need to be familiar with this body of literature in order to further understand African American children and recent African immigrants' children and how black culture has evolved over the centuries, just like they need to be well-versed with other types of multicultural literature that are available to us.[2]

A good place for teachers to start looking for possible books to include in their curriculum would be with award-winning books that depict black culture in Africa and America. Why start here, some may ask? We would go ahead and acknowledge that whether educators would admit it or not, there is something magical about awards within the American culture. For lack of a better word, they seem to add more "value" to products, ideas, professionals, and, yes, to books as well, and as Kidd (2007) notes, they "prolong the shelf life of a book" (p. 178). Sometimes, we ponder the obsession over awards. However, having taught children's literature at the college level for more than ten years, in the departments of Education and English, we have come to appreciate the warm glow on our pre-service teachers' faces when they discover that a book they liked had won an award, regardless of how minor or major the award really is. So we reckon there's some cultural value in this word and/or idea called *award*.

Some key awards given out specifically to books that portray black cultural experiences include the Coretta Scott King Award and the Children Africana Book Award. However, there are other mainstream awards in the United States such as the Newbery Medal and the Caldecott Medal, and now the Notable Books for a Global Society award, that also recognize books that have depicted African and African American cultures.[3] However, some concerns have been raised about award-winning books. In his analysis of three award-winning historical fiction novels (*Words by Heart, The Slave Dancer,* and *Roll of Thunder, Hear My Cry*), Taxel (1986) draws readers' attention to the culturally flawed content of the first two books. In doing so, he reiterates the point of balancing aesthetic consideration with cultural and historical accuracy to establish quality. This is so that the "demands for realistic, non-stereotyped characters, and for historical and cultural accuracy and authenticity in writing about the black experience, need not conflict with the demand for literary excellence" (Taxel, 1986, p. 249). Thus, when selecting literature for a unit on Africans and African Americans, like literature from other ethnic and social groups, teachers should therefore remember that cultural content is equally a great indicator of quality as literary aesthetics, regardless of whether the book in question has won an award.

REPRESENTATIONS OF BLACK CULTURE
IN CHILDREN'S AND ADOLESCENT LITERATURE

When it comes to literature about Africa—its people and cultures—like African American literature, educators are still wrestling with issues of aesthetic sensibilities, cultural authenticity, and representation (Fox & Short, 2003; Harris, 1997; Henderson, 2005; Khorana, 1994, 1998; Osa, 1995a, 1995b; Randolph, 2004; Sims, 1982, 1983; Taxel, 1986; Yenika-Agbaw, 2008). Nancy Larrick (1965) drew people's attention to this a long time ago in her article "The All-White World of Children's Books." Since then, other educators have replicated the study with similar results, or they have identified stereotypes that persist despite the small gains made over the years (Chall, Radwin, French, & Hall, 1979; MacCann & Woodard, 1972; Martin, 2004; Osa, 1995b; Sims, 1982, 1983.) Karen Sands-O'Connor (2005a, 2005b) also detects similar stereotypes about West Indian blacks in British children's literature, just like Randolph (2002, 2004), Kuntz (2005), Yenika-Agbaw (2008), and other scholars have pointed out stereotypes in books about Africa set in the United States.

Although literature for children set in Africa continues to be dominated by stereotypes (Maddy & MacCann, 1996, 2002; Osa, 1995a; Yenika-Agbaw, 2008), some of the authors attempt to capture the complexity of the cultural experiences in their books. This notwithstanding, the problem remains endemic partly because of the capitalistic nature of our society and the role publishers play in aiding and abetting this socially irresponsible behavior from otherwise talented individuals. In an interview with Cristina Kessler, an award-winning author of several children's books that are set in Africa, Brenda Randolph remarks that Kessler was "dismayed to find the appended subtitle" "A Tale from Africa" added to her title (p. 77) *The Beekeeper of Lalibela: A Tale fom Africa* (2007). The understanding then is that a sub-title that mentions the continent will sound more appealing to the average American book buyer, hence adding more commercial value to the precious picture book. Dan Hade reiterated this point, emphasizing that "80 percent of children's books are published by only eight companies" and, in addition, that corporations such as Disney and Viacom "play an enormous role in deciding which children's books will meet commercial success" (Trotter, 2007). Moreover, McNair (2008) discovered that Scholastic, one of the major book clubs for students and teachers, did not include many selections of literature written or illustrated by people of color. From all indications, then, there is no doubt that corporations inadvertently decide what needs to be published and also who should author a particular book. We are drawing attention to these issues, so teachers should also be aware of this capitalistic frenzy that has taken hold of the publishing industry, forcing us to read only *what they want us to read*.

DOMESTIC AND INTERNATIONAL MULTICULTURAL LITERATURE IN THE CLASSROOM

As schoolteachers contemplate developing a unit on Africa and African Americans, the first thing we would recommend is for them to decide on a rich theme that has both a universal and specific cultural appeal. Next, they should consult their district curriculum guidelines or the National Council of Teachers of English and the International Reading Association websites for the necessary standards as they select the necessary resources and brainstorm possible activities for the unit.

Including both domestic and international multicultural literature in one's curriculum, especially as it pertains to black culture, is necessary. Not only do these literatures provide us with possible outlets through which we can further understand black cultures in the continent and in the diaspora, they can also enable us to be acquainted further with aspects of our socio-cultural history not necessarily covered in depth in the social studies curriculum. It is such gaps in our official stories that at times create tension between Eurocentric values and black people and between blacks from the continent and blacks in America. We do not expect miracles to happen overnight, for as Dianne Johnson reminds us, "Anglo-American parents and book buyers are not, for whatever reasons, consciously or not, purchasing books with images of non-white characters" (Henderson & May, 2005, p. 371). We believe, however, that as we evolve as an inclusive society, with time this may change, and we are eagerly looking forward to that moment.

This edited volume is broken down into three sections to represent the needs of the different teaching levels: Pre-K–3, Upper Elementary and Middle Grades 4–8, and High School Grades 9–12. There are seventeen chapters excluding the Introduction and Afterword, grouped under three sections according to grade levels. These chapters explore a variety of themes with six that stand out. Cultural identity/authenticity is the primary focus in chapters 10, 11, and 17; critical literacy and disability in chapters 7 and 14; family life in chapters 1, 5, 6, and 13; hopes and dreams in chapters 9 and 16; social class/justice and/or discrimination in chapters 3 and 12; and spirituality in chapters 8, 15, and 4. In addition to identifying issues directly related to blackness and how they are constructed, contributors provide pedagogical ideas for classroom implementation. In the chapters following this Introduction, contributors share their visions of multiculturalism and literary texts and how these create possibilities in the classroom, especially when informed by theory. Each chapter provides a window through which readers may further understand the diversity in experiences of black people and cultures in literature.

While we are particularly pleased with the wide selection of texts that in a way introduces us to literary experiences of blacks in the continent and the diaspora, we are hoping that readers would take advantage of some of the theoretical lenses that inform classroom practices in all of these chapters. In so doing, we are hoping this will enable schoolteachers to reflect further on the complexity of what it means to be black in Africa and America, and across the globe. This book is a peek at the fascinating diversity amongst black communities, demonstrating how historical factors and geographical landscapes continue to shape the experiences of people of African descent in our global society.

REFERENCES

Bishop, R. S. (2007). *Free within ourselves: The development of African American children's literature.* Portsmouth, NH: Heinemann.

Botelho, M. J., & Rudman, M. K. (2009). *Critical multicultural analysis of children's literature: Mirrors, windows, and doors.* New York, NY: Routledge.

Cai, M. (2003). Multiple definitions of multicultural literature: Is the debate really just "ivory tower" bickering? In Kathy G. Short & Dana L. Fox (Eds.), *Stories matter: The complexity of cultural authenticity in children's literature* (pp. 269–283). Urbana, IL: NCTE.

Cai, M., & Sims Bishop, R. (1994). Multicultural literature for children: Towards a clarification of a concept. In A. H. Dyson & C. Denishi (Eds.), *The need for story.* Urbana, Il: National Council of Teachers of English.

Chall, J., Radwin, E., French, V., & Hall, C. (Eds.). (1979). Blacks in the world of children's books. *The Reading Teacher, 32*(5), 527–533.

Fox, D., & Short, K. (Eds.). (2003). *Stories matter: The complexity of cultural authenticity in children's literature.* Urbana, IL: NCTE.

Freeman, E., & Lehman, B. (2001). *Global perspectives in children's literature.* Boston, MA: Allyn & Bacon.

Gates, P., & Mark, D. L. H. (2006). *Cultural journeys: Multicultural literature for children and young adults.* Lanham, MD: The Scarecrow Press.

Harris, J. (Ed.). (1997). *Using multiethnic literature in the K–8 classroom.* Norwood, MA: Christopher-Gordon.

Henderson, D. (2005). Authenticity and accuracy: The continuing debate. In D. Henderson & J. May (Eds.), *Exploring culturally diverse literature for children and adolescents: Learning to listen in new ways* (pp. 266–276). Boston, MA: Allyn & Bacon.

Henderson, D., & May, J. P. (2005). Final notes: Continuing our conversation. In D. Henderson & J. May (Eds.), *Exploring culturally diverse literature for children and adolescents: Learning to listen in new ways* (pp. 369–371). Boston, MA: Allyn & Bacon.

Khorana, M. (1994). *Africa in literature for children and young adults: An annotated bibliography of English-language books.* Westport, CT: Greenwood.

Khorana, M. (Ed.). (1998). *Children's publishing in Africa: Can the colonial past be forgotten?: Critical perspectives on postcolonial African children's and young adult literature.* Westport, CT: Greenwood.

Kidd, K. (2007). Prizing children's literature: The case of Newbery gold. *Children's Literature, 35,* 166–190.

Kessler, C. (2006). *The Beekeeper of Lalibela: A Tale from Africa.* New York, NY: Holiday House.

Kuntz, P. (2005). Children's picture book about Africa: The children's Africana book awards 1992–2003.

In M. Afolayan & D. Jules (Eds.), *Current discourse on education in developing nations: Essays in honor of B. Robert Tabachnick and Robert Koehl* (pp. 289–299). New York, NY: Nova Science

Larrick, N. (1965). The all-white world of children's books. *Saturday Review, 48*, 63–85.

Lynch-Brown, C., & Tomlinson, C. (2005). *Essentials of children's literature* (5th Edition). Boston: Allyn and Bacon.

MacCann, D. (2001). *Apartheid and racism in South African children's literature, 1985–1995*. London: Routledge.

MacCann, D., & Woodard, G. (Eds.). (1972). *The black American in books for children*. Metuchen, NJ: The Scarecrow Press.

Maddy, A., & MacCann, D. (1996). *African images on juvenile literature*. Jefferson, NC: McFarland.

Maddy, Y. A., & MacCann, D. (2002). Anti-African themes in 'liberal' young adult novels. *Children's Literature Association Quarterly*, 27(2), 92–99.

Martin, M. (2004). *Brown gold: Milestones of African-American children's picture books, 1845–2002*. New York, NY: Routledge.

McNair, J. C. (2008). The representation of authors and illustrators of color in school-based book clubs. *Language Arts*, 85(3), 193–201.

Norton, D. (2005). *Multicultural children's literature: Through the eyes of many children* (2nd ed.). Columbus, Ohio: Pearson.

Norton, D., & Norton, S. (2007). *Through the eyes of a child: An introduction to children's literature* (8th Edition). Boston: Pearson.

Osa, O. (1995a). *African children's and youth literature*. New York, NY: Twayne Publishers.

Osa, O. (1995b). *The all-white world of children's books and African American children's literature*. Trenton, NJ: Africa World Press.

Randolph, B. (2002). Children's Africana book awards 2002 [Inaugural issue]. *Sankofa: Journal of African Children's and Young Adult Literature*, 59–68.

Randolph, B. (2004). Cultural authenticity and CABA 2004. *Sankofa: Journal of African Children's and Young Adult Literature, 3*, 74–82.

Randolph, B. (2007). Picture books sweep the 2007: Children's Africana Book Awards. *Sankofa: Journal of African Children's and Young Adult Literature, 3*, 74–84.

Sands-O'Connor, K. (2005a). The alphabet begins with e: England, empire, & everybody else. Paper presented at Children's Literature International Summer School (CLISS3), Roehampton University, London. August.

Sands-O'Connor, K. (2005b). Home lessons: Immigrant culture and early concept books. Paper presented at Children's Literature International Summer School (CLISS3). Roehampton University, London. August.

Sims, R. (1982). *Shadows and substance: Afro-American experience in contemporary children's books*. Urbana, IL: NCTE.

Sims, R. (1983). What happened to the "all-white" world of children's books? *Phi Delta Kappan, 65*, 650–653.

Taxel, J. (1986). The black experience in children's fiction: Controversies surrounding award winning books. Curriculum Inquiry, 16(13), 145–181.

Taxel, J. (2003). Multicultural literature and the politics of reaction. In K. Short & D. Fox (Eds.), *Stories matter: The complexity of cultural authenticity in children's literature* (pp. 143–164). Urbana, IL: NCTE.

Temple, C., Martinez, M., Yokota, J., & Naylor, A. (2002). *Children's books in children's hands: An introduction to their literature* (2nd ed.). Boston, MA: Allyn & Bacon.

Trotter, A. (2007). Story power! The impact of children's Literature. Retrieved from http://www.rps.psu.edu/unplugged/spring07/hade.html

Yenika-Agbaw, V. (2008). *Representing Africa in children's literature: Old and new ways of seeing*. New York, NY: Routledge.

NOTES

1. As a matter of fact, in "Using International Literature to Enhance the Curriculum," Clark, Cox, White, and Bluemel (2004) define international literature as "books originally written in English by authors in countries such as New Zealand, England, Australia or Canada, then published or distributed in the U. S." and as "books first published in a foreign language, then translated and published in the U.S." (unpaged in the online version of an article that was originally published in *Teacher Librarian, 31*(5), 12–15). Nowhere in their definition does a list of books published in continental Africa feature; one could only speculate that they might have insinuated this in the second half of their definition. Even then, it is not clear.

2. See suggestions on selection criteria for multicultural literature and some possible instructional ideas in Violet Harris' (1997) *Using Multiethnic Literature in the K–12 Classroom* and Pamela Gates and Dianne L. Mark's (2006) *Cultural Journeys*

3. See The American Library Association website for a complete listing; also check out the websites of the different awarding institutions for specific titles.

SECTION I

BLACK MULTICULTURAL LITERATURE THAT TARGETS PRE-K–3

CHAPTER 1

Fathers Know Best

Traditional Families in Recently Published African American Children's Literature for the Early Grades

RUTH MCKOY LOWERY

January 20, 2009, marked a historic day, when President Barack Obama took the presidential oath of office; his wife and two young daughters were proudly positioned by his side. This image of a traditional African American family—father, mother, and young children—has spurred multiple dialogues of the current state or fate of the traditional African American family. The perception that this traditional family structure is not typical of the African American culture continues to stir the debate across the United States. The first ten years of the twenty-first century has further sparked numerous roundtable discussions and debates about African American fathers and their involvement in their young children's lives (Gordon, 2010; Marks, Hopkins-Williams, Chaney, Nesteruk & Sasser, 2010; Raikes, Summers, & Roggman, 2005).

The reality of the portrait the President and his family represents for African American families is important in discussions across families, schools, communities, and all media and social spaces. The cliché that "Father knows best" seems an incongruous concept in the African American father, as the African American family is most often depicted as a family in crisis (Thomas, Krampe, & Newton, 2010). Unfortunately, this depiction permeates across all spectrums of the research. When one reads, speaks, or hears of the African American family, the popular image is that of the single mother raising several children and with an absent father who is oftentimes uninvolved in his children's lives (Coles & Green, 2010). Coles and Green (2010) posited that African American fathers are "rarely depicted as deeply embedded within and essential to their families of procreation" (p. 1); articulating further, the image of the absent father is so pervasive, when African American fathers are involved in their children's lives they are "virtually offered a Nobel Prize" (p. 1).

As a literacy teacher educator, responsible for preparing culturally responsive teachers to meet the needs of their diverse student population, I am always cognizant of the need to present contemporary issues through the medium of children's literature to my preservice teachers. In this chapter, I discuss the contemporary portrayal of African American fathers in traditional families in picture books for young children in prekindergarten to grade three. I concur with Lamorey (2010) when she articulated that "one way to add to our understanding of African American fathers is to analyze the roles of African American fathers in children's story books" (p. 280). Lamorey further noted that picture books for young children can be considered "cultural capital" for them to "value and emulate" (p. 280). Young children need to see positive representations of all structures of the African American family in the books they are exposed to, and the traditional father needs to be an evident part of this representation.

I situate this discussion within a culturally responsive pedagogical framework (Gay, 2000; Ladson-Billings, 1992). Ladson-Billings (1992) articulated that culturally responsive teachers develop the whole child, using their cultural mores and understanding to inform the teaching and learning process. Gay (2000) also found that teachers who practice culturally responsive pedagogy use "cultural knowledge, prior experiences, frames of reference, and performance styles of ethnically diverse students to make learning encounters more relevant to and effective for them" (p. 29). They practice concrete meaning-making for their students and work to provide a plethora of experiences that positively enhance their students and others' lives.

For the purposes of this discussion, I focus on the traditional African American father figure and traditional African American family in children's literature. I use the terminology "traditional father" to mean a father who shares a household with a wife and children and "traditional African American family" to mean a family consisting of father, mother, and children. I look first at the literature about African American fathers, situating it in the general research on fathers, and then I focus on the picture books for young children, limiting the discussion to books written in 2000 and beyond. Although I acknowledge the importance of honoring the diversity in different family structures (Gilmore & Bell, 2006), this chapter focuses on the traditional family. My rationale for this narrow focus is to highlight contemporary positive images of African American fathers that are being presented to children at the dawn of the twenty-first century, querying the notion that African American families are not reflective of the image President Obama and his family presents.

REPRESENTATIONS OF FATHERS:
A BRIEF LOOK AT THE RESEARCH

The topic of the African American father as a fundamental member of the traditional family is deeply embedded in the discussions about fathers in general, looking across mainstream culture to ascertain the role of fathers. Parke (2004) articulated that in "the 21st century, fathers are clearly recognized as central players in the family and major contributors to children's social, emotional, and cognitive development" (p. 456). There has also been an increase in the research on fathers' involvement in their children's development (Coley, 2003; Doherty, Kouneski, & Erickson, 1998). Gadsden and Smith (1994), in their study of the research centered on fathers, determined that such research has increased and has been more targeted on investigating fathers' involvement in their children's lives. Gadsden and Smith further posited that "implications of this body of work are that the role of fathers, and of the family itself, contributes to the affective development of children; to the shaping of personality; and eventually to a sense of belonging, meaning, and socioemotional stability" (p. 640).

The image of the married father who is involved in his children's lives is also gaining prominence in contemporary research. In their study of working-class fathers in dual-income earning families where both parents work outside of the home, Meteyer and Perry-Jenkins (2010) determined that these families constituted over 53 percent of the married couples in the United States. Thomas et al. (2010) advocated for children living in homes where both parents are present, noting the following:

> Children feel the closest to their fathers when they live with both biological parents. Although this does not mean that children do not feel close to their fathers when they do not live in the same household, it does show that a loving, two-parent household is still the optimum familial arrangement. (p. 544)

Fagan (2009) also articulated that a "growing body of research suggests that married couples experience fewer symptoms of depression, less stress, better health, and a higher sense of well-being than couples who are unmarried" (p. 259). King (2003) advocated for religion in parent involvement, asserting that religious fathers are more involved with their children.

Although a majority of African American children younger than eighteen do not live in a home with their father, this reality was not always the norm in American society. In 2004, only 33 percent of African American children lived in households where their parents were married (Coles & Green, 2010). Harris and Graham (2007) articulated that until the 1970s, over 58 percent of African American children lived in two-parent households. Marks et al. (2010) delve further historically, finding that in 1925, six of every seven black households consisted of a husband or father. Marks et al. further noted that different factors have contributed to the "eight-year decline in black married fathers" (p. 21). These factors include "an imbalanced gender ration, lack of mate availability, criminality, and many other issues" (p. 21).

As studies on fathers' involvement in their families increase, so too must the targeted studies on African American fathers. Gadsden and Smith (1994) asserted that the research focus on African American males is recent, scant, and more often "focuses typically on discussions that both characterize and put these males 'at risk,' either as learners in school or as adolescent or absent fathers" (p. 634). The research on African American fathers needs to move beyond the deficit model that is the present focus in the broader research (Baghban, 1994; Blankenhorn & Clayton, 2003). Conversations about African American fathers and their involvement in the lives of their children need to be broad in focus and must address the many layers that have persistently contributed to the absences being articulated in the literature. Factors such as racism and discrimination must be a part of the discussion that more accurately represents African American fathers and their involvement or lack thereof in their children's lives (Hall, Livingston, Henderson, Fisher, & Hines, 2007). Marks et al. (2010) found that of over seventy studies conducted since 1980 based on fathers' involvement in their children's well-being, more than 80 percent showed significant positive relationships between fathers and their children. These positive findings need to be better disseminated to the society at large.

CONTEMPORARY REPRESENTATIONS
OF FATHERS IN PICTURE BOOKS

Children's literature is a vital instrument in the education process for young children. It is also a great tool for examining family relationships (Quinn, 2009). Before children can decipher letters and sounds, they are bombarded with images in picture books as parents, teachers, librarians, and others read to them and help them make sense of their world. McNair (2008) positioned that children's literature "functions as an important tool in the educative process within schools, and it serves to socialize children and shape their values, cultural norms, and worldviews" (p. 3). It is important to understand how fathers are portrayed in books for young children because these books could provide cultural and symbolic information that men might use to construct their identity as a father (Quinn, 2009). It can also be the catalyst that helps others see the positive representations in books and further authenticate the realization that fathers, particularly African American fathers, are involved in their children's lives.

In an analysis of 200 picture books for young children representing families, Anderson and Hamilton (2005) found stereotypical portrayals of parents and determined that fathers were "significantly under-represented, and they were presented as unaffectionate and as indolent in terms of feeding, carrying babies, and talking with children" (p. 149). As a contrast, in her examination of the representations of fathers in Caldecott Award winning books from 1938 to 2002, Quinn (2006) found that fathers provided more verbal affection, taught children, and played with them more than mothers.

Gilmore and Bell (2006) affirmed that the image of the traditional family is still dominant in children's literature, but they argue that families are not what they used to be fifty years ago and advocate for a diverse perspective where children can see other family structures represented in picture books shared with them. With these varying representations of fathers in children's literature, it is important then to appreciate the importance for this further exploration of the representation of African American fathers in picture books for young children. LaFaye and Hendrickson (2001) posited that the absence of strong father figures in children's literature is most noticeable in books about African American families than any other group. Given the research discussed about the presence and/or absence of African American fathers, I wanted to focus on books about traditional African American fathers in positive portrayals in picture books. Referring back to President Obama and his family, I wanted to identify those stories that shine a positive light on fathers who are present in the home and are actively involved in their children's lives. I wanted to represent stories of those "Nobel Prize" winners articulated by Coles and Green (2010).

THE BOOKS: STORIES FOR THE EARLY YEARS

In my search to find positive and engaging contemporary literature portraying traditional African American fathers, I explored various databases, for example, the Database for Award-Winning Children's Literature (DAWCL) and the Children's Literature Comprehensive Database (CLCD). I then perused the local library to determine availability of books. I first gathered all the books that featured an African American father in the story, sorting through the forty-three books gathered to separate books that were published in 2000 and beyond. I did a quick read of these books to determine how the families were structured in the stories. Because the goal was to find stories that were written at the beginning of the twenty-first century, the selection was further narrowed to separate those books that were appropriate, those that represented a positive story about the traditional father figure.

Eleven books from the collection met three basic requirements: (a) they were published in 2000 or after, (b) they were suitable for preschool to grade three children, and (c) they represent contemporary African American fathers in a traditional family. Nine of the eleven books were written by African American authors and two by white female authors (see Table 1). Of the nine books, seven were written by females and two by males. Two female authors, Nikki Grimes and Angela Johnson, each wrote two books. Eight of the eleven titles were illustrated by African American males, with E. B. Lewis illustrating three. The remaining three books were illustrated by two white females and one white male.

I reread through each book several times to determine feasibility, themes, and overall representation of positive images of African American fathers. In the remainder of this chapter I discuss the eleven books, focusing on three larger subcategories determined from multiple readings of the stories: Fathers as captains: Daddy knows best; Adventuring with Dad: Oh the places we will go; and Fathers as anchors: Always my Daddy. I bring to bear Kelly's (2009) assertion that children's books are "widely recognized as a reflection of cultural conceptions of gender roles, parenting, and family relationships" (p. 109), in my sense-making of positive representations of contemporary African American fathers in children's literature.

FATHERS AS CAPTAINS: DADDY KNOWS BEST

A common representation of the fathers as the captain or leader in the family is often noted in various settings: "If daddy is there, everything will be alright." "Daddy can make it better." Don't worry; daddy will take care of it." These are some of the sentiments often attributed to fathers who are there for their children. Five of the eleven books fit this category.

In *You Can Do It* (2008), written by Tony Dungy, Linden envies his brother and sisters because they know exactly what they want to be when they grow up. When his teacher asks him what he dreams of being someday, Linden has no idea and unwittingly replies, "Maybe a duck?" (unpaged). This, of course, gets him in trouble, as the teacher calls home. All he seems to do is constantly get in trouble and the main reason does not seem to be his nagging toothache. When his father queries the real reason for his sadness, Linden admits to being sad because he does not know his "it," what he wants to be when he grows up. Dad reassures him that when the time is right, he will find his dream. Desiring to alleviate his worry, dad takes Linden to his science lab on their way to the dentist the next morning. At the dentist, Linden learns a lot about dentistry, and a few weeks later, he shares his new knowledge with his classmates. Linden discovers his passion and tries to find his "it," as his father encourages him to "dream big." Dad is the gentle anchor that keeps Linden steady during his tumultuous drifting. It is his initiative to comfort Linden that soon sets the boy on the wonderful path of discovery toward identifying his "it."

TABLE 1. Children's Literature Portraying African American Fathers in Traditional Families

Author	M/F	Race	Title	Illustrator	M/F	Race
Asim, Jabari	M	AA	*Daddy Goes to Work* (2006)	Aaron Boyd	M	AA
Dungy, Tony	M	AA	*You Can Do It* (2008)	Amy June Bates	F	W
Frame, Jeron Ashford	F	AA	*Yesterday I Had the Blues* (2003)	R. Gregory Christie	M	AA
Grimes, Nikki	F	AA	*When Daddy Prays* (2002)	Tim Ladwig	M	W
Grimes, Nikki	F	AA	*Welcome, Precious* (2006)	Bryan Collier	M	AA
Johnson, Angela	F	AA	*Down the Winding Road* (2000)	Shane W. Evans	M	AA
Johnson, Angela	F	AA	*Lily Brown's Paintings* (2007)	E. B. Lewis	M	AA
Kurtz, Jane	F	W	*Faraway Home* (2000)	E. B. Lewis	M	AA
McQuinn, Anna	F	W	*Lola Loves Stories* (2010)	Rosalind Beardshaw	F	W
Nelson, Vaunda Micheaux	F	AA	*Who Will I Be Lord?* (2009)	Sean Qualls	M	AA
Tarpley, Natasha Anastasia	F	AA	*Bippity Bop Barbershop* (2002)	E. B. Lewis	M	AA

Key: M/F (males/females), Race (AA: African American; W: White)

Nikki Grimes, in *When Daddy Prays* (2002), presents a beautiful collection of poems highlighting the love, faith, and hope a young boy experiences in his daily life as he watches his father in action and listens to him pray. He awakens some nights to hear daddy praying with tears in his voice; he models his father's clothes standing before the mirror, dreaming of the day the clothes will fit; he jealously listens to his father praying over his baby brother until he realizes that his father is also praying for him; when he becomes ill, his father soothes his pain, whispering a prayer for him. Each poem reinforces the young boy's faith in the power and might of his father. He knows that everything will be alright; his anchor is affirmed when his daddy prays. Daddy is constantly thinking of his well-being and is willing to do everything to keep his son safe and make him happy.

In *Welcome, Precious* (2006), Nikki Grimes presents the story of happy parents who excitedly welcome a new baby into their home. They lovingly introduce their baby to the sights and sounds of a world wrapped in rainbows: the robin's song, leaves swishing in the breeze, the sun and moon, grandmother's kisses, and so much more for little baby to enjoy. Throughout the story, the father actively participates in all facets of his new baby's life. He lovingly wraps the young baby in his arms and is ever attentive and involved in the baby's development.

Jane Kurtz creates a similar story of reassurance in *Faraway Home* (2000). Desta's father has received word that his mother is ill and he must go home to Ethiopia to visit her. Desta is worried that her father will fall in love again with his homeland and won't come back to the United States, and more importantly, to her. Her father soothes her uncertainties by reminiscing about his childhood growing up. When Desta worries that Ethiopia is too far away, her father encourages her to close her eyes and she vicariously experiences his childhood through his stories. Daddy promises to tell Desta stories about his homeland every night until he leaves, but he also reassures her that when he returns, he will have "new stories to tell" (unpaged). Desta's father soothes her uncertainties and reassures her that he will return to her. She determines to "hold his stories in her heart" (unpaged) until he does.

In *Bippity Bop Barbershop* (Tarpley, 2002), Miles is excited to get his first haircut at the barbershop, but he is also a little scared. With Mama and sister Keyana still asleep, he and daddy have the house to themselves as they prepare for the big event. They "dress in matching blue jeans and gym shoes" (unpaged) as they get ready for the important day. They stop for breakfast at Jack's Sweet Shop. Everyone tells him to be brave but he doesn't understand why. When the time comes for the actual haircut, however, he gets nervous. When Mr. Seymour, the barber, asks what style he wants, Miles decides he wants his hair to look just like his dad's: "Cut low on top and shaved clean all around, just like his" (unpaged). Miles and daddy hum a happy "bippity bop" tune as they walk home, "two cool cats, side by side" (unpaged). Although getting a haircut is scary, Miles relies on the strength and presence of his dad. With his father by his side, Miles soon learns there is nothing to be afraid of and enjoys every part of the thrilling experience.

All five stories in this category highlighted proud fathers who stood tall as they actively participated in their children's lives. Fathers alleviated their children's fears and reassured them with their presence that all will be well. The fathers proved to be the captain and leader for their children. They knew best how to solve problems that arose. Their presence in these children's lives was significant. Threaded throughout the stories were images of fathers hugging, cuddling, listening, and just being there for their children. Linden's father in *You Can Do It* was willing to share his youthful vulnerability to alleviate his son's worries, when he told him that he didn't know what he wanted to be when he was Linden's age. He assures Linden that he still has plenty of time to figure it out. Like Linden's father, Desta's father in *Faraway Home* alleviates her fears by taking her concerns seriously and providing an outlet for her. In so doing, he helps Desta enjoy the last days at home with him before he leaves for Ethiopia. *When Daddy Prays* presents a father who believes strongly in interceding for his children. He tries to lead by example, and his son is reassured when he consistently witnesses his father doing something that seems rather natural. *Welcome, Precious* illuminates a father who actively participates in his new child's life, helping to awaken this child to the wonders of the world around. Finally, Miles, in *Bippity Bop Barbershop,* shares a loving relationship with his family, but he gets to have a wonderful rite of passage experience with his father; all attention is focused on him.

ADVENTURING WITH DAD: OH THE PLACES WE WILL GO

Young children find it exciting to go on adventures with their fathers. They bask in the special attention given them. Three of the books aptly fit this category, as they presented stories of young children traveling with their fathers to memorable places. In *Daddy Goes to Work* (Asim, 2006), a young girl tells about spending the day with her father at his office (Take Your Child to Work Day). After she and daddy ride the subway together, she meets his coworkers and they all know her name. She is proud to see that her father has the family's pictures displayed on the walls of his office. Her father tells his workers that they have a new boss as "Today my daughter runs the show" (unpaged). She helps him write a memo to his client overseas, and at midday, they head outside for lunch and a walk through the park. After lunch she helps daddy conduct a meeting in the conference room. At five o'clock, they call mom and tell her they are on their way home. The daughter is very proud of her father and the work they did together.

Lola in *Lola Loves Stories* (McQuinn, 2010) also ventures out with her father as he takes her to the library every Saturday. As daddy and mommy read stories to Lola, she aesthetically lives through the experiences. She transforms into a fairy princess after daddy reads a story about a fairy princess. She goes on an amazing journey to Paris and Lagos after her mother reads a story about an amazing journey. The excitement never ends as Lola discovers new adventures in the pages of her books. After daddy reads a story about a wild and wicked monster, we know what Lola will be tomorrow.

Down the Winding Road (Johnson, 2000) also presents an adventure, as a father takes his young son and daughter from the city out to the country for their annual summer visit to see the Old Ones, the seven aunts and uncles who raised him. The children are excited to spend time with their elders, learn about their father's escapades as a young child, and just enjoy the countryside. When it's time to go back to the city, they start missing the relatives as they travel the winding road back home.

All three stories positively illuminated the excitement and wonder of young children going on a journey with their fathers. In *Daddy Goes to Work,* the father's pleasant disposition shows that he is having a wonderful day with his daughter. He involves her in all his activities throughout the day, and he even checks in at the end of day to ascertain that she indeed had a great time. *Lola Loves Stories* presents a refreshing story of a father who is deeply involved in his daughter's literacy development. He takes her to the library and then he animatedly reads to her, sparking her imagination in living through the story. In *Down the Winding Road,* the father maintains connections with his elders and ensures that his children do the same. The children are very familiar with them and can recollect stories they have heard over the years. They express sadness when it's time to say goodbye, ascertaining that they had a good time visiting. Their fond memories of the vacation will fortify them until the next trip back down the winding road.

FATHERS AS ANCHORS: ALWAYS MY DADDY

As young children in traditional families go through various stages of growing up, they come to realize that daddy is there for them no matter what. This fact is sometimes taken for granted, as children may be accustomed to always having their fathers there, hovering in the background, coming to their aid, offering solace, or just simply being their father or daddy. The final three books fit this category.

In *Yesterday I Had the Blues* (Frame, 2003), a young boy realizes everyone in his family goes through various moods, depicted through an array of colors, from shades of blue, to gray, to pink, to red. One day he awakes with "those deep down in my shoes blues, the go away, Mr. Sun, quit smilin' at me blues" (unpaged). The next day all is green and it is the kind of green, that makes him "want to be somebody" (unpaged). He knows all is not well when "Daddy says he got the grays. . . . The don't ask for a new skateboard till tomorrow grays" (unpaged). He feels sorry for "poor daddy" who has been cited for parking in a no-parking zone, an inconvenient added expense the family could obviously do without. As he experiences the various moods of each family member, he determines that it is okay because, "We got a family—the kind of family makes you feel like it's all golden" (unpaged).

Young Lily, in *Lily Brown's Paintings* (Johnson, 2007), loves the wonderful world she lives in with her mother, father, and baby brother, but when she paints, her world begins to change. Lily vicariously escapes to exciting places and times through her paintings. In her artistic world, anything is possible as the universe becomes "one big colorful splash" (unpaged) as stars come down to dance and alligators communicate by phone. When Lily returns from her adventures, she "remembers her mama's smile, her daddy's eyes, and the way her baby brother holds her hand before he goes to sleep" (unpaged), and she knows her loving family is still there for her. All is well in Lily's world.

In *Who Will I Be Lord?* (Nelson, 2009), a young girl struggles to decide what she will be when she grows up. She reflects on her great-grandparents, grandparents, parents, and other relatives, but she still cannot decide who she would like to emulate. Great-grandfather was a musician, grandmother a teacher, and grandfather a preacher. Her father is a mechanic who willingly helps his neighbors when they cannot afford to pay him. She loves to "curl up beside him" (unpaged) when he comes home from work even though, when he takes off his boots, his "feet are a little stinky" (unpaged). Her mother, too, is always busy helping others. In the end, she decides to follow mother's advice that it's all up to her to decide what she will be when she grows up.

The stories in this category mainly represented examples of fathers who were anchors for their children, not always visible but always working behind the scenes. In the three stories, the fathers remained in the background, but the children knew they were there at all times. In *Yesterday I Had the Blues*, the young boy recognized the reasons his father had the "grays." A parking ticket meant daddy would have to spend money he was not planning to. Thus, he knew it would not be a good time to ask for a new skateboard. He understands his father's frustration and voices his empathy, "Poor Daddy" (unpaged). In *Lily Brown's Paintings*, Lily gets to experience life through her paintings, but her family is always in the background. She is secure in this realization, so she has no fear journeying through time, experiencing the pleasures of growing up without a worry or care for her daily existence. Her daddy's eyes are always there. In *Who Will I Be Lord?* The young girl enjoys curling up by her father even when he has just come home tired and exhausted from work. Her father has a kind heart and helps others. She shares that almost "everybody in town owes Papa money" (unpaged), but Mama tells people to leave him alone when they complain that it was "bad business." Her father is a positive example following in the footsteps of his forefathers.

CONCLUSION

The eleven books discussed in this chapter clearly illuminated positive representations of African American fathers in traditional families. Again, after reviewing the research on African American fathers, the focus of this chapter was to highlight children's books that offered a positive story about the role of the father in traditional family relationships. It was interesting to discover that a large majority of the stories were written by people of the culture. In her research on culturally responsive pedagogy, Gay (2000) found that the "quantity and variety of culturally validating books, written in authentic voices and providing insider perspectives, are numerous for African Americans" (p. 123). African American students must become familiar with African American authors so they are aware of where to find book selections (Gray, 2009, p. 480).

Gray (2009) determined that more African American literature is being published and is readily available in mainstream outlets. Books representing diverse experiences can enrich student learning about the culture, history, and life experiences of ethnically diverse groups (Gay, 2000, p 123). These books, which highlight the experiences of children who are culturally similar, are an asset to young African American children. All eleven stories presented fathers who were actively involved in their children's lives, either orchestrating or staying in the background and scaffolding their lived experiences. These are positive stories that should be shared with young children across the prekindergarten to grade three age groups. Young children need to see their lives reflected through the metaphorical mirrors, windows, and doors (Botelho & Rudman, 2009). Botelho and Rudman further delineated the metaphors and their relationship with literature, positing that mirrors allow children to "see themselves reflected so as to affirm who they and their communities are. They also require windows through which they may view a variety of differences . . . literature can become a conduit—a door—to engage children in social practices that function for social justice" (p. 1).

All children can experience the mirrors, windows, and doors through positive portrayals in children's literature. Books representing positive family relationships, particularly positive African American fathers, should be more visible so young African American children and their peers can see them and be exposed to them in their formative years. Educators, parents, media personnel, and all involved in educating young children should be culturally responsive in providing them the diverse cultural lenses through which they may view the world around them. It is vital that the literature presenting positive images of African American fathers in traditional families be a part of this literature presented to young children.

Culturally responsive teachers can help their students better appreciate all families by actively incorporating diverse types of literature in their curriculum and classroom libraries. Books highlighting positive representations of the traditional African American father and family must be consciously integrated in social studies lessons and everyday reading activities as young children learn about families and family structures. For example, young children enjoy going to work or traveling with their parents. After reading *Daddy Goes to Work* and *Bippity Bop Barbershop*, children can reminisce about a time they visited their father's or mother's place of employment. They can also share about a time they went on an outing with just their father. They can also "dream up" a trip they would like to take with their fathers or what they would do if they visited their father's workplace. Teachers can also develop a unit on African American writers who write about African American families. They can solicit the media specialist to help them collect and assemble text sets for the classroom project. Having these text sets in the classroom provides opportunities for young children to see themselves and others reflected in picture books. The early childhood classroom is a visual space, and young children learn from the images that surround them. Children's literature portraying positive images of the traditional African American family should not only be a part of a multicultural literature unit. Rather, it should be an integral part of the regular curriculum for all students.

CHILDREN'S BOOKS CITED

Asim, J. (2006). *Daddy goes to work.* Illustrated by A. Boyd. New York, NY: Little, Brown and Company.

Dungy, T. (2008). *You can do it.* Illustrated by A. J. Bates. New York, NY: Little Simon Inspirations.

Frame, J. A. (2003). *Yesterday I had the blues.* Illustrated by R. G. Christie. Berkeley, CA: Tricycle Press.

Grimes, N. (2002). *When daddy prays.* Illustrated by T. Ladwig. Grand Rapids, MI: Eerdmans.

Grimes, N. (2006). *Welcome, precious.* Illustrated by B. Collier. New York, NY: Orchard Books.

Johnson, A. (2000). *Down the winding road.* Illustrated by S. W. Evans. New York, NY: Dorling Kindersley.

Johnson, A. (2007). *Lily Brown's paintings.* Illustrated by E. B. Lewis. New York, NY: Orchard Books.

Kurtz, J. (2000). *Faraway home.* Illustrated by E. B. Lewis. Orlando, FL: Harcourt.

McQuinn, A. (2010). *Lola loves stories.* Illustrated by R. Beardshaw. Watertown, MA: Charlesbridge.

Nelson, V. M. (2009). *Who will I be Lord?* Illustrated by S. Qualls. New York, NY: Random House.

Tarpley, N. A. (2002). *Bippity bop barbershop.* Illustrated by E. B. Lewis. New York, NY: Megan Tingley Books.

REFERENCES

Anderson, D. A., & Hamilton, M. (2005). Gender role stereotyping of parents in children's picture books: The invisible father. *Sex Roles, 52*(3/4), 145–151.

Baghban, M. (1994). Through the glass clearly: Positive images of African-American fathers in young adult literature. In K. P. Smith (Ed.) *African-American voices in young adult literature: Tradition, transition, transformation* (p. 232). Lanham, MD: Scarecrow Press.

Blankenhorn, D., & Clayton, O. (2003). Introduction. In O. Clayton, R. B. Mincy, & D. Blankenhorn, (Eds.), *Black fathers in contemporary American society: Strengths, weaknesses, and strategies for change* (pp. 1–5). New York, NY: Russell Sage.

Botelho, M. J., & Rudman, M. K. (2009). *Critical multicultural analysis of children's literature: Mirrors, windows, and doors.* New York, NY: Routledge.

Coles, R. L., & Green, C. (Eds.). (2010). *The myth of the missing black father.* New York, NY: Columbia University Press.

Coley, R. L. (2003). Daughter-father relationships and adolescent psychosocial functioning in low-income African American families. *Journal of Marriage and Family, 65*(4), 867–875.

Doherty, W. J., Kouneski, E. F., & Erickson, M. F. (1998). Responsible fathering: An overview and conceptual framework. *Journal of Marriage and the Family, 60*(2), 277–292.

Fagan, J. (2009). Relationship quality and changes in depressive symptoms among urban, married African Americans, Hispanics, and Whites. *Family Relations, 58*(3), 259–274.

Gadsden, V. L., & Smith, R. R. (1994). African American males and fatherhood: Issues in research and practice. *The Journal of Negro Education, 63*(4), 634–648.

Gay, G. (2000). *Culturally responsive teaching: Theory, research & practice.* New York, NY: Teachers College Press.

Gilmore, D. P., & Bell, K. (2006). We are family: Using diverse family structure literature with children. *Reading Horizons, 46*(4), 279–299.

Gordon, E. (2010). The Ebony roundtable: Who's your daddy? *Ebony, LXV*(8), 88.

Gray, E. S. (2009). The importance of visibility: Students' and teachers' criteria for selecting African American literature. *The Reading Teacher, 62*(6), 472–481.

Hall, R. E., Livingston, J. N., Henderson, V. V., Fisher, G. O., & Hines, R. (2007). Post-modern perspective on the economics of African American fatherhood. *Journal of African American Studies, 10,* 110–121.

Harris, Y. R., & Graham, J. A. (2007). *The African American child: Development and challenges.* New York, NY: Springer.

Kelly, J. (2009). Fathers and the media: Introduction to the special issue. *Fathering, 7*(2), 107–113.

King, V. (2003). The influence of religion on fathers' relationships with their children. *Journal of Marriage and Family, 65*(2), 382–395.

Ladson-Billings, G. (1992). Reading between the lines and beyond the pages: A culturally relevant pedagogy. *Theory Into Practice, 31*(4), 312–320.

LaFaye, A., & Hendrickson, L. (2001). You've come a long way, daddy: Affirmations of fatherhood in recent African American picture books. *Bookbird, 39*(2), 28–33.

Lamorey, S. (2010). Where's your daddy? African American father figures in children's story books. In R. L. Coles & C. Green (Eds.), *The myth of the missing black father* (pp. 279–295). New York, NY: Columbia University Press.

Marks, L., Hopkins-Williams, K., Chaney, C., Nesteruk, O., & Sasser, D. (2010). "My kids and wife have been my life": Married African American fathers staying the course. In R. L. Coles & C. Green (Eds.), *The myth of the missing black father* (pp. 19–46). New York, NY: Columbia University Press.

McNair, J. C. (2008). A comparative analysis of *The Brownies' Book* and contemporary African American children's literature written by Patricia C. McKissack. In W. M. Brooks & J. C. McNair (Eds.),

Embracing evaluating, and examining African American children's & young adult literature (pp. 3–29). Lanham, MD: Scarecrow Press.

Meteyer, K., & Perry-Jenkins, M. (2010). Father involvement among working-class, dual-earner couples. *Fathering, 8*(3), 379–403.

Parke, R. D. (2004). Fathers, families, and the future: A plethora of plausible predictions. *Merrill-Palmer Quarterly, 50*(4), 456–470.

Quinn, S. M. F. (2006). Examining the culture of fatherhood in American children's literature: Presence, interactions, and nurturing behaviors of fathers in Caldecott Award winning picture books (1938–2002). *Fathering, 4*(1), 71–95.

Quinn, S. M. F. (2009). The depictions of fathers and children in best-selling picture books in the United States: A hybrid semiotic analysis. *Fathering, 7*(2), 140–158.

Raikes, H. H., Summers, J. A., & Roggman, L. A. (2005). Father involvement in early head start programs. *Fathering, 3*(1), 29–58.

Thomas, P. A., Krampe, E. M., & Newton, R. R. (2010). Father presence, family structure, and feelings of closeness to the father among adult African American children. *Journal of Black Studies, 38*(4), 529–546.

CHAPTER 2

Powerful Words

Celebrating Poetry with Young Children

MARY NAPOLI

INTRODUCTION

One of the benefits of sharing quality African American and African poetry with young children is to provide a context for celebrating diversity, identity, and social justice. Reading poetry is just one way to help empower the lives of young children and to shape an emancipatory curriculum. As Rudine Sims Bishop (2007) noted, "The dominant impulse of late twentieth century African American children's poetry has been to affirm the worth and beauty of Black children and their lives" (p. 95). By sharing poetry that speaks to the everyday details of children's lives, young children can develop a deeper awareness of their sense of self and the possibilities of their world.

As I reflect upon my early teaching career (1990s) working with kindergarten and first-grade students, my collective memories are alive with children who showed me the power and place that poetry can have in their lives. Adrienne[1] was one of the first students who reinforced the importance of creating a context for playing with language. She loved reading and she loved writing about her family, her interests, and her friends. While browsing Eloise Greenfield's highly acclaimed poetry collection, she often sang and hummed the words to her own beat. In my classroom library, I always highlighted poets, authors, or illustrators, including the work of African American poets such as Greenfield, Arnold Adoff, Gwendolyn

Brooks, and Nikki Giovanni, to name a few. Later on, I was introduced to the works of Nikki Grimes, Joyce Carol Thomas, and Ashley Bryan's *Sing to the Sun* (1992), and I weaved their work into the fabric of my early literacy program.

I always began the year by reading Greenfield's *Honey, I Love and Other Love Poems* (1978), which contains sixteen poems that celebrate the myriad of daily activities that there are to love in the world, including family, words, friends, music, and oneself. As Bishop (2007) noted, love is a common theme in African American children's literature, and poetry is no exception. The poetry in Greenfield's collection captures childlike sensibilities that echo the lives and concerns of children. Greenfield (1975/1990) wrote that one of her purposes for writing for children is to awaken them to the beauty of words and to instill a love for the arts. One day, during a writing workshop, I noticed that Adrienne was humming and writing. When she volunteered to share her writing with the rest of the class, she beamed with delight at the words on the page. She mirrored the style of Greenfield's *Honey, I Love* by celebrating her family and life. She wrote this (featured below with correct spelling):

> *I love the way my auntie visits me.*
> *She always gives me hugs and kisses.*
> *I love the way my auntie brings me presents.*
> *Like chocolate kisses and doll baby clothes.*
> *I love the way she sings with me.*
> *But honey, let me tell you that I love when she brings me hugs and kisses.*

Through the captivating rhyme and rhythm of this poem that celebrates the simple things in a child's life, Adrienne taught me a valuable lesson that day—to immerse children in quality selections of poetry to celebrate language and to give children a voice. In addition, teachers must provide young listeners with varied opportunities to explore poetry selections that embrace an imaginative quality of language, filled with sensory expressions but also a range of emotional depth and insight into cultural diversity and appreciation.

SELECTING AND USING QUALITY AFRICAN AMERICAN AND AFRICAN POETRY WITH YOUNG CHILDREN

Poetry is entwined in the lives of children. From infancy to early childhood, young listeners are exposed to lullabies, nursery rhymes, street rhymes, and jump rope chants. Poetry for the very young should be playful; as Lee Bennett Hopkins suggests, "[P]oetry for children should appeal to them and meet their emotional needs and interests" (1987, p. 9). As young children grow, so does their immersion in listening to poetry selections that mirror their lives. Using high-quality African American and African poetry in the early childhood classroom offers teachers and students many opportunities to gain broader understandings about the world while making connections to their everyday lives. Children need to receive affirmation of themselves and their culture through literature (Bieger, 1995/1996; Bishop, 2007) and be able to connect the text to self in order to promote greater meaning (Rosenblatt, 1978). Thus, poetry appreciation begins in a child's formative years. When poetry is an integral part of the early childhood classroom, it can truly help children see, feel, and respond to things, people, and typical events in unique ways. Therefore, quality poetry must satisfy similar criteria as any other genre of children's literature. As literature experts (e.g., Kiefer, Hepler, & Hickman, 2007; Sloan, 2003) note, teachers who select poems for children should consider the overall appeal and whether the words will stir emotions like delight, sadness, or nostalgia. As collections of African and African American poetry become increasingly available for classroom library collections, it is also important to consider the following checklist based on professional sources (Harris, 1990; Sims-Bishop, 1990, 1992; Webster & Walters, 2008).

1. Is the poet's voice authentic?
2. Is the language used authentic?
3. Is the culture portrayed from the point of view of someone inside the cultural group?
4. Is the culture portrayed multidimensionally?
5. Are cultural details naturally integrated within the text?
6. Are characters portrayed as individuals without stereotyping?
7. Are issues presented in their true complexity?
8. Will children see "mirrors" of their own heritage?
9. Will children see many "windows" into other people's lives?

The poetry highlighted in this chapter is included because it meets the aforementioned criteria and has been notated on various award lists. In addition, the selections have been successfully used in my work with prospective teachers and young children. Moreover, the poems echo familiar themes of love, joy, identity, and daily life. Poetry and song have been the impetus for cultural sharing with children for many generations, and there are many reasons for teachers to include high-quality selections in their curriculum. Some of these include the exposure to patterns in language and the history of the past, present, and future of people of African descent in the continent and in the African diaspora.

One reputable place for selecting quality poetry is to examine the National Council of Teachers of English award for Excellence in Poetry for Children, which is presented every two years to honor a living American poet for his or her aggregate body of work for children. The following African American poets have been recognized with this honor: Eloise Greenfield (1997), Arnold Adoff (1988), and Nikki Grimes (2006). Oftentimes, poetry titles appear on the Coretta Scott King Award list, such as *My People* (2009), illustrated by Charles R. Smith, based on a poem written by Langston Hughes, or *The Blacker the Berry* (2009), illustrated by Floyd Cooper and written by Joyce Carole Thomas. In addition, teachers can refer to the Lee Bennett Hopkins poetry award winners and honor books (http://www.pabook.libraries.psu.edu/activities/hopkins/), such as *Stitchin' and Pullin' a Gee's Bend Quilt* (2008), by Patricia McKissack, or *Jazz* (2006), by Walter Dean Myers and illustrated by Christopher Myers. Finally, some other award-winning poetry is frequently included on the following lists: The Notable Books for a Global Society (http://clrsig.org), The Notable Children's Books in the Language Arts (http://www.childrensliteratureassembly.org/), and the Notable Trade Books for Young People (http://www.socialstudies.org/notable). Many of the poetry titles written expressly for young children address social, cultural, and identity issues to celebrate childhood and emotions. According to Rochman (1993), "Books can make a difference in dispelling prejudice and building community; not with role models and literal recipes, not with noble messages about the human family, but with enthralling stories that make us imagine the lives of others" (p. 19). Poetry selections with a global focus present readers with language and situations which allow them to broaden their perspectives and foster new understandings. There are many outstanding poetry collections, anthologies, and single book length titles available to educators. An examination of these works reveals recurring themes in African American poetry. Poetry reveals what a people values or experiences through generations. It is a window into the soul (Hammontree, 2009), which can provide insight into the lives of a people. Some themes in African American poetry include family life, history, freedom, urban culture, songs, jazz, blues, friends, daily activities, church (call and response), and identity. Providing quality poetry can help children find poems that reflect their own feelings and even find poems that they can perform or dramatize.

In Table 1, I have included a sample list of award-winning poetry selections from 2000–2010 aimed at young children (Pre-K–3), organized by several popular themes found in African American poetry.

TABLE 1.

Theme	Poetry Collection or Anthology	Award(s) Received
Friendship	*Danitra Brown Leaves Town* (2002) by Nikki Grimes; illustrated by Floyd Cooper	
Daily life (celebration of family, things, routines, etc.)	*Brothers & Sisters: Family Poems* (2009) by Eloise Greenfield; illustrated by Jan Spivey Gilchrest	
	Some Kind of Love: A Family Reunion in Poems (2009) by Traci Dant; illustrated by Eric Velasquez	
	Stitchin' and Pullin' a Gee's Bend Quilt (2008) by Patricia C. McKissack; illustrated by Cozi Cabrera	Lee Bennett Hopkins Poetry Honor award (2009)
	Young Cornrows Callin' Out the Moon (2007) by Ruth Forman; illustrated by Cbabi Bayoc	Notable Children's Books in the Language Arts (2008)
	Under the Christmas Tree (2002) by Nikki Grimes; illustrated by Kadir Nelson	
	Short Takes: Fast-Break Basketball Poetry (2001) by Charles R. Smith	Lee Bennett Hopkins Poetry Honor award (2002)
	Shoe Magic (2000) by Nikki Grimes; illustrated by Terry Widener	
	Touch the Poem (2000) by Arnold Adoff; illustrated by Lisa Desimini	Notable Children's Books in the Language Arts (2001)
Identity and heritage	*The Blacker the Berry* (2008) by Joyce Carole Thomas; illustrated by Floyd Cooper	Coretta Scott King Book Award winner for illustrator (2009) and Honor Book for author (2009) Notable Children's Books in the Language Arts (2009)
	Bronzeville Boys and Girls (2007) by Gwendolyn Brooks; illustrated by Faith Ringgold	
	Crowning Glory (2002) by Joyce Carol Thomas; illustrated by Brenda Joysmith	

TABLE 1. *continued*

Theme	Poetry Collection or Anthology	Award(s) Received
History, culture, and music	*My People* (2009) by Langston Hughes; photographs by Charles R. Smith, Jr.	Coretta Scott King Book Award for illustration (2010)
	Hip Hop Speaks to Children: A Celebration of Poetry with a Beat (2008) edited by Nikki Giovanni	Notable Children's Books in the Language Arts (2009)
	My America (2007) by Jan Spivey Gilchrist; illustrated by Ashley Bryan and Jan Spivey Gilchrist	
	Let It Shine: Three Favorite Spirituals (2007); illustrated by Ashley Bryan	Coretta Scott King Book Award for illustration (2008) Notable Books for a Global Society (2008)
	God Bless the Child (2004) by Billie Holiday & Arthur Herzog, Jr.; illustrated by Jerry Pinkney	Coretta Scott King Honor Book for illustration (2005)
	Ellington Was Not a Street (2004) by Ntozake Shange; illustrated by Kadir Nelson	Notable Children's Books in the Language Arts (2005) Coretta Scott King Book Award winner for illustration (2005)
	Love to Langston (2002) by Tony Medina; illustrated by R. Gregory Christie	Notable Children's Books in the Language Arts (2003)
	Rock of Ages: A Tribute to the Black Church (2001) by Tonya Bolden; illustrated by R. Gregory Christie	

CLASSROOM APPROACHES: EXPLORING AFRICAN AMERICAN POETRY FOR YOUNG CHILDREN

After selecting various titles from well-known and contemporary African and African American children's poets, teachers need to also find CD readings of poets reading their work and conduct poetry studies to help students learn more about the life of the poet. Some good reference materials include the following: Sylvia Vardell's *Poetry Aloud Here!: Sharing Poetry with Children in the Library* (2006) and *Poetry People: A Practical Guide to Children's Poets* (2007) and Lee Bennett Hopkins' *Pass the Poetry Please!* (1988).

According to Rudine Sims Bishop (2003), a culturally authentic work of literature captures the particular and unique qualities of a group's experience, thereby opening a window to the understanding of universal human experiences. Thus, as poems are shared with children, observe their reactions to the language, sound, repetition, and rhyme to spark conversations about their feelings toward the poems and what memories are triggered. Poetry with clear-cut rhymes or rhythm is well-liked by young children, and reading poetry on a daily basis will not only provide meaningful and purposeful experiences for them, but it will also honor and affirm their identity. As we invite students' responses, we can ask them various questions to facilitate critical reading (McClure, 1990), such as the following:

1. What do you think the poem will be about?
2. What did you like about this poem?
3. What does this poem remind you of?

In addition, inviting students to dramatize poetry could also expand their perspectives and appreciation about their world. For example, the poetry in Nikki Giovanni's (2008) edited collection, *Hip Hop Speaks to Children: A Celebration of Poetry with a Beat,* can be woven into the curriculum for arts, music, and dramatic performance. Children need to choose and create poetry that expresses their own personal lives. Since poetry is by nature an aural encounter, it is logical that teachers provide children with opportunities to gesture, act out, speak in expressive tones, participate chorally, motion, and dance to the meaning of words. Young children can also respond to poetry through music and art. Providing students with various colors, textures, and materials will invite them to transfer their feelings and emotions about poetry. As poetry is read aloud, children will also be captivated by the poet's technique and the interplay between text and illustration. Helping students evoke meanings (Rosenblatt, 1993), coupled with critical conversation, will guide them to develop an appreciation for the genre while healing their souls and spirits. At a time when early childhood teachers are experiencing significant mandates related to high-stakes assessment and the related pressures that accompany such mandates (Darling-Hammond, 2000; Greene, 1988), arts integration continues to be a meaningful and developmentally appropriate avenue to intellectually stimulate and nourish the needs of young learners.

For early childhood teachers who must meet a variety of standards within a limited time frame, teachers can incorporate the thematic strands of social studies using poetry (see Vardell, 2003, for suggested poems for the thematic strands). Moreover, poetry can serve as a model for writing. Young children also have an awareness of audience; therefore, an opportunity for sharing their writing is an important component as they make their poetry public. Kroll (1978) argues, "When children realize that peers, instead of a teacher, will read their compositions, an audience of 'significant others' is created, making audience sensitivity more meaningful. Powerful learning occurs when children experience the failure or success of their words to communicate to peers" (p. 831). Creating poetry forums, including in-class writing celebrations with friends and family, publishing class poetry journals, and hosting poetry festivals, will not only improve upon young students' literacy skills, but also facilitates new understanding about their lives. Calkins and Parsons (2003) point out, "As teachers, we need to move heaven and earth to be sure every child knows what it is to be a published author. Help children make their poems public by posting them in the community and reading them to various audiences" (p. 131). Thus, as teachers immerse younger students in a wide selection of African American poetry, they introduce them to new language patterns and messages. Children should be encouraged to "play" in the syntax of the author's work, use scaffolds, examine the poet's craft, or simply share their feelings and personal reflections about the poem.

CLASSROOM APPROACHES:
EXPLORING AFRICAN POETRY FOR YOUNG CHILDREN

There are many selections of African poetry that teachers can integrate into the early childhood curriculum. My hope is that as early childhood teachers expose their students to poetry about Africa, they will also educate them about Africa's culture, landscape, animals, and traditions and help them foster a global awareness about their world. Poetry selections such as *Is It Far to Zanzibar: Poems About Tanzania* (2000) by Nikki Grimes or *Off to the Sweet Shores of Africa and Other Talking Drum Rhymes* (2000) by Uzoamaka Chinyelu Unobagha will afford young children with new understandings about the people, animals, and cultures of Africa.

In Grimes' collection of over a dozen poems about Tanzania, she presents playful rhymes and singsong verse about the local children, tourists, and daily life ("I safari, you safari. / Everyone is on safari."). Not only do the poems invite dramatization and motion, but they will prompt further inquiry about the culture and people. Teachers can use the back matter with a list of Swahili words and a map of the country to integrate geography and language arts. In *Off to the Sweet Shores of Africa and Other Talking Drum Rhymes* (Unobagha, 2000), the poems derive from the poet's Nigerian cultural heritage and her interest in Mother Goose rhymes. The poems feature cultural objects and ideas such as the use of the drum, the animals and fruits, the market, rivers, and the desert to tell the story of village life. The rhythmic language is simple and delightful ("Round and round the mango tree, / Who did run but little me / With ten bananas in my pail / And ten red monkeys at my tail!"), and teachers can provide students with musical instruments to accompany the poetry reading.

Another collection that describes the life and customs in a Nigerian village is *The Distant Talking Drum: Poems from Nigeria* (1995), by Isaac Olaleye, which received The Notable Books for a Global Society distinctive award. This collection of vignettes explores the typical life in the rural Yoruba community in Nigeria. Traditionally, the talking drum was a means of communication between members in the village, but today, the drum is used for ceremonial celebrations as echoed in the title poem: The drum "... Is calling the mighty rain forest / For me to come, / For me to dance. / Now the sound of sweet songs / I hear. / Beautifully they flow!" The poems, accompanied by exuberant, childlike paintings, describe the weather, farming, domestic work, and recreational life of the village. Lastly, in *Talking Drums: A Selection of Poems from Africa South of the Sahara* (2004), edited and illustrated by Veronique Tadjo, which was included on The Notable Children's Books in Language Arts list and received the Children's Africana Honor Book Award, features poems that celebrate nature, beauty, and the universe of black Africa. The versatility of the poems makes it a wonderful collection for all ages. Most impressive is the depth and range of the poems, including oral poems passed down through the generations as well as more contemporary work by individual poets. Many of the poems can be used with dramatization or simple motions such as the extract from "The Lion Roars with a Fearful Sound" or "Songs of the Animal World," as well as music and artistic responses.

Infusing poetry selections about African culture is one way to develop relevant critical thinking skills while addressing common core standards in social studies and language arts. As Peter Hunt (1992) noted in Botelho and Rudman (2009), poetry, out of all the genres, is the one that challenges our notion of comprehension. No single meaning is intended in a poem. Words, phrases, images, ideas, all convey different shades of meaning and a range of feelings. Using global titles from The Notable Books for a Global Society list, the Children's Africana Book Award list (http://www.africaaccessreview.org/aar/news.html), and reviewing the International Board on Books for Young People (IBBY) website will promote international understanding through children's books. Therefore, I begin this next section by suggesting a few interdisciplinary activities to enable students to understand some basic information about Africa.

Activity # 1: Sharing Poetry and Music to Generate Interest

To introduce a unit about Africa to students from preschool to grade three, teachers can weave various poetry selections and then lead students in a large group inquiry about what they want they know about Africa and what they learned about Africa (Ogle, 1986). Teachers can also play music during transition times and during independent reading and writing.

Activity #2: Geographical Exploration

Since literature provides a rich foray into another culture, excellent nonfiction selections as well as traditional literature can be used to help students understand that Africa is a continent and not a country and that there is diversity in the land, people, languages, cultures, and histories. Two excellent books to use include the Children Africana Book Award (CABA) winners *Africa Is Not a Country* (Knight, & Melnicove, 2000) and *Ikenna Goes to Nigeria* (Onyefulu, 2008). The book, *Africa Is Not a Country,* takes its readers through what the children in the country may be doing. For instance, in the first country discussed, Eritrea, two boys named Arim and Efrem are preparing for school as they are reminded by their mother to respect their elders. Children are shown doing normal activities that any student would do in the United States including running, participating in choir, playing leapfrog, watching cartoons, and listening to bedtime stories. The book also shows some things that African children may do that are different from what American children might do in their daily lives. These activities include carrying fresh milk in a gourd on one's head, seeing camels, or wearing traditional outfits to do ancient dances. From reading about leisure activities of the different countries to what happens at mealtimes, all of the text and activities that children read about the different countries will show readers that Africa is a very diverse continent and help them become culturally aware. The illustrations aid the text to show diversity. Different social classes, geographies, and living styles are shown. It helps the reader gain an understanding that though people may live differently, all of them are enjoying their lives. The illustrations and text together promote awareness and acceptance. Teachers can also go on a virtual tour of Africa and chart their observations about the names of the countries and the types of daily activities, including work and recreation. Some other titles that would be excellent additions to a text set (Kurkjian, Livingston, & Siu-Runyan, 2004) include the following: *Africatrek: A Journey by Bicycle Through Africa,* by Dan Buettner (1997), and *Ogbo: Sharing Life in an African Village,* by Ifeoma Onyefulu (1996). Finally, students can also learn about African animals while reading nonfiction selections and poetry excerpts such as "The Lion" by Nigerian poet Uzo Nwokedi: "The lion has a golden mane. / A golden coat / and golden eyes / The gazelle leaps across the plain/and seems to float./Across the skies.

Activity #3: Pair Poetry with Folktales

Poetry can be read before sharing African folktales. Poems and songs, like traditional literature, transcend time and space and are meant to be shared from generation to generation, with varying interpretations and meanings well into the future. There are many African folktales available for early childhood teachers to teach reading and to explore storytelling. Students and teachers can compare and contrast various African folktales to those that they are familiar with to broaden their perspectives on literature and culture. One excellent title is *The Hatseller and the Monkeys: A West African Folktale,* by Baba Wagué Diakité (1999). In this story, readers will meet BaMusa, a hatseller who is very happy in his livelihood. He was taught how to make wide-brimmed dibiri hats woven from rice stalks and intricately embroidered fugulan caps from his parents and grandparents. One day, he traveled to a neighboring village with a stack of his hats on his head, intending to sell them at the festival. But he neglected to eat breakfast, and on the way, he became tired and fell asleep under a mango tree.

Unfortunately, his snoring attracted some monkeys, who crawled around BaMusa and cleverly took all of his hats except the one covering his face. The monkeys hid in the mango tree and waited until BaMusa woke up. He realized what happened and tried to think of a creative way to retrieve his hats. He yelled at the monkeys, and they yelled back. He threw a branch at them, and they threw leaves. Then he threw a stone, and they retaliated with mangoes. BaMusa took the opportunity to eat some of the mangoes, and once his stomach was full, he thought of a solution. He took off his remaining hat, waved it at the monkeys, and threw it to the ground. As he expected, the monkeys followed suit, and he was able to gather his hats and proceed to the festival, coming to the conclusion that it is best to think on a full stomach. Teachers can use African poetry about monkeys as an introduction to this folktale and also explore the beautiful illustrations painted on ceramic tiles in soft colors.

Teachers can also weave math and literacy with poetry by sharing simple counting poems and other award-winning books such as *One Child, One Seed: A South African Counting Book* by Kathryn Cave (2003). If we follow a constructivist approach, children should be allowed to interact with the multicultural materials, to discover on their own, and to come up with explanations and hypotheses to situations and events. The role of the teacher is to serve as a facilitator, motivator, and guide, and to allow and take into consideration the students' input in identifying problems and solutions. Based on Vygotsky's theory, this type of teaching approach and collaboration between the teacher and the learner (scaffolding) fosters cognitive growth and increases the child's performance (Berk & Winsler, 1995).

Activity #4: Art, Culture, and Poetry

The multiple selections of quality poetry titles and literature about Africa include beautiful artwork to explore style and theme. Students can experiment with various materials to respond to poetry. Teachers should provide magazines or newspaper supplements they can use to make a collage or mixed media piece. Furthermore, teachers can show young children various murals and discuss the similarities and differences in the artwork and encourage them to write their own poetry. Students can write a collaborative poem or use a scaffold to write a poem that touches upon their emotions to the artwork.

FINAL THOUGHTS

Overall, weaving both African American and African children's poetry in the early childhood program will promote cultural and global awareness for young learners. In many classrooms, poetry remains an untapped resource for exploring African American and African themes. With the aim of educating young children about the world around them, I suggest that classroom teachers use the poetry selections in this chapter to provide opportunities to address the developmental needs of the young child while infusing critical literacy, integrated learning, and social justice. Poetry speaks to the hearts and minds of young learners and can be a powerful way to transform students' understanding about the world around them.

NOTE

1. Pseudonym used.

CHILDREN'S POETRY CITED

Adoff, A. (2000). *Touch the poem*. Illus. by Lisa Desimini. New York, NY: Blue Sky Press/Scholastic.
Bolden, T. (2001). *Rock of ages: A tribute to the black church*. Illus. by R. Gregory Christie. New York, NY: Random House.
Brooks, G. (2007). *Bronzeville boys and girls*. Illus. by Faith Ringgold. New York, NY: Amistad/HarperCollins.

Bryan, A. (1992). *Sing to the sun: Poems and pictures*. New York, NY: HarperCollins.

Bryan, A. (2007). *Let it shine: Three favorite spirituals*. New York, NY: Atheneum Books for Young Readers.

Dant, T. (2009). *Some kind of love: A family reunion in poems*. Illus. by Eric Velasquez. New York, NY: Marshall Cavendish.

Forman, R. (2007). *Young cornrows callin' out the moon*. Illus. by Cbabi Bayoc. San Francisco, CA: Children's Book Press.

Gilchrist, J. S. (2007). *My America*. Illus. by Ashley Bryan and Jan Spivey Gilchrist. New York, NY: HarperCollins.

Giovanni, N. (Ed.). (2008). *Hip hop speaks to children: A celebration of poetry with a beat.* Naperville, IL: Sourcebooks.

Greenfield, E. (1978). *Honey, I love and other love poems*. Illus. by Leo and Diane Dillon. New York, NY: Harper & Row.

Greenfield, E. (2009). *Brothers & sisters: Family poems*. Illus. by Jan Spivey Gilchrist. New York, NY: HarperCollins.

Grimes, N. (2000). *Is it far to Zanzibar: Poems about Tanzania*. Illus. by Betsy Lewin. New York, NY: Lee & Low.

Grimes, N. (2000). *Shoe magic*. Illus. by Terry Widener. New York, NY: Orchard Books.

Grimes, N. (2002). *Danitra Brown leaves town*. Illus. by Floyd Cooper. New York, NY: HarperCollins.

Grimes, N. (2002). *Under the Christmas tree*. Illus. by Kadir Nelson. New York, NY: HarperCollins.

Holiday, B., & Herzog, Jr., A. (2004). *God bless the child*. Illus. by Jerry Pinkney. New York, NY: HarperCollins.

Hughes, L. (2009). *My people*. Photographs by Charles R. Smith, Jr. New York, NY: Atheneum.

Jjuko, Dominic Mwasa. (1993). *How Lion Became King*. Kampala, Uganda: Fountain Publishers.

McKissack, P. C. (2008). *Stitchin' and pullin' a gee's bend quilt*. Illus. by Cozi Cabrera. New York, NY: Random House.

Medina, T. (2002). *Love to Langston*. Illus. by R. Gregory Christie. New York, NY: Lee & Low.

Myers, W. D. (2006). *Jazz*. Illus. by Christopher Myers. New York, NY: Holiday House.

Olaleye, I. (1995). *The distant talking drum: Poems from Nigeria*. Illus. by Frané Lessac. Honesdale, PA: Wordsong.

Shange, N. (2004). *Ellington was not a street*. Illus. by Kadir Nelson. New York, NY: Simon & Schuster.

Smith, C. R. (2001). *Short takes: Fast-break basketball poetry*. New York, NY: Dutton.

Tadjo, V. (2004). *Talking drums: A selection of poems from Africa South of the Sahara*. New York, NY: Bloomsbury.

Thomas, J. C. (2002). *Crowning glory*. Illus. by Brenda Joysmith. New York, NY: Joanna Cotler Books.

Thomas, J. C. (2008). *The blacker the berry*. Illus. by Floyd Cooper. New York, NY: HarperCollins.

Unobagha, U. C. (2000). *Off to the sweet shores of Africa and other talking drum rhymes*. Illus. by Julia Cairns. San Francisco, CA: Chronicle Books.

OTHER CHILDREN'S LITERATURE SELECTIONS CITED

Buettner, D. (1997). *Africatrek: A journey by bicycle through Africa*. Minneapolis, MN: Lerner.

Cave, K. (2003). *One child, one seed: A South African counting book*. Photographs by Gisèle Wulfsohn. New York, NY: Henry Holt.

Diakité, B. W. (1999). *The hatseller and the monkeys: A West African folktale.* New York, NY: Scholastic.

Knight, M. B., & Melnicove, M. (2000). *Africa is not a country.* Illus. by Anne Sibley O'Brien. Brookfield, CT: Millbrook Press.

Onyefulu, I. (1996). *Ogbo: Sharing life in an African village* (U.S. ed.). New York, NY: Gulliver/Harcourt Brace.

Onyefulu, I. (2007). *Ikenna goes to Nigeria.* London: Frances Lincoln.

REFERENCES

Berk, L. E., & Winsler, A. (1995). *Scaffolding children's learning: Vygotsky and early childhood education.* Washington, DC: National Association for the Education of Young Children.

Bieger, E. M. (1995/1996). Promoting multicultural education through a literature-based approach. *The Reading Teacher, 49*(4), 308–312.

Bishop, R. S. (2003). Reframing the debate about cultural authenticity. In D. L Fox & K. G Short (Eds.), *Stories matter: The complexity of cultural authenticity in children's literature* (pp. 25–37). Urbana, IL: National Council of Teachers of English.

Bishop, R. S. (2007). *Free within ourselves: The development of African American children's literature.* Portsmouth, NH: Heinemann.

Botelho, M. J., & Rudman, M. K. (2009). *Critical multicultural analysis of children's literature: Mirrors, windows, and doors.* New York, NY: Routledge.

Calkins, L. M., & Parsons, S. (2003). *Units of study for primary writing/poetry: Powerful thoughts in tiny packages.* Portsmouth, NH: Heinemann.

Darling-Hammond, L. (2000, December 7–8). *Transforming public schools: The role of standards and accountability.* Paper presented at the Creating Change in Public Education seminar, John F. Kennedy School of Government, Harvard University, Cambridge, MA. Retrieved from http://www.ksg.harvard.edu/urbanpoverty/Urban%20Seminars/December2000/hammond.pdf

Greene, M. (1988). *The dialectic of freedom.* New York, NY: Teachers College Press.

Greenfield, E. (1975). Something to shout about. *The Horn Book Magazine, 41,* 624–626.

Greenfield, E. (1990). Eloise Greenfield. In *Something about the author.* Vol. 61. Ed. by A. Commire. Detroit: Gale Research, 89–102.

Hammontree, B. (2009). "Poetry is . . ." Poems for the people . . . poems by the people. Retrieved from http://www.netpoets.com/poems/beauty/0061002.htm

Harris, V. (1990). African American children's literature: The first one hundred years. *Journal of Negro Education, 59*(4), 540–555.

Hopkins, L. B. (1987). *Pass the poetry please!* New York, NY: Harper & Row.

Hunt, P. (Ed.). (1992). *Literature for children: Contemporary criticism.* New York, NY: Routledge.

Kiefer, B., with S. Hepler & J. Hickman. (2007). *Charlotte Huck's children's literature* (9th ed.). New York, NY: McGraw-Hill.

Kroll, B. (1978). Developing a sense of audience. *Language Arts, 55,* 828–831.

Kurkjian, C., Livingston, N., & Siu-Runyan, Y. (2004). Building text sets from the Notable Books for a Global Society lists. *The Reading Teacher, 57*(4), 390–398.

McClure, A. (1990). *Sunrises and songs: Reading and writing poetry in the classroom.* Portsmouth, NH: Heinemann.

Ogle, D. (1986). K-W-L: A teaching model that develops active reading of expository text. *The Reading Teacher, 39,* 564–570.

Rochman, H. (1993). *Against borders: Promoting books for a multicultural world.* Chicago, IL: American Library Association.

Rosenblatt, L. M. (1978). *The reader, the text, the poem: The transactional theory of the literary work.* Carbondale: Southern Illinois University Press.

Rosenblatt, L. M. (1993). The transactional theory: Against dualisms. *College English, 55* (4), 377–386.

Sims-Bishop, R. (1990). Mirrors, windows and sliding glass doors. *Perspectives, 6*(3), ix–xi.

Sims-Bishop, R. (1992). Multicultural literature for children: Making informed choices. In V. J. Harris (Ed.), *Teaching multicultural literature in grades K-8* (pp. 37–53). Norwood, MA: Christopher Gordon.

Sloan, G. (2003). *Give them poetry!: A guide to sharing poetry with children, K-8.* New York, NY: Teachers College Press.

Vardell, S. M. (2003). Poetry for social studies: Poems, standards, and strategies. *Social Education, 67,* 206–211.

Vardell, S. M. (2006). *Poetry aloud here!: Sharing poetry with children in the library.* Chicago, IL. American Library Association.

Vardell, S. M. (2007). *Poetry people: A practical guide to children's poets.* Santa Barbara, CA: Libraries Unlimited.

Webster, P. S., & Walters, T. (2008). Bridges to cultural understanding: Using poetry to promote multiethnic awareness. *Multicultural Education, 15*(3), 44–49.

CHAPTER 3

Representing Cultural Identity in Children's Literature

Black Children in Their Communities

JANET HELMBERGER

Children's engagements with literature have the potential to transform their world-views through understanding their current lives and imagining beyond themselves. Students do need to find their lives reflected in books, but if what they read in school only mirrors their own views of the world, they cannot envision alternative ways of thinking and being (Short, 1999, p. 10).

Children find substance and a sense of self in stories. As they read, they can use stories to think about their own experiences and those of other people. In the stories suggested here, children can see their lives and the lives of other people in their communities reflected.

As I selected the children's books for this project, I kept in mind Freire and Macedo's (1987) observation: "Reading the world always precedes reading the word, and reading the word implies continually reading the world. . . . this move-ment from the word to the world is always present; even the spoken word flows from our reading of the world" (p. 35). Therefore when children discuss stories, they need to connect their readings of these stories to their own experiences as they occur in their own communities. As they become more and more literate, they can see across the range of social classes within their communities. Their reading of the world can and should be reflected in the words they read.

Enciso (1994) urges us to remember that children come to us with "a vast store-house of cultural knowledge as they explore and declare who they are and how they want to be seen as members of a classroom and community" (p. 524). We must help them use their knowledge as they learn more about their communities and increase their powers of literacy.

PRIMARY DISCOURSES AND BEYOND

A person's interactions with the world reflect a strong influence from his or her primary discourse, which exists within the context of a cultural group, as a way of viewing the world (Darder, 1991; Freire & Macedo, 1987; Lankshear, Gee, Knobel, & Searle, 1997). A child's primary discourse frames his or her core identity and learning that come from living and interacting with family at home and in the neighborhood. How we read texts written about various cultural groups depends upon our primary discourses. These discourses begin within the diversity of our own cultural contexts and contribute to our individual sense of self. Secondary discourses emerge from the kinds of learning that happen when we incorporate new experiences—at school, in scouting and clubs, sports activities, travel experiences, and so forth. The following questions are at the heart of this chapter:

- How do multicultural children's books represent students' culture, identity, and language, as they live in their communities?
- How can we use multicultural children's books to help students bridge gaps in their knowledge, to grow toward mutual understanding through dialogue in the classroom (a micro-community)?
- How do images reflected in children's books lend themselves to dialogue among students?
- How can students' responses to books inform understanding and contribute to border crossing?

As we read books with children, we should focus on the connections between culture, identity, and language use found in the interaction of the characters. How this interaction plays out represents a cultural border crossing that can make and remake cultural and linguistic realities, as we read and respond to literature together.

CHILDREN'S LITERATURE AND BORDER CROSSING

Literature can be used by students and teachers to get to know each other and learn more about each other's cultures in the process of border crossing (Dilg, 1999; McGinley et al., 1997; Yokota, 1993). One challenge for students involves the link between their own cultures and their identities. Dilg (1999) observed the following: "For many students today, a working familiarity with their own cultural history and the wish for that history to be known by others are essential steps in the formation of their identities" (p. 100). Using literature to read about a variety of cultural groups, as Dilg indicated, can bring to light aspects of these histories and help students meet the challenge of connecting their identities to their own cultures and others. Important in this process is this:

> [W]hen students and teachers recognize the cultures that influence their own lives and thinking, each becomes more aware of how and why culture is important to everyone else. These understandings do not devalue culture or promote cultural "sameness," rather, they highlight differences across cultures as important and valuable in creating community and pushing everyone's learning. (Kaser & Short, 1998, p. 189)

Our classrooms are spaces in which we can provide opportunities for serious cultural communication to take place in story discussion, beginning with their shared search for meaning. This shared search happens as children read books that reflect or resemble their own personal cultural experiences, as well as those of their peers whose cultural experiences may be different. Through this communication process around text, children not only learn about their peers, they also develop awareness of their own sense of themselves.

Many people believe that group membership "giv[es] definition and meaning to the individual" (Ferdman, 1990, p. 185). By purposefully incorporating children's books representing various cultural groups into our literacy curriculum, students can recognize and discover the diversity across groups. As children read the stories included in this chapter, some may meet characters whose experiences and viewpoints are similar to their own. Alternatively, some may encounter viewpoints and events that could challenge their own lived experiences.

All of the stories suggested here tell us in varying ways how it feels to have alternate ways of being. For instance, they capture the experiences of moving from a rural area to an urban area, from one city to another, or one neighborhood to another; from one country to another; and the adjustments characters make in such moves. They also reveal how people have depended upon one another for support (both social and economic), whether they live together in one neighborhood or further away. They demonstrate how people have shaped and reshaped their goals and dreams to fit into their changing lives, in various living situations. They tell how people have withstood dominance and oppression and how these experiences have been ignored by dominant groups (Darder, 1991; Enciso, 1997; Rochman, 1993; Sleeter & Grant, 1999); Taxel, 1994; Wink, 2000). These are all important concepts children need to explore as they read and interact with literary texts about children and

communities of color. As mentioned earlier, I wanted to see how black cultural identity and communities are represented in books.

SELECTION OF STORIES AND THEIR SETTINGS

To select the stories for this chapter, I searched the listings of the Coretta Scott King
Book Awards from its inception in 1970, the Ezra Jack Keats Awards, Africana
Awards, and Caldecott Awards. Several titles were award winners or honor books
for the author and/or illustrator. As I perused library shelves and Internet listings,
I located additional books that told stories of African American children in their
communities. For this chapter I have limited myself to twenty-seven picture books.

Most of the stories take place in urban locations around the United States, in
cities large and small, from New York (Collier's *Uptown*, 2003; Ringgold's *Tar
Beach*, 1991; Shange's *Ellington Was Not a Street*, 1983; Steptoe's *Creativity*, 1997)
to Columbus, Ohio (Rosen's *Elijah's Angel*, 1992); Wilmington, North Carolina
(Jordan and Jordan's *Salt in His Shoes*, 2000); New Orleans (Coles' *The Story of Ruby
Bridges*, 1995); Los Angeles (Bunting's *Smoky Night*, 1994); Houston and
Washington, DC (Allen's *Dancing in the Wings*, 2000); and Texas and Chicago
(Grimes' *Talkin' About Bessie*, 2002).

Some stories take place in rural areas in the South (Howard's *Virgie Goes to
School with Us Boys*, 2000; McKissack's *Goin' Someplace Special*, 2001, and *Mirandy
and Brother Wind*, 1988; Smalls' *A Strawbeater's Thanksgiving*, 1998) and Midwest
(Thomas' *I Have Heard of a Land*, 1999). Igus' *Going Back Home*, 2004, takes place
both in the South and the Midwest.

Other picture books take place in areas of the United States that are not clearly
identified, such as Curtis' *The Bat Boy and His Violin*, 1998; Flournoy's *The Patchwork
Quilt*, 1985; Hoffman's *Amazing Grace*, 1991; Obama's *Change Has Come*, 2009; and
Yarbrough's *Cornrows*, 1997.

Five picture books reflect the voices of poets writing about the experiences of
African Americans in various parts of the United States: Cook's *Our Children Can
Soar*, 2009; Greenfield's *Nathaniel Talking*, 1989; Holiday and Herzog's *God Bless
the Child*, 2004; Steptoe's *In Daddy's Arms I Am Tall*, 1997; and Thomas' *The Blacker
the Berry*, 2008.

Nineteen of the twenty-four authors of the suggested children's books are
African Americans. Five are not. In all cases, the authors and illustrators celebrate
the variety of African American communities represented in their books.

Language use varies across the books. It is generally descriptive, in several
cases lyrical (not limited only to the poetry collections) and declarative, showing the
variety of language use across communities. In some cases, the dialogue in the books

reflects certain words and slang used in some communities; in no way does this distract or confuse the reader, or take away from the storytelling.

As noted earlier, the books reflect both urban and rural communities; the latter may include both farms and small towns in more rural areas. The books represent the variety in these communities fairly, showing the usual, expected commonalities and variations across family relationships, connections within local communities, and in movement between communities. While all of the books suggested earlier reflect a range of experiences, Curtis' *The Bat Boy and His Violin*, 1998; Flournoy's *The Patchwork Quilt*, 1985; Hoffman's *Amazing Grace*, 1991; Howard's *Virgie Goes to School with Us Boys*, 2000; McKissack's *Goin' Someplace Special*, 2001; Ringgold's *Tar Beach*, 1991; Rosen's *Elijah's Angel*, 1992; Steptoe's *Creativity*, 1997; and Yarbrough's *Cornrows*, 1997, are particularly strong as they portray variations in such relationships, both positive and not-so-positive, from rural to urban areas. They all reflect the importance of family, heritage, education, and persistence.

Across twenty-six years of teaching students in diverse classrooms in both English and Spanish, I have experienced the significance for children of stories like these that reflect part of the diversity in our classroom community. Careful readings of these books generate important conversations and thinking about our own experiences as we connect with those of the characters.

HOW WE SELECT BOOKS FOR OUR STUDENTS

As teachers, we must be meticulous as we choose books to use in our classrooms. Bishop (1992) described the consequences of our choices:

> If literature is a mirror that reflects human life, then all children who read or are read to need to see themselves reflected as part of humanity. If they are not, or if their reflections are distorted and ridiculous, there is the danger that they will absorb negative messages about themselves and people like them. Those who see only themselves or who [are] exposed to errors and misrepresentations are miseducated into a false sense of superiority, and the harm is double done. (p. 43)

The books we choose should be related to events and issues that children experience in their own lives. Story dialogue should focus on identifying the challenges found in the stories and how they are solved. Pertinent for both teachers and students, according to Cai (2003), is that "[r]eading multiculturally enhances our multicultural awareness and helps us see multicultural issues that are not readily apparent" (p. 279). He later reminded us that "[t]o see commonalities between cultures is important, but to study the differences is equally or more important" (p. 280).

We must look carefully at issues of cultural authenticity when we choose books to use in our classrooms. We need to be aware of the authors' own stories. Fang, Fu, and Lamme (2003) indicated the complexity of authenticity:

> [That] racial, ethnic, religious, and gender identities do not always ensure that writers will accurately portray their own group cultures, and outsiders can write sympathetic and historically accurate fictional stories. . . . Writers who step beyond their lived experiences need to carefully research the cultural group they portray in order to avoid using stereotypical images and erroneous cultural information. (p. 286)

Those of us who are non-African Americans and work with African American students must include in our preparation additional reading that will "acquaint [us] with the variety and diversity to be found *within* the culture. No one book can represent the literature of an entire cultural group" (Bishop, 1992, p. 47). We also need to be sure to include stories that represent people with a variety of experiences.

Doing this preparation work will make us stronger teachers; as Fang, Fu, and Lamme (2003) wrote, "Genuine understanding of literature requires knowledge of the contexts in which it was originally written and has since been read by others. [We should] teach students strategies for reflectively and critically interpreting the texts they read" (pp. 295–296).

Especially significant in the study of picture books are the illustrations, equal in importance to the text. Sipe (2000) described the synergy between illustrations and text, saying this: "In picture books, the illustrations act to fill in gaps in the text, and the text acts to fill in gaps in the illustrations" (p. 272). Nodelman (1996) added that "[Illustrations] are representations—signs whose meaning depends on a repertoire of learned strategies. . . . Because pictures are permeated by the ideological assumptions of their culture, children won't understand pictures until they develop some understanding of the culture" (pp. 216–217).

As we contemplate cultural authenticity in picture books, we must consider the illustrations, "based on whether the art form serves its purpose in relation to the story. . . . an authentic form does not have to be rigidly interpreted as the typical traditional style" (Short, 2006, p. 4). Bishop (1992) listed specific questions that we should ask when we study the pictures:

> Do they present accurate, authentic, non-stereotypical presentations of people of color? Do they show variety of physical features among the people of any one group, or do they all look alike?—Do pictures show the diversity of people who would naturally be present in certain settings such as urban centers? (p. 50)

While there are similarities between and across cultures, there are also significant differences; our interactions with texts and illustrations, and with each other around the texts, will affect what we thought we knew. As children see these interactions within the covers of books they read, the interchange can function in classrooms around children's books to lead to better understanding and knowledge among children. These interactions, based on changing perspectives, can in turn impact the functioning and workings of people in their broader communities. As we work on literacy acquisition, we want children to *really* want to read. However, as Rochman (2003) postulates, "For books to give pleasure there has to be tension and personality, laughter and. . . . conflict. That's what will grab kids and touch them deeply—and make them want to read" (p. 104). The challenge then is on how to facilitate learning around issues in literary texts that cause these tensions. Furthermore, this is impacted by the cultural images that our students bring to the stories we read together, most of which are stereotypes of the "other." We need to work with students to relate children's experiences with what we read in these stories and their representations. The next section provides a scaffolding that we can use to structure our discussions.

CULTURAL AWARENESS AND CULTURAL KNOWLEDGE SURROUNDS US

Theories of reader responses as transactions with texts provide the frame of pedagogical structures in this section. Literature discussion sessions are ways that students can bridge gaps in knowledge and mutual understanding that exist when cultural groups are valued differently. Students use a shared focus of discussion to relate to their own experiences and those of people they know. Together we perform aesthetic readings of books, in which "we. . . . participate in the story, we identify with the characters, we share their conflicts and their feelings" (Rosenblatt, 1993, p. 7). We interact with each other to negotiate our understanding of the story.

When using the suggested strategies with the children's books, there are limitations in observable, quantitative correlation with the standardized tests required by the pressures of No Child Left Behind legislation, state Adequate Yearly Progress demands, and the required use of basal anthologies and reading "programs" in public school districts. On the other hand, good children's trade books are integral components in the acquisition of real literacy. As Clarke (2006) wrote, "With texts and the students' lives at the center of [a] unit, students [can] critically interrogate voice and begin to develop a positive sense of self-worth" (p. 60).

We want to help students connect with the realness and the authenticity in the story. How do they identify with the characters in the story? Do the stories reflect their experiences or the experiences of people they know?

Variations on the following scaffolding can be used by teachers and students as criteria for analysis of multicultural children's books:

Literary Merit

1. How are the problems involved in the story handled? (Could these situations happen in real life?)
2. How are dialogues handled? (How do they reflect dialogues of people in the community?)
3. Are the problems handled by the characters themselves, are they solved by the intervention of others, or by a combination of "solvers"?
4. How are themes and issues developed in the stories and illustrations?

Cultural Accuracy and Representation

1. How do the books portray characters in their environment, both in terms of location (between neighbors and neighborhoods, between urban and rural areas, etc.) and economic situation, both in the text and illustrations?
2. How are urban groups and rural groups portrayed around the United States?
3. How are traditional features of a particular heritage regarding importance of family and religion treated and incorporated into the threads of the story?
4. Related to the previous question, do the traditional features of particular heritage portrayed in the books indicate the gradual changes that occur in any dynamic cultural milieu?
5. Are the gradual changes that occur naturally with cyclical migration around the United States reflected in the story?
6. What issues are represented in the story?
7. How do the illustrations reflect the cultural components?

Character Portrayal Found in the Books

1. How is language used to refer to or depict the characters?
2. What values and traditions are represented in both the text and illustrations?
3. How do the story and illustrations depict individuals?

On occasion, the teacher or a student could conduct a read-aloud of a particular story, followed by discussion, using selected questions from those listed earlier. It is important that the teacher does a minimal amount of talking in this dialogue. Eventually, we want students to dialogue directly with each other, with questions asked by the teacher as needed. (At times, it would be appropriate for the teacher to share opinions and ideas—but to limit his or her questions.) We want students to jump right into the discussion, without waiting for the teacher to get them going.

All of the books suggested in this chapter could be read aloud, especially the selections in which poetry serves as the text (Cook's *Our Children Can Soar*, 2009; Greenfield's *Nathanial Talking*, 1989; Shange's *Ellington Was Not a Street*, 1983; the work of the poets in Steptoe's *In Daddy's Arms I Am Tall*, 1997; and Thomas' *The Blacker the Berry*, 2008). Holiday and Herzog's *God Bless the Child* (2004) includes a CD that could be played while displaying the illustrations.

Another good strategy involves dialogue journals, in which students write about their reactions to what they read or hear in read-alouds. Students may begin writing in their journals using the questions that follow, intended to provide guidelines for their responses:

- What did you find interesting about the culture represented in the story?
- What puzzled you?
- What are some tensions you saw in the story?
- What words or special ways of telling an idea were new for you?
- Has anything that happened in this story ever happened to you?
- What was your favorite part of the story?
- What was the author telling us in this story?
- What do you think about this author's message?

Depending on the writing strengths of students, they could also use some of the questions in the scaffolding on literary merit, cultural accuracy and representation, and character portrayal, provided earlier.

Students could also participate in literature discussion groups, organized in flexible, heterogeneous groupings. Sometimes these groups would be chosen by the teacher, sometimes by the students themselves. They could share their responses to the questions from their dialogue journals, use questions from the scaffolding provided earlier, or respond to thoughts that may emerge through their discussion.

Beyond the read-alouds, dialogue journals, and literature discussion groups, students can write their own stories; they become "storyteller[s] in a social and cultural context. . . . the student must be writing for self and community rather than simply for [school]. . . . In essence, we use writing to learn about ourselves and to communicate that understanding with real people" (Shafer, 2003, p. 17). If we incorporate writers' workshop into our reader response work, we can help students *think* like writers, which "supports the development of critical literacy. Frequent discussions that speculate about the author's purpose and audience help students realize the intentionality behind the texts they read" (Juel, Hebard, Huabner, & Moran, 2010, para. 32).

As a further extension, students can also bring in their own family stories in the form of artwork and quilts, created by extended families members that connect with the stories read in class. Some of the titles that are linked to this extension in particular include the following: Flournoy's *The Patchwork Quilt*, 1985; Greenfield's *Nathanial Talking*, 1989; Hoffman's *Amazing Grace*, 1991; Howard's *Virgie Goes to School with Us Boys*, 2000; Igus' *Going Back Home*, 2004 (which showcases Michele Wood's artwork); and Ringgold's *Tar Beach*, 1991.

CONCLUSION

As we select books to read in our classrooms, we can give voice to the cultural lives of our students. The books included here are representations of African American children and their communities, with cultural expressions that help readers see and learn other people's stories. We need to work with students to carefully consider how we reflect on and absorb our cultural histories as we read. As Taxel (1995) attests, "[We must consider] the insistence of peoples from many of the diverse cultures that comprise our multiracial, multicultural nation to have their history and culture treated with respect, dignity, and sensitivity" (p. 164).

SUGGESTED CHILDREN'S BOOKS

Allen, D. (2000). *Dancing in the wings.* (K. Nelson, Illus.). New York, NY: Dial Books.

Bunting, E. (1994). *Smoky night.* (D. Diaz, Illus.). San Diego, CA: Harcourt.

Coles, R. (1995). *The story of Ruby Bridges.* (G. Ford, Illus.). New York, NY: Scholastic.

Collier, B. (2003). *Uptown.* (G. Ford, Illus.) New York, NY: Henry Holt.

Cook, M. (2009). *Our children can soar: A celebration of Rosa, Barack, and the pioneers of change.* (P. Cummings, J. Ransome, E. Velasquez, and L. Dillon, Illus.). New York, NY: Bloomsbury.

Curtis, G. (1998). *The bat boy and his violin.* (E. B. Lewis, Illus.). New York, NY: Simon & Schuster.

Flournoy, V. (1985). *The patchwork quilt.* (J. Pinkney, Illus.). New York, NY: Penguin.

Greenfield, E. (1989). *Nathaniel talking.* (J. Spivey Gilchrist, Illus.). New York, NY: Writers & Readers Publishing.

Grimes, N. (2002). *Talkin' about Bessie: The story of aviator Elizabeth Colman.* (E.B. Lewis, Illus.). New York, NY: Orchard Books.

Hoffman, M. (1991). *Amazing Grace.* (C. Binch, Illus.). New York, NY: Penguin.

Holiday, B., & A. Herzog, Jr. (2004). *God bless the child.* (J. Pinkney, Illus.). New York, NY: HarperCollins.

Howard, E. F. (2000). *Virgie goes to school with us boys.* (E. B. Lewis, Illus.). New York, NY: Simon & Schuster.

Igus, T. (2004). *Going back home: An artist returns to the South.* (M. Wood, Illus.). San Francisco, CA: Children's Book Press.

Jordan, D., & R. M. Jordan. (2000). *Salt in his shoes. Michael Jordan. In pursuit of a dream.* (K. Nelson, Illus.). New York, NY: Simon & Schuster.

McKissack, P. C. (1988). *Mirandy and brother wind.* (J. Pinkney, Illus.). New York, NY: Alfred A. Knopf.

McKissack, P. C. (2001). *Goin' someplace special.* (J. Pinkney, Illus.). New York, NY: Scholastic.

Obama, B. (2009). *Change has come. An artist celebrates our American spirit.* (K. Nelson, Illus.). New York, NY: Simon & Schuster.

Ringgold, F. (1991). *Tar beach.* (F. Ringgold, Illus.). New York, NY: Crown.

Rosen, M. J. (1992). *Elijah's angel. A story for Chanukah and Christmas.* (A. B. L. Robinson, Illus.). San Diego, CA: Harcourt.

Shange, N. (1983). *Ellington was not a street.* (K. Nelson, Illus.). New York, NY: Simon & Schuster. (Illus. copyright, 2004)

Smalls, I. (1998). *A strawbeater's thanksgiving.* (M. Benson Rosales, Illus.). Boston, MA: Little Brown.

Steptoe, J., Illus. (1997). *In daddy's arms I am tall: African Americans celebrating fathers.* New York, NY: Lee & Low. (Text copyright by individual poets)

Steptoe, J. (1997). *Creativity.* (E. B. Lewis, Illus.). New York, NY: Clarion.

Thomas, J. C. (2008). *The blacker the berry.* (F. Cooper, Illus.). New York, NY: HarperCollins.

Thomas, J. C. (1999). *I have heard of a land.* (F. Cooper, Illus.). New York, NY: HarperCollins.

Yarbrough, C. (1997). *Cornrows.* (C. Byard, Illus.). New York, NY: Penguin.

REFERENCES

Bishop, R. S. (1992). Multicultural literature for children. Making informed choices. In V. J. Harris (Ed.), *Teaching multicultural literature in grades K-8* (pp. 39–53). Norwood, MA: Christopher-Gordon.

Cai, M. (2003). Multiple definitions of multicultural literature: Is the debate really just "ivory tower" bickering? In D. L. Fox & K. G. Short (Eds.), *Stories matter. The complexity of cultural authenticity in children's literature* (pp. 269–283). Urbana, IL: National Council of Teachers of English.

Clarke, L. W. (2006, January). "Talk to the hand, girl"; Using texts to explore student voice. *English Journal, 95*(3), 56–60.

Darder, A. (1991). *Cultural and power in the classroom. A critical foundation for bicultural education.* New York, NY: Bergin & Garvey.

Dilg, M. (1999). *Race and culture in the classroom. Teaching and learning through multicultural education.* New York, NY: Teachers College Press.

Enciso, P. E. (1994, November). Cultural identity and response to literature: Running lessons from *Maniac Magee. Language Arts, 71*, 524–533.

Enciso, P. E. (1997). Negotiating the meaning of difference. Talking back to multicultural literature. In T. Rogers & A. O. Soter (Eds.), *Reading across cultures. Teaching literature in a diverse society* (pp. 13–41). New York, NY: Teachers College Press.

Fang, Z., Fu, D., & Lamme, L. L. (2003). The trivialization and misuse of multicultural literature: Issues of representation and communication. In D. L. Fox & K. G. Short (Eds.), *Stories matter. The complexity of cultural authenticity in children's literature* (pp. 284–303). Urbana, IL: National Council of Teachers of English.

Ferdman, B. M. (1990). Literacy and cultural identity. *Harvard Educational Review, 60*(2), 181–203.

Freire, P., & Macedo, D. (1987). *Literacy. Reading the word and the world.* New York, NY: Bergin & Garvey.

Juel, C., Hebard, H., Huabner, J. P., & Moran, M. (2010, March). Reading through a disciplinary lens. *Reading to Learn, 67*(6), 12–17. Retrieved from: http://www.ascd.org/publications/educational_leadership/mar10/vol67/num06/Reading_through_a_disciplinary_lens.

Kaser, S., & Short, K. G. (1998, March). Exploring culture through children's connections. *Language Arts, 75*(2), 185–192.

Lankshear, C., Gee, J. P., Knobel, M., & Searle, C. (1997). *Changing literacies.* Buckingham, UK: Open University Press.

McGinley, W., Kamberelis, G., Mahoney, T. Madigan, D., Rybicki, V., & Oliver, J. (1997). Re-visioning reading and teaching literature through the lens of narrative theory. In T. Roberts & A. O. Soter (Eds.), *Reading across cultures. Teaching literature in a diverse society* (pp. 42–68). New York, NY: Teachers College Press.

Nodelman, P. (1996). *The pleasures of children's literature.* (2nd ed.). White Plains, NY: Longman.

Rochman, H. (1993). *Against borders. Promoting books for a multicultural world.* Chicago, IL: American Library Association.

Rochman, H. (2003). Beyond political correctness. In D. L. Fox & K.G. Short (Eds.), S*tories matter. The complexity of cultural authenticity in children's literature* (pp. 101–115). Urbana, IL: National Council of Teachers of English.

Rosenblatt, L. M. (1993). The literary transactions: Evocation and response. In K E. Holland, R. A. Hungerford, & S. B. Ernst (Eds.), *Journeying. Children responding to literature* (pp. 6–23). Portsmouth, NH: Heinemann.

Shafer, G. (2003, September). Imagine you're a writer. *TETYC 31*(1), 16–23.

Short, K. G. (1999). Critically reading the word and the world. Building intercultural understanding through literature. *Bookbird, 2,* 1–10.

Short, K. G. (2006, September). *Ethics and cultural authenticity in international children's literature.* Paper presented at the meeting of the International Board on Books for Young People, Macau, China.

Sipe, L. R. (2000). The construction of literary understanding by first and second graders in oral response to picture storybook read-alouds. *Reading Research Quarterly, 35*(2), 252–275.

Sleeter, C. E., & Grant, C. A. (1999). *Making choices for multicultural education. Five approaches to race, class, and gender.* Upper Saddle River, NJ: Prentice Hall.

Taxel, J. L. (1994). Political correctness, cultural politics, and writing for young people. *New Advocate, 7*(2), 93–108.

Taxel, J. L. (1995). Cultural politics and writing for young people. In S. Lehr (Ed.), *Battling dragons. Issues and controversy in children's literature* (pp. 155–169). Portsmouth, NH: Heinemann.

Wink, J. (2000). *Critical pedagogy. Notes from the real world.* (2nd ed.). New York, NY: Longman.

Yokota, J. (1993). Issues in selecting multicultural children's literature. *Language Arts, 70,* 156–167.

CHAPTER 4

Spirituality and Young Children

Literature as a Support for Resilience and Coping

PATRICIA CRAWFORD

At Pine Valley Elementary School, Ms. Collins reads stories aloud to her first graders on a daily basis. In an effort to honor children's interests and make a stronger connection with families, she sponsors a month-long story fest, inviting each student to bring in a favorite book from home that will be read aloud in class. The first days go well. Ms. Collins reads each of the children's favorite books in turn, including Eric Carle's (1985) *The Very Busy Spider*, Kevin Henkes' (2000) *Wemberly Worried*, a Sesame Street book, and a smattering of fairy tales. She becomes anxious, however, when Tamera brings in a well-worn, and obviously much loved, collection of Bible stories. Ms. Collins responds, "That's a very special book. It's one that would be great to read at home or church. Why don't you read it there? Do you have another book you'd like to read at school?" Tamera is puzzled by her teacher's response and replies, "This book was my mom's when she was little. It's my favorite. Why can't we read it here?"

Down the hall in the kindergarten classroom, a related scene unfolds. Mrs. Jones and her student teacher are displaying a host of wordless picture books for their students to enjoy. They place old and new favorites in the reading center, including *Pancakes for Breakfast* (dePaolo, 1978), *The Red Book* (Lehman, 2004), and *The Lion and the Mouse* (Pinkney, 2009). Mrs. Jones does not include her copy of Peter Spier's (1977) Caldecott-winning wordless text, *Noah's Ark*. As she places this book behind her desk and out of the children's reach, her student teacher notes, "That looks good." Mrs. Jones responds, "It is—but you can't mix religion with school. It's not right, and you can get into trouble."

Finally, in a second-grade classroom across town, Mr. Jenkins prepares to read Margaret Wise Brown's (1949) classic text, *The Important Book*, as a prompt to a lesson. He begins the read-aloud by saying, "This book is about different things and what makes them important." Jana offers, "I saw something important at church yesterday." A classmate joins the discussion: "Church is important." Another adds, "So is God. God is very important." Mr. Jenkins thanks the students for their comments and then quickly guides the conversation back to safer territory. "Let's read and find out about the important things in this book," he says.

Vignettes such as these play out in primary classrooms on a regular basis (Mardell & Abo-Zena, 2010; Myers & Martin, 1993). Not only are these situations indicative of the discomfort many teachers experience in dealing with religion in the classroom context, but they also serve as dual reminders that children's spiritual wonderings are often prompted, supported, and problematized by the literature that is shared with them (Green & Oldendorf, 2005; Zeece, 1998), and that spirituality is an ongoing and important aspect in the lives of young children (Coles, 1986, 1990; Myers 1997; Myers & Myers, 1999).

This centrality of a spiritual focus may be particularly evident among children who come from cultures in which religious traditions, houses of worship, and spiritual leaders play a central role in their family and community lives. In many African American communities, spirituality has been identified as a salient, shared, cultural value, one that not only helps to define and express belief systems but also offers protective qualities and coping skills for dealing with life's difficult challenges (Boykin, 1994; Haight, 1998; Mattis, 2002). In the United States, African American churches have historically served as community gathering spots, as centers of political organization, and as places that offer emotional solace and practical support within communities that were unwelcoming or hostile to people of color. Tonya Bolden (2001, n.p.) wrote the following in her poetic and informative picture book tribute to the black church:

> She has done so much
> to make her people strong.
> to keep so many alive in their bodies, in their souls.
> in times of dense distress.

Her words continue on, painting vivid images of the crucial role that spiritual nurturing has played:

Arms ever-always open
through the neglect and disrespect,
lack, attacks,
ashes
to embrace the children of her children's children and their child
to be born.

Children's spirituality lays both within and transcends beyond elements typically defined as religious, impacting many different domains of life experience. The purposes of this chapter are to consider the nature of this spirituality of young children and to explore the ways in which the spirited nature of children can be nurtured through thoughtfully chosen children's literature and related learning experiences. Books featuring African American characters, settings, and other elements of culture will receive specific attention.

YOUNG CHILDREN, SPIRITUALITY, AND LITERATURE

The term "spirituality" is one that is widely used but for which there is no universally accepted definition (Trousdale, 2004). While most people associate some type of religious connotation with the term, others position spirituality within a broader framework, one that addresses the very human desire to make sense of life through relationships with the sacred, the secular, and the self (Nye, 2006; Myers & Myers, 1999). Young children often display inclinations across all of these contexts: expressing religious convictions, considering "why" questions about the seemingly unexplainable events in their personal and collective lives, and tapping into important relationships with others, both divine and human, to cope with loss and deal with life's challenges (Coles, 1986, 1990; Myers, 1997).

Teachers of young children have no easy task in guiding them as they grapple with challenging spiritual topics. At first brush, their wonderings may seem to belong more to the territory of philosophers and theologians. However, these are joys and struggles that are wrestled with by even the youngest learners. Thus, in order to teach the whole child, primary teachers must be ready to support learning across all domains, including the spiritual (Buchanan & Baumgartner, 2009). This readiness will take different forms, depending on both the context and purposes of the setting in which teachers work.

In faith-based settings, spiritual support may include intentional forays into religion, spirituality, and morals, as informed by the guiding principles of the school. Parents who have enrolled their children in faith-based schools have implicitly or explicitly given their permission for their children to participate in faith explorations, at least to the extent outlined by school policy. An excellent example of an authentic literacy-rich spiritual exploration within a faith-based setting has been documented in *God's Photo Album: How We Looked for God and Saved Our School* (Mecum, 2001). This extended photo essay, aimed at both juvenile and adult audiences, documents one school's quest to "look for God" in the world around it. With disposable cameras and pencils in hand, children and their families from a small school set out to find God and document their journey along the way. They did so by capturing images of nature, other people, and the work of human hands. By making their work public, they not only raised proceeds to help their struggling school, but they also raised the conscience of others who were spiritually like-minded about their world.

While a project like *God's Photo Album* may be inappropriate or difficult to implement in settings that are not faith-based, some programs have also recognized that all children need opportunities to explore their important spiritual questions. For example, kindergartners at the Tufts University laboratory school, a private but secular setting, engaged in a study of spiritual beliefs (Mardell & Abo-Zena, 2010). Using a project approach framework (Katz & Chard, 1989), teachers facilitated a range of learning experiences, even forming a "God Study Group" for interested classroom participants. They used literature, discussion, dramatic play, interviews with resource people, and response projects to support children's inquiries. The teachers and associated researchers acknowledge that there are innate challenges in exploring such controversial topics with young children. However, they also point to the significance of such work, as an important part of an antibias curriculum, as a contribution to children's cultural literacy, and as a help for children to become more cognizant and valuing of their own belief systems (Derman-Sparks & Edwards, 2010; Mardell & Abo-Zena, 2010).

Although it can be difficult to navigate, even students in public settings benefit from an opportunity and safe space in which they can consider spiritual differences and similarities between themselves and others (Baumgartner & Buchanan, 2010; Myers & Martin, 1993; Peyton & Jalongo, 2008). They want to know not only why things happen but also why their perspective of events may be similar to or different from others. Silvern (2006) suggests that this can be facilitated by listening closely to children's conversations, responding authentically to their concerns, and acknowledging their unique perspectives.

Children's spirituality also extends beyond religious inquiries to their authentic explorations and search for explanations about the world and people that surround them. This perspective of spirituality touches the very depths of human nature and focuses not only on the "other worldliness" of spiritual wonderings but on the spirited nature of children, of their resiliency and modes of coping with life's challenges (Myers & Myers, 1999).

Literature provides a powerful opportunity to support children in their spiritual wonderings and concerns about both the sacred and the secular (Peyton & Jalongo, 2008; Pike, 2004; Trousdale, 2004; Zeece, 1998). Through quality literature, young readers have the opportunity to explore sensitive topics, challenging contexts, and even situations that probe pain and loss, all within the safe confines of the pages of a book. Picture books, in particular, provide an abbreviated format in which tough topics can be broached using an economy of words and a plethora of images that convey meaning beyond the printed text (Roberts & Crawford, 2008; Sipe, 2007). Picture books serve as material tools that help to both reflect and shape images of cultural and spiritual understandings for young learners. Through them, readers can find comfort, question behaviors, and wrestle with moral dilemmas (Johnson, 2009). Books invite children to relate vicariously to characters; they have the opportunity to safely consider the motivations, personality, and life circumstances that make them similar to or different from the real and fictional people they encounter within the bound pages.

BOOKS THAT NURTURE THE SPIRIT FOR EVERY CHILD

The past three decades have seen the publication of many children's books that address sensitive topics or deep, challenging issues in a didactic manner. While these can be helpful sources of information, most children prefer texts that provide authentic storylines and literary contexts for engagement (Sipe, 2007). The following section provides an exploration of authentic children's literature that has some type of spiritual component. The first part considers books that explore issues that surround faith or elements explicitly related to the sacred. The second part presents an exploration of texts that model the spirited nature of human beings and the coping skills used to maintain and restore resilience in the face of life's challenges. Pedagogical considerations are presented at the conclusion of the chapter.

Books that Explore Issues of Faith and the Sacred

Sacred texts play an important role in the lives of young children. In many faith communities, children often read, recite, and memorize passages from Scripture, which is a form of traditional literature. Perhaps few passages are as familiar to Christian communities as that found in the 23rd Psalm. Tim Ladwig (1997) presents this ancient text and translates it for a contemporary audience in *Psalm Twenty-three*. Each verse is paired with images from an urban setting and features African American characters. The text introduces a young brother and sister duo as they encounter both the nurturing and challenging circumstances that reside in their immediate neighborhood, following them as they proceed through a host of daily rituals. Nestled in their warm bed and waking to the embrace of a caring extended family, they are reminded that they are provided for and that they "shall not be in want." A romp in a nearby park is reminiscent of "green pastures." Images of caring teachers and supportive school environments are reminders that they are guided in "paths of righteousness" and that familiar places and loving relationships do indeed "restore [their] soul[s]." These hopeful scenes are made more powerful by their juxtaposition with images of threatening street scenes ("the shadow of death") and bullies who lurk nearby ("I will fear no evil . . ."). The centrality of their church and images of the Good Shepherd are woven throughout the book.

Traditional literature also finds its form in the words of African American spirituals. "This Little Light of Mine" provides a terrific example of a joyful spiritual song that has been passed from generation to generation and continues to be sung by children today. With its roots in the biblical text (Matthew 5:14–16), the original lyrics reference the manner in which the light of faith shines through individuals. It provides hope and light and therefore should not be hidden. Several illustrators have brought the familiar words to life through their vibrant artwork. Ashley Bryan's (2007) version presents the song, along with two other well-known spirituals, each extended with his characteristically vivid, colorful, and somewhat abstract style of illustration. In an illustrator's note, Bryan recounts the powerful role that spirituals played in African American history. During the time when it was illegal to teach a slave to read or write, these songs provided an outlet for creativity and a mode through which expressive thoughts and hopes for freedom could be conveyed to the world. Bryan notes that as part of his honoring of these songs, he has "made an effort to create the most forceful illustrations that will capture the underlying meaning of the Spiritual" (Bryan, 2007, n.p.). He urges readers to keep this spirit alive by joining in and singing along.

E. B. Lewis (2005) has developed a different type of book in response to "This Little Light of Mine." In this version, realistic paintings capture the sentiment of each line of familiar lyrics. In the opening pages, readers are introduced to a young African American boy who first looks at himself in a mirror and then looks out of a window to see the world. Paired with the lyrics, it becomes clear that the child sees a light in himself and either consciously or unconsciously recognizes that this light needs to be shared with the world. Successive pages reveal him sharing this light in the form of hugs to family members, in friendly waves to neighbors, in the act of consoling friends and providing practical assistance to those in need. The light within him is significant, needed by others, and made manifest in the most ordinary, but intentional, daily interactions. The child depicted in the pages of this text has made a choice. Just like the generations of women and men who have preceded him, he will share his light and make a difference to others:

Hide it under a bushel? No!
I'm gonna let it shine . . .
Won't let no one blow it out,
I'm gonna let it shine. (Lewis, 2005, n.p.)

In addition to traditional texts, belief systems and their application to everyday life can also be probed by investigating the writings and works of spiritual leaders. For example, *Martin's Big Words* (Rappaport, 2007) presents the story of Martin Luther King by drawing on both biographical information and Dr. King's own words. This verbiage, paired with Bryan Collier's illustrations, inspired by stained glass windows, demonstrates the transformative power of faith both in the personal and public life of the civil rights leader. The book not only inspires, but it also sheds the false sanitization that exists in portraying the civil rights movement as one that had no spiritual component. The concepts of faith in action, and as action, are reinforced by the interjection of Dr. King's words: "Remember, if I am stopped, this movement will not be stopped, because God is with this movement" (Rappaport, 2007, p. 20). Dr. King is not portrayed as only a spiritual leader; however, this role is not minimized either and is recognized as one important component that helped to shape his identity and the powerful work that he was to accomplish.

Words of a more recent spiritual leader are presented in *God's Dream* (Tutu & Abrams, 2008). In this work, Archbishop Desmond Tutu puts forth a child-appropriate version of the nonsectarian, peace-filled spiritual statements for which he is known among adults. The illustrations depict children of many different cultures, ethnicities, and religious affiliations, with the text suggesting that through their actions and choices, all children can participate in God's dream of building a compassionate, respectful, and loving world. No doubt, the creation of this book was influenced deeply by the experiences of the author, well-known for having lived out his spirituality in both the midst and aftermath of South Africa's apartheid era, and those of the illustrator, who was born into war-torn Vietnam. Together, they have woven words and pictures in a manner that conveys the significance of spirituality in daily life. Although this text provides a somewhat simplistic approach to very complex world problems, it also offers an introduction to the thoughts of a respected religious leader and a springboard for developing a perspective that values a diversity of approaches and practices within the spiritual domain.

Finally, the relationship between the sacred and everyday life can be explored by reading stories that demonstrate the manner in which ordinary people choose to implement their lives of faith, which can have a transforming effect on the world. An example of this can be found in the ways in which the intersection between belief and educational opportunity is portrayed in books.

Perhaps one of the most familiar and well-documented historical examples of this relationship can be found in *The Story of Ruby Bridges* (Coles, 1995). In this true story of how a young girl integrated the all-white Frantz Elementary School in 1960 New Orleans, the author conveys the intense psychological pressure exerted on six-year-old Ruby as she deals with jeers, angry mobs, and classroom isolation. The text shows that faith played a significant part in the Bridges' family life, with Ruby's mother noting, "We wanted our children to be near God's spirit. . . . We wanted them to feel close to Him from the very start!" (Coles, 1995, n.p.). Drawing on this spiritual foundation, Ruby finds the strength to endure tremendous hardship in the midst of the integration process and emerges not just surviving but responding to those who are cruel to her by offering forgiveness and prayer. This biographical picture book provides a model of the interweaving of family support, spiritual rootedness, and a personal determination that triumphs in the midst of historic and systemic injustice.

An exploration of the interplay among spirituality, education, and civil rights is also explored in *Sister Anne's Hands* (Lorbiecki, 2000). In this poignant story set during the civil rights movement, Sister Anne is an African American nun who comes to teach in an all-white parochial school. Neither her students nor their families are quite sure what to expect from this nun, who looks different from any teacher they have encountered in their past. All goes well until someone sails a paper airplane with hurtful comments about Sister Anne across the room. As Sister Anne processes the event and responds thoughtfully to the words, her students learn much more than the math and reading lessons that were planned for them. This is a powerful story that exposes the hurt and remorse that accompany racist acts, for both the participants and those who are only tangentially involved. Again, a spiritual context conveys the fact that characters live, love, and learn across all domains.

In another example, Elizabeth Fitzgerald Howard (2000) teams with illustrator E. B. Lewis in *Virgie Goes to School with Us Boys* to tell the story of a young girl who longs to go to school with her brothers. Set in the post-Civil War era, the text mentions that the school was established by Quakers or "some folks who love the Lord" (n.p.). In order to attend school, the children have to walk many miles and demonstrate bravery along the journey. They sing traditional spirituals to give them courage and to pass the time en route. The book portrays the right to an education for people of every race, culture, and gender as a principle that cannot be separated from a life of faith. The author provides additional personal and historical information related to this in her postscript.

Books That Demonstrate Spirit in the Challenges of Daily Life

Children's lives demand resilience and support for a spirited response in situations both large and small. Picture book models offer children tools for coping across a full range of these types of challenges. In *The Hello, Goodbye Window* (Juster, 2005), a young child deals with a repeated ritual of loss and consolation within the scope of a caring, multiracial family. Each day she stays at Nanna and Poppy's house while her parents go to work. Although the days are joyful, she still must navigate the comings and goings—saying farewell to her parents on one end of the day and then doing the same with her grandparents on the other. Her grandparents console her with kind words and by introducing her to the magic window for hellos and goodbyes. The child knows that eventually the person she misses most will appear in this window. Chris Raschka's Caldecott-winning illustrations provide an understated, yet reassuring perspective on the comfort of people and routines that can be counted upon during momentary uncertainties.

Peer relationships take on a new importance during the primary years. Children grow in both the ability and desire to develop close friendships. Although some friendships develop easily, others require a greater level of intention and effort. A story of challenges in building peer relationships is presented in Mary Ann Rodman's (2005) *My Best Friend.* Six-year-old Lily desperately wants seven-year-old Tamika to be her best friend. When Tamika seems uninterested, Lilly does everything in her power to move the relationship forward: She manages to be at the pool at the same play time, buys a matching bathing suit, and offers to share her Popsicle. In spite of all her efforts, Tamika remains aloof, referring to Lilly's actions as babyish, and she is only interested in playing when no one else is around. It takes many rounds of subtle rejection before Lilly decides to pursue a different friendship. Lilly's character shows tremendous growth in the course of a few pages, as she moves from neediness to agency and as she comes to understand that she can move on to a friendship that will be more reciprocal in nature. This provocative picture book raises many questions about the nature of friendship and shows that the relational road that children travel is not always a smooth one. The sensitively rendered text and E. B. Lewis' luminous watercolor illustrations convey a sense of honest, and at times, painful reality. Young readers are invited to thoughtfully consider Lilly's discovery that friendship is not something that can be forced on another person, that it requires cooperation on the part of both parties. Readers are also presented with the hopeful thought that there may be many potential friends right near them, waiting to be discovered.

Lucille Clifton's (1983) *Everett Anderson's Goodbye* presents a very definitive model of spirited coping, in the midst of a substantial and permanent loss. In this now classic text, little Everett Anderson mourns the loss of his father. The sparse text leads readers through Everett's journey through the stages of grief, as his denial, anger, bargaining, depression, and finally acceptance of this traumatic event are lived out in the scope of everyday life. This book echoes the life-changing sadness that accompanies such a profound loss but also offers hope of endurance. Surrounded by his mother's love and support, Everett manages to survive and learns that even in death, "love doesn't stop" (n.p.).

A spirituality of resilience is demonstrated in the ways in which individuals respond to life's challenges over both the short and long terms. *Mr. George Baker* (Hest, 2004) provides an excellent example of the latter. The story introduces two characters who, by external appearances, appear to have little in common. Mr. George Baker is an African American centenarian who never learned to read. Harry is a young white schoolboy. They are bound together by proximity in their neighborhood and in spirit by their desire to learn to read. Each day they head off to school together: Mr. Baker to adult education courses and Harry to the first grade. By word and example, Mr. Baker provides a model of kindness and caring. His character exemplifies the value of hard work and education for his young friend. Harry, for his part, is mesmerized by Mr. Baker and the fascinating life he has lived for 100 years.

Perhaps the most important elements of this story are the ones left unstated. Although no explanation is given as to why Mr. Baker did not learn to read, it can be inferred that circumstances did not permit him to obtain a quality education during his early life. Perhaps this was due to segregation, a poor educational system, or the need to leave school in order to make a living. What is made explicit in the text is that in spite of circumstances, Mr. Baker views himself as a lifelong learner, one whose illiteracy is a situation that "must be corrected" (Hest, 2004, n.p.). Mr. Baker's resilience is buoyed by the loving relationship he has with his wife, the joy he takes in the talents he has displayed in other facets of life, and an inner optimism. These qualities not only help propel him toward his goal of learning to read, but they also strengthen his capacity for mentoring Harry in a friendship that transcends the boundaries of both race and age.

Readers who find the exploration of Mr. Baker's boundary-crossing relationship to be compelling may also enjoy reading *Miz Berlin Walks* (Yolen, 1997) as a companion piece. In this story, Mary Louise is a young African American girl who observes Miz Berlin, an older, eccentric, white woman who walks the neighborhood each evening. As she walks, she sings and recounts fanciful stories of days gone by. One day, Mary Louise finds herself brave enough to join Miz Berlin's stroll, and she is soon delighted and overcome by the woman's amazing stories. As they become nightly walking partners, the two forge an unlikely friendship that is interrupted only by Miz Berlin's fall and eventual death. Yolen's text, enhanced by Floyd Cooper's rich and poignant illustrations, conveys the joy of this relationship and the pain of loss that comes with Miz Berlin's passing. In spite of Mary Louise's grief, the message is clear: Miz Berlin and her legacy continue to live on. Daily events and simple gestures such as taking walks and telling stories have brought delight and strength to all involved; they have connected generations and hearts, giving hope even in the face of a painful loss.

Another type of deep loss demanding a spirited resilience is explored in *Visiting Day* (Woodson, 2002). In this text, a young girl and her grandmother prepare for a family visit. They are going to see Daddy. Every effort is made to make this day a special one: favorite food is lovingly cooked, hair is neatly braided, and mementos are prepared. From the opening pages, the anticipation of parent, child, and grandparent are tangible. Only when the story unfolds does it become clear that this visit will take place at a prison. In one of the few picture books that features an incarcerated parent, *Visiting Day* tackles a difficult topic of loss in a manner that is at once poignant and hopeful. Although prison life is clearly presented as bleak and undesirable, the father and his fellow prisoners are portrayed in a manner that is dignified and humane. The poetic print text, combined with James Ransome's powerful illustrations, capture the little girl's sense of sadness and longing for the father who is absent. However, they also present a clear sense of resilience, a hopeful and positive look forward to the future when together time will not be limited to a single monthly visiting day. Coping mechanisms to deal with this type of loss are artfully woven into the storyline, showing that small actions can make big differences in the lives of both those who give and receive. Sharing artwork and cards, engaging in good laughs and conversation, and breaking bread together are all small things that can make a seemingly intolerable situation much more livable and help to shorten the distance between loved ones.

PEDAGOGICAL CONSIDERATIONS FOR SPIRITUAL EXPLORATIONS

The exploration of literacy-based spirituality requires careful consideration on the part of the teacher. Clearly, educators who work in public settings have a different set of expectations and protocols than those who work in faith-based ones. Teachers of young children must find and navigate a path that honors children's spiritual explorations, questions, and concerns. Furthermore, they must do this without either minimizing children's belief systems or presenting material in a manner that could be construed as either implicitly or explicitly proselytizing. In preparing to do this, teachers might consider the following recommendations:

- *Create an intentional environment to support children and families:* Researchers and practitioners have found that responsiveness is the key to creating a classroom setting that is supportive to children's spiritual development. Engage in active listening and respond thoughtfully to children's questions or concerns. It is essential that family members be informed and involved with spiritual explorations and discussions that occur in the classroom (Mardell & Abo-Zena, 2010; Myers & Myers, 1999; Silvern, 2006).
- *Include appropriate literature that explores spiritual topics in the classroom library:* Appropriate literature will vary from classroom to classroom and be dependent on curricular issues and school expectations. If the social studies curriculum includes explorations of cultural issues, it seems reasonable that children be able to explore literature that addresses spiritual similarities and differences.
- *Provide appropriate response projects:* Children will benefit from exploring texts within a historical context with art and literacy extensions. For example, they may enjoy illustrating their own versions of illustrated spiritual songs as part of a unit on folk songs or other song picture books.
- *Model a spirit of resilience by including literature that explores a range of life circumstances:* No single text will fulfill the spiritual wonderings of every child, and not every child is ready to explore specific sensitive topics. Teachers will feel more comfortable in sharing literature on these issues if they have a strong familiarity with the children and families with whom they work. Teachers will also want to consider whether it would be more appropriate to share specific books and related discussions in large-group, small-group, or individual read-aloud sessions.

The real-life circumstances of children are diverse and complicated. Therefore, the literature that we share with them must also be diverse, and in some cases, complicated. By choosing and using literature wisely, we can address children's concerns with care and support their spirited lives and spiritual wonderings along the way.

CHILDREN'S BOOKS CITED

Bolden, T. (2001). *Rock of ages: A tribute to the African American church.* Illus. by R. G. Christie. New York, NY: Alfred A. Knopf.
Brown, M. W. (1949). *The important book.* New York, NY: HarperCollins.

Bryan, A. (2007). *Let it shine.* New York, NY: Atheneum.

Carle, E. (1985). *The very busy spider.* New York, NY: Philomel.

Clifton, L. (1983). *Everett Anderson's goodbye.* Illus. by A. Grifalconi. New York, NY: Holt, Rinehart & Winston.

Coles, R. (1995). *The story of Ruby Bridges.* Illus. by G. Ford. New York, NY: Scholastic.

dePaolo, T. (1978). *Pancakes for breakfast.* Boston, MA: Houghton Mifflin.

Henkes, K. (2000). *Wemberly worried.* New York, NY: Greenwillow.

Hest, A. (2004). *Mr. George Baker.* Cambridge, MA: Candlewick.

Howard, E. F. (2000). *Virgie goes to school with us boys.* Illus. by E. B. Lewis. New York, NY: Simon & Schuster.

Juster, N. (2005). *The hello, goodbye window.* Illus. by C. Raschka. New York, NY: Scholastic.

Ladwig, T. (1997). *Psalm twenty-three.* Grand Rapids, MI: Eerdmans.

Lewis, E. B. (2005). *This little light of mine.* New York, NY: Simon & Schuster.

Lehman, B. (2004). *The red book.* Boston, MA: Houghton Mifflin.

Lorbiecki, M. (2000). *Sister Anne's hands.* Illus. by W. Popp. New York, NY: Puffin.

Pinkney, J. (2009). *The lion and the mouse.* Boston, MA: Little, Brown.

Rappaport, D. (2007). *Martin's big words.* Illus. by B. Collier. New York, NY: Hyperion.

Rodman, M. A. (2005). *My best friend.* Illus. by E. B. Lewis. New York, NY: Viking.

Spier, P. (1977). *Noah's ark.* New York, NY: Doubleday.

Tutu, D., & Abrams, D. C. (2008). *God's dream.* Illus. by L. Pham. Cambridge, MA: Candlewick.

Woodson, J. (2002). *Visiting day.* Illus. by J. E. Ransome. New York, NY: Scholastic.

Yolen, J. (1997). *Miz Berlin walks.* Illus. by F. Cooper. New York, NY: Philomel.

REFERENCES

Baumgartner, J., & Buchanan, T. (2010). Supporting each child's spirit. *Young Children, 65*(2), 90–95.

Boykin, W. (1994). Harvesting talent and culture: African American children and educational reform. In R. Rossi (Ed.), *Schools and students at risk: Context and framework for positive change* (pp. 116–138). New York, NY: Teachers College Press.

Buchanan, T., & Baumgartner, J. (2009). Appropriately and intentionally teaching the whole child: Rediscovering spirituality. *Focus on Pre-K and K, 22*(3), 4–7.

Coles, R. (1986). *The moral life of children.* New York, NY: Atlantic Monthly Press.

Coles, R. (1990). *The spiritual life of children.* Boston, MA: Houghton Mifflin.

Derman-Sparks, L., & Edwards, J. O. (2010). *Anti-bias education for young children and ourselves.* Washington, DC: National Association for the Education of Young Children.

Green, C., & Oldendorf, S. (2005). Teaching religious diversity through children's literature. *Childhood Education, 81,* 209–218.

Haight, W. L. (1998). "Gathering the spirit" at First Baptist Church: Spirituality as a protective factor in the lives of African American children. *Social Work, 43*(3), 213–221.

Johnson, D. (2009). *The joy of children's literature.* Boston, MA: Harcourt.

Katz, L., & Chard, S. (1989). *Engaging children's minds: The project approach.* Norwood, NJ: Ablex.

Mardell, B., & Abo-Zena, M. M. (2010). Kindergartners explore spirituality. *Young Children, 65*(4), 12–17.

Mattis, J. S. (2002). Religion and spirituality in the meaning-making and coping experiences of African-American women. *Psychology of Women Quarterly, 26,* 309–321.

Mecum, S. (2001). *God's photo album: How we looked for God and saved our school.* San Francisco, CA: Harper.

Myers, B. K. (1997). *Young children and spirituality.* New York, NY: Routledge.

Myers, B. K., & Martin, M. P. (1993). Faith foundations for all of our children. *Young Children, 48*(2), 49–55.

Myers, B. K., & Myers, M. E. (1999). Engaging children's spirit and spirituality through literature. *Childhood Education, 76,* 28–32.

Nye, R. (2006). Identifying the core of children's spirituality. In D. Hay & R. Nye (Eds.), *The spirit of the child* (Rev. ed.) (pp. 108–128). London: Jessica Kingsley Publishers.

Peyton, M. R., & Jalongo, M. R. (2008). Make me an instrument of your peace: Honoring religious diversity and modeling respect for faiths through children's literature. *Early Childhood Education Journal, 35,* 301–303.

Pike, M. A. (2004). 'Well-being' through reading: Drawing upon literature and literacy in spiritual education. *International Journal of Children's Spirituality, 9,* 155–162.

Roberts, S. K., & Crawford, P. A. (2008). Real life calls for real books: Literature to help children cope with family stressors. *Young Children, 63*(5), 12–17.

Silvern, S. (2006). Educating mind and spirit: Embracing a confluence of cultures in the education of children. *Childhood Education, 83,* 2–5.

Sipe, L. (2007). *Storytime: Young children's literary understanding in the classroom.* New York, NY: Teachers College Press.

Trousdale, A. M. (2004). Black and white fire: The interplay of stories, imagination, and children's spirituality. *International Journal of Children's Spirituality, 9,* 177–188.

Zeece, P. D. (1998). "Can God come here?" Using religion-based literature in early childhood settings. *Early Childhood Education Journal, 25,* 243–246.

CHAPTER 5

Sharing Culturally Relevant Literature with Preschool Children and Their Families

April Whatley Bedford & Renée Casbergue

In 2008, we received a three-year Early Reading First (ERF) grant, a component of No Child Left Behind legislation focusing on three- and four-year-olds. All ERF projects were designed to enhance the literacy development of at-risk preschool children through enriching classroom environments, literacy curriculum and instruction, and family literacy practices, and by engaging preschool teachers in high-quality, literacy-focused, professional development. Our particular project, Project Recovery, included seven prekindergarten classrooms in New Orleans public schools. One hundred percent of the children in these classes were African American, as identified by their parents. Six of the seven teachers and all of the teaching assistants were also African American. To involve teachers, students, and families in a variety of culturally meaningful literacy experiences, we carefully chose children's literature by and about African American and African individuals.

BUILDING UPON A THEORETICAL FOUNDATION

We strongly believe that *all* children deserve the opportunity to see themselves represented in books, and we used the often-cited work of Rudine Sims Bishop (1990) to guide us in selecting books for our project that would serve as mirrors reflecting students' cultural identities as well as windows through which to learn more about others different from themselves. We concur with Brooks and McNair (2009) that "African American children's literature can . . . assist readers with establishing beliefs, racial and literate identities, as well as sets of literacy, social, and cultural practices" (p. 126). Not *all* children's books about African Americans will promote such positive outcomes for readers, however.

A number of scholars like Mikkelsen (1998) have questioned whether authors who are not African American can write credibly and authentically about African American experiences. Some researchers go so far as to define African American children's literature as "books that are written by and about African Americans" (Brooks & McNair, 2009, p. 134). Recently, experts in children's literature have extended this "insider/outsider" debate to the work of the illustrator, arguing that African American illustrators bring a valuable insider's perspective to picture books and children's book cover design (Johnson, 1990; Roethler, 1998; Thompson, 2001). Roethler (1998) asserts that the images young children "soak up" during their earliest school experiences will "remain with them for the rest of their lives" (p. 96). Because the books we purchased for our project classrooms were primarily picture books, these were important considerations for us.

Sadly, the number of books available that fit the accepted scholarly definition of African American children's literature is small. In 2009 (the latest publication year for which data are available), the Cooperative Children's Book Center received and reviewed approximately 3,000 of the estimated 5,000 children's books published that year. Of these, 157 books were about African Americans, and 83 of these books, or 53 percent, were written by African American authors (Horning, Lindgren, & Schliesman, 2010). The number of picture books illustrated by African American illustrators was not reported. Of the books that we purchased for the Project Recovery classrooms that featured African American characters and experiences, some but not all were written and/or illustrated by African American authors and illustrators. (A full list of African American and African children's books we selected can be found in the Appendix on pp. 70-71.)

ENRICHING THE LITERACY ENVIRONMENT

A number of studies have shown the importance of accessibility of a large number of children's books to the literacy development of young children. For example, Neuman (1999) and her colleagues (Neuman, Celano, Greco, & Shue, 2003) provide strong statistical evidence for surrounding young children with books in order to increase their gains in reading and writing skills. Because of findings like these, all ERF grants provide substantial funding for purchasing books for classrooms.

While not all the books we purchased included African American characters, we tried to provide as many as possible that would reflect the identities and experiences of the children in our particular project. We began by taking stock of what was already available in each classroom. Of our seven classrooms, three had no books available at all when the teachers began teaching in them. The other four classrooms all had children's books available, but only two of them had books by or about African Americans: three books in one classroom and nine in another. Four of the seven teachers had purchased books for the classrooms themselves prior to participating in our project, ranging from one to twelve books about African Americans. The twenty-nine different picture books by or about African Americans that were present in the seven participating classrooms before our project began included all genres with the majority (twelve) being realistic fiction. Six of the twenty-nine included African settings. Fifteen were written by African American authors, and sixteen were illustrated by African American illustrators.

After this initial inventory of each classroom, we began ordering books and provided the children with immediate access to them as soon as they arrived. We placed a number of books in the classroom library center. Every ERF classroom is required to have a reading center with bookshelves and soft furniture, like beanbag chairs or child-sized foam couches, where children are encouraged—and allowed time—to interact with books of their own choosing. We also placed topically related books in every other learning center in the classroom so that children could explore books in a variety of settings (Casbergue, McGee, & Bedford, 2007). When possible, we selected books to purchase that extended the subject of each center. We also featured African American characters by placing books like *Violet's Music* (Johnson, 2004) in the music center; *Full, Full, Full of Love* (Cooke, 2003), a book that highlights the special foods eaten by an African American family at Sunday dinner, in the housekeeping center; and *Bippity Bop Barbershop* (Tarpley, 2002) in the second dramatic play center, set up as a hair salon.

SUPPLEMENTING A LITERACY-FOCUSED CURRICULUM

Because all ERF projects in 2008 were required to purchase a preschool curriculum, we chose Opening the World of Learning, or OWL (Schickedanz, Dickinson, & Charlotte-Mecklenburg Schools, 2005), primarily because it is literature-based and includes forty-eight individual titles with purchase. Within these fiction and nonfiction picture books, we found a diverse range of cultures and ethnicities represented. However, when we examined the OWL curriculum for specific titles by and about African Americans and Africans, we found only four. *Peter's Chair* (Keats, 1967), *Whistle for Willie* (Keats, 1964), and *Corduroy* (Freeman, 1968) feature

African American characters, and *Bringing the Rain to Kapiti Plain* (Aardema, 1986) is set in Africa. All three of the authors/illustrators of these books are white.

To make the curriculum more culturally relevant for the students in our project, we purchased books that reflect African American culture to incorporate into the six curricular units of OWL. We added books such as *Bigmama's* (Crews, 1991) to the family unit; *Please, Puppy, Please* (Lee & Lee, 2005) to a unit on friends; *Looking Like Me* (Myers, 2009) when learning about shadows and reflections; *One Hot Summer Day* (Crews, 1995) to the wind and water unit; *I Love My Hair!* (Tarpley, 2001) to a unit on things that grow; and *Beautiful Blackbird* (Bryan, 2003) when studying colors. Many of these books easily fit within more than one curricular unit, and teachers often returned to the books for repeated readings in a different context when appropriate.

IMPLEMENTING LITERATURE-BASED INSTRUCTION

There is a wealth of professional literature that recommends the use of picture books to support the literacy development of young children (see Strasser & Seplocha, 2007, for an excellent overview). Much of the professional development we provided for our teachers centered around effective strategies for sharing books with children and extending reading experiences to develop particular literacy skills. These included specific models for reading aloud, retelling and building comprehension, using shared writing, fostering phonemic awareness, and developing oral language and vocabulary (see McGee, 2007; McGee & Schickedanz, 2007; Schickedanz & Casbergue, 2009).

According to Harris (1990), "Literature created by African Americans has never been a central component of schooling" (p. 540). We hoped to change this in the classrooms in our project by centering as much instruction as possible on picture books by and about African Americans. We purchased books like *The Neighborhood Mother Goose* (Crews, 2003), a collection of over forty traditional nursery rhymes illustrated by whimsical photographs of African American children and families in urban environments, to foster language play and recognition of rhyming words. To build vocabulary, we looked for very simple texts like *Peekaboo Morning* (Isadora, 2002), about which teachers and children could discuss the illustrations in detail, as well as books with rich, advanced vocabulary that teachers could define in context while reading aloud, like Marilyn Nelson's (2009) *Beautiful Ballerina*, illustrated by photographs of lovely African American dancers. Vocabulary words and concepts introduced by these books were then further developed during dramatic play in centers. To promote comprehension by forming personal connections to texts and activating prior knowledge, we selected books by local authors highlighting local cultural events like *Mardi Gras* (Shaik, 1999) and *Jazz Fest* (McConduit, 1997).

SHARING BOOKS WITH FAMILIES:
THE FAMILY BOOK CLUB MODEL

While Project Recovery is primarily classroom based, we have also developed many strategies for involving families in extending students' literacy development at home. One of these is the Family Book Club. Modeled after other ERF projects that included Community Book Clubs (Dail, McGee, & Edwards, 2009), we presented families of our prekindergarten students with the opportunity to come to school three evenings during the school year to discuss books with one another. A few weeks prior to each book club meeting, we sent home two books with each child, and these books were theirs to keep whether or not a child's family attended the Family Book Club. For these selections, we focused solely on books by and about African Americans.

Like our colleagues from other ERF projects, we began by pairing an adult book with a picture book on the same theme so that adult family members might have an independent reading experience to enjoy as well as an experience of shared reading with the children in their household. Through these meetings, we hoped to provide guidance to families in selecting books for their children and in sharing and discussing books as a family as well as providing a small collection upon which each family could build a home library. By requiring teachers to attend the Family Book Club meetings and providing them with their own books to keep, we also extended guidance to them in selecting books for instruction and continuing to build classroom libraries.

Book Club One: A Focus on Local Culture

For our first book club, we chose books that focused on our local New Orleans culture in order to help families make personal connections to the books, build a sense of community, and prompt readers to tell or even write their own stories. The adult book, *Coming Out the Door for the Ninth Ward*, by Nine Times Social and Pleasure Club (2009), published by the New Orleans-based Neighborhood Story Project, is a book of personal narratives and oral histories about a Second Line parading club, an African American community tradition in New Orleans. The related picture book we introduced was *Jazz*, written by Walter Dean Myers and illustrated by Christopher Myers (2006), a collection of poems about jazz music with New Orleans settings.

Five of the authors of *Coming Out the Door for the Ninth Ward*, all African American men who grew up in the Ninth Ward neighborhood, narrated a slideshow about their neighborhood, read excerpts from their book, and led the book club participants in a Second Line dance. The adults present, both students' family members and teachers, made numerous personal connections to this book and its authors. Some parents admitted that they hadn't read the book before the meeting, but the authors' presentation had motivated them to read it now. The authors also described how they sought out the opportunity to tell their own stories after hearing about other books published by the Neighborhood Story Project. Although none of the men who authored *Coming Out the Door for the Ninth Ward* had been particularly strong students in school, and they had not envisioned themselves as published authors prior to their experience with the Neighborhood Story Project, they discussed the empowerment they felt from seeing themselves as writers. They strongly urged adult family members to write their own stories and to encourage their children to do so as well.

We then led the participants in a discussion of the picture book *Jazz* (Myers, 2006). We began by providing biographical information about the author and illustrator and their relationship as father and son and shared how even though Walter Dean and Christopher Myers are not from Louisiana, they dedicated this book to the children of New Orleans. Further, we recommended reading the dedications of books and discussing with children what the dedication reveals about what is important to the author. Throughout the discussion of *Jazz*, we focused on the local New Orleans traditions that were the subjects of the poems, asked participants— both children and adults—to identify their favorite poems and why they liked them, and highlighted the ways in which the written text was extended through the visual details of the illustrations. We also taught adult family members a specific strategy for sharing poetry with their children by leading them in a choral reading of a poem about Louis Armstrong, a very familiar figure to New Orleans residents.

The children present eagerly discussed the poems and illustrations in *Jazz*. Most of the adults present seemed familiar with *Jazz*, but it was evident that older siblings of our students had also read the book prior to the meeting. Everyone present enthusiastically participated in the choral reading of the poem "Louie, Louie, How You Play So Sweet." We concluded the book club with refreshments and informal discussion about the books among authors, teachers, families, and ERF project staff members.

Book Club Two: Jerry Pinkney Author and Illustrator Study

For our second book club, we chose to focus on author and illustrator Jerry Pinkney in order to extend the strategy of forming personal connections to books established during the first book club, to highlight award-winning African American children's literature, and to introduce participants to other authors and illustrators in the "Pinkney Dynasty" (Minzesheimer, 2010), as well as African American poet Marilyn Nelson. Instead of pairing an adult book with a picture book, we selected two picture books illustrated by Pinkney. We chose *Sweethearts of Rhythm* (Nelson, 2009) as a replacement for an "adult" book because we discovered from the first book club that many of the parents of our students were not avid readers, and we thought they might appreciate a relatively quick read. Also, this book has New Orleans connections that we thought would interest readers.

Written by Marilyn Nelson, *Sweethearts of Rhythm* is a lengthy picture book of poems about a nonfiction topic, the International Sweethearts of Rhythm, an all-female swing band made up of members from multiple different races, but primarily African American, that gained popularity during World War II. This little-known slice of history was beautifully captured in Nelson's evocative poems, told from the perspective of the instruments in the band and Pinkney's lush watercolor and collage illustrations. Because Marilyn Nelson chose to begin the book with an imagined conversation among the instruments in a New Orleans pawn shop on the eve of Hurricane Katrina, *Sweethearts of Rhythm* provided natural avenues for our book club participants to make personal connections to the book, and the subject of swing music afforded them opportunities to make intertexual connections between *Sweethearts of Rhythm* and *Jazz*.

At the time of this book club, Pinkney had recently become the first African American illustrator to receive the Caldecott Medal for his nearly wordless picture book retelling of the traditional fable *The Lion and the Mouse* (2009), set in the African Serengeti. We chose this book not only for its acclaim but also for the opportunities it provided for family members to create their own verbal texts while viewing the pictures together.

As an introduction, we shared biographical information about and photos of Pinkney and gave a brief introduction to his large body of work focused on African and African American experiences. We also introduced members of his family who create children's books: wife Gloria Jean Pinkney, who has authored family stories such as *Back Home* (Pinkney, 1999), illustrated by Jerry; son Brian Pinkney, who has illustrated a number of picture book biographies like *Sojourner Truth's Step-Stomp Stride*, written by his wife, Andrea Davis Pinkney (2009); and son Myles Pinkney, whose photographs illustrate books like *Shades of Black*, authored by his wife, Sandra Pinkney (2000). Additionally, we provided background information about Marilyn Nelson as well as an introduction to her other books, many of which are award-winning works of poetic nonfiction about important African American historical figures and events. We ended the introduction by showing a video performance by the International Sweethearts of Rhythm and providing participants with a handout including all the information discussed in the introduction as well as websites where they might learn more about the Pinkneys, Marilyn Nelson, and the Caldecott Award.

During the open-ended discussion that followed, several adult participants mentioned their favorite poems from *Sweethearts of Rhythm* (Nelson, 2009), and they seemed particularly interested in discussing what they had learned about the band as well as the historical time period in which the book was set. We prompted participants to consider how the text and illustrations interacted to extend their knowledge of the historical era portrayed and how Nelson's decision to combine poetry, fantasy, and nonfiction created a reading experience different from a straightforward nonfiction account. Adult participants were especially responsive to the author's inclusion of Hurricane Katrina.

Both adults and children participated in the discussion of *The Lion and the Mouse* (Pinkney, 2009). Some parents at first expressed skepticism about the value of wordless books in developing reading skills, so we discussed how narrating wordless books—especially with scaffolding provided by more knowledgeable authors—can help young children build vocabulary and understand the elements of story. As with *Jazz*, we discussed the dedication of *The Lion and the Mouse* and what it revealed to us about the author. Both participants and we, as discussion leaders, commented on details of particular illustrations and how Pinkney portrayed the animal characters' emotions in his paintings. Finally, we nudged participants to compare the illustrators' styles across both books and discuss which illustrations they liked better and why.

Book Club Three: Jacqueline Woodson Author Study

For our third book club, we chose to explore the works of Jacqueline Woodson, because she has written a range of award-winning literature—from picture books, through upper elementary and middle-grade chapter books, to young adult novels—on a variety of historical and contemporary African American experiences that families can read together throughout a child's development. We selected *After Tupac and D Foster* (Woodson, 2008) because of its recognition as a Newbery Honor book and because some of the teachers in our project were enthusiastic about the connections to Tupac Shakur. The book is a slim, young adult novel that we thought might be at both the reading and interest levels of many of the parents of our prekindergarteners. We selected *The Other Side* (Woodson, 2001) because we had quite a bit of knowledge of the "back story" of the creation of this book from hearing Woodson and illustrator E. B. Lewis discuss this book at conferences that we thought families in our project might find interesting. Also, we hoped a shared reading of *The Other Side* might facilitate an open discussion of issues of racial intolerance with which we are all still confronted frequently.

After Tupac and D Foster (Woodson, 2008) is a realistic fiction novel about the friendship of three middle-school girls living in Queens in 1996. D, a new friend, exposes the other two girls to many aspects of life they have not known about in their middle-class existence. As a foster child, D has experienced hardships of which her two friends are unaware, but they envy her freedom and independence. All three girls are deeply affected by the songs of Tupac Shakur and later by his death. Much of the book is written in the Black Vernacular English spoken by the girls.

The Other Side (Woodson, 2001) is a picture book about the friendship between a white child and an African American child, neighbors who live separated by a fence. The mother of each girl tells her not to cross the fence to play with the other girl, but the girls continue to draw closer to one another until eventually, they sit together on the fence and ultimately begin to play together despite their mother's warnings. Beautiful watercolor illustrations by E. B. Lewis depict the setting as possibly the 1950s, although Jackie Woodson has stated that she wrote a contemporary story.

As we had done with the Pinkneys, we began by presenting biographical information about Jacqueline Woodson, a brief introduction to her books, and a video of her reading aloud from *Peace, Locomotion* (Woodson, 2009). We also provided biographical information about illustrator E. B. Lewis, the Newbery Medal, and the Coretta Scott King children's book award. After these presentations, we engaged participants in open-ended discussions about both books.

Responses to the two books by the adults in attendance were varied. We discovered that the majority of adult participants were unfamiliar with the concept of "young adult literature" and had mistakenly believed that *After Tupac and D Foster* was written for a much younger audience. Once we cleared up this misconception, many parents expressed a more accepting view of the book. A number of parents and teachers, of varied ages, didn't like the topic of *After Tupac and D Foster*. Several felt that the vernacular language in which the book was written is not an appropriate language model for African American middle-school students to be reading, although they acknowledged that it contributed to the book's realism. When a young teacher from one school discussed her personal connections to the book and what the music of Tupac Shakur meant to her, and another teacher and her husband led a presentation because the husband had met Tupac, other adult participants expressed positive responses as well.

Adults and children at all three locations were eager to discuss *The Other Side*. The adults were surprised to learn that Jacqueline Woodson had envisioned a contemporary setting for the book in her mind and were also surprised that the illustrator created his illustrations without consultation with the author. They acknowledged that the story could just as easily take place today as fifty years ago, but they also agreed that setting the book in the past (as the illustrations did) made it easier for them to discuss racial issues, a reflection Jackie Woodson made herself after the book was published. All participants were captivated by the illustrations and pointed out details they had observed.

REFLECTING ON OUR EXPERIENCES

In her study of students' and teachers' criteria for choosing African American literature, teacher Erika Gray (2009) asks, "Can you imagine going through elementary school without ever finding a book that includes characters that look like you or remind you of your family?" (p. 472). We cannot; in fact, it was precisely these kinds of experiences that made us both readers, and we wanted to provide these kinds of connections to books for the children in the prekindergarten classrooms of our ERF project. In looking back at our experiences toward meeting that goal, we have, at times, been surprised, disappointed, and encouraged.

We were disappointed, but not particularly surprised, by the availability of books in general, much less culturally relevant books, in our classrooms prior to the beginning of our project. We were pleased to see that some teachers had purchased books for their classrooms themselves (although this should not have been necessary) but a little surprised that few had made a conscious effort to provide African American literature for their African American students, especially since all but one of them were African American themselves. This is in keeping, however, with Gray's (2009) findings of the teachers in her school. In talking with our teachers, we don't believe it was a lack of awareness on their part of the importance of providing their students with books that mirrored their own racial identities but rather a lack of accessibility of those books and limited funding. For example, one teacher stated that she had only been able to purchase books at garage and yard sales; the likelihood that she would find African American literature in such places is slim. We are encouraged, however, by the comments of one of our newer teachers. At the time of this writing, two years after the project began, she stated, "I am presently purchasing lots of books. I am consciously choosing African American books and stories using different languages."

We were also somewhat surprised as well as disappointed by our efforts to extend the curriculum to include "culturally conscious literature" (Harris, 1990). We realize that a curriculum like OWL, that is used in classrooms throughout the country, must represent diversity rather than focus on a specific racial or ethnic group, and it does do that very well. However, of the four titles that include African American or African characters, all were created by white authors and/or illustrators, and all of the books were more than twenty years old. While all four of these books might be considered classics, there were certainly more recent titles included in the curriculum. We wonder if this represents the authors' lack of familiarity with African American literature, and we would advocate for the inclusion in any commercial curriculum of current books by African American authors and illustrators. These books will act as "mirrors" for African American students while providing a culturally authentic "window" (Bishop, 1990) for students of other backgrounds.

Also related to curriculum, we were able to find books with African American characters that could be connected to all six themes of OWL—family, friends, wind and water, shadows and reflections, world of color, and things that grow—but they were not all "African American literature" as defined in the current literature (Brooks & McNair, 2009). In other words, many of them were not written by African American authors or illustrated by African American illustrators (or both). Not all were necessarily high-quality literature, either. While none perpetuated stereotypes or misconceptions or were overtly negative in any way, they would not all be recognized as excellent. They were simply "good enough" for our particular purposes. Still, we felt that the books we selected prompted valuable literacy experiences for our students because of the ways in which our teachers shared them. We voice strong support, however, for the increased publication of high-quality African American children's literature for young children across all genres and a wide range of topics.

Our experiences with Family Book Club covered the gamut from disappointing to surprising to encouraging. We were discouraged that not many families actually attended our Family Book Clubs; however, all families in our project over a four-year period will have received six books that represent outstanding African American literature. We were also somewhat disappointed in the lack of participation by the adults in attendance. Each time, we hoped for more open-ended discussion by parents and caregivers, but because this rarely happened, we prepared presentations and handouts that provided more information about the selected authors, illustrators, and literary awards. We were encouraged that participants seemed to appreciate this information, and we were not surprised by their lack of awareness of African American authors and illustrators, since that is very much in keeping with previous research findings.

What we were most pleased by was how everyone present at Family Book Clubs had read the picture books we provided and how much all types of participants seemed to enjoy talking about them. Adult family members engaged in the most discussion about picture books as did the teachers present, and this seemed to break down some of the walls between families and school professionals that might have existed. Our prekindergarteners were also eager to share their experiences with the picture books in these settings, but by far the most responsive group of readers was the older siblings who attended. From these responses, we did see evidence of true family literacy experiences that had taken place at home and were shared at school, and we believe that the books themselves fostered these experiences.

WHERE DO WE GO FROM HERE?

Certainly, immersing ourselves in the current, vibrant scholarship about African American children's literature has raised our awareness of many issues to consider when selecting books to share with teachers, students, and families. In particular, we have become much more conscious of how books about African Americans might not have been created by African Americans and what this might mean to readers. For future professional development, we plan to engage teachers in close analysis of picture books featuring African American characters created by "outsider" as well as "insider" authors and illustrators. While we personally believe that there are some outstanding African American books written by authors who are not African American, as well as outstanding books written by African American authors but illustrated by artists who are not African American, we look forward to the kinds of conversations we will have with our teachers around these issues.

We will continue to immerse ourselves, and the teachers in our project, in the latest scholarship about African American children's literature and use it to guide our continued purchasing of books for the classrooms. However, where we have focused the past two years on developing skills and strategies of literacy and nurturing a love of literature, we now plan to shift to a more critical view of children's literature. We know the teachers are ready for this, although most have not been exposed to critical literacy perspectives. We also believe the children in our ERF classrooms, despite their young age, can also respond critically to the books they encounter, whether those books be mirror or window.

APPENDIX

African American Picture Books Purchased for Prekindergarten Classrooms

Bryan, A. (2003). *Beautiful blackbird*. New York, NY: Atheneum.
Bryan, A. (2007). *Let it shine*. New York, NY: Simon & Schuster.
Cook, M. (2009). *Our children can soar*. New York, NY: Bloomsbury.
Cooke, T. (2003). *Full, full, full of love*. Illus. P. Howard. Cambridge, MA: Candlewick.
Cox, J. (2003). *My family plays music*. Illus. E. Brown. New York, NY: Holiday House.
Crews, D. (1991). *Bigmama's*. New York, NY: HarperCollins
Crews, N. (1995). *One hot summer day*. New York, NY: Greenwillow Books.
Crews, N. (2003). *The neighborhood Mother Goose*. New York, NY: Greenwillow Books.

Dillon, L., & Dillon, D. (2007). *Jazz on a Saturday night.* New York, NY: Blue Sky Press.

Falwell, C. (2005). *David's drawings.* New York, NY: Lee & Low.

Grimes, N. (2006). *Welcome, precious.* Illus. B. Collier. New York, NY: Orchard Books.

Isadora, R. (2002). *Peekaboo morning.* New York, NY: Putnam.

Johnson, A. (2004). *Violet's music.* Illus. L. Huliska-Beith. New York, NY: Dial.

Katz, K. (1999). *The colors of us.* New York, NY: Henry Holt.

Lee, S., & Lee, T. L. (2002). *Please, baby, please.* Illus. K. Nelson. New York, NY: Simon & Schuster.

Lee, S., & Lee, T. L. (2005). *Please, puppy, please.* Illus. K. Nelson. New York, NY: Simon & Schuster.

McConduit, D. W. (1997). *D. J. and the jazz fest.* Illus. E. F. Henriquez. Gretna, LA: Pelican Publishing.

Myers, W. D. (2009). *Looking like me.* Illus. C. Myers. New York, NY: Egmont.

Nelson, M. (2009). *Beautiful ballerina.* Photographs by S. Kuklin. New York, NY: Scholastic.

Pinkney, S. (2000). *Shades of black.* Illus. M. Pinkney. New York, NY: Scholastic.

Shaik, F. (1998). *The jazz of our street.* Illus. E. B. Lewis. New York, NY: Dial.

Shaik, F. (1999). *On Mardi Gras day.* Illus. F. Cooper. New York, NY: Dial.

Tarpley, N. A. (2001). *I love my hair!* Illus. E. B. Lewis. New York, NY: Little, Brown.

Tarpley, N. A. (2002). *Bippity bop barbershop.* Illus. E. B. Lewis. New York, NY: Little, Brown.

CHILDREN'S BOOKS CITED

Aardema, V. (1986). *Bringing the rain to Kapiti Plain.* New York, NY: Macmillan.

Bryan, A. (2003). *Beautiful blackbird.* New York, NY: Atheneum.

Cooke, T. (2003). *Full, full, full of love.* Illus. P. Howard. Cambridge, MA: Candlewick.

Crews, D. (1991). *Bigmama's.* New York, NY: HarperCollins.

Crews, N. (1995). *One hot summer day.* New York, NY: Greenwillow Books.

Isadora, R. (2002). *Peekaboo morning.* New York, NY: Putnam.

Johnson, A. (2004). *Violet's music.* Illus. L. Huliska-Beith. New York, NY: Dial.

Keats, E. J. (1964). *Whistle for Willie.* New York, NY: Puffin.

Keats, E. J. (1967). *Peter's chair.* New York, NY: Harper & Row.

Lee, S., & Lee, T. L. (2005). *Please, puppy, please.* Illus. K. Nelson. New York, NY: Simon & Schuster.

McConduit, D. W. (1997). *D. J. and the jazz fest.* Illus. E. F. Henriquez. Gretna, LA: Pelican Publishing.

Myers, W. D. (2006). *Jazz.* Illus. C. Myers. New York, NY: Holiday House.

Myers, W. D. (2009). *Looking like me.* Illus. C. Myers. New York, NY: Egmont.

Nelson, M. (2009). *Beautiful ballerina.* Photographs by S. Kuklin. New York, NY: Scholastic.

Nelson, M. (2009). *Sweethearts of rhythm.* Illus. J. Pinkney. New York, NY: Penguin.

Pinkney, A. (2009). *Sojourner Truth's step-stomp stride.* Illus. B. Pinkney. New York, NY: Hyperion.

Pinkney, G. J. (1999). *Back home.* Illus. J. Pinkney. New York, NY: Puffin.

Pinkney, J. (2009). *The lion and the mouse.* New York, NY: Little, Brown.

Pinkney, S. (2000). *Shades of black.* Illus. M. Pinkney. New York, NY: Scholastic.

Shaik, F. (1999). *On Mardi Gras day.* Illus. F. Cooper. New York, NY: Dial.

Tarpley, N. A. (2001). *I love my hair!* Illus. E. B. Lewis. New York, NY: Little, Brown.

Tarpley, N. A. (2002). *Bippity bop barbershop.* Illus. E. B. Lewis. New York, NY: Little, Brown.

Woodson, J. (2001). *The other side.* Illus. E. B. Lewis. New York, NY: Putnam.

Woodson, J. (2008). *After Tupac and D Foster.* New York, NY: Penguin.

Woodson, J. (2009). *Peace, locomotion.* New York, NY: Putnam.

REFERENCES

Bishop, R. S. (1990). Mirrors, windows, and sliding glass doors. *Perspectives, 6,* ix–xi.

Brooks, W., & McNair, J. C. (2009). "But this story of mine is not unique": A review of research on African American children's literature. *Review of Educational Research, 79*(1), 125–162.

Casbergue, R., McGee, L., & Bedford, A. (2007). Characteristics of classroom environments associated with accelerated literacy development. In L. Justice & C. Vukelich (Eds.), *Achieving excellence in preschool language and literacy instruction.* New York, NY: Guilford.

Dail, A. R., McGee, L. M., & Edwards, P. A. (2009). The role of community book club in changing literacy practices. *Literacy Teaching and Learning, 13,* 25–56.

Gray, E. S. (2009). The importance of visibility: Students' and teachers' criteria for selecting African American literature. *The Reading Teacher, 62*(6), 472–481.

Harris, V. J. (1990). African American children's literature: The first one hundred years. *Journal of Negro Education, 59,* 540–554.

Horning, K. T., Lindgren, M. V., & Schliesman, M. (2010). *Thoughts on publishing in 2009.* Retrieved from http://www.education.wisc.edu/ccbc/books/choiceintr010.asp

Johnson, D. (1990). "I see me in the book": Visual literacy and African-American children's literature. *Children's Literature Association Quarterly, 15,* 10–13.

McGee, L. M. (2007). *Transforming literacy practices in preschool: Research-based practices that give all children the opportunity to reach their potential as learners.* New York, NY: Scholastic.

McGee, L. M., & Schickedanz, J. A. (2007). Repeated interactive read-alouds in preschool and kindergarten. *Reading Teacher, 60*(8), 742–751.

Mikkelsen, N. (1998). Insiders, outsiders, and the question of authenticity: Who shall write for African American children? *African American Review, 32,* 33–49.

Minzesheimer, B. (2010, February 3). For Jerry Pinkney's bunch, books bind a literary dynasty. *USA Today.* Retrieved from http://www.usatoday.com/life/books/news/2010-02-04-pinkney04_CV _N.htm

Neuman, S. B. (1999). Books make a difference: A study of access to literacy. *Reading Research Quarterly, 34*(3), 286–311.

Neuman, S. B., Celano, D. C., Greco, A. N., & Shue, P. (Eds.). (2003). *Access for all: Closing the book gap for children in early education.* Newark, DE: International Reading Association.

Nine Times Social and Pleasure Club. (2009). *Coming out the door for the Ninth Ward.* New Orleans, LA: UNO Press.

Roethler, J. (1998). Reading in color: Children's book illustrations and identity formation for black children in the United States. *African American Review, 32,* 95–105.

Schickedanz, J., & Casbergue, R. (2009). *Writing in preschool: Learning to orchestrate meaning and marks.* Newark, DE: International Reading Association.

Schickedanz, J. A., Dickinson, D. K., & Charlotte-Mecklenburg Schools. (2005). *Opening the world of learning: A comprehensive early literacy program.* Parsippany, NJ: Pearson Early Learning.

Strasser, J., and Seplocha, H. (2007). Using picture books to support young children's literacy. *Childhood Education, 83,* 219–224.

Thompson, A. (2001). Harriet Tubman in pictures: Cultural consciousness and the art of picture books. *The Lion and the Unicorn, 25,* 81–114.

SECTION II

BLACK MULTICULTURAL LITERATURE THAT TARGETS UPPER ELEMENTARY AND MIDDLE GRADES: 4–8

CHAPTER 6

"I Want My Mama!"

Young Black Adolescents Reading through the Grief

Shanetia Clark & Kimetta Hairston

HICCUPS

Ms. Jenkins sat patiently waiting in her classroom. Outside the rain poured down, leaving the sky gloomy and dark, darker than any other day she could remember. She was waiting for Gloria, one of her seventh-grade English students, to come in for afternoon detention. Earlier that day during third period, Gloria had gotten into a heated argument with another student during journal sharing. Today's prompt sprang from previous discussions about young adult texts that were written by black authors: "What makes you the person you are? Who or what experiences have the largest effect on your world?" Ms. Jenkins thought it would be a great spark to get her students to share about their personal inspirations, values, and beliefs; she had no idea that these questions would ignite a vast array of emotions ranging from anger to grief to acceptance.

Third period had been going well. With some time remaining at the end of the period, Ms. Jenkins presented a prompt to the class and invited the students to write in their journals quietly. She and her class wrote, and after time was called, Ms. Jenkins encouraged the students to share their writing. Gloria sat there listening to the other students read their reflections. Ms. Jenkins could see her getting antsy in her seat; she watched her wring her hands and wipe them on her dark blue jeans. Finding confidence, Gloria raised her hand and asked if she could share. After receiving approval from Ms. Jenkins, Gloria sat up in her chair, cleared her throat, and started to read with a soft voice.

> As I lay there, curled up in a fetal position, my head and stomach ached with pains. I reflected on how I got to the age of 13 and why I am finally able to fully see that my momma left me and she is not coming back.

Silence enveloped the room. The majority directed its gaze to Gloria and listened intently. Ms. Jenkins noticed Marcus, a black male student, lower his head and slouch deep into his chair. She also noticed another classmate, Tonia, who sucked her teeth and began tapping her pencil on her desk. Gloria glared at Tonia, sighed, and continued.

> When I was still in my mother's womb, she left me. I know that sounds crazy, but just listen to my teenage thoughts. She was on crack, she never went to the doctor, and she did not care about the egg that grew inside her. But for some reason, God allowed that egg to grow and I arrived. For a moment in my early years, I can remember my momma. Then it gets cloudy, and I remember my grandmother and aunties always taking care of me. Around five, my momma came back. She met a great guy, not my biological dad but a man who took on the role of father to me. They had my brother in the first year of the marriage. For about two years, I can remember happiness. Life was good. So good! My brother and I loved one another. I remember smiling and laughing. Then my mother started to disappear again. The crack was back. I thought momma loved us more than crack. I was wrong. She deserted us—me—again!

Tonia began to chuckle nervously and Ms. Jenkins could see the anger and uneasiness on her face. Ms. Jenkins moved her index finger to her lips signaling for Tonia to be quiet. Gloria cleared her throat and continued.

> When I was about eight years old, I awakened one night in the middle of a dream. (I remember this because I always wish that I had kept dreaming.) Unfortunately it was real. My mother stood over me and sobbed. "What's wrong, momma?" I asked. She leaned in to hug me, squeezed me tight, and kissed my forehead.
>
> "Goodbye, sweetheart," she said as she walked away. I pressed my hand to my cheek and rubbed away my and my momma's tears. It wasn't until the next week that I realized once again . . . momma was gone. The pain was heavy. I could not figure out why my mother did not want me. Was I ugly or stupid or both? I hated myself.
>
> I screamed and cried. I turned on my dad. I called him ugly names. Even though I treated my dad like crap, when he filed to divorce my mother, he also requested and got full custody of my brother and me. I guess you can say he won. The judge found my mother as "unfit" and once again she had left me. From that point on, my mother was absent from my life and in and out of my world until about two years ago.
>
> It was a Saturday. Saturday morning at 11:00, Momma called me! She wanted to see

me and she was planning on coming to my basketball awards banquet the next week. I begged my dad to take me to get a new outfit and to take me to the beauty shop to get my hair done. He did. Although, he looked so concerned and sad and when I asked him what was wrong, he just smiled. "You're beautiful inside and out. Gloria, life is like a huge hiccup—disappointments come and go, but regardless, there will always be enough water to drown them out." I could not figure out why he said this until later that night when I found myself at the banquet watching the door and waiting for my mother who never showed. She must have gotten stuck in traffic. Maybe she forgot where the banquet was, I rationalized. When I got home, I raced to the caller id. She called! She promised to come and see me the next day.

She never came.

My relationship with my mother existed only in my mind. I fantasized a lot about the two of us going shopping, talking about boys, and even spending hours laughing at the silliest things. I retreated internally. I was lonely and depressed. My dad did not know how to handle me, and I could tell he was giving up on me, but he never left. I gained a lot of weight, I stopped playing sports, and I began to treat my little brother pretty badly. Was I becoming my mother?

Tonia murmured, "Yup, don't we all and yes you are fat and ugly."

Gloria stopped. She tried so hard to hold back her tears, but the anger took over and she yelled at the top of her lungs, "Shut up, Tonia! It's your dad who's the drug dealer! He's the one who kept giving my mom the drugs. That's why he beats you and your momma up every day! That's why you are an ignorant bitch!" At that point the classroom erupted. Tonia and Gloria lunged toward one another, ready to fight. Ms. Jenkins stepped in right on time. She grabbed both girls by the arm and escorted them to the office, both still spewing insults.

When Ms. Jenkins returned to the classroom, the students stopped recapping what had transpired. No one looked at her. A few had tears in their eyes. Others had their heads down on the desks. But Marcus had Gloria's journal. Ms. Jenkins demanded that he give it to her: "That is Gloria's journal and no one else should read it without permission." It was obvious that Marcus had already read the journal, but he did not say a word and just handed it to Ms. Jenkins. The bell rang.

As the students exited the room, Marcus stopped by Ms. Jenkins' desk. He stood there for a few seconds and then he said, "My momma left me when I was seven years old. She left me, my brother, and my dad. She never came back to see me. I wanted her to, but she didn't. When Gloria was reading, I was thinking that she was lucky because at least her mother would resurface and check on her. My momma left me. She's not dead; she's just gone. Am I wrong to still want her and to still miss her? But most of all, am I wrong because I have accepted her absence and understand that I am a better person without her?" Ms. Jenkins was about to answer, but Marcus cut her off and said, "Thank you, Ms. Jenkins, for giving us the opportunity to read those books the past few weeks. They gave me a chance to look inside myself, share these feelings with you, and write my reflection today in class. Thanks."

He walked out of the room with his head high and his shoulders back. On her desk was Gloria's journal. Hesitantly, Ms. Jenkins began to read the journal.

> One day my dad came to me and we had a very long talk. He arranged for me to spend more time with my aunts and grandmother. I started to see how much once again he just wanted me to be happy and he wanted me to understand that it was not my fault that my mother had deserted me. Although sad and still longing for the woman who left me, I knew that I would be okay. Yesterday when I got home from school, my dad was waiting for me in the kitchen. He said he needed to talk to me. I knew what was coming—whenever my mother in the past was about to disappear again or go back on crack, my dad always came to me to prepare me for it. What was it this time? How much had she stolen, was she in jail, or was she sick again? My world was so upside down, and I was trying to turn around so I thought how could she possibly abandon me any more than she already had? But this time, the conversation was a little different. "Your mother is dead," he whispered. My dad proceeded to tell me that my mother was dead. It's crazy; I've been crying since my father told me my mother is dead.
>
> Ms. Jenkins gave us the book *What Momma Left Me* to read. It was that book that gave me a reason to understand and to appreciate that I am a good person. It is because of my mother, my experiences, my dad and myself that I am able to be me.
>
> Thanks, Ms. Jenkins. I miss my mother, but I have always missed my mother. She was never really there. A girl needs to know that her mother cares, but she also needs to understand that just because a person delivers a child from her womb, it does not make her a great mother or role model. Ms. Jenkins is a role model. My mother? I'm not sure. I think she was just my momma and everybody wants momma, right? In her defense, I do believe that she tried to love me. I believe that she loved crack more.
>
> So, there I was this morning on my bed in a puddle of tears and years of feeling sorry for myself and I could hear the rain outside on my windowsill. For the first time I could breathe. I took the deepest breath and I felt myself turning upward in my thoughts and feelings. I think my hiccups are finally going away. I got up and I decided to come to school.

This story, "Hiccups," is a composite reflection collected from interactions with young black adolescents who were abandoned in one way or another by their mothers (Hairston, 2010). It is a literary work that incorporates students reflecting on personal experiences, as well as relating to novels that were introduced to them in the classroom. The story represents the significant impact of both mental and physical abandonment and how teachers can impact the lives of their students through literature, character identification, and reflective writing and experiences.

Gladding and Gladding (1991) state that "identification with literary characters similar to themselves [is] helpful in releasing emotions, gaining new directions in life, and promoting new ways of interacting" (p. 7). By providing access to stories, teachers are holding the space for their students to deal with loss of a parent and the young adult literature serves as a "transactional object" (Wilhelm, 2010). In other words, like Ms. Jenkins in "Hiccups," the teacher invites the students to engage their active energies to juxtapose their lives and the text. Furthermore,

DeMinco (1995) adds that, "With the help of books, undaunted adults [teachers] can make bereavement a therapeutic experience which may even pave the way for future trusting and supportive interactions" (p. 184).

Research reveals that grief is an "oscillatory process in which the bereaved can experience a variety of feelings and emotions, both positive and negative" (Trunnell, Caserta, & White, 1992, p. 275; see also DeMinco, 1995). Although grief is not considered an illness, it may cause upset stomach, headaches, loss of appetite, uncontrollable crying, anger, and depression. All of these are characteristics of the seven stages of grief. Kubler-Ross (1969) discovered that the grieving process varies depending on the nature of the loss as well as the individual going through it. The Kubler-Ross Stages of Grief model was introduced in the book *On Death and Dying* (1969). As an extension of her original five stages, the grieving process has gained additional steps by other researchers (Wright, 2009). These stages are comprised of the following: (1) shock and denial; (2) pain and guilt; (3) anger and bargaining; (4) depression, reflection, and loneliness; (5) the upward turn; (6) reconstruction and working it through; and (7) acceptance and hope. The third, fourth, and fifth stages of grief are the focal points in the literary works discussed in this chapter.

GRIEVING THE ABSENT MOTHER IN YOUNG ADULT LITERATURE

A mother's presence and impact linger throughout her children's lives. From the very beginning, the connection between mother and children is a dynamic force. For example, by interacting and engaging in conversation with her children, she provides the best foundation for the development of oral language, cognition, and writing (Wolf, 2007). Given that the mother has a direct link to the manner in which her children make sense of their world, her absence forces them to adjust to life without her. This readjustment manifests itself through the seven stages of grief. While all mothers have an impact on the emotional and psychological experiences of their children, the stories in this chapter focus specifically on the relationships between absent black mothers and their children.

When a black mother is absent from her children's lives, what does that mean? Her absence can be categorized as an emotional absence or a physical absence, but regardless, her children are left behind. Mother, mommy, momma, ma, mom—whatever the title, her multifaceted roles are inclusive of protector, teacher, counselor, nurturer, and friend. The mother's presence in her child's life is directly connected to the way her children will thrive. For example, Crew (2002) found that a "mother's emotional relationship with her [son and] daughter is thus considered in relation to the pressing demands of ensuring physical nurturance" (p. 5). The children confront ongoing processes of neglect and anger, which result in low self-esteem and grief. Ormrod (2006) found that low self-esteem among young black adolescents is an ongoing concern in America.

This section explores stages three, four, and five—(3) anger and bargaining; (4) depression, reflection, and loneliness; (5) the upward turn—through the lens of a collection of young adult literature. The stories—*Bud, Not Buddy* (Curtis, 1999), *Miracle's Boys* (Woodson, 2000), *Ninth Ward* (Rhodes, 2010), "The Untitled Story" (Stimpson, 2011), and *What Momma Left Me* (Watson, 2010)—beautifully and with great sensitivity explore the protagonists' adjustment to a new life without their mothers, who died or chose to leave the home. As we discover, just as in life, the young characters grieve differently, in their own way and according to their own time.

STAGE THREE: ANGER AND BARGAINING

Anger is a powerful and destructive emotion. To ease of this heightened emotional state, one retreats to the bargaining stage. The black male adolescents in *Bud, Not Buddy* (Curtis, 1999); *Miracle's Boys* (Woodson, 2000); *Ninth Ward* (Rhodes, 2010); *What Momma Left Me* (Watson, 2010); and "The Untitled Story" (Stimpson, 2011) experience this stage in reaction to their mother's death or desertion.

Bud, *not* Buddy, Caldwell, of the Newbery Award winning book by Christopher Paul Curtis (2000), cries at night remembering the moment when he walked into his mother's room and was unable to awaken her. His world changes immediately. He is sent to live in an orphanage. After enduring the uncertainty and despair in the orphanage, he goes to live with the Amos family. The Amos' son, Todd, who was spoiled despite his mischievous behavior, relentlessly tortures Bud. Refusing to take the abuse anymore, Bud goes on the lam. Anger at the abuse within the Amos household galvanizes Bud to leave and search for the man he believes is his father.

Miracle's Boys, by Jacqueline Woodson (2000), is the story of three brothers who live on their own in New York City. The boys' mother, Milagro, which means "miracle" in Spanish, has died, and Lafayette, the youngest son, takes Spanish in school so that he'll "have a little bit more of her to hold on to" (p. 19). Tyree, the eldest, who resembles her physically and spiritually, raises his younger brothers. Newcharlie feels guilty that the last images his mother saw of him before she died was in handcuffs being carted off to juvenile detention. He wishes that her last memories of him were of the two of them sitting and laughing on the couch. Newcharlie's anger and malcontent are directed toward Lafayette: "How come you ain't save her, huh?. . . . If I was here, I would've saved her" (p. 40). By lashing out at his younger brother, Newcharlie actually begins to bargain. He implores that if time could be rewound, Miracle would still be alive; he pleads that he should have been there and the anger and bargaining blur into one explosive emotion.

Similarly, Miracle's other two sons experience the anger and bargaining stage. They are at odds with one another and at their situation of being alone. Tyree is frustrated at Lafayette for covering for Newcharlie when he doesn't do the chores; he goes into the kitchen, pretends to sweep, and breaks down to weep. Tyree has to put his own dreams aside so that he can raise his siblings. Such an awesome responsibility certainly bears a heavy weight on him, as manifested through his raising his voice at Newcharlie for getting into trouble again.

Renee Watson's *What Momma Left Me* (2010) opens with a free verse poem entitled "Our Father." Thirteen-year-old Serenity Evans, the narrator, writes the following:

> I don't have many good memories of my daddy.
> He was hardly home. And when he was,
> he was mad
> at my momma,
> or me,
> or my younger brother, Danny. (p. 1)

Serenity and Danny's father was a physical abuser; in a fit of rage, he brutally killed Loretta, his wife and mother of his children. They now live with their maternal grandparents, Grandma Claire and Grandpa James.

The siblings work through their anger of their mother's death in different ways. Danny exhibits the most anger during the story; he acts out at home and at school. Danny begins to socialize with a dangerous crowd. He lashes out at his grandparents. In addition, he skips classes. Danny does not have an outlet, like his sister Serenity, to positively release his anger. The way in which Serenity begins to ease her grief and develop as a young woman is through her poetry workshop class.

Ninth Ward, written by award-winning author Jewell Parker Rhodes (2010), is set in New Orleans leading up to Hurricane Katrina. The story centers around Lanesha, a twelve-year-old who is raised by her maternal grandmother Mama Ya-Ya because her mother died in childbirth; her mother's ghost remains with Lanesha "until she finds her purpose" (p. 54). Lanesha expresses her anger at her maternal and paternal relatives who neither visit nor welcome her into their homes in the higher elevated parts of the city. She transforms her anger and frustration by forming a sweet friendship with TaShon, a quiet boy who is teased by their classmates. Together, they rescue a dog, Spot, that had been attacked by a group of boys.

The mother in the story, "The Untitled Story," left her husband and two sons; she "decided not to come back home" (Stimpson, 2011, para. 12). Her dream was to be a Hollywood film screenwriter, and staying with her family stifled that dream. She deliberately chose to be absent. Seven years pass, and this is where the story begins. DeMarcus Polk, the younger brother of Ronald Polk, works hard in school and has visions of going to college. Ronald, the eldest, had to assume more of a parental role due to their father having to work two jobs. DeMarcus "believed that his father still wanted the best for them, but the best was far beyond his father's reach now. Survival was the only thing he could provide for them after his mother's leaving and lay-off" (Stimpson, 2011, para. 8). With the new survival mode, these men have to expand their roles within the household. DeMarcus had to vacuum, get the mail, and make sandwiches two days a week; Ronald had to do the laundry and cook hot dogs two days a week. Ronald protested, "That's girl stuff" (Stimpson, 2009, para. 19). The identity of the males shifts beyond the traditional gender roles, and the father explained this necessary shift: "Well, there are no girls around here anymore. It's just us men from now on" (Stimpson, 2011, para. 20).

Stage three, anger and bargaining, looks differently in each of these texts. The young black protagonists range in their level of anger: Bud ran away, Newcharlie got arrested, Danny skipped school and began to associate with a dangerous crowd, and Ronald protested having to do "girl stuff." Just as in the introductory anecdote of this chapter, the anger is the first outward manifestation of the child's grief in the classroom. The teacher may not know the cause of the anger, which in the cases of these stories, is the mother who has either died or abandoned the family. The root of the anger is from characters missing their mother and searching for a way to regain order in their world. Still, order is not achieved until they have navigated through the stages of grief.

STAGE FOUR: DEPRESSION, REFLECTION, AND LONELINESS

After the anger and bargaining stage manifests itself outwardly and disrupts classroom dynamics, teachers have the ability to support students who enter into the fourth stage of grief. Students turn inward, becoming more introspective, during this stage. Wright (2009, para. 11) explains what this stage looks like to "well-meaning outsiders":

> Just when your friends may think you should be getting on with your life, a long period of sad reflection will likely overtake you. . . . During this time, you finally realize the true magnitude of your loss, and it depresses you. You may isolate yourself on purpose, reflect on things you did with your lost one, and focus on memories of the past. You may sense feelings of emptiness or despair.

Serenity's English teacher in *What Momma Left Me* (Watson, 2010) provides the space—more specifically Serenity's writer's notebook—for her to reflect and unpack her grief and to make sense of her new world. Serenity writes to release the secrets that she had guarded so closely:

> [Momma] made excuses for him, trying to convince us that he really did care, but I think even she stopped believing her lies . . . I'm really good at keeping secrets. I still haven't told any of my momma's. (pp. 3–4).

The teacher assigns a variety of poetry forms and literary devices such as list poems, an anaphora, acrostic poems, hyperbole, metaphor, sensory details, personification, and haikus. The writings enable Serenity to concretely work through her feelings toward her first crush, a neighborhood boy named Jay; her friendship with her new best friend, Maria; and her inability to cook and bake just as her mother had done.

The writing within the poetry workshop class proved to be the catalyst for Serenity to work through the stages of grief.

Armed with his briefcase that is bound with tight twine and filled with sentimental treasures and the official "Bud Caldwell's Rules and Things to Have a Funner Life and Make a Better Liar of Yourself" (Curtis, 1999), Bud attempts to make sense of his world. Episodic and sensory memories are triggered by a collection of objects: a dated picture of his mother secured in an envelope, flyers of Mr. Herman E. Calloway and his bands, a collection of rocks with letters and numbers written on them, and a blanket. Bud travels throughout Michigan and finally finds Herman E. Calloway, the man who he believes is his father. He talks about his memories:

> Me and momma having the same conversations lots of times is one of the main things I can remember about her now. Maybe that's because when she'd tell me these things she used to squeeze my arms and look right hard in my face to make sure I was listening, but maybe I remember because those arm-squeezing, face-looking times were the only times that things slowed down a bit when Momma was around. (Curtis, 1999, p. 41)

Driven by the mission to find this man who could be his father, Bud risks his life during the search, overcoming dangerous areas and situations. With the aid of some good Samaritans and quick wit, Bud safely reaches Herman and his bandmates.

STAGE FIVE: THE UPWARD TURN

The upward turn is the transitional stage toward acceptance and peace. This stage is an active release for those whose grief is starting to lessen and they begin to regain order in their worlds. Again, Wright (2009) explains this dynamic stage: "As you start to adjust to life without your dear one, your life becomes a little calmer and more organized. Your physical symptoms lessen, and your 'depression' begins to lift slightly" (para. 15). The space between depression and epiphany is the upturn.

Within the collection of these stories, the characters in each of these texts achieve the upturn. Bud's upturn comes when he hears Herman Calloway, who is actually his maternal grandfather, weeping in his bedroom. Until that moment, Bud had held onto hope that this man was his father or at least could direct him to his father. Finding family, though unexpected, enables Bud to move toward healing. At the heart of *Miracle's Boys* (Woodson, 2000) is the death of the boys' mother and father. Lafayette did not know his father because he died before he was born. His father succumbed to illness after saving a stranger's life. With the most internal conflict, Newcharlie initially channeled his guilt into negative behavior; yet, after being arrested for the last time, he begins to reach solace and decides to turn his life around. His decision to stay out of trouble and to reconnect with his brothers is the upturn. Likewise, Danny, in *What Momma Left Me* (Watson, 2010), stops with the negative behavior. Serenity, who had been outwardly resistant to helping her mother cook and bake in the kitchen, chooses to make her mother's famous red velvet cake. Baking the cake is a monumental moment in Watson's story.

In "The Untitled Story" (Stimpson, 2011), the culmination of the ability to become self-reliant and move beyond the mother's absence is evident when DeMarcus goes to check the mail and a package is on the doorstep. He notices that the package is from California and reads a note from his mother written on a movie flyer—"I finally made it!—Mom" (Stimpson, 2011, para. 32). DeMarcus, in a bold move, "tore the flyer to pieces and threw them into the wind" (Stimpson, 2011, para. 33). The floating remnants of the flyer releases his grief.

READING (AND WRITING) THROUGH THE GRIEF

Over the past few decades, young adult literature has gained momentum to tell richer and bolder stories about and for young people (Alvine, 2010). These texts illuminate the for real and gritty stories of youth culture. Kelly Gallagher (2009) extols the benefits of inviting and honoring such texts into the classroom:

> If we want kinds to become better readers, they have to read a lot more than they are currently reading. And if we want our students to do a lot more reading than they are currently doing, they need to be immersed in a pool of high-interest reading material. (p. 30).

The readers' active relationship with texts is where literacy develops. Personal growth also occurs. As classrooms continue to evolve, teachers increasingly find themselves faced with the challenge to develop literacy experiences that might allow students to delve more deeply with texts, ones that embrace their background and learning needs (International Reading Association, 2010).

A viable avenue for teachers to honor the life and literacy experiences of their students is to go against the "devaluing [of] adolescents' out-of-school reading and by not stocking the kinds of texts students want to read" (Lenters, 2006). Rosenblatt (1938) posited that it is important

> for the teacher to acquire some general understanding of the possible experiences and pre-occupations typical of the particular group of students with which he [or she] is dealing. This will aid him [or her] in his [or her] choice of appropriate literary works and in his [or her] handling of the students' spontaneous responses to literature. (p. 78)

Teachers have the unique opportunity to invite the out-of-school stories of their adolescent students into the class. Characters who overcome devastating loss, such as an absent mother, demonstrate the unbreakable spirit of resilience. Within the framework of the seven stages of grief, students oftentimes demonstrate stages three to five: anger and bargaining; depression, reflection, and loneliness; and the upward turn.

What follows are several instructional suggestions for teachers to utilize in their classrooms in order to provide aesthetic experiences for students to read (and write) through their grief. And while the venues for these transactions range from traditional discussions to artistic sharing, each supports students in their journey to cope with loss.

INVITATION OF STUDENT-SELECTED TEXTS

A safe way to support adolescents as they develop their own sense of self, particularly if they have an absent mother, is to invite students to select texts that tell their stories. Students may introduce their books to their classmates through "book talks." Sharing these books and stories provides automatic credibility. See Table 1 for some guiding questions that could further initiate conversations that are grounded in the student-selected texts.

Young people will be able to relate to the characters and/or situations. Literature affords students the ability to explore the characters' lives (as well as their own) through the "veil of anonymity" (Clark & Marinak, 2010). By introducing real literature that tells real stories, students can identify with the protagonists and/or antagonists. Self-selected texts enable students to gain new ownership of the literature. The teacher may also introduce additional stories that mirror the students' lives.

TABLE 1. Guiding Questions

Emotional-Level Questions	Intellectual-Level Questions
1. What is your first reaction to the work?	1. Would you change the ending of the work? Why or why not? If so, how?
2. What feeling and/or emotions does the work evoke in you?	2. What fears and/or concerns do you have for the characters?
3. What character(s) do you particularly like or dislike?	3. What stage(s) of grief do(es) the protagonist and/or antagonist exhibit within the story?
4. Do any of the characters remind you of people you know?	4. What is the major point of this work?
5. What memory does the work help you recall?	5. What is your final reaction to the work?
6. Have you been in a similar situation?	

Adapted from Metzger, K., and Adams, J. (2007). Opening dialogue amidst conflict: Utilizing young adult literature in the classroom. *ALAN Review, 34*(3), 61–66.

ARTISTIC INTERPRETATIONS OF GRIEF

Art is the transmission of discovery. Thus, honor students' artistic and digital talents. Students may create an artistic text that responds to the stages of grief. Teachers who welcome students' artistic talents into the classroom support their visual literacies. These artistic expressions are viable vehicles for students to showcase "their perceptions of the meanings, implications, and consequences of [grief]" (Metzger & Adams, 2007, p. 63). At times, words may not be the best medium through which students can articulate themselves; therefore, it is up to the teacher to welcome other forms expression.

There is the potential for powerful musical and dramatic connections. For example, students could compose a song, which expresses a character's emotions during a pivotal moment in the story. In addition, students may compile or compose a soundtrack that traces a character's grief from shock and denial to acceptance and hope. Dramatic performances add a deeper level of engagement with the stories. Students may write scripts that retell key episodes in the stories or are based on emotionally charged moments in their own lives. Dramatic performances welcome students to draw upon, as Beach, Appleman, Hynds, and Wilhelm (2001) proclaim, "their own ideas, beliefs, attitudes, and understandings to employ dialogue, define their roles, make decisions, adopt certain stances, or recognize the consequences of their actions. They need to activate relevant schema and relate their personal experiences to create and sustain a drama world" (p. 73).

We live in a digital, multimodal world. Encouraging students to utilize computer technology to create new texts is important. Students may create digital stories or other video presentations that fuse images, written text, and music. This sophisticated composing disrupts the "literacy hierarchy" by expanding the view of authentic literacy (Bruce, 2008). These multimedia presentations may be based on the stories discussed in this chapter, ones that students bring to the class, or episodes in their own lives.

LETTERS TO AND FROM THE ABSENT MOTHER

What would Bud, Newcharlie, DeMarcus, and Serenity say to their mothers? Invite students to assume a character's identity and write a letter to the absent mother. With support from the stories, students will be deliberate in their choice of tone and voice. Some questions for them to follow: *Why did she go away? Does she regret her (lack of) choice? Does she miss her children? Would she want to be reunited with her children? Why or why not?* If students become the characters, they can make connections to the stories and their lives.

What would the mothers' response be to her children? What would Miracle say to her sons today? Is Serenity and Danny's mother proud of them? How does Lanesha's mother feel about her daughter? Is Bud's mother happy that he found his grandfather? These are some guiding questions that could spark a powerful expository or narrative response from the perspective of the absent mother. Teachers will enable students to engage in authentic writing where voice, style, and content are paramount. Having students write from various points of view allows them to unpack these texts beyond the surface. Through these letters, the teachers recognize students' anger and offer a venue to bargain with the absent mother.

FINAL THOUGHTS

With the expectation that the mother is the primary caregiver, when she is absent from her children's lives, young people must endure a radical cognitive and social adjustment. They, in essence, grieve for their mother's absence and strive to reach the final stage of acceptance that she is not coming back. The mothers' physical absence from the home has a tremendous, long-lasting impact on the children's development of their own sense of self.

There is not an abundance of young adult novels and stories in which the black mother is absent. These stories should be included in the scope and sequence of the English or language arts classrooms. We, the authors, have chosen to focus on a small selection of stories within this chapter. A common thread among each of the stories and those like them is that a mother's presence lingers even though she is absent.

Like the characters in the stories, our students must overcome loss. To assist in coping with loss, such as an absent mother, teachers can offer literature as an outlet for grief. Interacting with the literature through the stages of grief framework can serve as an anchor for students who may not explicitly state what has happened in their lives outside of school. Those who grieve typically exhibit in the classroom anger and bargaining; depression, reflection, and loneliness; and an upturn. With the teachers' guidance, students will positively and safely grieve. Once the students openly reflect on the stories and possibly connect their reflections to true circumstances, they move toward the process of healing and acceptance. By encouraging students to read texts that mirror their lives, teachers help students navigate through the seven stages of grief. Classroom teachers have the awesome responsibility to provide a safe space for students to make sense of their world.

REFERENCES

Alvine, L. (2010). Young adult literature as genre: Shifting teacher perceptions. *SIGNAL Journal, XXXIII*(2), 2–5.

Beach, R., Appleman, D., Hynds, S., & Wilhelm, J. (2001). *Teaching literature to adolescents*. Mahwah, NJ: Lawrence Erlbaum.

Bruce, D. L. (2008). Visualizing literacy: Building bridges with media. *Reading & Writing Quarterly, 24,* 264–282.

Clark, S. P., & Marinak, B.A. (2010). Striving to be better people: Unpacking "kind" texts to confront victimization. *SIGNAL Journal, XXXIII*(2), 24–30.

Crew, H. S. (2002). *Feminist theories and the voices of mothers and daughters in selected African-American literature for young adults*. Retrieved from http://comminfo.rutgers.edu/professional-development/childlit/books/CREW65.pdf

Curtis, C. P. (1999). *Bud, not Buddy*. New York, NY: Random House.

DeMinco, S. (1995). Young adult reactions to death in literature and life. *Adolescence, 30* (117), 179–185.

Gallagher, K. (2009). *Readicide: How schools are killing reading and what you can do about it*. Portland, ME: Stenhouse Publishers.

Gladding, S. T., & Gladding, C. (1991). The ABCs of bibliotherapy for school counselors. *The School Counselor, 39,* 7–13.

Hairston, K. R. (2010, July). *Anonymous reflections from teenage daughters*. Unpublished paper presented at the African American Chamber of Commerce of Central Pennsylvania Community Training Event, Harrisburg.

International Reading Association. (2010). *Standards for reading professionals—Revised 2010.* Newark, DE: Author.

Lenters, K. (2006). Resistance, struggle, and the adolescent reader. *Journal of Adolescent and Adult Literacy, 50*(2), 136–146.

Kubler-Ross, E. (1969). *On death and dying*. New York, NY: Scribner.

Ormrod, J. E. (2006). *Educational psychology: Developing learners*. Upper Saddle River, NJ: Merrill Prentice Hall.

Metzger, K., & Adams, J. (2007). Opening dialogue amidst conflict: Utilizing young adult literature in the classroom. *The ALAN Review, 34*(3), 61–66.

Rhodes, J. P. (2010). *Ninth ward*. New York, NY: Little, Brown.

Rosenblatt, L. (1938) *Literature as exploration*. New York, NY: Modern Language Association.

Stimpson, M. (2011). *The untitled story*. Retrieved from http://www.wegottaread.com/downloads/20110202_41.

Trunnell, E. P., Caserta, M. S., & White, G. L. (1992). Bereavement: Current issues in intervention and prevention. *Journal of Health Education, 23*, 275–280.

Watson, R. (2010). *What momma left me*. New York, NY: Bloomsbury USA Children's Books.

Wilhelm, J. (2010, November). Teaching for joy and wisdom: Being the book and being the change. In S. Hayes (Chair), *Middle Mosaic: Writers and Readers Together*. Symposium conducted at the 99th Annual Convention of the National Council of Teachers of English, Orlando, Florida.

Wright, J. (2009). 7 Stages of grief: Through the Process and Back to Life. Retrieved from http://www.recover-from-grief.com/7-stages-of-grief.html

Wolf, M. (2007). *Proust and the squid: The story and science of the reading brain*. New York, NY: HarperCollins.

Woodson, J. (2000). *Miracle's boys*. New York, NY: G. P. Putnam's Sons.

CHAPTER 7

African American Female Literacies and the Role of Double Dutch in the Lives and Literature for Black Girls

RACHEL GRANT

Down in the meadow where the corn cobs grow,
A grasshopper jumped on an elephant's toe. The elephant cried with tears in his eyes,
"Why don't you pick on someone your size."

—DOUBLE DUTCH RHYME

Perhaps at no other time in history have we looked to education and educators as crucial forces for advancing enlightenment and global harmony, competition and nationalism as we prepare children for a world that is more diverse, more dangerous, more interconnected, and more divided. This appears to be the case especially in countries such as the United States, where schools have experienced increases in the numbers of racial, linguistic, and culturally diverse students. "We know for certain that teaching in U.S. schools is increasingly a cross-cultural phenomenon, in that teachers are frequently not the same race, ethnicity, [social] class, and linguistic dominance as their students" (Gay, 2003, p. 1). Nowhere is this situation more visible than in the urban school setting, where, even there, teachers are overwhelmingly white, female, and middle class.

How can teachers support intellectual, cultural, social, political, and "human" growth for children and youth through literature? What theoretical frameworks can inform teacher selection of literature to integrate books on black culture into their curriculum? What themes can teachers use in promoting specific cultural resources of Africa and African Americans for engaging children in literature and literacy activities? There are no simplistic answers to these questions that can provide a road map for teachers to use in addressing the vast range of backgrounds, needs, and interests of African ancestry children. The multicultural movement of the 1990s helped increase awareness of the growing demographic and cultural divide that exist between teachers and their students by stressing the need to celebrate and incorporate into the curriculum the histories, peoples, and traditions of the indigenous and people of African ancestry. However, there is still much work that is needed.

In the United States, the African American personage is an inescapable vessel of American history, culture, society, and literature. The history of African American children's literature reflects the same racialized attitudes as in the U.S. society, which means that the literature included limited self-awareness among readers; circumscribed publication and distribution; omitted from libraries, schools, and bookstores; and subjected to uninformed criticism (Harris, 1990). Above all else, literature for children of color was not considered part of the literary canons that included the sanctioned lists of works perpetuated by critics, educators, and cultural guardians. As a result, for many decades, African American children's literature did not constitute the literature read by many children, black or otherwise.

Throughout their history in the United States, people of African ancestry and those who advocate on their behalf have made great strides to tell, through narrative and other genres, the experiences and stories of African heritage people. During the past thirty years, in literary circles and the wider society, work "for, by, and about" Africa and African Americans has become more visible and is enjoyed by a broad range of readers. There is also a rich and growing body of work addressing the stories of Africans in America, reflecting the perspectives and experiences of young African Americans. A major objective in the multicultural movement has been to infuse into U.S. education a more balanced perspective about the role of African Americans and other people of color as children come to understand how "others" helped in shaping the development of this country. A challenge for today's classroom teacher is to sustain gains made during the era of multiculturalism in what is now a climate in which cultural enrichment through literature often must take a back seat to high-stakes testing and teacher accountability.

This chapter has four interrelated goals: (a) introduce the theoretical framework of African American female literacies; (b) connect this framework to a specific cultural tool, double dutch rope jumping; (c) provide an overview of one book in which double dutch is the prominent theme; and (d) suggest activities for using the book to engage students in writing activities. I begin by providing a brief history of African American children's literacy, emphasizing the important role of literature as a component of schooling. Next, I introduce African American female literacies as a theoretical framework for utilizing culture in themes for children's literature. Then, I highlight double dutch rope jumping as a theme used in literature targeting young girls, especially African American girls living in urban communities. In the final sections, I introduce a book that uses double dutch as the theme in a coming-of-age story in which the principle characters are African American middle-school girls. I conclude with suggestions for writing activities and other ideas for using cultural tools to engage young African American girls in literacy practices.

AFRICAN AMERICAN CHILDREN'S LITERATURE

By all accounts, African Americans have been depicted in general literature since the seventeenth century (Harris, 1990; Broderick, 1973; Kline, 1992); however, the 1890s was the first decade in which books written for children of color were published. In early works, depictions of African American children and their families were often stereotyped, pejorative, and unauthentic. The characters were submissive or depicted in ways that would not offend "white sensibilities" or call in question the social, economic, or political inequalities that existed between blacks and whites in America. In her chronicle of the first hundred years of African American children's literature, Harris (1990) identifies major periods of development: the beginnings, 1890–1900; emergent tradition, 1900–1920s; strengthening of the tradition, 1930–1940; shift to assimilation, 1940–1970; and culturally conscious literature, 1970s and beyond.

An overview of the major periods reveals the following. During the *beginnings* (1890–1900), the earliest works were not intended to entertain but instead contained themes and motifs stressing, for example, perseverance, love of family, goodness, and kindness (Harris, 1990). Harris suggests that in the earliest books and writings, children were engaged in activities that were deemed to bring joy; for example, going to church, dancing, attending a picnic, or daily tasks. Harris identified two related conditions influencing literary expansion for African American children's literature after the 1890s: improved educational opportunities for blacks and the advent of a black middle class.

During the *emergent tradition* period (1900–1920s), writers began to produce more culturally authentic literature for African American children, and many of the texts were viewed as oppositional because the writers wanted to contradict a theme (the benevolent white), motif (happy, content black), or stereotype (lazy trickster). Many texts during this period sought to bring to life sociocultural realities faced by children and their families. Common themes were intended to help black children realize that being "colored" was normal, inform them about the accomplishments of black people, teach codes of honor and respect, instill pride in home and family, provide a model for how to interact with whites, and entertain. During this period, more African Americans began to see that writing had potential as an avocation and vocation. As well, more white publishers were willing to publish literature targeting black children. In other words, publishers realized there was profit in making available texts designed for the black consumer.

The next period of African American children's literature, *strengthening of the tradition* (1930–1940), saw efforts to build on accomplishments made during the previous period as themes in children's literature expanded to include individual advancement, critical thinking, and personal commitment to advancing the race. Harris credits educator Carter G. Woodson as the major influence during the period. Woodson's accomplishments included spearheading the movement for Negro history week and being a founding member of the Associated Publishers and the Association for the Study of Negro Life and History. Perhaps Woodson's most important accomplishment was his book, *The Mis-Education of the Negro* (1933), which is still regarded as a most important work on education and the descendants of African slaves. In his book, Woodson stressed that what he proposed, although seen at the time as radical change for the education of African American children, actually was not, for he believed U.S. schools were not devised to "uplift" black children. Rather, schools worked to maintain economic and political power for whites.

The period of *strengthening of the tradition* also overlapped with an important historic period for African Americans known as the Harlem Renaissance (1920–1930). The Harlem Renaissance was a cultural movement that represented a literary and intellectual flowering that fostered a new cultural identity for African Americans. The period is marked by the growth of black-owned newspapers and magazines and black art, music, and theater. Although New York City became the epicenter of this movement, many French-speaking black writers, originally from African and Caribbean colonies, and living in Paris at the time, were also influenced by the Harlem Renaissance. The Harlem Renaissance grew out of changes that had taken place in African American communities since the end of slavery and was preceded by the first "Great Migration" of blacks from the South to work in the factories of cities in the North. The economic downturn of the Great Depression was a major factor that decreased publishing opportunities and notoriety of many black writers of adult and children's literature during the late 1930s. However, the Harlem Renaissance remains a major influence today on American culture, literature, and music.

The next period of African American children's literature, recognized as the *shift to assimilation* (1940–1970), saw greater mass acceptance of African American children's literature. However, a subtle shift in tone and ideology occurred. Arna Bontemps, considered by many to be the "father" of African American children's literature, created an extensive body of work during the 1940s and 1950s. Bontemps, like many writers before, wrote novels, biographies, and histories, and contributed to an already impressive body of poetry anthologies and folktales for children. Much of the literature during this period was labeled "social conscience literature" because, according to Sims (1982), a goal for many of the authors was to develop a "social conscience—mainly in non-Afro-American readers, to encourage them to develop empathy, sympathy, and tolerance for Afro-American children and their problems" (p. 17). Many of the themes in children's literature of this period emphasized the universal qualities and experiences of African Americans as they promoted integration and advanced notions of the American "melting pot" and cultural diversity.

The current and fifth period of African American children's literature is characterized as the period of *culturally conscious literature* and includes work created after the 1970s. The language, characters, and cultural traditions depicted in *culturally conscious literature* reflect a decidedly African American tone, content, and perspective. Harris declares that the literary quality of the work during this period "equals and, in many cases, surpasses the quality of general children's literature" (1990, p. 550). A notable feature of texts from this period is that they present the range of African American experience and do not hesitate to describe historically accurate events and situations to convey the full extent of treatment blacks have experienced in the United States. Another notable feature of literature during the current period has been to present the complexity of African American life as it is influenced by poverty, crime, racism, and economic conditions.

AFRICAN AMERICAN FEMALE LITERACIES

The primary theoretical perspective undergirding this chapter is research on African American female literacies (Collins, 2000; Richardson, 2003). Critical race (Ladson-Billings & Tate, 1995) and intersectionality theory (Collins, 1998a, 1998b; Glenn, 2002), as well as critical race feminism (Grant, 1992; Wing, 1997), undergird African American female literacies perspective. I find these are useful frameworks for representing and speaking to the experiences of black girls and women in educational spaces. The premise for an African American female literacies perspective is that ideologies of women's knowledge are shaped by women, by virtue of their unique biological function, mothering and nurturing experiences, role assignment and work, sociohistoric treatment, ethnic and cultural tradition, and by discursive ways in which class, race, and gender interact and react. Further, this premise suggests that ways of acting in, living in, understanding, responding to, shaping, and as well, being shaped by the world, give rise to female, in particular African American female, consciousness, voice, and literacies. Patricia Hill Collins describes this as " . . . this private, hidden space of Black women's consciousness, the 'inside' ideas that allow Black women to cope with and in many cases, transcend the confines of intersecting oppressions of race, class, gender, and sexuality" (2000, p. 98).

Elaine Richardson (2003) and others (Smitherman, 2006; Lanehart, 2002) describe African American female literacy practices as these: storytelling (using stories to transmit special knowledge), performative silence (communicative style of "keeping your business to yourself"), strategic use of polite and assertive language (navigating between verbal and nonverbal communication, e.g., smiles, eye and head movements), style shifting and codeswitching (moving between or among different linguistic or language systems, usually African American language and Standard English), indirection (making the point with words that on the surface "say one thing, but mean another"), stepping and rhyming (the verse and rhyming routines recited during jump rope routines, hand clap, and dance performance), and preaching (taking from the communicative style associated with ministers of the black church, e.g., call-response, repetition of language, voice modulation, emotion, etc.).

In the United States, black female consciousness grows out of a constructed knowledge and voice from which she learns "to speak in unique and authentic voice, women must 'jump outside' the frames and systems authorities provide and create their own frame" (Murray, 1987, p. 134, as cited in Collins, 2000). One need not subscribe to the cliché, "Women are from Venus, men are from Mars," to acknowledge that, frequently, as a result of sociocultural, sociohistoric, and ethnic and religious conditions, women and men in a given society differ in their ways of doing, knowing, and being in the world. In addition to gendered influences, differences in the literacy status of African Americans reflect broader sociohistoric factors related to the following: (a) the African Holocaust of Enslavement, (b) antiliteracy campaigns to contain and repress literacy for formerly enslaved Americans, (c) segregated and poor quality schools, (d) large number of underfunded and underresourced schools, (e) overrepresentation of blacks in the military and prisons (Blackmon, 2008; Davis, 2005; Russell, 1998), and (f) high rates of poverty in African American communities (Anderson, 1988; Harris, Kamhi, & Pollock, 2001; Williams, 2005). The impact of these legacies today supports the need for literature that presents the cultural knowledge, histories, perspectives, and personages of Africa and African Americans. This is important not just for African heritage children but for other children who represent the many heritages in American schools and society.

AFRICAN AMERICAN GIRLS

The fifty years since the landmark U.S. Supreme Court decision in *Brown v. Board of Education* have been marked by mixed results in a continuing struggle to end the unequal and poor quality education many African American children still receive. This is especially the case for black children attending school in rural as well as urban communities. Of late, much attention is paid to differences in the literacy performance of urban students who are largely African American and Hispanic, and poor, and their white counterparts, who in larger numbers are middle class and attend suburban schools. In the public discourse, literacy has long been associated with schooling, and children's literature has long been recognized as an important tool for cultivating reading that can improve children's chances for success in school.

Few would argue that literature is a developmental asset when readers have opportunity to see themselves reflected in the personages and circumstances depicted in books and other forms of literacy. Moreover, literature is an important conduit for the formation of culture, which depends on the capacity of a group to transmit customary beliefs, social forms, and material characteristics. This is the case for all groups but especially blacks, who are so often missing and underrepresented in traditional publishing and emerging technologies. As the U.S. school population becomes more diverse, the challenge for teachers is to make available more literature that reflects the interests and realities of all learners, especially those to whom "mainstream" American personages and stories will have less appeal.

Recently, there has been growing concern for the well-being of young African American males. While this attention is not without merit, there is still a need to look at the educational experiences and schooling processes of African American girls in urban school settings. Black girls are represented in large numbers in urban schools; however, "the educational needs of Black girls have fallen through the cracks" (Evans-Winters & Esposito, 2010, p. 11). This is especially the case for middle and high school girls attending school in communities where poverty and racial isolation are implacable and teaching often is ineffective. In her work *Teaching Black Girls: Resiliency in Urban Classrooms*, Venus Evans-Winters focused on the pedagogical and educational needs of urban poor and working-class African American female students who, as a group, "remain whited out (subsumed under White girls' experiences), blacked out (generalized within Black male experience), or simply pathologized" (2007, p. 9). It is clear that African American girls remain venerable to many of the same conditions that diminish academic success and life chances for their male counterparts (Fordham, 1993, 1996; The Black Girls, 1995). Space does not permit me to examine the full range of issues that impact schooling for African American girls; however, what we do know is that race, gender, and class combine to shape the educational and life experiences of black girls, creating unique obstacles for them (Morris, 2007). I believe that teachers who incorporate themes reflecting the cultural tools and social practices, especially those focused on the resiliency and resiliency-fostering factors of black girls, provide opportunities for them to connect to literacy through meaningful literature that showcases black female ingenuity.

DOUBLE DUTCH

Gaunt (2006) asserts that, although present in the South, double dutch is largely based in the multiethnic streets in the North and it is impossible to determine where African American or other ethnic groups got the idea to practice it. Double dutch is a two-rope jumping sport that probably originated with ancient Phoenician, Egyptian, and Chinese rope makers. These ancient craftsmen, lore has it, used a series of footwork and precise jumps as part of a rope manufacturing process. Brought to the United States by Dutch settlers, double dutch grew popular as a mostly urban game in which young girls often sang rhymes or chanted while turning and jumping.

The art of rope jumping, especially double dutch, has a long history within African American communities, both rural and urban, often serving as a cultural resource because of the "capital" afforded those more adept at performing the intricate moves and endurance needed in this jumping style. "There is a whole world of insight about racial and gender socialization and ethnic identification within African American culture that is hidden within the seemingly trivial maneuvers of games like double-dutch" (Gaunt, 2006, p. 14). Viewed within the context of cultural politics, rope jumping in African American communities is cultural capital. "Such capital is not simply something one has, but something that has different value in different contexts" (Grant & Wong, 2008, p. 176).

In 1973, two African American New York police detectives, David Walker and Ulysses Williams, organized the first competition of double dutch, and in 1975, the American Double Dutch League (ADDL) was founded. Since then, double dutch has evolved and grown in popularity such that local competitions and a "world invitational" tournament are held annually, attracting teams from as far away as Japan. There is even support for making it an Olympic event (McManus, 1995).

In spite of its popularity outside urban communities, double dutch remains a mainstay for black girls and offers "insight into the *learned* ways of being that foster and reflect individual and group identity within African American communities" (Gaunt, 2006, p. 13, emphasis in original). Moreover, for black girls, the double dutch street game displays not just complex physical ability but offers opportunity for advancing "kinetic orality" or metacommunication, terms used by Cornel West, that in his words are "dynamic repetitive and energetic rhetorical styles that form communities, e.g., antiphonal styles and linguistic innovations that accent fluid, improvisational identities . . ." (1989, p. 93).

Everyday girls generate and pass on a unique repertoire of hand-clapping games, chants, and rhymes through the game of double dutch. However, this play, over time and across generations, has evolved and become something much more for urban black girls. Indeed it has become a symbol of black female ingenuity, a shared social practice that is part of the black private and public sphere. Double dutch rope play, for black girls and women, is a space where they learn, share, and sustain gendered and raced identities in ways that empower and "uplift" the individual and collective. Therefore, it seems reasonable within the framework of cultural work that themed literature focused on double dutch can be used to engage young African American girls in literate activities and at the same time promote literature.

DOUBLE DUTCH—THE BOOK

Written by Sharon Draper (2002), the story's setting is a "big-city school" much like those potential young readers attend. The opening lines set the stage for drama, tension, and twists and turns that run throughout the story:

> Look Out Girl, Here Come The Tolliver Twins! Have mercy! They look like they're ready to bite something. Delia pulled her books close to her body and tried to avoid what looked like was going to be a direct confrontation with two of the most feared boys at the school—Tabu and Titan Tolliver. (p. 1)

The reader prepares to take a journey through the lives of a cohort of young girls and boys, situated differently in terms of family and circumstance but who are oddly connected by one common element, double dutch.

The principal characters are four friends, Delia, Charlene, Yolanda, and Randy, who are, for the most part, successfully navigating the perils of middle school, but Delia and Randy have secrets that threaten to destroy their friendship. Draper assigns qualities to each character that I believe resonate well with young girls, especially those who live in large cities and attend urban schools. Although many of the perils associated with urban school life (violence, bullying, and divorce) lurch on the periphery, these elements are not central to Draper's story. Instead, she has chosen to feature the genuine "connectedness" among friends within seemingly normal life, then links these characters to each other, and in meaningful and realistic ways, to their elders, parents, and other adults. However, "story is story," so there is the predictable romantic attraction, "girl talk," mystery, and tension. Overall, *Double Dutch* is refreshing and an enjoyable read for middle or high school. I also believe the book has strong cross-cultural appeal, in particular for urban adolescent readers, because double dutch rope jumping is practiced by other ethnic groups who will find a comfortable familiarity with the various relationships and situations depicted in the story, enabling them to relate these to their own lives.

The theme of double dutch provides a powerful social connection for each character in the story for obvious, and some less obvious, reasons. Draper's use of rope jumping sustains an atmosphere of personal challenge, group effort, and individual and team competition that demonstrates how, through double dutch, young female members of black culture learn, share, sustain, and connect to each other and adults. Gaunt notes that within the realm of double dutch, black girls and women alike engage interdependent social practices that demonstrate "an ongoing process of rhythmic consciousness and improvisational social interaction . . . individuality within collectivity, social and musical aesthetics, and metrical complexity" (2006, p. 179). In Draper's story, the theme of double dutch is used as catalyst for motivating characters to value teamwork, maintain high grades, connect to community, fuel budding romances, and relate across gendered, raced, and intergenerational divides.

ACTIVITIES FOR BUILDING LITERACY AND HONORING AFRICAN AMERICAN FEMALE LITERACIES

In this last section, I present some of the literacy activities Draper includes at the end of her book and juxtapose them with other ways to incorporate discussion and writing activities that are informed by African American female literacies and critical race feminism. Teachers choosing to incorporate *Double Dutch* (Draper, 2002) into their curriculum will be delighted by the menu of literacy ideas Draper presents. My intention is not to exhaust the instructional possibilities for using *Double Dutch* but to offer a few suggestions that can be expanded or adapted for appropriate use in any classroom. It is my hope that these ideas can be the springboard for activities informed by ways of being, thinking, and looking at the world through a lens informed by African American female literacies and other critical perspectives. Indeed, the suggestions are intended as a beginning.

When teachers integrate literature into the curriculum, students are given the opportunity to learn about themselves and the world during a critical period in their development. This is especially the case because adolescence is a stressful period involving a pivotal transition from childhood dependency to adulthood independence and self-sufficiency. Literature merits a place in the curriculum for adolescents, because when young readers find text they "connect to," it has the potential to inform, to offer a perspective and an insight that they can bring to their own experiences, and to provide spaces for responding to literature through discussion and in writing. Literature can indeed be a powerful tool for reading and writing.

Recent research on literacy suggests a growing number of evidence-based practices that can help children with the complex process of reading to make meaning.

However, there remain significant gaps in achievement on literacy performance indicators for black and Hispanic students as compared to white students, suburban students, and their urban and rural counterparts, and students living in poverty as compared to those privileged by middle and upper income. Although black females, in general, typically outperform their male counterparts, literacy achievement in high-stakes tests for black girls, in particular those living in urban areas, still lags behind white female and male students (National Assessment of Educational Progress, 2006). I suggest that when viewed within critical pedagogical frameworks such as critical race theory (CRT), critical race feminism (CRF), and African American female literacies (AAFL), literature can be a useful tool for young readers to improve reading because the text used can (a) strengthen bonds within groups who experience raced, gendered, and classed identities; (b) provide space for critical questioning of the "acceptable" and "unacceptable"; and (c) strengthen development of personal agency, which can often be difficult for individuals who historically have been "Othered" within U.S. society.

Also informative for this chapter is a small but growing body of work known as *resiliency research* that examines resiliency-fostering factors for black girls in urban areas (Evans-Winters, 2007; Ladner, 1987; O'Connor, 1997; Ward, 1996; Wang & Gordon, 1994). Resiliency, simply put, "is the ability to recover from or adjust to problems, adversities, and stress" (Evans-Winters, 2007, p. 20). I believe instruction framed by the type of critical perspectives mentioned here allows teachers to present a "strength-based model" that can be a mediator to enhance literacy. When books such as *Double Dutch* are incorporated into the curriculum, black girls have opportunity to see themselves depicted in ways to promote "strength-building" and literacy.

The end-of-the-book activities are organized into three broad categories: reading group discussion topics, writing, and critical investigation. In this last section, I present three examples and then juxtapose what they might look like when critical theory frames are posed. This I believe will help teachers in (re)thinking the use of literature for urban students, especially girls and black girls, in particular.

DISCUSSION AND WRITING ACTIVITIES

The following chart offers discussion and writing activities based on characters and/or events in the story. Alongside them I offer options for (re)thinking the activity informed by CRF and AAFL perspectives.

Text Idea	CRF/AAFL Modification
Double Dutch begins with a discussion of the characters' fear of the Tolliver twins. Trace how the idea of fear and the results of fear are developed throughout the story.	*Double Dutch* begins with a discussion of the characters' fear of the Tolliver twins. Why do you think the author chose to cast boys and not girls as characters who perpetuated violence? If girls, not boys, had been cast as the school bullies, how might their acts of violence differ from the Tolliver twins? In your own school or communities, in what ways do you see acts of bullying? Who is most likely to be depicted as committing these acts, girl or boy, black, Hispanic, Asian, or white student? Why?
Why is the television program, in which the twins appear, an effective way to increase their negative reputation? Discuss the effects of these types of talk shows.	Television shows like the one in which the Tolliver twins appear and the new "reality shows" have become increasingly popular. What "type" of story is most likely to be featured on these shows? What images of women do you see depicted on the shows? How do you feel about these images?
"Double dutch requires an intricate display of skill, agility, and strength. It encourages creativity, teamwork, and sportsmanship, and it develops physical fitness and mental discipline" (Draper, 2002, p. 188). Write an expository paper on sport. Tell how the game is played, give some of its rules, and explain why it is successful as an enjoyable physical activity.	"Double dutch requires an intricate display of skill, agility, and strength. It encourages creativity, teamwork, and sportsmanship, and it develops physical fitness and mental discipline (Draper, 2002, p. 188)." The sport of double dutch is practiced around the world and has become popular in countries as far away as Japan. In spite of the similarities in how people engage the sport of double dutch, one major difference is that black girls have always incorporated chants, rhymes, and music into their rope jumping play. Research the inclusion of these literacies in the rope jumping play of African American girls.

Text Idea	CRF/AAFL Modification
Additional Discussion and Writing Ideas	(1) Why do you think the author selects a white male as the team coach? Is this realistic? If the story took place in your school, who might be the coach? Why?
	(2) Why do you think the author selects Randy as the team's unofficial manager? Why do you believe a boy was selected for this role? (3) Did your mother practice double dutch as a girl? Does she still enjoy the game? If not, why do you think she doesn't? (4) Why do you think girls stop playing games like double dutch as they grow older? Why is it that boys continue playing games well into adulthood?
	(5) Research the presence of double dutch rope jumping in your community.
	(6) Research the history of double dutch in the United States. In your paper, be sure to discuss reasons for its ongoing popularity in urban African American communities.
	(7) There is some research (Story et al., 2003) that suggests double dutch should be used to reduce or prevent obesity among young black girls. How do you feel about using double dutch for this purpose? If this program was to be offered in your school, would you participate?

After reading the book or as students finish key chapters, I recommend teachers engage them first in small-group discussion and then expand this to "grand conversation." Initially, literature discussion group frameworks could be utilized, but in addition to organizing the groups around typical group characteristics, for example, interest or ability, I encourage teachers to consider gender, race and ethnicity, and personal circumstance when organizing discussion groups. Shared race and ethnicity or gender might allow for more candid responses that could later be compared across groups and "deconstructed" during grand conversation. This would help students examine gendered and raced responses to the story. Building on the discussion, teachers could have students extend their responses through shared writing for coconstructed responses, interactive writing across groups to support struggling writers, or journal writing for self-reflection or character study. Another useful writing activity would be to have students "rethink" the actions of characters, especially when the actions they take seem not to serve their own best interest.

It is clear that much more is needed to incorporate the literature of Africa and African Americans into U.S. school curriculum. Teachers need to be aware of critical theory that would be helpful in utilizing literature in ways that engage young readers, especially those in urban areas, so students connect situations and personages to their own lives. This is especially important, as I pointed out in this chapter, for young African American girls because, "By ignoring or subsuming Black girls' experiences within White girls' and Black boys' experiences, we overlook the inimitable experience of the Black girl. Her experiences as a racialized "other," girl, and of the lower caste in the United States, makes oppression nearly ineluctable" (Evans-Winters, 2007, pp. 9–10).

CHILDREN'S LITERATURE

Chambers, V. (2002). *Double dutch: A celebration of jump rope, rhyme, and sisterhood*. New York, NY: Author.
Draper, S. M. (2002). *Double dutch*. New York, NY: Aladdin Paperbacks.
Hru, D. (1996). *The magic moonberry jump ropes*. New York, NY: Dial.
Singletary, M. E. (2007). *Just jump: The double dutch club series #1*. Chicago, IL: Moody Publishers.
Singletary, M. E. (2008). *Something to jump about: The double dutch series #2*. Chicago, IL: Moody Publishers.

REFERENCES

Anderson, J. D. (1988). *The education of blacks in the South, 1860–1935*. Chapel Hill: University of North Carolina Press.

Blackmon, D. A. (2008). *Slavery by another name: The re-enslavement of black Americans from the Civil War to World War II*. New York, NY: Anchor Books.

Broderick, D. (1973). *Image of the black in children's fiction*. New York, NY: Bowker.

Collins, P. H. (1998a). *Fighting words: Black women and the search for social justice*. Minneapolis: University of Minnesota Press.

Collins, P. H. (1998b). Intersections of race, class, gender, and nation: Some implications for black family studies. *Journal of Comparative Family Studies, 29*, 27–36.

Collins, P. H. (2000). *Black feminist thought: Knowledge, consciousness, and the politics of empowerment*. New York, NY: Routledge

Davis, A. Y. (2005). *Abolition democracy: Beyond empire, prisons, and torture*. New York, NY: Seven Stories Press.

Evans-Winters, V. E. (2007). *Teaching black girls: Resiliency in urban classrooms*. New York, NY: Peter Lang.

Evans-Winters, V. E., & Esposito, J. (2010). Other people's daughters: Critical race feminism and black girls' education. *Educational Foundations, 4*, 11–24.

Fordham, S. (1993). "Those loud black girls": (Black) women, silence, and gender "passing" in the academy. *Anthropology and Education Quarterly, 24*(1), 3–32.

Fordham, S. (1996). *Blacked out: Dilemmas of race, identity and success at Capital High*. Chicago, IL: The University of Chicago Press.

Gay, G. (2003). *Becoming multicultural educators: Personal journey towards professional agency*. New York, NY: Jossey-Bass.

Glenn, E. N. (2002). Unequal freedom: How race and gender shaped American citizenship and labor. Cambridge, MA: Harvard University Press.

Grant, L. (1992). Race and schooling of young girls. In J. Wrigley (Ed.), *Education and gender inequality* (pp. 91–114). New York, NY: Falmer.

Grant, R. A., & Wong, S. D. (2008). Critical race perspectives, Bourdieu, and language education. In J. Albright & A. Luke (Eds.), *Pierre Bourdieu and literacy education* (pp. 162–184). London, UK: Routledge.

Gaunt, K. D. (2006). *The games black girls play: Learning the ropes from double-dutch to hip-hop*. New York, NY: New York University Press.

Harris. J. L., Kamhi, A. G., & Pollock, K. E. (Eds.). (2001). *Literacy in African American communities*. Mahwah, NJ: Lawrence Erlbaum.

Harris, V. J. (1990). African American children's literature: The first hundred years. *The Journal of Negro Education, 59*, 540–555.

Kline, L. (1992). *African-American children's literature*. Washington, DC: U.S. Department of Education. (ERIC Document Reproduction Service No. ED 355 520)

Ladner, J. A. (1987). Introduction of tomorrow's tomorrow: The black women. In S. Harding (Ed.), *Feminism and methodology* (pp. 74–83). Bloomington: Indiana University Press.

Ladson-Billings, G., & Tate, W. (1995). Towards a critical race theory of education. *Teachers College Record, 97*(1), 47–60.

Lanehart, S. L. (2002). *Sista speak! Black women kinfolk talk about language and literacy*. Austin: University of Texas Press.

McManus, K. (1995, April 21). Knowing the ropes. *The Washington Post: Weekend*, pp. 6–7.

Morris, E. W. (2007). "Ladies" or "Loudies"? Perceptions and experiences of black girls in classrooms. *Youth & Society, 38*, 490–515.

Murray, P. (1987). *Song of a weary throat: An American pilgrimage*. New York, NY: Harper & Row.

National Assessment of Educational Progress. (2006). Report prepared by the Office of Educational Research and Improvement. Washington, DC: U.S. Department of Education.

O'Connor, C. (1997). Disposition toward (collective) struggle and educational resilience in the inner-city: A case study of six African American high school students. *American Educational Research Journal, 34,* 593–629.

Richardson, E. (2003). *African American literacies.* London, UK: Routledge.

Sims, R. (1982). *Shadow and substance: Afro-American experience in contemporary children's fiction.* Urbana, IL: National Council of Teachers of English.

Smitherman, G. (2006). *Talkin that talk: Language, culture, and education in African Americans.* New York, NY: Routledge.

Story, M., Sherwood, N. E., Himes, J. H., Davis, M., Jacobs, D. R., Cartwright, Y., Smyth, M., & Rochon, J. (2003). An after-school obesity prevention program for African American girls: The Minnesota GEMS pilot study. *Ethnicity & Disease, 13,* 54–64.

The Black Girls. (Eds.). (1995). *Black girl talk.* Toronto, Ontario, Canada: Sister Vision.

Wang, M. C., & Gordon, E. W. (Eds.). (1994). *Educational reisilence in inner city America.* Mahwah, NJ: Lawrence Erlbaum.

Ward, J. V. (1996). Raising resisters: The role of truth in the psychological development of African American girls. In B. J. R. Leadbeater & N. Way (Eds.), *Urban girls: Resisting stereotypes, creating identities* (pp. 85–99). New York, NY: New York University Press.

West, C. (1989). Black culture and postmodernism. In B. Kruger & P. Mariani (Eds.), *Remaking history: Discussion in contemporary culture* (pp. 87–96, Vol. 4). Seattle, WA: Bay Press.

Wing, A. K. (Ed.). (1997). *Critical race feminism: A reader.* New York, NY: New York University Press.

Williams, H. A. (2005). *Self-taught: African American education in slavery and freedom.* Chapel Hill: University of North Carolina Press.

Woodson, C. G. (1933). *The mis-education of the Negro.* Asmara, Eritrea: Africa World Press.

CHAPTER 8

Discrimination and Preadolescence

Two Readers' Constructions

ANN BERGER-KNORR

As an informal summer reading opportunity, I invited two preadolescent girls to read and respond to *Roll of Thunder, Hear My Cry*, by notable author and Newbery Award winner Mildred Taylor (1976). Curious about preadolescents' constructions of racial discrimination, I was interested in examining how they read and responded to various depictions of discrimination in the context of the novel. Moreover, I was interested in what sense they made of particular scenes from the novel that portray various forms of racial discrimination and, consequently, how sophisticated their understandings of those depictions might be. Further, I was curious as to whether providing them with a framework—or a lens—for viewing and conceptualizing racial discrimination would help them better understand the complexities of discrimination, in general, and scenes from the novel, in particular. And furthermore, I wondered whether this lens might serve as a pedagogical tool for helping teachers better discuss and "take up" issues involving race and race relations with students in classroom settings.

I chose the historical fiction novel *Roll of Thunder, Hear My Cry* for several reasons. First, it was important to select a piece of literature which represented the "best of the best" in terms of quality for adolescent and young adult readers. *Roll of Thunder, Hear My Cry* has received many accolades over the years, but, most importantly, it has received the prestigious Newbery Award given to the most distinguished contribution to American literature for children. "[L]auded for both its literary qualities and its perspective on black history" (Taxel, 1986, p. 249), *Roll of Thunder, Hear My Cry* is considered a "classic" within the field of children and adolescent literature.

A second reason for selecting *Roll of Thunder, Hear My Cry* was the opportunity for sharing with students—and teachers—an authentic way for discussing race and racial relations via African American literature. As a teacher educator, I often hear teachers remark upon reading *Roll of Thunder, Hear My Cry*: "What a great book. Reading it with students would serve as a wonderful way to teach about racial discrimination, racism, or prejudice, etcetera." I am always intrigued hearing such comments from teachers. Yet, I find when I probe for specific ways in which teachers actually go about teaching discrimination and/or prejudice using this novel, such claims are often left unanswered.

As a teacher educator, I believe multicultural literature, in general, and African American literature, in particular, are ideal for discussing important social issues with children and young adults. Both carry the potential for raising students' awareness about issues of race and racial relations. My concern, however, is whether teachers (read: white teachers) are equipped with the knowledge necessary for carrying out these tasks in their classrooms. More to the point, I wonder whether teachers are pedagogically prepared for exploring and discussing racial issues with students. After all, *knowing* that a book contains sociopolitical themes such as racial discrimination is very different than actually *teaching* about it. Others have shared a similar concern with respect to teachers' abilities to address race and race relations with students, in general (see, e.g., Berger-Knorr, 1997; Ladson-Billings, 2003; Picower, 2009; Sleeter, 1995), and within the context of children's and adolescents' literature, in particular (see, e.g., Brooks & Hampton, 2005); Copenhaver, 2000; Fondre, 2001; Rogers & Christian, 2007).

While I believe most in our society, teachers included, would agree that racial discrimination is a negative thing, and they would most assuredly like to see it eradicated, identifying and naming what it is and how it is manifested in our society is a often a difficult task. Using literature for the purposes of exploring sociopolitical themes such as discrimination provides many opportunities for both teachers and students to develop more sophisticated understandings of literature as well as the broader society.

Thus, the purpose of this paper is, at least, twofold. First, I attempt to understand two preadolescents' interpretations (read: constructions) of racial discrimination in the context of the novel *Roll of Thunder, Hear My Cry*. Second, based on these constructions, I share a critical lens for helping students, and teachers, better understand racial discrimination in an attempt to bring about social change.

I define discrimination as the following: "[B]ehavior that disadvantages one group in relation to another group and maintains and perpetuates conditions of inequality" (Fiske-Rusciano & Cyrus, 2005, p. 195). Racial discrimination, or racism, the "discrimination against and the subordination of a person or group because of color" (Fiske-Rusciano & Cyrus, p. 195), is the main focus of this paper. I differentiate racial *discrimination* (behaviors and practices) from racial *prejudice* (beliefs and attitudes) because "one can be **prejudiced,** believing in the inferiority of certain kinds of individuals based on their membership in a certain group, but not **discriminate,** not act on those beliefs" (Fiske-Rusciano & Cyrus, 2005, p. 198, emphasis in original). Thus, racial discrimination as "the behavioral extension of racial prejudice" (Fiske-Rusciano & Cyrus, 2005, p. 198) includes "those policies, procedures, decisions, habits, and acts that overlook, ignore or subjugate members of certain groups or that enable one group of people to maintain control over another group . . ." (Fiske-Rusciano & Cyrus, 2005, p. 195), based on the color of one's skin.

Prior to the 1960s, discrimination was viewed as a "creature of prejudice" (Feagin & Feagin, 1988, p. 41). What this means is that the problem of discrimination was viewed as one motivated primarily by individuals (or groups of individuals) on the basis of prejudice or hatred. Implicit in this "prejudice-causes-discrimination-model" (Feagin & Feagin, 1988, p. 42) was the assumption that the solution to discrimination was one of simply eliminating prejudice. Thus, the elimination of prejudicial behavior would lead to the eradication of discrimination. Since the 1960s, however, a more comprehensive conceptualization of discrimination has evolved.

According to the U.S. Commission on Civil Rights, there are two forms of racial discrimination (Fiske-Rusciano & Cyrus, 2005): overt racial discrimination and institutional racial discrimination. Overt racial discrimination relies on the "use of color and other visible characteristics related to color as subordinating factors" (Fiske-Rusciano & Cyrus, 2005, p. 197). Institutionalized racism, a "more subtle and often invisible" (Fiske-Rusciano & Cyrus, 2005, p. 197) form of racial discrimination, "does not explicitly use color as the subordinating mechanism. Instead, decisions are based on such other factors as skill level, residential location, income, and education—factors that appear to be racially neutral" (Fiske-Rusciano & Cyrus, 2005, p. 197).

Along similar lines, Fiske-Rusciano and Cyrus (2005) and Rothenberg (1988, 2007) conceptualize three different types of racial discrimination in our society: (a) individual, (b) organizational, and (c) structural. Individual racial discrimination refers to the prejudicial attitudes and behaviors of one group of individuals toward another. Organizational discrimination refers to "the well-established rules, policies, and practices of organizations" (Rothenberg, 2007, p. 257), including education, government, places of employment, and family institutions. Structural discrimination refers to the cyclical nature of discrimination and how it reproduces itself within society. While on the surface most acts of discrimination appear to be inflicted against an individual—or groups of individuals—most are embedded in the very social fabric of society in the policies and practices and, consequently, are much harder to detect. All forms of discrimination, however, serve to reproduce or maintain structural forms of discrimination. These forms can be either conscious or unconscious, subtle or obvious (Fiske-Rusciano & Cyrus, 2005).

Chafe (1988, 2007) conceptualizes discrimination in terms of social control, which operates to subjugate blacks in a society dominated by whites. He offers four distinct ways in which discrimination inflicts "pervasive and insidious control upon blacks" (2007, p. 661). The four forms of social control include the following:

1. Physical intimidation, which includes "[p]hysical force, and ultimately the threat of death" (p. 660), which serves "as a constant reminder that whites [hold] complete power over black lives" (p. 660). Thus, lynchings, burnings, beatings, killings, and so forth, result in "pervasive fear, anchored in the knowledge that whites [can] unleash vicious and irrational attacks without warning" (p. 660).
2. Psychological power, which is "the ability of whites to intimidate [blacks] psychologically" (p. 661), which serves to "define and limit the reach of black aspirations" (p. 661). Here, verbal taunts, discouraging words, and name-calling all reduce "the chance that [blacks] [are] able to aspire realistically to a life other than that assigned them within a white racist social structure" (p. 661).
3. Economic control, or the "white domination of the economic status of black people" (p. 660), which results in the fear of economic sanctions against blacks, including the loss of work or being fired. Thus, if rules are not followed or duties not executed "in a deferential manner," jobs will be lost. According to Chafe, "The fundamental precondition for success in the black community . . . [is] acting in ways that [will not] upset the status quo" (p. 661).
4. Internal pressure, which is "exercised by the black community itself out of self-defense" (p. 662), and is, according to Chafe, the "most devastating control of all" (p. 662). In a society organized by white power, instances of telling one to "hush up," "be quiet," or "mind one's way"—out of self-defense—result in the "urgent necessity that black people train each other to adapt in order to survive" (p. 662).

My plan for the girls' reading of the novel was quite simple. Because the opportunity played out over the duration of a summer, I asked that the girls read and respond to the novel independently and meet with me upon the completion of their reading. To assist them with the task, I asked that they keep a journal of their reading and document any incidences or events that they believed portrayed discriminatory acts or behaviors as carried out by the characters in the story. I also asked that they write a brief summary after reading each chapter and record any thoughts, reactions, or questions that they might have as a result of their reading.

As a way to help the girls focus their attention on the task of documenting racial discrimination during the reading of the novel, I provided them with a bookmark highlighting several definitions of racial discrimination. Following are the definitions that were listed on the bookmark:

- The unjust or prejudicial treatment of people on the grounds of race.
- Behaviors or actions that disadvantage one group in relation to another group and maintain and perpetuate conditions of inequality.
- When people are treated badly, not given respect, or are considered inferior because of the color of their skin.

IDENTIFYING DISCRIMINATION: ACTIVITY 1

On our first meeting, I asked the girls to share with me their overall reactions to the story, including their opinions, likes, dislikes, and any questions or concerns they had about the novel. Additionally, I asked them to read out loud their summaries to one another, chapter by chapter, so that we, as a group, could discern their overall understanding of the story. In doing so, we discussed the many important events of the story as they played out across the beginning, middle, and end of the novel. In the final chapters, we pondered the fate of T. J. and the Logan family.

After discussing the novel by chapters, we proceeded to identify the various incidences of discrimination the girls had recorded in their journals. In doing so, we made a list of these incidences, across each of the twelve chapters, and recorded them on chart paper. While compiling the list, I asked two central questions of the girls: (a) What examples of racial discrimination did you find (e.g., incidences from the text)? (b) Why is this an example of racial discrimination (e.g., specific discriminatory act)?

Together, we documented thirty-nine incidences from the novel. Thirty-five of these incidences involved specific discriminatory acts as carried out by whites toward blacks. Of these thirty-five, eighteen made reference to overt racial discrimination. Specifically, seven referenced the physical intimidation and/or violence of whites toward blacks, including the following: burnings, beatings, killings, a shooting, an incident of tar and feathering, and a pushing. Additionally, eight referenced the psychological power of whites over blacks, including the following: threats, laughing, teasing, and name-calling.

The remaining seventeen of the thirty-five incidences made reference to covert or more subtle forms of racial discrimination, that is, the unfair practices, policies, and/or rules that are often embedded in institutions, including places of employment, government, education, and so forth. Specifically, six of the seventeen incidences referenced the unfair economic (i.e., monetary) control of whites over blacks, five referenced the unfair laws and/or policies involving schools, four referenced the unfair practices as inscribed in the legal system, and three made reference to the unfair laws and/or policies established in towns or stores.

Based on these findings, it was clear the girls were capable of identifying specific discriminatory acts—be they overt or covert—on individual and organizational levels, across physical, psychological, and/or economic forms of discrimination. While the girls did not have the language or the conceptual knowledge to name the acts as such, they were clearly able to differentiate physical acts of discrimination (e.g., violence, killings) versus psychological acts of discrimination (e.g., teasing and name-calling) versus economic acts of discrimination (e.g., firings) and other unfair acts of discrimination.

Moreover, it was clear the girls had a relatively "high level of awareness" (Lobron & Selman, 2007, p. 531) in terms of understanding and conceptualizing racial discrimination. That is, not only were they capable of identifying the various acts *as* discriminatory, they were able to "accurately identify white people as the source of discrimination" (Lobron & Selman, 2007, p. 531).

Interestingly, while the girls appeared to have a firm understanding of discriminatory actions as carried out by whites toward blacks (of which there were many in the text), they were less certain about the unfair actions and behaviors as carried out by whites toward whites, blacks toward blacks, and blacks toward whites. For example, of the thirty-nine documented incidences, four required specific attention. As we compiled the list, the girls deliberated on the following: (a) whether the actions of a white person against another white person (who was a friend of a black person) was a form of racial discrimination, (b) whether a black person's actions against another black person (in the form of social control) was a form of racial discrimination, and (c) whether a black person's actions against a white person (in the form of revenge or retaliation) was a form of racial discrimination.

Whites Toward Whites

In their journals, both girls documented at least one incident involving a white person's actions toward another white person as discriminatory in nature. During our talk, both pondered whether the actions of a white person against another white person (who is a friend of a black person) was a form of racial discrimination. For example, when discussing the friendship between Jeremy Simms (a white boy) and Stacey Logan (a black boy), Teresa wondered whether it was discrimination when Jeremy's sister, Lillian Jean, chastised and beat her brother for being friends with Stacey. On a similar note, Jessica wondered whether it was discrimination when the white kids laughed and made fun of Jeremy for walking to school with the black kids.

Blacks Toward Blacks

Both girls, in their journals, documented a specific incident involving a black person's actions toward another black person. Specifically, the girls referenced the scene in the story where Miss Crocker, the teacher, whips Little Man and Cassie for their refusal to accept the worn and tattered textbooks offered to them. During our discussion, both girls grappled with the notion of whether Miss Crocker's actions against Little Man and Cassie were a form of racial discrimination. Jessica, in her journal, wrote the following: "I thought what Little Man did was right. But, what Miss Crocker did was just wrong. She didn't have to whip him. Isn't this discrimination?"

Blacks Toward Whites

In her journal, Jessica wrote the following: "I think [it] is discrimination when the bus splashed Cassie and her brothers when they were walking to school. But is it discrimination against white people when Cassie and her brothers dig that big hole in the road and made the bus tip over?" Teresa wrote the following in her journal: "The Logan kids are splashed by the bus again and the White kids laugh. [The Logans] got revenge, though!" During our discussion, this issue of whether a black person's actions toward a white person (in the form of revenge) is discriminatory in nature sparked an interesting debate.

Given the girls' attempts to identify and understand discrimination, it was important to challenge the taken-for-granted assumptions about discrimination and clear up any misconceptions (e.g., reverse discrimination) regarding the concept. After all, it was just as important for the girls to understand what racial discrimi-

DISCRIMINATION AND PREADOLESCENCE | 113

nation was as it was for them to understand what it was not. Rothenberg (1988) reminds us that racial discrimination or racism

> involves the subordination of people of color by white people. While an individual person of color may discriminate against white people or even hate them, his or her behavior or attitude cannot be called "racist." He or she may be considered prejudiced against whites and we may all agree that the person acts unfairly or unjustly, but racism requires something more than anger, hatred, or prejudice; at the very least, it requires prejudice plus power. The history of the world provides us with a long record of white people holding power and using it to maintain that power and privilege over people of color, not the reverse. (p. 6)

Thus, referring to the aforementioned examples as documented in the text, we concluded that a black person's actions against a white person (in the form of revenge) was not considered racial discrimination. While the act itself may not have been fair or right, it was not a form of racial discrimination. Furthermore, we concluded that a white person's actions against another white person (who was friends with a black person) was not considered racial discrimination. Moreover, we also concluded that a black person's actions against another black person was not considered racial discrimination. However, it could be viewed as form of social control (e.g., internal pressure) within the black community (see more on this later).

EXAMINING AND EXPLAINING DISCRIMINATION: ACTIVITY 2

On our second meeting, the girls and I categorized the thirty-five incidences of racial discrimination into eleven "scenes," so that we could more easily discuss the acts in the context of the novel.

As a way to examine and make better sense of the scenes, I asked the girls to complete individual event maps. Highlighting the scenes via an event map provided a unique way to flesh out the reasons and motivations behind each of the acts, all the while providing for me a way to examine the girls' conceptualization of the acts themselves. Before completing the maps, however, the girls and I revisited each scene by rereading the corresponding pages in the novel in an attempt to refamiliarize ourselves with the events from story. (As an aside, the girls enjoyed doing this, as I modeled for them the reading of the scenes with fluency and expression.) We then took turns reading each scene individually, out loud. Once completed, I asked the girls to document the following for each scene on the event map: (a) Who? (b) Did what? (c) How? and (d) Why? Furthermore, I asked that they include their overall thoughts regarding the event as well.

Based on my observations, the girls were clearly capable of identifying the important elements—across the eleven scenes—in terms of who (the perpetrator), what (the action), how (how the act was carried out), and why (the reasons or motives behind the act). Undoubtedly, they demonstrated their ability to not only *identify* the various discriminatory acts but *explain* why they happened within the context of the story.

In their attempts to explain why the discriminatory acts happened, the girls often couched their responses around notions of whites (from the story), believing they were "in control of blacks" and/or "better than Blacks" and/or "more important than Blacks." Concepts such as power, control, and domination cannot be removed from discussions regarding discrimination, race, and race relations. (Three cheers for the girls for sensing this and attempting to name it as such!) While, again, they did not have the language to articulate these concepts, per se, they certainly recognized them, conceptually, as critical components in their understanding of racial discrimination. For example, when sharing the reasons as to why the night men made threats and harassed members of the black community in the context of the story, Jessica, on her event map, wrote the following: "It's unfair. They [the night men] think they are so scary, but are they really? *They think they are in control of blacks*" [emphasis added]. Teresa wrote the following: "This is unfair business when the night men make threats or show up in the middle of the night. *The night men do this because they want control and want to scare everybody so the blacks will obey them out of fear*" [emphasis added].

Along similar lines, when discussing the scene in which Mr. Barnett overlooks T. J. as a patron in Barnett's Mercantile and waits on a white lady instead, Jessica, in her attempt to explain the reason for this, suggests the following: "*Because the white men think they are more important than the blacks*. This is not fair because T. J.'s list is shorter and he was there first. They [whites and blacks] should be given the same respect; they are both people. Mr. Barnett should have waited on T. J. first!" [emphasis added]. Likewise, Teresa provides a similar reason: "*Because Mr. Barnett thinks whites, himself included, are better than the blacks*. NOT FAIR! T. J. was there first, so, he should have been served first. This is unfair because they should [both] be given the same respect, regardless of the color of their skin" [emphasis added].

Notice, also, in the aforementioned examples, that the girls' responses are couched in a language of fairness. In many instances across the eleven scenes, the girls emphasized in their responses the concept of unfair treatment of whites toward blacks. For example, when asked to describe their thoughts about the scene involving the white bus driver who repeatedly taunts the Logan kids by splashing them on their way to school, Jessica remarked as follows: "It isn't fair because the blacks don't get a bus but the whites do. Why do the white kids have to treat blacks like that? That isn't fair either." And Teresa commented as follows: "It is not fair because the blacks should have a bus also. The whites should not make fun of the blacks because they have less than they do. I feel bad for the blacks."

Just as feelings of unfairness were embedded in concepts of control, power, and domination, so, too, were feelings of empathy embedded in the girls' responses. For example, when asked to provide their thoughts regarding the incident when Cassie accidently bumped into Lillian Jean on the sidewalk and Lillian Jean forced Cassie to apologize, Jessica remarked as follows: "Cassie said she was sorry, but Lillian Jean made her apologize in the street. Lillian Jean thinks she is the best thing in the world. She is not. She discriminates against Cassie. *I feel sorry for Cassie*" [emphasis added]. On a similar note, regarding the same scene, Teresa remarked on the actions of Mr. Simms when he pushes Cassie into the road: "Mr. Simms thinks Lillian Jean (his daughter) is better than Cassie. Even though Lillian Jean is his daughter, he shouldn't have done that to Cassie. Lillian Jean and Mr. Simms think they are better than blacks. Isn't saying sorry enough? *I feel bad for Cassie*" [emphasis added].

Feelings of right versus wrong and anger also emerged in the girls' responses. For example, in the final scene of the novel where the night men break into T. J.'s home and beat up T. J. and his family, Jessica, describing her thoughts, commented in the following way: "*This makes me angry.* The night men should get in trouble for hurting and killing people for no reason. I am wondering: Are they going to court?" (emphasis added). Likewise, Teresa commented as follows: "The night men should not be [allowed] to treat people that way. The night men were dragging [T. J.'s parents] by their ankles, and smashing [the] kids through windows. It's just awful. *And wrong.* The night men should get in trouble for killing (and almost killing) innocent people! Where are the police?" [emphasis added].

The fact that the girls couched their responses in terms of fairness and empathy toward black people suggests to me they not only connected with the text emotionally (i.e., the characters toward whom the act was carried out), but they also conceptualized discrimination in an *affective* way. Moreover, it suggests their ability to not only recognize the injustices of discriminatory acts of whites against blacks but their ability to determine what is right and wrong in terms of human decency and equitable treatment toward *all* people. Questions that arose, such as "Are they going to court?" and "Where are the police?" indicate the girls' desire for some type of action (read: FAIR action) to be taken against the perpetrators.

When we explored the notion of whether the police would fairly treat T. J. or whether there would be a fair trial for T. J., both girls suggested to the contrary. That is, both predicted T. J.'s fate with negative outcomes. In her journal regarding T. J.'s fate, Jessica bluntly stated the following: "I think T. J. will die." And, Teresa concurred: "I think T. J. will eventually die because he'll be sent to the chain gang."

And this leads me to the following question: Why? Why do the girls believe this? What leads them (and us!) to infer this by the end of the novel? Is it perhaps because we know, intuitively, that racial discrimination is not a "personal deviation"

(Rogers & Mosley, 2006, p. 467) but, rather, a societal ill embedded in the very social fabric of our society? That is, T. J.'s fate is no fault of his own but the result of the institutional and systemic nature of racism inscribed in our society at large. Is it because we know, as Rogers and Mosley (2006) suggest, that " . . . changing racist practices and policies needs to include *[both]* changes in habits of mind , , , *[and]* changes in economic and political structures" (p. 467, emphasis added)? If so, how might we help students, teachers, and others to understand this?

It is precisely for this reason that I wanted to provide for the girls (as well as students and teachers) a critical framework—or lens—for helping them better understand the complexities of racial discrimination, across individual, organizational, and structural levels. Doing so, I believed, would enable them to better *name* the various forms of social control and discrimination that keep blacks (read: T. J., the Logans, and the rest of the black community) in their place, thus preventing them from challenging the status quo. It would also help them, I believe, better understand the complexities of racial discrimination in the context of the novel, in particular, and in society, in general.

NAMING DISCRIMINATION: ACTIVITY 3

Utilizing Chafe's (1988; 2007) framework for social control and Rothenberg's (1988; 2007) conceptualization of racial discrimination, the girls, at our next meeting, set out to categorize the various scenes of discrimination as depicted in the novel. Specifically, we considered whether the depictions of racial discrimination and social control were examples of the following: (a) physical intimidation, (b) psychological power, (c) economic control, and/or (d) internal pressure (Chafee, 1988; 2007). And, moreover, we considered whether the scenes were depictions of the following: (a) individual, (b) organizational, or (c) structural levels of racial discrimination (Rothenberg, 1988, 2007).

The two girls worked collaboratively as they applied the aforementioned frameworks to the eleven scenes from the novel. Table 1 highlights Teresa's and Jessica's conceptualizations of the various forms and levels of social control and racial discrimination across those scenes.

Based on my observations, this activity was, by far, the most meaningful for the girls to complete. In fact, the girls stated as much. My overall sense of asking them to name the forms and levels of social control and racial discrimination was that it did, indeed, help them to better understand discrimination both in terms of the story and in terms of the larger society, as well. It also provided them with a language in which to discuss discrimination, enabling them to talk about the various forms and levels using concrete terminology.

TABLE 1. Forms and Levels of Social Control and Discrimination

Scene	Discriminatory Act	Form of Social Control And Discrimination	Level of Discrimination
Berry's Burning	Burning	Physical Intimidation	Individual
White Bus	Threat and Unfair Practice	Psychological Power and Economic Control	Individual and Organizational
Inferior Books	Unfair Practice	Economic Control and Internal Pressure	Organizational
Night Men	Threat and Killing	Psychological Power and Physical Intimidation	Structural
Market in Strawberry	Unfair Practice	Economic Control	Organizational
Barnett's Mercantile	Unfair Practice	Psychological Power	Individual
Sidewalk in Strawberry	Threat and Pushing	Psychological Power and Physical Intimidation and Internal Pressure	Individual
Ma Gets Fired	Unfair Practice	Economic Control and Psychological Power	Organizational
Pa Gets Shot	Shooting	Physical Intimidation and Economic Control and Psychological Power	Individual and Structural
Bank Loan Called	Unfair Practice	Economic Control	Organizational
T. J's Arrest	Beating and Unfair Practice	Physical Intimidation	Individual and Structural

In their attempts to complete this activity, I can state the following with considerable confidence. First, the girls clearly demonstrated the ability to name the various forms of social control and discrimination across the eleven scenes. Specifically, they understood the concepts of physical intimidation, psychological power, economic control, and internal pressure, as forms of social control and racial discrimination. More specifically, they were able to name these forms, as such, appropriately across the discriminatory acts and scenes. Moreover, it was apparent the girls understood physical intimidation to mean the physical actions taken by a white person against a black person and to include the following: burnings, beatings, killings, and so forth. It was apparent they understood psychological power to mean the mental control that whites held over blacks and to include the following: taunts, teasing, threats, name-calling, and so forth. It was apparent the girls understood the concept of economic control to include the following: unfair practices of whites against blacks involving money, whether that issue of money involved selling goods, paying back loans, losing a job, or the economic control of keeping blacks in their place (economically) via unfair social practices. And last, it was apparent the girls understood the concept of internal pressure as a form of social control and understood it to include the following: the actions taken within the black community or by members of the black community to protect another member, out of self-defense, including examples such as Miss Crocker's whipping of Little Man and Cassie and Big Ma scolding Cassie in public and making her apologize to Lillian Jean.

Second, the girls clearly demonstrated their ability to name the various *levels* of discrimination, including individual, organizational, and structural. Specifically, they understood racial discrimination at the individual level to include various forms of physical and psychological control as inflicted by whites over blacks (e.g., burnings, killings, threats, etc.). Moreover, they understood racial discrimination at an organizational level to include unfair practices, policies, and rules across various institutions, including schools, banks, the government (town laws), and the workplace. Furthermore, the girls seemed to understand racial discrimination at the structural level, referencing the cyclical (albeit) repetitive nature of the night men's actions and how those actions played out across the various scenes—for example, the threat of the night men at night, Pa's shooting, and T. J's arrest. While it is true that the girls' conceptualizations are not completely thorough—or as sophisticated as we might want them to be—one can argue that their conceptual understanding is certainly commendable for their age and intellectual development as preadolescents. Moreover, their conceptual understanding is reflective and indicative of their understanding and response, at this particular moment in time. Later, when we discussed their overall conceptualizations and understanding of the forms and levels of racial discrimination, it became apparent that, with further examination and reflection, their (our) constructions of these events could or would change and morph into more thorough and sophisticated understandings. Consequently, as a result of our discussions, we continued to broaden our understandings of racial discrimination—on many levels—learning and growing together.

For example, with further examination and reflection, we determined together that there were multiple effects (e.g., forms) of racial discrimination—beyond the initial act—which lent itself to the structural nature of discrimination. Thus, one could actually apply *all the levels of discrimination*, that is, individual, organizational, and structural, collectively, across each of the scenes depicted. For example, while many of the discriminatory acts appear on the surface to happen at the individual level (e.g., a discriminatory act inflicted against one person by another person on a onetime basis), when one begins to probe deeper, one finds that these acts are not, in fact, isolated acts; rather, they are embedded in the very social fabric of society, happening not on an individual basis and one time only, but inflicted against many people, many times over. For example, each of the aforementioned scenes appear to happen at the individual level. However, we know this not to be the case. We know that these acts are not insulated or isolated; rather, they happened over again, only in different places, at different times, involving different people. Once these acts become inscribed in the practices, policies, and rules and occur time and time again, thus, reinforcing themselves, they are considered organizational and structural forms of discrimination.

Moreover, we discerned that one could find evidence of internal pressure from within the black community as a form of social control, across each of the scenes depicted. That is, when a discriminatory act took place, there was always a response to that act, be it an inward response in terms of a thought or a belief (by the inflicted person) or an internal response from within the black community itself. For example, out of the eleven scenes, we found evidence of internal pressure (in the text) as a form of social control in at least nine of them. (As an aside, we also found many outward responses against the acts of discrimination, in the form of resistance, revenge, or retaliation. What is interesting about these forms of resistance, however, is that although they show signs of resourcefulness on the part of the blacks or black community, these very acts often served to reinforce themselves, thus perpetuating the very system the individuals were trying to resist.)

The point, here, is not that we must come to an overall consensus about discrimination, or the forms and levels of discrimination, per se, but to embark on a journey of learning in an attempt to understand the complexities and nuances of racial discrimination, in general. That is, we must engage in the process of dialogue and conversation and exchange, with the hope of broadening our understanding of race and relations in the larger society. Thus, the role of conversation is critical in the development of social awareness (Lobron & Selman, 2007). Copenhaver (2000) reminded us as follows: "[U]nless teachers and [students] have these critical discussions [regarding race], the silence will not be broken. . . . When teachers provide the books and the conversations, we open the door to dialogue that can allow our students to grow in their understandings . . ." (p. 15).

This project, however, is only a beginning, a springboard from which we can build future conversations about racial discrimination with students. It provides only a window into students' conceptualizations, which sheds light on the important question as to whether preadolescents are capable of holding intellectual discussions regarding racial discrimination. To this question I answer an emphatic YES! It also begs the question: Are teachers capable of having those conversations and discussions with students? I certainly hope so. For, as a teacher educator, I agree with Nieto (2003), who suggested the following: "The responsibility for exposing and confronting racism has for too long been on the shoulders of African Americans and other people of color; it is time to share the burden and up to teachers of all backgrounds to do this; white educators need to make the problem of racism their problem" (p. 203).

I offer this project as a theoretical and pedagogical tool for helping teachers move in this direction with the keen understanding that racism and racial discrimination "must be dealt with on two levels: personal and societal, emotional and institutional" (Yamato, 2005, p. 217). The goal is to reveal the complex nature of racial discrimination so it can be identified, examined, and named in an attempt to bring about social change. For once, students—and teachers—can name racial discrimination; they can take action against it and work in ways to change it and eliminate it.

REFERENCES

Berger-Knorr, A. (1997). *Unlearning privilege: Gender, race, and class in reading methods* (Unpublished doctoral dissertation). The Pennsylvania State University, Ann Arbor, MI.

Brooks, W., & Hampton, G. (2005). Safe discussion rather than first hand encounters: Adolescents examine racism through one historical fiction text. *Children's Literature in Education, 36*(1), 83–98.

Chafe, W. (1988). Sex and race: The analogy of social control. In P. Rothenberg (Ed.), *Racism and sexism: An integrated study* (pp. 334–348). New York, NY: St. Martin's Press.

Chafe, W. (2007). Sex and race. The analogy of social control. In P. Rothenberg (Ed.), *Race, class, and gender in the United States* (pp. 659–673). New York, NY: Worth Publishers.

Copenhaver, J. (2000). Silence in the classroom: Learning to talk about issues of race. *The Dragon Lode, 18*(2), 8–16.

Feagin, J. R., & Feagin, C. B. (1988). Theories of discrimination. In P. S. Rothenberg (Ed.), *Racism and sexism: An integrated study* (pp. 41–48). New York, NY: St. Martin's Press.

Fiske-Rusciano, R., & Cyrus, V. (2005). *Experiencing race, class, and gender in the United States* (4th ed.). New York, NY: McGraw Hill.

Fondre, S. (2001). Gentle doses of racism. *Journal of Children's Literature, 27*(2), 8–13.

Ladson-Billings, G. (2003). Foreword. In S. Greene & D. D. Abt-Perkins (Eds.), *Making race visible: Literacy research for cultural understanding* (pp. vii–xi). New York, NY: Teachers College Press.

Lobron, A., & Selman, R. (2007). The interdependence of social awareness and literacy instruction. *The Reading Teacher, 60*(6), 528–535.

Nieto, S. (2003). Afterword. In S. Greene & D. Abt-Perkins (Eds.), *Making race visible: Literacy research for cultural understanding* (pp. 201–205). New York, NY: Teachers College Press.

Picower, B. (2009). The unexamined whiteness of teaching: How white teachers maintain and enact dominant racial ideologies. *Race Ethnicity and Education, 12*(2), 197–215.

Rogers, R., & Christian, J. (2007). 'What could I say?' A critical discourse analysis of the construction of race in children's literature. *Race Ethnicity and Education, 10*(1), 21–46.

Rothenberg, P. S. (1988). The problem: Discrimination. In P. S. Rothenberg (Ed.), *Racism and sexism: An integrated study* (pp. 9–19). New York, NY: St. Martin's Press.

Rothenberg, P. S. (2007). *Race, class, and gender in the United States: An integrated study* (7th ed.). New York, NY: Worth Publishers.

Sleeter, C. (1995). Reflections on my use of multicultural and critical pedagogy when students are white. In C. Sleeter & P. McLaren (Eds.), *Multicultural education, critical pedagogy, and the politics of difference* (pp. 415–438). New York, NY. State University of New York Press.

Taylor, M. (1976). *Roll of thunder, hear my cry.* New York, NY: Bantam.

Taxel, J. (1986). The black experience in children's fiction: Controversies surrounding award winning books. *Curriculum Inquiry, 16*(3), 245–281.

Yamato, G. (2005). Something about the subject makes it hard to name. In R. Fiske-Rusciano & V. Cyrus (Eds.), *Experiencing race, class, and gender in the United States* (4th ed., pp. 215–218). New York, NY: McGraw-Hill.

CHAPTER 9

Daring to Dream

Characters in Coretta Scott King Author Award-Winning Books and Their Pursuits of the American Dream

LINDA T. PARSONS & MICHELE D. CASTLEMAN

Created in 1969 and recognized as an official award by the American Library Association (ALA) in 1982, the Coretta Scott King (CSK) Award recognizes outstanding books for children and young adults written and illustrated by African American authors. The award was created, in part, because no African American author had won the prestigious Newbery Medal and only twice had an African American writer been recognized by a Newbery Honor: Arna Bontemps in 1949 and Julius Lester in 1968 (Bishop, 2007). The selection criteria for the CSK Award states that books receiving the award "promote understanding and appreciation of the culture of all peoples and their contribution to the realization of the American dream of a pluralistic society" (American Library Association, 2009). The criteria also states that "particular attention will be paid to titles which seek to motivate readers to develop their own attitudes and behaviors as well as comprehend their personal duty and responsibility as citizens in a pluralistic society" (American Library Association, 2009). But what is the American dream? How is it constructed and manifested in this award-winning literature by African American authors? With these questions and the award selection criteria in mind, we set out to discover the American dream as expressed by characters in a set of CSK author award-winning and honor books.

Historically, there have been liberal/individualist and conservative/nationalist interpretations of the American dream (Beach, 2007). Embedded in the Declaration of Independence, the liberal/individualist version specifies the democratic ideals of equality and the inalienable rights of life, liberty, and the pursuit of happiness. It proposes that any American may pursue a decent standard of living through hard work and responsible behavior. Throughout the 1900s, standard of living was equated with "a steady job, owning a house in a safe neighborhood with decent schools, and believing that your children would have a chance to go to college" (Jencks, 2008, p. B6). Educational and economic opportunities and the right of the individual to make choices theoretically transcend restrictions of class, religion, race, or ethnic group. In reality, however, this iteration of the American dream was not extended to enslaved people, people of color, and women.

The aristocratic, conservative/nationalist construct of the American dream is based on "authority, order, inequitable property distribution, submissive masses, and a ruling elite" (Beach, 2007, p. 151). It cedes to a talented few with resources and connections the right to take advantage of and benefit from opportunities. While this meritocratic version of the American dream ostensibly praises "self-reliance, hard work, frugality, dutiful industry, success, and prosperity" (Beach, 2007, p. 151), it is falsely empowering. It blames and condemns those individuals who do not succeed, solidifying extant class and power structures rather than granting equal opportunity to all. Individuals with status, wealth, and/or power are privileged while disenfranchised others encounter insurmountable obstacles in their pursuit of this American dream.

Christopher Jencks (2008) suggests that a re-visioned American dream must emphasize service rendered to others over accumulating material possessions. Similarly, Beach (2007, p. 160) states, "Either one is living and working to eradicate injustice and structural inequality or one is living and working to support such a system." Believing texts are cultural constructs "promot[ing] a certain *version* of reality" (Apol, 1998, p. 34), we asked what American dream the characters in CSK award-winning and honor titles express. As they re-vision the dream for themselves, do they work to eradicate or to support injustice and inequality? How might adolescents who read these books "make sense of themselves and their place in the adult world they will soon enter" (Glenn, 2008, p. 34)? In the remainder of this chapter, we explore the American dream as envisioned by the characters in CSK author award-winning and honor titles.

DISCOVERING THE DREAMS

We adopted an interpretive, qualitative approach to content analysis rooted in literary theory consistent with reader response and poststructuralist theories. We believe that meaning does not reside in the text alone. "There is nothing inherent in a text; the meanings of a text are always brought to it by someone" (Krippendorff, 2004, p. 22). Furthermore, there are many possible and valid interpretations of a text rather than a single meaning to be discovered (Rosenblatt, 2005). Given this theoretical grounding, we approached this research with the belief that thematic categories would emerge during our transaction with and analysis of each text and across texts. We examined thirty-five CSK author award-winning and honor titles to acertain how the award criteria were exemplified in these books, and we limited our analysis to books from 2000–2010, since they are representative of the new millennium. Our research question focused our reading: What dreams do the main characters in these books express?

The books we analyzed included individual and collective biography, informational books, historical fiction, and contemporary realistic fiction. We analyzed the dreams of real and fictional characters in the same manner, drawing inferences from the characters' thoughts and statements. Inference is at the heart of content analysis. Krippendorff (2004) tells us this:

> Content analysts infer answers to particular research questions from their texts. Their inferences are merely more systematic, explicitly informed, and (ideally) verifiable than what ordinary readers do with texts. Recognizing this apparent generality, our definition of content analysis makes the drawing of inferences the centerpiece of this research technique. (p. 25)

As we read, the characters' dreams formed loose categories that became initial codes. This open coding (Strauss & Corbin, 1998) enabled us to identify themes that exposed the dreams each character expressed. We continued to refine codes, made iterative passes through the data, identified the components and subcomponents within codes, and moved from open coding to consistent and verifiable codes.

During the final phase of analysis, we systematically checked each component of the dreams and constantly sought evidence from the books to justify our interpretation of the data. As we moved toward finalizing our categories, we refined our terminology by merging, eliminating, or renaming codes to accurately identify the characters' dreams. We ultimately identified six interwoven dreams: the dreams of mobility, achievement, selfhood, and family, and the dreams of remaining a child and promoting social justice. Furthermore, in many instances, the character's dream evolved. Table 1 delineates the dreams and their components. Additionally, each book included in the study is listed in the Appendix (pp. 134–137). The chart in the Appendix indicates the complex overlap of the various components in the dreams expressed by each main character. It may be noted that we analyzed thirty-five books yet only thirty-two are listed in the Appendix. There were no discernible dreams in the three books not included in the chart: *Bad News for Outlaws: The Remarkable Life of Bass Reeves, Deputy U.S. Marshal* (Nelson, 2009); *The Blacker the Berry* (Thomas, 2008); and *Fortune's Bones: The Manumission Requiem* (Nelson, 2004).

TABLE 1. The American Dream Re-visioned by Characters in CSK Award-Winning Books

Dream of Mobility	• Escaping • Arriving
Dream of Achievement	• Academic • Economic
Dream of Selfhood	• Artistic Expression • Battling Perceptions
Dream of Family	• Creating • Saving
Dream of Remaining a Child	• Avoiding Adulthood and Responsibility • Missing Childhood
Dream of Promoting Social Justice	

Characters who dreamt of mobility dreamt of escaping current circumstances and/or of arriving at a specific location. Characters who wanted to escape their situation were prevalent in, though not restricted to, historical fiction about slavery wherein freedom from bondage could be achieved only through escape. Other characters, however, dreamt of escaping the drudgery of their lives, discrimination and prejudice, pregnancy, or incarceration. Characters also dreamt of arriving at a specific location. Most often, they wanted to improve the quality of their lives, envisioning a greater level of freedom, opportunity, or equality in another place. A few characters dreamt of traveling and arriving at exotic destinations. Several characters dreamt of both escaping a particular situation and of arriving at a particular location.

Academic and/or economic achievement was another dream. The dream of education and academic achievement was spurred by three motivations: the intrinsic love of learning, the use of education as a stepping-stone to another goal, or the desire for an equal education. In the books that featured characters who dreamt of economic achievement, the characters hoped economic security would allow them to rise above their current situation. In many books with a historical setting, this dream involved the characters' desire to own land as an expression of freedom, power, or respectability within the community.

The dream of selfhood took two different forms in the books whose characters expressed this dream: artistic expression and battling perceptions. Some characters wanted to express themselves artistically, hoped for an artistic career, or based their identity on their art and were empowered by it. Characters who dreamt of battling the ways others perceived them focused on expressing their personal identity and dreams rather than adopting others' constructions or dreamt of being perceived as equal, resisting ethnic or racial stereotypes.

Some CSK protagonists dreamt of saving or of creating family. The overwhelming need for connection with others was the driving force behind this dream. Characters dreamt of saving families that had been separated. Many families in historical novels were sold apart in slavery, while in contemporary novels abandonment, divorce, or death were more common reasons for separation. Other characters sought to create new, chosen families. Some characters overlapped these categories, struggling to let go of a biological family that could not, or perhaps should not, be saved and coming to accept others as chosen family.

Characters dreamt of maintaining or reclaiming childhood in some instances. Characters who wished to prolong their childhood often wished to do so because they themselves were about to become parents. Their dream was to avoid adulthood and responsibility. Other characters missed childhood and dreamt of returning to its innocence or naiveté. Missing childhood was often a natural result of entering adolescence. At other times, characters' lives changed due to divorce or death, and they longed to return to a state of innocence rather than face the reality of their changing lives and the emotional pain these changes caused.

Characters who expressed the dream of promoting social justice often hoped to improve their communities or the living conditions of their people. Some characters participated in service organizations or chose careers that would allow them to give back to their communities. Historical characters brought others out of bondage or fought figuratively or literally for freedom and equality. Some biographical characters used their fame to promote social justice. The dream of promoting social justice was taken up by characters in various, personal ways.

Although this discussion has separated out the various components of the characters' dreams, in the next section of this chapter we take an in-depth look at four characters. These characters reveal the multilayered nature of their American dream and the ways the components of their dreams converge and connect. These analyses reveal the complex and sometimes evolving nature of their dreams.

DARING TO DREAM: THE CHARACTERS

Leah Hopper

The Red Rose Box (Woods, 2002) began in June 1953, on Leah Hopper's tenth birthday, when she received the red rose box as a present from her Aunt Olivia. When Leah subsequently visited Olivia in California, she learned that Sulphur, Alabama, and Los Angeles, California, were literally worlds apart and experienced a place where segregation was not a way of life. Childless but financially secure, Aunt Olivia and Uncle Bill sent money and presents to Leah and her sister Ruth and invited them to vacation in New York City. While they were on vacation, the girls' parents and twenty-five other townspeople were killed when a hurricane hit Sulphur. Leah and Ruth moved in with their aunt and uncle, healed from their terrible loss, and learned to live with and love a new family. Leah's complex American dream includes the escaping and arriving elements of mobility, the dream of academic achievement spurred by her intrinsic love of learning, a dream of selfhood that involves battling others' perceptions, and a dream of family: the impossibility of restoring her birth family and the possibility of creating a new family.

Leah dreamt of traveling to exotic places. Before blowing out the candles on her birthday cake, she reflected, "I wished that I wouldn't spend all of my life in Sulphur. . . . I wanted to send Mama a postcard from Paris once, maybe twice" (Woods, 2002, p. 15). While eating in Chinatown during her first trip to Los Angeles, Leah dreamt of going to China someday. Leah's dream of mobility entangled the desire to travel with the desire to escape the strictures of the Jim Crow South. Leah noted that in Los Angeles, colored sat anywhere on buses, there were no colored entrances to movie theaters, and shops and restaurants did not display Whites Only signs, and she began "to think about the word freedom" (p. 27). When it was time to go back to Sulphur, Leah wondered "why any colored man or woman would ever go back to the South, below the Mason-Dixon line, after knowing what freedom felt like" (p. 46).

Leah's dream of mobility went beyond traveling to exotic destinations and escaping the South to focus on arriving at a destination where she could know freedom. Exemplifying the complexity and interwoven nature of these dreams, the dream of selfhood is implicated here. Leah dreamt of battling others' perceptions of her inferiority. While in the back of the bus returning from shopping in Sulphur, where she experienced one humiliation after another, Leah "wanted to tell everybody in the town that [she] was going to be somebody, someday" (Woods, 2002, p. 64). The somebody she wanted to be was a teacher. Her dream of academic achievement was fueled by her intrinsic love of learning. Leah loved the used books her father frequently bought her. Leah reflected, "Those books kept the ambition hovering around me. I learned many things from those frayed pages, and though the words rolling off my tongue still sounded Louisiana country, the words themselves started to change" (p. 51).

A powerful and poignant component of Leah's American dream was that of family. In a complex dance of loss and longing, she dreamt of the family she had lost and gradually dreamt of the family she, Ruth, Aunt Olivia, and Uncle Bill could become. Reflecting on her loss, she stated, "I wanted to see my daddy, tall and brown, to feel my mama's lips on my right cheek, to smell apple cobbler cooking in her oven" (Woods, 2002, p. 82). In the depth of her despair, Leah said, "I was empty. I was hungry for love and kisses, hungry for Daddy's little pats on the head, hungry for the smells that came from Mama's kitchen" (p. 87). Rather than allowing Aunt Olivia to console her, Leah wanted to tell her, "She wasn't my mama, sassy and strong, that Uncle Bill wasn't my daddy, who dreamed out loud. Instead I leaned into her and soaked up some love. I hoped Mama and Daddy would understand" (p. 97). This was the moment when Leah adopted a dream of creating family. A new family was ultimately created, and Leah felt she and Ruth "had a place where [they] belonged" (p. 135).

Billie Holiday

Becoming Billie Holiday (Weatherford, 2008) is a fictionalized memoir written as poems titled after her songs. Beginning with Eleanor Fagan's birth in 1915, the memoir traces her metamorphosis into Billie Holiday. Eleanor's early life included little adult supervision or love, time spent in reform school, rape, prostitution, drug use, and survival on the streets of Baltimore. By the time she was fifteen, she knew her voice could change her life. Even after making her way to Harlem, Billie Holiday experienced hatred and prejudice as a black female artist. The dream Billie Holiday passionately pursued was extremely complex. Holiday dreamt of mobility; economic achievement; creating family; selfhood, in which she could express herself artistically and also battle prejudice; and promoting social justice to improve her life and the lives of others.

The various components of Billie Holiday's American dream were inextricably interwoven. Home literally and metaphorically represented family, security, and a place of self-expression. Born to an unwed mother who frequently abandoned her to the care of friends and relatives, Billie Holiday dreamt of creating family. Her father's path and her own intersected at various points in her life, and she longed particularly for his love. Billie stated, "I prayed for my mother / to stay put for a while, / my father to stick around/for more than a few hours, / and a place to call home" (Weatherford, 2008, p. 42). Once she asked her father for rent money, and when he gave it to her and told her to "scram," she reflected, "I would've paid / for a chance to call him 'Daddy'" (p. 69).

Having grown up in poverty, Billie Holiday dreamt of economic achievement and knew her voice would help her realize that dream. She wondered if her songs "could lift [her] / from hometown haunts / to center stage" (Weatherford, 2008, p. 48). Her dream of artistic expression afforded her another sense of home. She stated, "I toted my songs / like a satchel and felt most / at home when I sang" (p. 47). Harlem represented home, a safe haven from racial prejudice and arrival at a place where she could realize her dream of artistic expression. When she was twelve, her mother hired her out as a live-in maid and sent her by train to Long Branch, New Jersey. Billie said, "My heart was set on Harlem / and my mind was made up. / I ditched the kiddie nametag / and rode to New York" (p. 56). Years later, when the boss at the Fox Theater in Detroit contended she was "too high yellow, / too light-skinned, to share / the stage with black musicians" (p. 100) and insisted she darken her skin with greasepaint, she "smiled to keep from throwing up / and never missed Harlem more" (p. 100). Billie Holiday dreamt of a time and a place where she would have "the chance to sing in [her] own skin" (p. 108).

Home was implicated in her dream of promoting social justice. Billie observed that as racism ripped America apart, jazz mended it together. However, she stated, "But music / alone couldn't mend the tear. / The needle pricked my fingers / till my soul was sore, and I longed / to hop a train for home" (Weatherford, 2008, p. 103). The number of black men lynched during this era of the Ku Klux Klan and the Jim Crow south inflamed her dream of combating racism, and she did it through song. She wondered, "How could I not long to voice outrage?" (p. 100). Regarding Lewis Allan's protest poem that became the lyrics for her most famous song, "Strange Fruit," Billie asked, "How could I let that tune slip away / without passing through my lips?" (p. 109). Artistic expression, the mobility of arriving in Harlem, creating family, achieving economic security, and promoting social justice are inextricably intertwined in Billie Holiday's multilayered American dream.

November Nelson

Family is also a central dream in *November Blues* (Draper, 2007). This contemporary realistic novel is the sequel to *The Battle of Jericho* (2003), also a CSK award-winning book. In *November Blues*, sixteen-year-old November Nelson and her mom were making college plans. Their goals were disrupted when November informed her mom that she was pregnant by her deceased boyfriend, Josh. Although she decided not to have an abortion, throughout the novel, November vacillated between keeping the baby or allowing Josh's parents to adopt and raise the baby so she could continue her dream of going to college as a stepping-stone to her future career. As her pregnancy progressed, November felt trapped by her own body and dreamt of escaping her circumstances and avoiding the responsibilities of adulthood and parenthood. Although November missed the freedom of childhood, she eventually decided to keep her daughter, committing to the dream of creating a new family above all her other dreams.

Before November told her mom she was pregnant, Ms. Nelson was excited by November's acceptance into Cornell University's Summer College program. Her mom exclaimed, "This is going to get you into an Ivy League school!" (Draper, 2007, p. 32). November's academic achievements were a stepping-stone to further success at school, a hope both she and her mother held for her. But after November informed her mom of her pregnancy, her mom stated, "There's no sense in going [to the Cornell program] now. This was your stepping stone to get into one of the best schools in the country next year. There goes that dream" (p. 50). Due to her changed circumstances, November had to adjust and shift her dream as she determined what she and her mom wanted.

At times, November had trouble letting go of the dreams and plans common among her friends, and she missed and longed for her own childhood. As she moved into her second and third trimesters of pregnancy, November had trouble engaging in common activities like going to the mall with her friends. At a summer cookout, November "listened to her friends chatter about the beginning of school, she envied them, sadly aware that she would be able to participate in none of the very ordinary school activities they mentioned. None" (Draper, 2007, p. 191). November dreamt of a childhood she could never return to. But by the time her daughter was born, November had chosen a new dream for herself, creating a family with her mother and baby daughter.

When November originally dreamt of having a family, she had "always imagined that when she got married and had kids she'd have it all together with a fine husband, a great career, and a nice house in the burbs—the story book stuff. By then she'd be able to welcome a new baby with the best of everything" (Draper, 2007, p. 170). Throughout the novel, November struggled with this dream, wondering whether it would still be available to her if she allowed her boyfriend's parents, the Prescotts, to adopt her child.

Even after the baby was born and they learned that she had some developmental delays, the Prescotts still considered adopting the child if she was tested in a few months and they determined that she was healthy. The Prescotts' lawyer, Mr. Grant, informed November of this possibility in the hospital, holding the legal documents in his hands:

"You still have the opportunity for a college scholarship and a sizable check, don't forget. If everything works out," he added.

November glanced at her mother, who seemed to know what her daughter was thinking. Both of them smiled....

November took the papers and, without glancing at them, ripped the pile in half, and then in half once more. She tossed them to the floor. (Draper, 2007, p. 303)

By tearing the contract, November resisted clinging to the dreams she had had before her daughter's birth and her dreams of escaping her situation. She instead committed herself to raising her daughter, to choosing her new family, and to taking on the responsibility of parenthood over all of her other possible dreams.

Steve Harmon

The realistic novel *Monster* (1999) by Walter Dean Myers also deals with the dream of escape, but in a very different manner. Written in alternating screenplay and journal formats, *Monster* is the story of sixteen-year-old Steve Harmon, who stood trial for his role as lookout in a robbery that resulted in the death of a drugstore owner. While in jail, Steve's one hope was to be found not guilty and to be released from jail. He wrote, "I wanted to be away from this place so bad, away from this place, *away from this place*" (Myers, 1999, p. 130). To deal with the difficult reality of jail, he recorded his trial as a screenplay and journal notes, expressing himself artistically and hoping that it would help battle the perception that he was a monster. Throughout his trial and time in jail, Steve wished to remain a child and wanted to avoid the responsibility of adulthood and the consequences of his possible role in the death of the storeowner, Mr. Nesbitt.

In his journal, Steve expressed his desire to battle the way others perceived him. He wrote, "I want to look like a good person. I want to feel like I'm a good person because I believe I am. But being in [jail] here with these guys makes it hard to think about yourself as being different" (Myers, 1999, p. 62). Steve wanted to battle the perception of being seen as guilty or as a monster. He wanted to be viewed as a human and as a young boy, perhaps feeding into his larger dream of being freed from jail. In fact, his defense attorney, Mrs. O'Brien, informed Steve that it was his job in the courtroom to present himself positively to the jurors: "I do know you'd better put some distance between yourself and whatever being a tough guy represents. You need to present yourself as someone the jurors can believe in" (p. 216). Steve's attempt to battle the perception that he was a monster was a central dream for him throughout the trial and even after he was released from jail.

Steve also expressed the desire to remain a child and to be perceived by others as a child. When his parents visited him in jail, he noted, "They didn't allow kids in the visiting area, which was funny. It was funny because if I wasn't locked up, I wouldn't be allowed to come into the visiting room" (Myers, 1999, p. 156). The dream of being perceived as a child served as a way for him to avoid accepting responsibility for his possible role in the robbery. When writing in his journal about the day of the robbery, Steve noted, "I walked into a drugstore to look for some mints, and then I walked out" (p. 140). He avoided any responsibility for his potential part in the robbery. While Steve may have viewed himself as being completely innocent, it was also possible that he described the day in these terms to battle the perceptions that others had of him. During the closing statements of the trial, the prosecutor, Ms. Petrocelli, made note of Steve's hopes throughout the trial:

> Mr. Harmon wants us to look at him as a high school student and as a filmmaker. He wants us to think, well, he didn't pull the trigger. He didn't wrestle with Mr. Nesbitt. He wants us to be believe that because he wasn't in the drugstore when the robbery went down, he wasn't involved. Again, perhaps he has even convinced himself that he wasn't involved. (pp. 261–262)

Steve's dreams of battling perceptions, missing childhood, avoiding adulthood, and of expressing himself artistically all overlapped with his overriding dream of escaping his current situation.

DARING TO DREAM: TEACHERS AND STUDENTS

Our critical analysis of the thirty-five Coretta Scott King award and honor books revealed six interrelated dreams. Characters who dreamt of mobility hoped to better their lives by escaping their present situation or by arriving at a particular destination. Other characters dreamt of economic and academic achievement that would offer security as well as personal satisfaction. They emphasized living life fully and meeting their basic needs rather than amassing possessions. Another dream was that of selfhood, wherein characters could express themselves and be perceived by others in ways that were personally liberating and satisfying. These characters hoped to transcend stereotypes and others' expectations. The security and support of familial relationships were paramount in the dreams of characters who sought to save an existent family or to create bonds with biological or chosen family. Another category comprised those adolescents who dreamt of remaining a child. Some characters simply missed the innocence, naiveté, or happiness associated with their childhood, while others, facing imminent parenthood themselves, dreamt of avoiding the harsh realities of adult responsibility. It is of note that in the construction of reality in these books, each teen eventually embraced the parenting role. Finally, a significant number of characters dreamt of promoting social justice in substantive ways.

Representing a broad spectrum of African American adolescents, the characters ranged from historic to contemporary figures, real and fictional, and from those in abject poverty to those with middle-class privilege. The characters in these CSK Award books dreamt of creating a life wherein they could freely be themselves, live safely and comfortably within a family group or community, and contribute to the common good. These characters and the dreams they express embody Bishop's (1990) and Galda's (1998) metaphors of literature as mirrors and windows: mirrors that reflect the readers' dreams and windows that allow readers to see and consider the dreams of others.

We encourage teachers and students to approach any consideration of the American dream as a critical and a political act, for "literacy is empowering only if one is a critical reader—one that analyzes, questions, and critically evaluates that which is being read" (Glenn, 2008, p. 40). Teachers and students may be empowered through critical readings and discussions of the American dream as it has been traditionally constructed, as these characters articulate it, and as it may be personally re-visioned. Students may consider whose dreams are represented and whose are not, and they may be encouraged to critique loci of power, agency, and voice. Readers may also consider the potential impact of the characters' dreams on the individual and on society. Discussions about the American dream may also serve as a catalyst for adolescent readers to crystallize their own dreams. Adolescent readers may be guided to critically examine the cultural messages contained in the novels by considering questions like the following that draw from Apol (1998), Rosenblatt (2005), and our own experience:

1. What was your response or reaction to the character and his or her dream? What caused you to have this reaction?
2. Whose voice is not heard or who is absent from the novel, and therefore, whose dream is not represented? Are your dreams represented?
3. What assumptions about your personal beliefs and experiences are implied as you consider the characters' dreams?
4. Are there dreams you as a reader want to resist? Are there dreams you share?
5. Do the character's world and the character's dreams reflect your own experiences and dreams? How do you understand the world differently from the character?
6. What do you consider to be the most important aspects of the American dream in your own life?

7. Who benefits and who is harmed by the dreams the character expresses? Consider your own dreams for your future. Who may benefit and who may be harmed?

8. When you hear the term *American dream*, what do you envision it meaning? Historically? Now? For yourself and your family?

If we accept that these books contain and convey cultural messages and values, then "examining the images and interrogating the messages given to children about themselves, their societies, and their futures becomes a political act" (Apol, 1998, p. 34). Identifying how these characters construct the American dream allows us to identify the cultural messages they convey and illuminates how they might influence adolescent readers to construct the American dream for themselves. How we envision and re-vision the American dream today has moral and political implications for current and future generations.

APPENDIX

Coretta Scott King Award Winners and the American Dream

Key to Chart

Dream of Mobility—ES: Escaping, AR: Arriving

Dream of Achievement—EC: Economic, ACA: Academic

Dream of Selfhood—AE: Artistic Expression, BP: Battling Perceptions

Dream of Family—CR: Creating, SA: Saving

Dream of Remaining a Child—AV: Avoiding Adulthood and Responsibility, MC: Missing Childhood

Dream of Promoting Social Justice:

CORETTA SCOTT KING AWARD WINNERS AND THE AMERICAN DREAM											
Coretta Scott King Award-Winning Book	Genre	Dream of Mobility		Dream of Achievement		Dream of Selfhood		Dream of Family		Dream of Remaining a Child		Dream of Promoting Social Justice
		ES	AR	EC	ACA	AE	BP	CR	SA	AV	MC	JU
The Battle of Jericho (Draper, 2003, Atheneum)	Contemp. Realistic Fiction				X	X				X	X	X
Becoming Billie Holiday (Weatherford, 2008, Wordsong)	Biography		X	X		X	X	X				X
Black Hands, White Sails (McKissack & McKissack, 1999, Scholastic)	Information	X	X	X		X						
Bronx Masquerade (Grimes, 2002, Dial)	Contemp. Realistic Fiction	X	X		X	X	X	X		X		X
Bud, Not Buddy (Curtis, 1999, Delacorte)	Historical Fiction		X					X				
Carver: A Life in Poems (Nelson, 2001, Front Street)	Biography		X		X							X
Copper Sun (Draper, 2006, Atheneum)	Historical Fiction	X	X					X	X			
Dark Sons (Grimes, 2005, Hyperion)	Contemp. Realistic Fiction/ Historical Fiction						X		X		X	
Day of Tears (Lester, 2005, Hyperion)	Historical Fiction	X						X	X			X
Days of Jubilee (McKissack & KcKissack, 2003, Scholastic)	Information	X	X	X					X			X
Elijah of Buxton (Curtis, 2007, Scholastic)	Historical Fiction		X				X					X

BOOK	GENRE	ES	AR	EC	ACA	AE	BP	CR	SA	AV	MC	JU
The First Part Last (Johnson, 2003, Simon & Schuster)	Contemp. Realistic Fiction	X	X		X	X		X		X		
Francie (English, 1999, Farrar, Straus & Giroux)	Historical Fiction	X	X	X	X							X
Keeping the Night Watch (Smith, 2008, Henry Holt)	Contemp. Realistic Fiction								X		X	
The Land (Taylor, 2001, Dial)	Historical Fiction		X	X			X	X				
The Legend of Buddy Bush (Moses, 2004, Margaret K. McElderry)	Historical Fiction		X	X			X					
Let It Shine (Pinkney, 2000, Harcourt)	Collective Biography		X	X	X	X	X		X			X
Locomotion (Woodson, 2003, Putnam)	Contemp. Realistic Fiction					X		X	X			
Mare's War (Davis, 2009, Knopf)	Historical/ Contemp. Realistic Fiction	X	X	X								
Maritcha: A Nineteenth Century American Girl (Bolden, 2005, Harry N. Abrams)	Biography				X							X
Miracle's Boys (Woodson, 2000, Putnam)	Contemp. Realistic Fiction		X	X	X				X			
Money Hungry (Flake, 2001, Hyperion)	Contemp. Realistic Fiction			X			X					
Monster (Myers, 1999, HarperCollins)	Contemp. Realistic Fiction	X				X	X			X	X	
November Blues (Draper, 2007, Atheneum)	Contemp. Realistic Fiction	X			X			X		X	X	

BOOK	GENRE	ES	AR	EC	ACA	AE	BP	CR	SA	AV	MC	JU
Red Rose Box (Woods, 2002, Perfection Learning)	Historical Fiction	X	X		X		X	X	X			
Remember: The Journey to School Integration (Morrison, 2004, Houghton Mifflin)	Historical Fiction				X		X					X
The Road to Paris (Grimes, 2006, Putnam)	Contemp. Realistic Fiction					X	X	X	X			
Talkin' About Bessie (Grimes, 2002, Orchard)	Biography		X	X	X							X
Twelve Rounds to Glory (Smith, 2007, Candlewick)	Biography			X		X	X					X
We Are the Ship (Nelson, 2008, Jump at the Sun)	Information		X				X					
Who Am I Without Him? (Flake, 2004, Hyperion)	Contemp. Realistic Fiction Short Stories			X			X					
A Wreath for Emmett Till (Nelson, 2005, Houghton Mifflin Harcourt)	Historical Fiction										X	X

Bad News for Outlaws: The Remarkable Life of Bass Reeves, Deputy U.S. Marshal (Nelson, 2009), *The Blacker the Berry* (Thomas, 2008), and *Fortune's Bones: The Manumission Requiem* (Nelson, 2004) are not listed on this chart, since our analysis did not reveal an expression of the characters' dreams.

NOTE

The results of the analysis that informed this chapter have been previously published in the article "I Have a Dream, Too!": The American Dream in Coretta Scott King Award-Winning Books, *Journal of Children's Literature*.

CHILDREN'S BOOKS CITED

Draper, S. M. (2003). *The Battle of Jericho*. New York, NY: Atheneum.
Draper, S. M. (2007). *November blues*. New York, NY: Atheneum.
Myers, W. D. (1999). *Monster*. Illus. by Christopher Myers. New York, NY: HarperCollins.

Nelson, M. (2004). *Fortune's bones: The manumission requiem.* New York, NY: Hand Print.
Nelson, V. M. (2009). *Bad news for outlaws: The remarkable life of Bass Reeves, deputy U.S. marshal.* Illus. by R. Gregory Christie. Minneapolis, MN: Carolrhoda.
Thomas, J. C. (2008). *The blacker the berry.* Illus. by Floyd Cooper. New York, NY: Amistad.
Weatherford, C. B. (2008). *Becoming Billie Holiday.* Illus. by Floyd Cooper. Honesdale, PA: Wordsong.
Woods, B. (2002). *The red rose box.* New York, NY: G. P. Putnam's Sons.

REFERENCES

American Library Association. (2009). The Coretta Scott King Book Awards for Authors and Illustrators. Retrieved from http: / /www.ala.org/ala/mgrps/rts/emiert/corettascottking-bookawards/corettascott.cfm/
Apol, L. (1998). "But what does this have to do with kids?": Literary theory and children's literature in the teacher education classroom. *Journal of Children's Literature, 24*(2), 32–46.
Beach, J. M. (2007). The ideology of the American dream: Two competing philosophies in education, 1776–2006. *Educational Studies, 41*(2), 148–164.
Bishop, R. S. (1990). Mirrors, windows, and sliding glass doors. *Perspectives, 6*(3), ix–xi.
Bishop, R. S. (2007). *Free within ourselves: The development of African American children's literature.* Portsmouth, NH: Heinemann.
Galda, L. (1998). Mirrors and windows: Reading as transformation. In T. E. Raphael & K. H. Au (Eds.), *Literature-based instruction: Reshaping the curriculum* (pp. 1–11). Norwood, MA: Christopher Gordon.
Glenn, W. (2008). Gossiping girls, insider boys, A-list achievement: Examining and exposing young adult novels consumed by conspicuous consumption. *Journal of Adolescent & Adult Literacy, 52*(1), 34–42.
Jencks, C. (2008, October 17). Reinventing the American dream. *The Chronicle of Higher Education, 55*(8), B6–8.
Krippendorff, K. (2004). *Content analysis: An introduction to its methodology.* (2nd ed.). Thousand Oaks, CA: Sage.
Rosenblatt, L. (2005). *Making meaning with texts: Selected essays.* Portsmouth, NH: Heinemann.
Strauss, A. L., & Corbin, J. M. (1998). *Basics of qualitative research: Grounded theory procedures and techniques.* Thousand Oaks, CA: Sage.

CHAPTER 10

Representing Black Experiences

Engaging Hearts and Minds with Excellent Nonfiction Literature

BARBARA MARINAK

Here I am, a white, 50-something woman writing about representing black experiences in nonfiction children's literature. How dare I? Or should I? Ultimately, after months of soul searching, the decision to attempt this chapter was made by honoring the deeply rooted fibers of my being. First and foremost, I have complete faith in the open-mindedness of young readers. Children thrive when invited to consider and discuss divergent points of view. Second is my passion for informational text. As educators, I believe we are obligated to seek and share credible books from a collection whose numbers are growing exponentially. And finally, I am drawn to this work by two life experiences—one heartening, the other haunting.

At age sixteen, while studying a long way from home on a National Science Foundation scholarship in Greensboro, North Carolina, I was welcomed into an African American Baptist Church. Then a few short years later, while teaching in Orangeburg, South Carolina, I encountered the Smith Hammond Middleton Memorial Center on the campus of South Carolina State College. My husband, then a faculty member at S.C. State, could see the Center from his office. During these pre-Google days, we asked people on campus and in town the significance of the names. Our inquiries were met with hushed whispers. We later learned that the gymnasium was erected in memory of three students. Delano Middleton, Samuel Hammond, and Henry Smith. The three were shot to death by South Carolina Highway Officers during a segregation protest in 1968. But in 1979, only eleven years after the massacre, few were ready to share. I am haunted by the names on the building. The Orangeburg Massacre remains one of the bloodiest tragedies of the civil rights era. And, even after four decades, it does not appear in any informational text for young readers.

Therefore, cognizant of inherent limitations but committed to the importance of choosing and using high-quality informational books with children, the ensuing chapter examines a variety of voices representing black experiences in the United States and around the world. The collection spans hundreds of years, crosses three continents, and includes perspectives on Negro League Baseball, the civil rights movement, lessons from a skeleton, life in African villages, and a view from Everest.

CHOOSING EXCELLENT NONFICTION FOR CHILDREN

The issues of ownership and appropriation in African and African American fiction have been raised in scholarly and popular discourse for years. Who can authentically and accurately represent black experiences in fiction? Must a fiction writer be African or African American to authentically represent black themes? These debates, clearly part of a greater societal conversation, have raged in the literature for several decades (Apple, 1993; Taxel, 1993). One thread in the discussions is the definition of multiculturalism and multicultural literature. There appears to be general agreement that multicultural literature is about an "identifiable other" (Cai & Bishop, 1994). Less agreement is seen when one considers the purpose it is "intended to serve" (p. 59). Little, however, is written about these questions as they relate to nonfiction children's literature.

This chapter explores excellence in nonfiction books about black experiences through two lenses. The first lens includes the agreed upon attributes of "excellent" informational text. First and foremost is accuracy. Excellent informational books must be factually correct. In addition, they should be significant, timeless, and provide connections to curricular concerns (Huck, 2003; National Council of Teachers of English, 2010). Determining significance and timelessness can be difficult. Considering the qualifications of the author and selecting books that have been recognized by awards given specifically for informational writing can prove helpful.

The second lens that informed this discussion is based on Cai and Bishop's (1994) suggestion that multicultural literature consists of at least three distinct text types. Their heuristic, comprised of world literature, cross-cultural literature, and parallel cultural literature, serves to clarify authenticity in informational text. World literature is generally defined as books about underrepresented peoples. Cross-cultural literature refers to works about the interrelations of peoples from different cultures as well as books about people from specific cultural groups that are written by individuals not of that group. And parallel culture literature refers to books written by individuals from parallel cultural groups such as African Americans, Native Americans, and Hispanic Americans. Their works represent the "experiences, consciousness, and self-image developed as a result of being acculturated and socialized within these groups" (Cai & Bishop, 1994, pp. 65–67). In addition, the concept of "cultural crossing" was also considered (Aronson, 1995). One example of cultural crossing is African Americans writing about nontraditional black issues.

Though these two lenses are important to consider when selecting multicultural nonfiction, all books are inherently biased by virtue of the information authors have included or excluded. Therefore, more than one text should be considered in order to most credibly represent a topic. It is only by exploring an event, era, place, or person from multiple perspectives that authenticity and accuracy about black experiences can be fully realized. Such perspective can be recorded in words or captured in illustrations, photographs, and artifacts. When possible, this chapter offers texts representing multiple perspectives. When only one perspective is available, credible sources for additional reading are suggested.

USING EXCELLENT NONFICTION TEXTS

Each section concludes with a method for engaging children in conversations about these important topics. The methods promote authentic and collaborative discourse. When used with compelling texts, they can engage the hearts and minds of young readers. Recommendations include I-Search (Short, Harste, & Burke 1996), Response Heuristic (Bleich, 1978), Socratic Questions (Gall, 1970), and Text Impression (McGinley & Denner, 1987) . By inviting such responses, teachers can challenge their students to read, think, and discuss nonfiction topics more critically.

Players on the Diamond

> For the heroic athletes who fought—and still fight—to level the playing field.
> —CAROLE BOSTON WEATHERFORD, 2005 (P. 5)

Choosing—There are those who say the civil rights movement began not in schools or on buses but in dugouts and on diamonds. In the mid-1860s, as the country moved from Civil War to Reconstruction, a few black players were hired by professional teams. Though treated disgracefully, players such as Bud Fowler, Charlie Grant, and Pete Hill persisted. They were talented athletes with a relentless passion for the game. But by the late 1800s, black players disappeared from professional teams. In a blatant but highly secretive attempt to segregate professional baseball, baseball owners had entered into a gentleman's agreement to let go of the current black players and not hire any new ones. That deal lasted for over sixty years and gave rise to a remarkable time in sports known as Negro League Baseball—an era that would pave the way for integration not only in sports but in all walks of American life.

From multiple perspectives, in words, photographs, artifacts, and illustrations, the story of Negro League Baseball is available in several texts for a variety of ages. Though many African Americans are responsible for the success of the Leagues, the talent and sacrifice of several extraordinary athletes can be seen and heard across five very different books. These individuals include John Jordan "Buck" O'Neil, Andrew "Rube Foster," Ted "Double Duty" Radcliff, Jackie Robinson, and Henry Aaron.

Negro League Baseball is part of a people's history in the beautifully illustrated *Our Children Can Soar* (Cook, 2009). This picture book, compile by Michelle Cook, was inspired by phrases that appeared at rallies, on blogs, and in text messages during the 2008 U.S. presidential campaign. The inspiring contributions of thirteen African Americans and their very different struggles for equality are portrayed by an equal number of today's premier illustrators. The contributions unfold chronologically in double-page, full-color illustrations with minimal words. However, the narrative gives nod to those who came before. Jackie Robinson, as drawn by Charlotte Riley-Webb, could score in 1945 (as the first African American to integrate professional baseball) because Ella Fitzgerald was on her way to becoming the "First Lady of Song" in 1935. And because Jackie scored, Rosa could sit in 1955. In addition to the symbolically arranged illustrations, readers can access brief biographies and descriptions by each illustrator in an afterword.

A Negro League Scrapbook, by Carole Boston Weatherford (2005), is an introduction to the era that was Negro League Baseball. In a foreword, Buck O'Neil provides his perspective of the Leagues. Former player, manager, and chairman of the Negro Leagues Baseball Museum until his death in 2006, O'Neil explains that the Leagues existed only because of segregation and suggests that Jackie Robinson becoming a Dodger in 1945 marked the beginning of the civil rights movement. The remainder of the scrapbook presents double-page spreads whereby each topic is described in a masterful arrangement of black and white photos with extended captions, quotes, text boxes, and color photographs of related memorabilia. Weatherford's book shares not only a brief history of the Negro Leagues but also the important role the Leagues played in the African American community. Profiled are Rube Foster, who formed the Negro National League in 1919; Ted Radcliff, who earned his "double duty" nickname by catching for Satchel Paige in one game and pitching a shutout in the second half of a remarkable double header; and Hammerin' Hank Aaron, who would someday break Babe Ruth's home run record. *A Negro League Scrapbook* chronicles the end of the Leagues after Jackie "crossed." However, the book does not end when the Leagues dissolved. Instead, Weatherford concludes by reminding readers that twenty-four players from the Negro Leagues (seven who also played in the major leagues; seventeen who did not) have been inducted into the Baseball Hall of Fame since 1962.

Kadir Nelson offers another perspective of the talented athletes that fought for equality on the field in *We Are the Ship: The Story of Negro League Baseball* (2008). In this highly personal account, Nelson uses an "Everyman" player as his narrator and carefully punctuates the lineup with stunning color illustrations. The resulting blend of history and art captures the drama that was Negro League Baseball. "Buck" O'Neil, Andrew "Rube Foster," Ted "Double Duty" Radcliff, Jackie Robinson, and Henry Aaron are all present, along with many other players, managers, and owners. The "story" of the Leagues is not over in nine innings. This game needs extra innings (ten chapters) to comprehensively capture the era.

We Are the Ship is dedicated to Buck O'Neil and opens with a foreword by Hank Aaron. What follows is an amazing game, from the beginning of African Americans playing baseball to the formation and eventual end of the Leagues. Throughout, Nelson provides dual perspectives—illustrations that require no words and an action-packed "story" rich in detail and accuracy. Nelson's dozens of oil paintings are so realistic that one can almost hear Wilber "Bullet" Rogan spinning a baseball in his huge hands or smell the leather of catcher Raleigh "Biz" Mackey's glove. They are so evocative that one must feel enraged at the sight of the "Cabins For Colored" sign and immense satisfaction as Jackie Robinson looms larger-than-life in front of his fellow Dodgers.

Comprehensive narrative introduces Rube Foster, the founder of the Negro National League. It hails Buck O'Neil and Ted "Double Duty" Radcliff as two of the greatest athletes to ever play the game. The entire 9th Inning" is devoted to Jackie Robinson's historic "crossing" and the grace he displayed during the dark days of baseball desegregation. "Extra Innings" is the end of Negro League Baseball. "Everyman" concludes that the African American players who never made it to the major leagues could not be bitter because there is no sadness in changing the course of history. In a concluding Author's Note, Nelson wonders if he has done justice to the history of Negro League Baseball. He need not worry. *We Are the Ship* is a verbal and visual tribute to the men whose vision and athleticism forced a reluctant national to grapple with racial equality on and off the diamond.

In a picture book biography, Matt Tavares shares a view of Hank Aaron that is richly different from that of Weatherford and Nelson. *A Negro League Scrapbook* (Weatherford, 2005) and *We Are the Ship* (Nelson, 2008) explain Aaron's playing days in the Negro Leagues but quickly transition to his enormous success in Major League Baseball. Both focus on his prowess as an athlete as well as the role the Negro Leagues played preparing him for life on predominately white teams during the early days of the civil rights movement. Tavares, on the other hand, explores the early of life of a skinny kid who once held his bat the wrong way. In tightly woven narrative, Tavares explains how Jackie Robinson would help Hank Aaron realize his dream. The opening of *Henry Aaron's Dream* (Tavares, 2010) sets the stage. The first image encountered is a full-color illustration of a sign hanging on a chain link fence that surrounds a baseball game in progress. The sign tells all: "whites only."

It was during the 1940s in Mobile, Alabama, that young Henry Aaron dreamt of becoming a big-league baseball player. But his father told him not to get his hopes up with the reminder, "Ain't no colored ballplayers." In fact, Henry was twelve before Mobile posted the sign "Colored Only" on Carver Park. Henry lived at the ballpark. Everyone noticed the skinny kid who held his bat the wrong way. Henry was a right hander and he kept his left hand on top. But before long, no one noticed how he held the bat. All they saw was Henry hitting the ball harder and farther than anyone else at Carver Park. Henry was thirteen when Jackie Robinson broke the color barrier in Major League Baseball and joined the Brooklyn Dodgers. The remainder of *Henry Aaron's Dream* chronicles Aaron's journey to the Boston Braves: There is the hard life on the road as a player on the Indianapolis Clowns of the Negro American League, talks amongst African American players as they helped each other cope with the taunts and jeers of racist fans, and the verbal and visual description of segregated ballparks in the South. Tavares concludes this stunning picture book with a unique, almost surreal, encounter. During a 1954 exhibition game between the Braves and the Dodgers in Mobile, Aaron outran a throw to Robinson to arrive safely at second base. And cheering him on, from the Colored section of Hartwell Field, were all the fans who remembered young Henry's dream. In an extended Author's Note, Tavares summarizes Aaron's long and successful career. However, the brief paragraphs and stats box don't do justice to "Hammerin' Hank's" remarkable career. *Henry Aaron's Dream* captures the days before the dream came true, the days when African American players fought to excel on the fields of Major League Baseball.

Some say Negro League Baseball ended in 1960 when the last of the Leagues folded. Buck O'Neil would disagree. This former player and manager might argue that the Leagues live on in the Negro Leagues Baseball Museum. O'Neil is mentioned in *A Negro League Scrapbook* (Weatherford, 2005) and *We Are the Ship: The Story of Negro League Baseball* (Nelson, 2008). But he is the sole player in sportswriter

Joe Posnanski's unique book, *The Soul of Baseball: A Road Trip Through Buck O'Neil's America* (2007). The idea for this journey (literally and figuratively) began when O'Neil asked Posnanski how he fell in love with baseball. Not quite sure how to respond, Posnanski decided to spend the 2005 baseball season "on the road" with the then ninety-four-year-old O'Neil. At the time, O'Neil was chairman of the Negro Leagues Baseball Museum—a commemoration he worked tirelessly to establish.

The Soul of Baseball offers an array of perspectives told through the voices of a passionate and optimistic former Negro Leagues player/manager and a somewhat cynical sportswriter. The words of Posnanski and O'Neil blend effortlessly as the two reflect on the past, present, and future of America's pastime. There are the descriptions of great Negro League players such as Satchel Paige and Willie Mays, remembrances of segregated restaurants and boarding houses, echoes of racist taunts, and the steadfast suggestion that the men of the Leagues were not only talented athletes but courageous activists. *The Soul of Baseball* invites readers (or listeners) into a wide range of emotions. Buck O'Neil was a humorous and generous man who approached life as a series of opportunities to be seized. However, like any great story, there are moments of gut-wrenching sadness. O'Neil and Posnanski attend the funeral of Ted "Double Duty" Radcliff. They deal with the shock and anger of O'Neil being passed over for admission to the Baseball Hall of Fame. And ultimately, Posnanski must cope alone with the passing of Buck O'Neil in 2006. *The Soul of Baseball* is a first-person perspective of segregated athletics shared by one of the game's greatest champions. The journey can be independently enjoyed by older readers or shared as a read-aloud with younger students.

Using—An I-Search (Short et al., 1996) is a reading-research strategy that invites readers to create their own questions, identify sources for research, formulate answers, and summarize their findings. I-Search honors that formulating questions and searching is, in and of itself, a valuable endeavor. An I-Search chart evolves when students create the guiding questions and potential sources for research *before* reading. The questions are answered during or after reading. Students then use the answers to their questions to write a summary of what they learned. Table 1 is an example of an I-Search matrix for Negro League Baseball. The questions were brainstormed by seventh graders studying the integration of athletics in the United States.

TABLE 1. I-Search for Negro League Baseball

QUESTIONS and SOURCES	What was Negro League Baseball?	Why did the Leagues flourish?	Who were some of the stars of the Leagues?	What hardships did the players endure?	Why were the Leagues important in the African American community?
Trade Books					
Journals					
Websites					
Reference Books					
Magazines					
Newspapers					
Summary					

Performances from the Stage

[On prejudice]: Sometimes, it's like a hair across your cheek. You can't see it, you can't find it with your fingers, but you keep brushing at it because the feel of it is irritating.

—MARIAN ANDERSON (1960)

Choosing—Both the Smithsonian Institution (2010) and the Library of Congress (2010) bookend the civil rights movement from 1955 to 1965. Clearly the fight for racial equity gained national and international prominence during the decade leading up to the passage of the Civil Rights Act of 1964 and the Voting Rights Act of 1965. Others, however, suggest that the fight for equality began long before 1955. As chronicled in books about the Negro Leagues, it happened on baseball diamonds beginning in the late 1800s. And, as told by poet Myra Cohn Livingston and authors Pam Munoz and Russell Freedman, the fight for racial equality was also heard on stage in the early decades of the twentieth century.

Marian Anderson was born in 1897 to a working-class family in South Philadelphia. Her magnificent contralto voice was first heard in the choir of Union Baptist Church. And, in the spirit of community that defines African American churches, it was the congregation of Union Baptist that established a Marian Anderson fund that enabled her to continue lessons when her family could no longer afford to pay. Most students learn about Marian Anderson's contributions to the world of music, including her debut at the New York Philharmonic in 1925, her first concert at Carnegie Hall, and her enormously successful European tour in the early 1930s. Sadly, however, many are completely unaware of a free concert offered by the gentle but persistent Anderson, a concert so significant that it began to erode the very fabric of racial segregation, and a concert venue where almost three decades later the civil rights movement would be propelled onto the national agenda.

After training and performing for several years in Europe, Anderson returned to the United States in the late 1930s. Although well-known and respected, she was still denied rooms in certain American hotels and was not allowed to eat in certain restaurants. The racism Anderson experienced came to the national stage when, in 1939, the Daughters of the American Revolution (DAR) refused to allow Anderson to sing for an integrated audience in Constitution Hall. As a result of the DAR's decision, thousands of DAR members, including First Lady Eleanor Roosevelt, resigned their membership. But that was only the beginning. Outraged by the DAR's refusal and wanting to spotlight the fact that the capital of the United States remained a segregated city, the Roosevelts arranged for Anderson to perform. On Easter Sunday, April 9, 1939, on the steps of the Lincoln Memorial, Anderson gave a free, open air concert. She sang for the nation on the very spot where Martin Luther King would continue the fight for equality on August 28, 1963. Amazingly, it took four more years for the doors of Constitution Hall to open for Anderson.

Three books for young readers tell the story of Marian Anderson. All three describe how she used her extraordinary talent to confront racial segregation in the arts. But the three titles represent the events from very different perspectives. In fact, reading and viewing the three is much like peeling the layers of an onion. *Keep on Singing: A Ballad of Marian Anderson,* by Myra Cohn Livingston with illustrations by Samuel Byrd (1994), is sparse and succinct. More detail and a completely different illustrative perspective can be found in *When Marian Sang,* by Pam Munoz Ryan and illustrator Brian Selznick (2002). The final and most complete accounting of Anderson's quiet but effective crusade is Russell Freedman's *The Voice That Challenged a Nation: Marian Anderson and the Struggle for Equal Rights* (2004).

Keep on Singing: A Ballad of Marian Anderson, by poet Myra Cohn Livingston (1994), is a picture book ballad penned in tribute to Anderson. It is beautifully brief, accurate, and poignant. However, the genre allows for so few carefully chosen words that only highlights of this extraordinary life are captured. Paired with colorful pastel illustrations by Samuel Byrd, Livingston includes Anderson's childhood in Philadelphia, her early training and career, the European tours, and her eventual return to the United States. *Keep on Singing* concludes with the concert at the Lincoln Memorial and the invitation to be the first African American woman to sing at the Metropolitan Opera House. Two double-page spreads capture Livingston and Byrd's juxtaposed perspective of the open air concert. One is Anderson at the feet of Lincoln alone. The other is Anderson in the foreground singing on the steps with a blurred background representing the huge crowd that came to the mall on that chilly Sunday morning. *Keep on Singing* contains an Author's Note where Livingston carefully footnotes facts from the ballad. Brief and beautiful, this text will surely leave readers wanting more.

When Marian Sang (Ryan, 2002), also a picture book, is more and different. It is told as a recital, with "libretto" by Pam Munoz Ryan and "staging" by Brian Selznick. In Ryan's biography, we learn important details that enrich the tapestry of Anderson's life. We come to know her sisters, her choir director at Union Baptist, and master teachers and conductors under whom she studied and performed. The events leading up to the open air concert are included; however, Ryan's narrative focuses on the hopes and fears of Anderson versus the political circumstances that resulted in the venue selection. Like *Keep on Singing, When Marian Sang* concludes with Anderson's performance at the Metropolitan Opera House. Unlike *Keep on Singing,* Selznick's stunning paintings are richly detailed yet quietly haunting. On the cover, Anderson is depicted in a cone of light behind a sky full of stars. In another, a young Anderson is standing on a chair among a choir of grownups and singing. Here the robes of the choir are parted to reveal a glimpse of the same starry sky on the cover. And the historic concert is painted in a fascinating trilogy—a huge American flag billowing in front of Constitution Hall, a close-up of Anderson singing with her eyes closed, and a double-page spread of the diverse audience that came to listen. All of Selznick's illustrations are shades of brown, cream, and gold, reminiscent of sepia-toned photographs. One can interpret the images a number of ways, depending upon perspective. Are the sepia-like hues meant to accurately portray the era of this biography? Is the peacefulness reflective of Anderson's "serene charm" (The Marian Anderson Historical Society, 2010)? Or is the dark detail symbolic of the racism and bigotry that overshadowed an otherwise colorful and majestic career? Ryan concludes with a comprehensive "encore" in an Author's Note that contextualizes many of the book's events.

The final, most comprehensive biography of Anderson is undoubtedly Russell Freedman's *The Voice That Challenged a Nation: Marian Anderson and the Struggle for*

Equal Rights (2004). With the meticulous attention to detail that this historian is known for, Freedman tells Anderson's story by expertly punctuating primary source material with only the words necessary to achieve coherence. The perspective in this text is that of Marian Anderson. This introspective diva kept journals, wrote many letters, and gave numerous speeches. In addition, she was frequently photographed and written about. By drawing on abundant archives from the Annenberg Foundation, Freedman represents the many dimensions of Anderson's life. In this biography, we learn about her as a daughter, wife, student, artist, performer, friend, and activist. There are numerous photographs of the events leading up to the concert at the Lincoln Memorial. However, unlike *Keep on Singing* (1994) and *When Marian Sang* (2002), the momentum of this biography accelerates after the open air performance in 1939. Anderson continued to advocate for equality in the arts, maintained a personal relationship with Eleanor Roosevelt, and served as a U.S. delegate to the United Nations. Perhaps the most memorable photograph Freedman includes was taken on the cold evening of January 7, 1943. There, amidst the snowflakes, is Anderson, descending the stairs of Constitution Hall following a benefit concert she performed during World War II—for an integrated audience. Anderson once reflected on her life and the fight for racial equality: "What I had was singing, and if my career has been of one consequence, then that's my contribution" (Anderson, 1977). This is a contribution not to be missed!

Using—Bleich's Response Heuristic (1978) encourages readers to think critically by considering the major ideas of a text, integrating them with prior knowledge, and reacting to them. Specifically, the Response Heuristic suggests a three-part framework to structure responses: text perceptions, reactions to the text, and associations with the text. The following contains an example of the Response Heuristic completed by Megan, an eighth grader, after reading *The Voice That Challenged a Nation: Marian Anderson and the Struggle for Equal Rights* (Freedman, 2004).

*****

Response Heuristic for *The Voice That Challenged a Nation: Marian Anderson and the Struggle for Equal Rights* (Freedman, 2004)

Text Perception is a summary statement about important information from the text.

> *On Easter Sunday, April 9, 1939, Marian Anderson sang to a crowd of 75,000 people on the steps of the Lincoln Memorial. She sang at the Lincoln Memorial because the DAR had a "whites only" rule at Constitution Hall.*

Reactions to Text are evaluative statements that ask students to express their opinion about the text.

> *I was outraged when I read this book. I had no idea that the Daughters of the American Revolution prohibited this great singer from performing at Constitution Hall.*

Associations with the Text are higher level evaluations that require students to associate information with their own prior knowledge or associate current reading with past readings.

> *Now I know why Martin Luther King, Jr. delivered his "I Have a Dream" speech on the steps of the Lincoln Memorial. Amazing that Dr. King's speech didn't happen until August 28, 1963!*

—MEGAN, GRADE 8

*****

A Requiem for Bones

Who speaks for Fortune? How is his legacy best served?
—MATTATUCK MUSEUM (2010)

Choosing—There is a skeleton on display at Mattatuck Museum in Waterbury, Connecticut. It was known as "Larry" and placed on exhibit beginning in the 1940s. There were many stories about Larry. Some said he died in the Revolutionary War. Other speculated he fell to his death or was drowned. In 1970, believing it was disrespectful to display the bones, the skeleton was removed from display. For more than twenty five years, the skeleton rested in storage. But in the 1990s, historians working in Waterbury discovered that "Larry" was actually the remains of a slave named Fortune. But the story does not end with the identification of Fortune's bones. What follows is a fascinating saga where debate still rages about the central question posed earlier. Who speaks for Fortune?

In an expertly crafted work of nonfiction that blends history, archeology, anthropology, music, and ethics, readers can learn about Fortune and wrestle with the question of how best to serve his legacy. Marilyn Nelson is the author of *Fortune's Bones: The Manumission Requiem* (2003). Thanks to Nelson's creativity, a requiem, a forensic examination, and the events of a slave's life are starkly presented in exposition, narration, maps, photographs, and paintings. In an introductory Author's Note, we are reminded that a requiem is words and music written to honor the dead. We learn that manumission is the formal release of someone who has been a slave. The Manumission Requiem, as Nelson explains, honors a slave freed not in life but in death.

TABLE 2. Socratic Question for *Fortune's Bones: The Manumission Requiem* (Nelson, 2003)

Questions that clarify	• Could you put that another way? • Can you give me an example?
Fortune's Bones	• **Can you give me an example of why the Mattatuck Museum once thought it was disrespectful to display human remains?**
Questions that probe reasons and evidence	• How do you know? • Why do you think that is true? • What would cause you to change your mind? • What do you think causes . . . to happen?
Fortune's Bones	• **What do you think caused historians at the Mattatuck Museum to search for the identity of the skeletal remains?**
Questions about viewpoints and perspectives	• What is another way to look at it? • Would you explain why it is necessary or beneficial and who benefits?
Fortune's Bones	• **Why do you think it was beneficial (or not) to identify the skeletal remains?**
Questions that probe implications and consequences	• Why is this issue important? • How does. . . tie in with what we learned before? • How can we find out?
Fortune's Bones	• **How can we find out if other museums are debating the issue of displaying human remains?**

The double-page spreads that comprise the remainder of this unique book pair the poems of the requiem with facts as they are known. There is information pieced together by historians about Fortune's life. He was a slave in Waterbury owned by Dr. Porter, a local physician. When Fortune died around the age of 60, the doctor rendered his bones for study. The modern forensic study of Fortune's bones is described. Included is a remarkable facial reconstruction by a forensic sculptor that eventually led to Fortune being brought to life in a full-color portrait. In an Afterword, Marie Galbraith of the Mattatuck Museum urges us to stay involved with Fortune's story. She invites readers to the museum's website where Fortune's story continues. Should Fortune's bones continue to teach us, as members of the African American History Project Committee contend? Or is it time to rest his bones in consecrated ground?

Unlike Negro League Baseball and the life of Marian Anderson, there are no other books about Fortune's bones. Therefore, in order to gain a second perspective, one must visit Mattatuck Museum's website (http://www.fortunestory.org). It is only by reading *Fortune's Bones* and exploring the ongoing work at the Mattatuck Museum that students can fully prepare for a critical conversation about Fortune's case and similar issues faced by museums all over the world.

Using—The mystery of the Waterbury skeleton, the debate regarding displaying human remains, and the ongoing controversy in Connecticut about Fortune's bones are perfect content for a Socratic discussion. Socratic inquiry encourages lively discussions by posing questions that explore complex ideas, air issues and problems, uncover assumptions, analyze concepts, and distinguish what is known from what is not known (Gall, 1970). Table 2 contains a sample of Socratic question stems and several specific inquiries for *Fortune's Bone: The Manumission Requiem* (Nelson, 2003).

Black Experiences Around the World

> E is for the embrace we give our loved one.
> —IFEOMA ONYEFULU, 1997 (P. 5)

Choosing—Life on two very different continents is the subject of the next collection of nonfiction books. Ifeoma Onyefulu was born into the Igbo tribe and raised in Eastern Nigeria. Today, she is a professional photographer who uses her stunning images and simple words to offer readers a glimpse into many aspects of African life. *A Is for Africa* (Onyefulu, 1997) is an alphabet book that depicts twenty-six examples of everyday life in Nigeria. *Emeka's Gift: An African Counting Story* (Onyefulu, 1995) presents through the eyes of a young child ten important African goods sold in local village markets. *One Big Family: Sharing Life in an African Village* (Onyefulu, 2006) explains how Nigerian villagers share, celebrate, and make important decisions. *Here Comes Our Bride!* (Onyefulu, 2004), also told from the perspective of a young child, captures the sights and sounds of a Nigerian wedding. And *Ikenna Goes to Nigeria* (Onyefulu, 2007) is a photo documentary chronicling a young girl's visit to the country where her mother was born. Onyefulu's books can certainly be shared individually, but taken together, they offer rich and varied perspectives about the people and culture of Nigeria.

In *Sacred Mountain Everest,* by Christine Taylor-Butler (2009), we travel to Asia for an encounter with the tallest peak on Earth. Many stories have been told about the dangers and triumphs surrounding the summit, but few describe the native people who serve as guides. In *Sacred Mountain Everest,* Taylor-Butler introduces the Sherpa of Nepal and Tibet. Famous for their bravery and navigational skills, Sherpas have played an important role in climbs since the 1920s. This text is not a traditional biographic presentation. Instead, it advocates for an understanding of the

Sherpas' way of life, their belief in the scared mountain, and their fight to protect a threatened and fragile ecosystem. *Sacred Mountain Everest* is illustrated with arti-facts, color photographs, maps, and diagrams. This important book is not as much about a mountain as it is a plea to respect the skilled and tolerant people charged with protecting it. Like *Fortune's Bones: The Manumission Requiem,* this is the only text for young readers about the Sherpa of Mount Everest. For a second perspec-tive, log on to Brian Handwerk's (2010) article on the website of *National Geographic.*

Using—*Sacred Mountain Everest* (Taylor-Butler, 2009) lends itself to a Text Impression (McGinley & Denner, 1987). The book contains interesting and chal-lenging words that should be discussed prior to reading. A Text Impression is a thinking-reading strategy that uses several important or interesting words to guide predictions. Using a Text Impression prior to reading not only promotes predictive discussion, but it also allows teachers to ascertain students' prior knowledge about a topic. Figure 1 contains directions and a sample Text Impression for *Sacred Mountain Everest.*

ecosystem

slopes

guide

treacherous

monastery

summit

Sherpa

tallest

FIGURE 1. Text Impression for *Sacred Mountain Everest* (Taylor-Butler, 2009)

Directions

1. Before reading, present five to ten important or interesting words from the book or selection. Introduce them on the board, one by one.
2. After presenting each word, pose questions such as these: What do you know? Now, what do you know? What do you think this book or selection will be about? What do you expect to read about if these words are in the book or selection?
3. During the discussion, note how the predictions change and evolve as words are introduced.
4. Record ideas. Leave the words posted during the reading of the book or selection. After reading, refer back to the words for additional discussion and/or clarification.

CONCLUDING THOUGHTS

This chapter sought to explore excellence in nonfiction books representing black experiences. Most of the suggested texts have been recognized for authenticity and accuracy by awards such as the Coretta Scott King Award, the Orbis Pictus, Notable Books for A Global Society, the Casey Award, the Sibert Medal, and the NAACP Image Award for Outstanding Literary Award for Children. In addition, the collection contains a sampling of the important multicultural attributes suggested by Cai and Bishop (1994) and Aronson (1995). Clearly all the books represent world literature. *The Soul of Baseball* (Posnanski, 2007) and *The Voice That Challenged a Nation* (Freedman, 2004) are examples of cross-cultural literature. Parallel culture literature can be seen in *A Negro League Scrapbook* (Weatherford, 2005), *We Are The Ship* (Nelson, 2008), and Onyefulu's African photo documentaries. And it is wonderful to offer an example of "cultural crossing." Taylor-Butler, an African American writer, contemplates the Sherpa in *Sacred Mountain Everest* (2009).

It is suggested that teachers can conduct a similar process as they search for and select accurate and authentic nonfiction books to represent black experiences. Further, by using the questions in Table 3, teachers can critically consider books for other multicultural topics. Perhaps Katherine Patterson said it best: "It is not enough to simply teach children to read; we have to give them something worth reading. Something that will stretch their imaginations—something that will help them make sense of their own lives and encourage them to reach out toward people whose lives are quite different from their own" (n.d.). What better way to engage the hearts and minds of young readers than with excellent nonfiction books that accurately and authentically represent black experiences?

TABLE 3. Framework for Critically Selecting Excellent Multicultural Nonfiction

Accuracy and Authenticity
Is the text factually correct?
Is the text about a significant topic?
Is the text timeless?
Is the text connected to my curriculum?
Has the text received an award for authenticity and accuracy?
Representation
Are world nonfiction texts available for instruction?
Are cross-cultural texts available for instruction?
Are parallel cultural texts available for instruction?
Are texts that represent cultural crossing available for instruction?

REFERENCES

Anderson, M. (1960). *Interview with Jet Magazine.* Retrieved from http://articles.baltimoresun.com

Anderson, M. (1977). *Interview with B. Klaw.* Retrieved from http://www.americanheritage.com/articles/magazine/ah/1977/2/1977_2_50.shtml

Apple, M. W. (1993). *Official knowledge: Democratic education in a conservative age.* New York, NY: Routledge.

Aronson, M. (1995). A mess of stories. *The Horn Book, 71*(2), 163–168.

Bleich, D. (1978). *Subjective criticism.* Baltimore, MD: Johns Hopkins University Press.

Cai, M., & Bishop, R. S. (1994). Multicultural literature for children: Towards a clarification of a concept, In A. H. Dyson & C. Genishi (Eds.), *The need for story* (pp. 57–71). Urbana, IL: NCTE.

Cook, M. (2009). *Our children can soar.* New York, NY: Bloomsbury USA Children's Books.

Freedman, R. (2004). *The voice that challenged a nation: Marian Anderson and the struggle for equal rights.* New York, NY: Clarion Books.

Gall, M. (1970). The use of questions in teaching. *Review of Educational Research, 40,* 707–721.

Handwerk, B. (2010). *The Sherpas of Mt. Everest.* Retrieved from http://news.nationalgeographic.com/news/2002/05/0507_020507_sherpas.html

Huck, C. (2003). *Children's literature in the elementary school* (8th ed.). New York, NY: McGraw-Hill.

Library of Congress. (2010). *Civil rights movement.* Retrieved from http://www.loc.gov/teachers/classroommaterials/themes/civil-rights/lessonplans.html

Livingston, M. (1994). *Keep on singing; A ballad of Marian Anderson.* New York, NY: Holiday House.

The Marian Anderson Historical Society. (2010). *Marian Anderson,* contralto. Retrieved from http://www.mariananderson.org/legacy/index.html

Mattatuck Museum. (2010). *Fortune's story*. Retrieved from http://fortunestory.org

McGinley, W., & Denner, P. (1987). Story impressions: A prereading/writing activity. *Journal of Reading, 31*(3), 248–253.

National Council of Teachers of English. (2010). *Orbis Pictus award for outstanding non-fiction for children*. Retrieved from http://www.ncte.org/awards/orbispictus

Nelson, K. (2008). *We are the ship: The story of Negro League baseball*. New York, NY: Hyperion.

Nelson, M. (2003). *Fortune's bones: The manumission requiem*. Ashville, NC: Front Street Books.

Onyefulu, I. (1995). *Emeka's gift: An African counting story*. New York, NY: Penguin.

Onyefulu, I. (1997). *A is for Africa*. New York, NY: Penguin.

Onyefulu, I. (2004). *Here comes our bride!* London: Francis Lincoln.

Onyefulu, I. (2006). *One big family: Sharing life in an African village*. London: Francis Lincoln.

Onyefulu, I. (2007). *Ikenna goes to Nigeria*. London: Francis Lincoln.

Patterson, K. (n.d.). Retrieved from http://www.readfaster.com/readingquotes.asp

Posnanski, J. (2007). *The soul of baseball: A road trip through Buck O'Neil's America*. New York, NY: Morrow.

Ryan, P. (2002). *When Marion sang*. New York, NY: Scholastic.

Short, K., Harste, J., & Burke, C. (1996). *Creating classrooms for authors and inquirers*. Portsmouth, NH: Heinemann.

Smithsonian Institution. (2010). *Civil rights movement*. Retrieved from http://search.si.edu

Tavares, M. (2010). *Henry Aaron's dream*. Somerville, MA: Candlewick Press.

Taxel, J. (1993). The politics of children's literature: Reflections on multiculturalism and Christopher Columbus. In V. Harris (Ed.), *Teaching multicultural literature in grades K–8* (pp. 1–36). Norwood, MA: Christopher-Gordon.

Taylor-Butler, C. (2009). *Sacred mountain Everest*. New York, NY: Lee & Low.

Weatherford, C. (2005). *A Negro league scrapbook*. Honesdale, PA: Boys Mills Press.

CHAPTER 11

Riddles as Critical Thinking Tools

A Case of African Traditional Oral Literature in the Social Studies Classroom

LEWIS ASIMENG-BOAHENE

INTRODUCTION

One of the strengths of inclusive schooling is the capability of the teacher to facilitate the active learning of all children using appropriate diverse materials and all available human resources in the classroom. The use of African oral traditions such as riddles can engender, even among illiterate communities, the knowledge, beliefs, and attitudes that could be learned through interactive process (Reagan, 2005). It is, therefore, not surprising that for some time, there have been calls for the inclusion of the perspectives of underrepresented classes into the curriculum (Delpit, 1995; Gay, 2000; Howard, 2003; Ladson-Billings, 1995). The hope of this call is to improve the academic performance of students who are culturally, ethnically, racially, and linguistically diverse, as globalization has created renewed interest in education in other cultures (Ladson-Billings, 1995; Nieto, 1999; Oakes & Lipton, 1999; Reagan, 2005). However, more often than not, such calls and efforts have time and again entailed little more than the addition of a short descriptive piece of literary writing, one that has rarely been articulated (Reagan, 2005). Consequently, in Western academia, non-Western perspectives in the form of cultural oral art like riddles are still accorded the status of a minor literary brand and thus remain at the peripheral part of Western academia—neglected, unexplored, and never becoming a full participant. This omission has been a common criticism of Western scholarship as very few individuals, according to Reagan (2005), have had any real exposure to non-Western educational traditions, and thus, perceptions remain deficient or stereotypical. This contention is further accentuated by Fafunwa (1974), who commented as follows:

> Because indigenous education failed to conform to the ways of the Westernized system, some less well-informed writers have considered it primitive, even savage and barbaric. But such contentions should be seen as the product of ignorance and due to a total misunderstanding of the inherent value of informal education. (p. 17)

Consequently, such naïve misunderstandings and misrepresentations remain all too common among some Western scholars who seek to understand the other. A call is therefore necessary for administrators and educators alike to expand their repertoire of understanding beyond the "conventional wisdom" of their pedagogic creed. This means learning to incorporate or delve into different non-Western cultural routes to accommodate the perspectives and cultural learning styles that promote other important communicative and educational inclusiveness in their diverse students.

As another form of fresh pedagogical perspective, my intent is not to argue for the debates about the field's various failings but rather to advance the discussion for the exploration of indigenous pedagogies like African riddles as pedagogical tools to develop critical thinking skills. Since there have been many stereotypical assumptions and speculations about both Africa and oral literature, it is necessary to expose these sometimes unsubstantiated views to open new landscape for a genuine appreciation of our present knowledge of the subject.

First, the context of this discussion focuses on conceptualizing African riddles and their ability to promote cognitive skills, thereby helping to extend and deepen our understanding of the world, while advancing our total capacity to think as educators. Second, the paper identifies and reviews the relationship between African riddles and critical thinking as useful partners in the Western/African scholarship. This connection is imperative, since critical thinking encourages innovation, creation, and use of various symbol systems of learning. The third factor describes the conceptual framework for the culturally responsive pedagogy and critical literacy that serve as the foundation for the development and implementation of the nonmainstream concept riddle as a pedagogic vehicle for critical thinking. The next discussion focuses on an outline of classroom-based pedagogical practice, using African riddles to promote critical thinking in an elementary social studies education class. Finally, concluding remarks are offered pertaining to the use of African riddles as knowledge tools for exploring critical thinking in social studies education.

WHAT IS CRITICAL THINKING?

Critical thinking is a contested territory with many competing views, beliefs, and practices. In fact, critical thinking is such a complex process that educators and psychologists have not yet been able to see eye to eye on a definition. However, in spite of this lack of agreement, some definitions merit highlighting. Maxim (2010) considers critical thinking as "the higher-order thought processes used to conceptualize and assess information for the purpose of detecting accuracy, biases, and suspend judgments, actions, or decisions until they view the issues" (p. 289). Although very embracing, Paul and Elder (2010), on the other hand, in their book, *The Miniature Guide to Critical Thinking,* define critical thinking as "the art of analyzing and evaluating thinking with a view to improving it" (p. 2). Differing from the aforementioned views, Nosich (2009), alternatively, dwells on prominent features of critical thinking like reflective, authentic, and standards.

However, Beyer (1995) considers critical thinking to mean making reasoned judgment by using criteria to judge the quality of something. In essence, critical thinking is a disciplined manner of thought that a person consciously uses to examine and assess the validity of something, or that of another, and evaluates that reasoning against universal intellectual standards like clarity, accuracy, precision, relevance, depth, breadth, and logic. Consequently, one can conclude that there are some common threads among scholars about what critical thinking entails. These threads include the ability to challenge common assumption by formulating questions, to identify and weigh appropriate evidence, and to reach reasoned conclusions. However, when conceptualizing it with riddles, one could consider critical thinking as the ability to critique puzzles, questions, or statements with a view to improve or answer them.

CRITICAL THINKING IN SOCIAL STUDIES

More significant than a definition of critical thinking by itself, however, is the belief that there are alternative paradigms of instructional path in social studies education other than the mainstream template which *forces* diverse children to live "their lives interpreted through the lens of the dominant" (Lynch & Baker, 2005, p. 143). National Council for the Social Studies (NCSS) takes a strong position on the role of critical thinking, as the concept is considered to be an unspoken associate of social studies education. Specifically, the NCSS Task Force on Early Childhood/Elementary Social Studies (1989) states as follows: "For children to develop citizenship skills appropriate to a democracy, they must be capable of thinking critically about complex societal problems and global problems. . . .

Children need to be equipped with the skills to cope with change" (p. 16). In addition, the council advocates for the inclusion of experiences that provide for the study of cultures and cultural diversity in social studies programs (NCSS, 1994). In other words, if social studies educators are to do justice to their diverse students, they must not present a culture that ignores or disparages other cultures. Oral traditions must be respected and viewed by educators as a unique intellectual institution, not merely as myths and legends. By instructing through the authentic and reflective words, experiences, and wisdom of diverse cultures, children become receptive to and are affected by events on a global level.

CONCEPTUAL FRAMEWORK ABOUT RIDDLES

Riddles have been told since ancient times, and one of the famous riddles is the riddle of the *Sphinx,* solved by Oedipus (Chatton, 2010). Thus, riddles and puzzles are some of the oral traditions or verbal art forms that have been handed down to us by our forefathers and mothers. Riddles are witty questions often imbued with wisdom. They require two parties, one to pose the question and the other to respond. In a general way, riddles are readily distinguishable by their question-and-answer statement form and by their succinctness. Very often, a riddle is a simple form of a phrase or statement referring to some familiar item in more or less shrouded language (Finnegan, 1970, p. 427).

Riddles as a widespread oral literature have been viewed differently, like critical thinking, by different scholars. Some argue that riddles just belong to the social circle of human race despite the fact that Aristotle several times amplified the close relation between metaphorical articulation and riddles (Chatton, 2010; Finnegan, 1970). Consequently, analyzing the cognitive value of riddles as metaphorical expressions related to sociocultural paradigm seems not to have sufficiently captured the ears and the eyes of anthropologists, philologists, psychologists, or students of folklore (Leach, 1950). While it constitutes a game that challenges the intellectual adroitness of the riddler's peers, it is a metaphor that confronts the apparently impossible with what is.

However, in spite of the aforementioned paucity, we used critical literacy as a guide to frame the rationale for teachers to develop a meaningful curriculum for critical thinking that draws from the cultural riches of the African American family and community. Thus, this paper is anchored in the principles of critical literacy (Freire & Macedo, 1987; Meacham, 2000) and critical/cultural responsive teaching (Moll, 1990; Waxman & Padron, 1995) in providing the theoretical frameworks. Critical literacy argues that academic success can be achieved through inclusive instruction, as critical responsive teaching is seen as the type of instruction that, like riddles, "focuses on the critical family and community issues that students encounter daily" (Waxman & Padron, 1995, p. 52). Consequently, African cultural heritage is nurtured through the pedagogic creed of African oral literature in the form of culturally sensitive teaching. This idea is forcefully illustrated by Lee (2000), who used culturally responsive teaching as the theoretical context to contend that "signifying as a form of social discourse in the African American community has the potential to serve as an effective scaffolding devise for teaching complex skills in the interpretation of literature" (p. 159). Thus, the same role can be said of riddles, which enjoy ubiquitous status in many African communities as channels of communication to promote cognitive development through exchange of ideas. Hence, this critical function of riddles is in congruence with the major elements in both critical literacy and critical/culturally responsive practice whereby teaching is used to promote racial, ethnic, linguistic, and economic equality and equity for all students (Grant & Asimeng-Boahene, 2006).

Thus, contrary to the common postulation that they are simply word puzzles sometimes presented by masters of ceremonies at evening gatherings, riddles are in the same stance with fables, folktales, and proverbs as one of the earliest and most pervasive types of created thought. One could further make a strong argument for their preeminence to all other forms of literature and to all other oral lore, for riddles "are essentially metaphors, and metaphors are the result of the primary mental processes of association, comparison, and the perception of likeness and differences" (Leach, 1950, p. 938). Some Western scholars generally classify riddles as enigmas or conundrums, which are problems or statements generally expressed in metaphorical or figurative language and which require ingenuity and careful thinking for their solution (Chatton, 2010; Finnegan, 1970). The essence of riddles as oral art is further captured when one is reminded how riddles played a prominent role in revitalizing the *Mercure de France,* which became a reservoir for riddles, the solution of which captured acclaimed eminence in the French society during the seventeenth and eighteenth centuries (Riddles, 1967). Furthermore, riddles as an element of critical thinking have found their presence in other forms of art. English composer Sir Edward Elgar, for instance, presented a string of musical riddles in his *Enigma Variations* (1899), which served as conundrum for the listeners by requiring them to identify the person to whom a particular rendition was dedicated. In fine arts, the charm of riddles is depicted in metaphysical paintings such as Giorgio de Chirico's (1910) figurative *Enigma of an Autumn Afternoon* (Riddles, 2005). Consequently, riddles, like other oral teachings rich in critical thinking processes, contribute to stimulating the creative thought process and wealth of ideas.

PERSPECTIVES OF RIDDLES IN AFRICA

The riddle is one of the most important forms of oral art in Africa, and even though it has played an important role in African culture, it remains undefined and for the most part undescribed.

Even though a significant amount of work has been published on African oral literature, the facts are scattered and uneven, often obscured in hard to find journals, coupled with occasional fleeting references, and as such their importance has not been universally cherished (Finnegan, 1970, p. 26; Harries, 1971; Reagan, 2005). The widely held impression of Africa as a continent devoid of indigenous literary practices continues to exist, and it is still, at times, uttered in a manner as unsophisticated as that stated by Burton in the late 1800s about Africa:

> The savage custom of going naked, we are told, "has denuded the minds. and destroyed all decorum in the language. Poetry there is none. . . . There is no metre, no rhyme, nothing that interests or soothes the feelings, or arrests the passions." (cited in Finnegan, 1970, p. 26)

Some scholars who would instantly rebuff such an extreme remark are notwithstanding, sometimes unconsciously swayed by such biased and uninformed assumptions about the descriptions of literary traditions among nonliterate peoples. Thus, there is still the widely held myth of Africa as continent either devoid of literature until its engagement with "civilized" nations which precipitated publications in European languages, or having just rudimentary or unrefined literary construct not requiring systematic study (Finnegan, 1970, p. 26; Harries, 1971).

However, we should be mindful that African riddles have their roots in folk literature and enjoy prominence in virtually all black African cultures (Reagan 2005). Thus, riddles in Africa have regularly been considered to be a type of art form, and like proverbs, they are expressed briefly and concisely; they involve analogy, whether in meaning, sound, rhythm, or tone. Riddles also sometimes have close connections with other aspects of literary expression—with such forms as enigmas and dilemma tales with stories and epigrams. In spite of such connections, however, riddles emerge as a distinct type of literary expression in most African countries (Finnegan, 1970, p. 426; Reagan, 2005).

The Characteristics and Functions

However, despite the fact that they are one of the most important forms of oral art in Africa, they remain infrequently discussed in Western/American classrooms.

Riddles in African societies function like a sort of initiation into poetic expression. It is, thus, a truly active learning process by which the intelligence of the individual is solicited. In effect, the efforts of the audience to find the correct answers are likewise very instructive. In this respect, incorrect answers are often as interesting as correct answers because they reveal the inductive mechanisms by which the listeners attempt to decode the images. The main purpose of posing a riddle is to outwit the respondent. In most African oral literature, the riddle is often posed with linguistic or contextual ambiguity in order to confuse the respondent and create difficulty in solving the problem.

In essence, riddles and other oral traditions such as folktales are important media for transmitting indigenous education, knowledge, and critical thinking skills to children in many parts of rural Africa. Cole-Beuchat (1957) argues that riddles combine recreational and educational needs to an unusual degree, providing an exercise in intellectual skill and quickness of wit and a test of memory. In a comparable way, Ishumi (1980) argued that traditional quizzes (riddles) could be equated in function to present-day psychological tests that assess knowledge and creativity in associating, differentiating, establishing cause-and-effect, and so forth.

Gwaravanda and Masaka (2008) also remark that African riddles are important logical tools in the traditional system of education. They function as socialization and recreation processes in addition to sharpening one's reasoning skills and quickness of wit, and riddles can foster quick mental flexibility on the part of the child as he or she grapples with different possibilities and probabilities in the search for correct answers to given riddles. Consequently, the process of solving riddles involves logical inferences and the justification for answers based on reasoned analysis of the posed riddle.

The following examples conceptualize how African riddles can serve as critical thinking tools:

BERBER (MOROCCO): I riddle it you, a storage jar without an opening.
ANSWER: God will not tell you otherwise than that, it is an EGG (Harries, 1971, p. 381).

RIDDLE 1: "A pair of shoes which are never worn out" (*Mpaboa a enhida.* . . . Akan, Ghana).
EXPECTED ANSWER: "A pair of feet" (*Enae.* . . . Akan, Ghana).

RIDDLE 2: "When father was departing, he left a gentle man; so long as he is alive, he is playful and harmless. But when he is dead, the least mistake you make, trying to touch him, he will bite you seriously (Akan, Ghana).
EXPECTED ANSWER: "Bottle" (*Pintoa* . . . Akan, Ghana), the time of its death is when it is broken. It is only when that can cut some one.

RIDDLE 3: *A be ori a be re, sibe-sibe o nsowo ola?* (We cut off the top and the bottom, yet it produces wealth?).
EXPECTED ANSWER: *Ilu.* (drum. . . . Yoruba, Nigeria).

These three examples illustrate how, for all intents and purposes, African communities have used riddles to uphold critical thinking in the traditional forms of education. The examples exercise the intellect, teach logic, and compel individuals to engage in the contemplation of a variety of paradoxes and enigmas to know about social norms, history, and sociocultural environment.

The Intersection of Critical Thinking and Riddles: What Do They Have in Common?

Full-fledged critical thinking is multifaceted. Like African riddles, both are reflective and authentic and thus involve asking questions that address the heart of the matter. Like riddles, critical thinking entails posing the problem in the first place and trying to answer those questions by reasoning them out. Quintessentially, what riddling and critical thinking have in common is that they both address a question or problem. Those trying to solve the riddle think it through using the rudiments of reasoning. As they do this, they monitor their reasoning using the critical thinking standards (Nosich, 2009). Consequently, riddling and critical thinking share common boundaries in terms of the following:

- Intellectual audacity: This entails their readiness to confront challenges about established principles and philosophical viewpoints. Both will undeniably face up to deep-rooted ways of judgment or thoughts one may entertain.
- Confidence in reasoning: This describes the willingness to try to figure things out, to rely on thinking through things, to the best of one's ability, rather than on all the other influences that shape thinking without knowing it.
- Intellectual firmness: This is the willingness to stick with an intellectual undertaking for as long as it takes to reach a realistic conclusion. This helps to push one's intellectual perseverance in the form of revising one's thinking.
- Intellectual autonomy: This is the willingness to think for oneself using the best reasoning one is capable of, including elements, standards, and discipline with awareness of the bigger picture (Nosich, 2009).

Thus, the commonalities between riddles and critical thinking, in an epistemological sense, cannot be overemphasized. They both promote the use of the intellect to address issues.

TABLE 1. Common Tenets of Critical Thinking and African Riddles

Critical Thinking Skills	African Riddles	Attributes
Infer	Young white men who look alike living in cave.	The teeth (Sotho) (Human body)
Compare and contrast	Men who do not put their sticks on the ground.	Dog (Sotho) (Flora & fauna)
Make decisions	Two paths lead up the mountain.	Nostrils (Human body)
Analyze	The plateau with one flower?	The Belly and navel (Sotho) (Human body and attributes) (Attributes) (Shona)
Evaluate	We cut off the top and bottom, yet it produces wealth.	Drum (Ndebele)

The interrelationship of the tenets of critical thinking and African riddles (see Table 1) underscores the use of African riddles as tools to promote critical thinking skills.

Table 1 illustrates how the interrelationship of African riddles and the basic tenets of critical thinking (infer, compare and contrast, make decisions, analyze, evaluate) can be woven to promote a new pedagogical approach besides the mainstream paradigm. Thus, the relationship between African riddles and critical thinking is self-evident as it calls to mind different ways of seeing and learning as they cross paths. In essence, Table 1 brings to light a conceptualization of critical thinking skills explicated through African riddles making use of human parts and attributes, flora and fauna, and cultural artifacts. The understanding of this intersection and linkage can help students acquire global knowledge with better appreciation of global perspectives as it exposes them to other uncharted paradigms which continue to appear too remote for them because of mainstream curricular approach (Maxim, 2010). In view of tremendous challenges facing racially and ethnically diverse children in the United States, this model could create multiple perspectives for teachers to become aware of the need for culturally responsive teaching practices within schools for their diverse students. In support of this view, Gloria Snively, (cited in Reagan, 2005) made a compelling argument:

> If schools are to do justice to native students, they must not represent a culture that ignores and denigrates the indigenous culture. Oral traditions must be respected and viewed by the teacher as a distinctive intellectual tradition, not simply as myths and legends.
>
> If the traditional beliefs, values, and ideas that have been taught to the children by their parents and grandparents are not important in the school curriculum, the message is obvious. (p. 128)

Gloria Snively's statement poignantly reminds us of Victor Hugo, the famous French poet, novelist, and dramatist of the nineteenth century, who is credited with the saying, "There is nothing more powerful than an idea whose time has come." The statement suggests a natural progression from inception to full-blown acceptance of an idea. With the renewed interest in the education of other cultures engendered by contemporary globalism, the same can be said of the idea of using African riddles as critical thinking tools to improve the academic performance of students who are culturally, ethnically, racially, and linguistically diverse. Consequently, it is because of this conviction that I find it academically disturbing that non-Western epistemologies as alternative paradigms continue to be at the peripheries in the Western academic landscape.

Furthermore, as triggers for reflection, I share the views of Semali and Kincheloe (1999), who argued the following:

> We find it pedagogically tragic that various knowledges of how action affects reality in particular locales have been dismissed from academic curricula. Such ways of knowing and acting could contribute so much to the educational experiences of all students; but because of the rules of evidence and the dominant epistemologies of Western knowledge production, such understandings are deemed irrelevant by the academic gatekeepers. . . . Our intention is to challenge the academy and its "normal science" with the questions indigenous knowledge raise about the nature of our existence, our consciousness, our knowledge production, and the "globalized" future. (p. 15)

Consequently, we all should be cognizant of Semali and Kincheloe's clarion reminder that there is much in non-Western societies' educational paradigms that is worthwhile and valuable and that educators need to learn to do a better job from learning from these exemplars. Thus, the value of indigenous knowledge like riddles is not only practical and pragmatic, but it is rather profoundly epistemological in nature. Accordingly, as widespread behavioral experience, riddles have the wherewithal to widen children's conceptual lenses by acting as catalyst for the development of critical thinking for both intercultural awareness and critical literacy, as they have the literary resources to engender cross-cultural communication across cultural and national frontiers. Rethink how you can tie these teaching ideas to critical literacy standards.

The following are examples of critical thinking activities using African riddles:

1. Instruction can range from simply incorporating "a riddle of the week" to having students interpret riddles.
2. Discuss the themes in Table 1, then ask students to search for riddles that relate to critical thinking.
3. In small groups, ask students to try to find at least four riddles for which they can determine the following:
   a) Riddle
   b) Underlying value
   c) Influence on critical thinking

The following are examples of riddles related to critical thinking:

- What is the difference between an elephant and a flea? An elephant has fleas, but a flea will never have an elephant.
- What runs all round the yard without moving? The fence.
- What is always before you, yet you can never see it? Your future.
- What increases the more you share it with others? Joy.
- Question: *Nzira mbiri dzinoenda mugomo?* [Two paths lead up the mountain?]
  Answer: *Mhino.* [Nostrils.]

- Question: *Ngabantwana bami bakha indlu banganamanzi?* [My children burning a house without water?]
  Answer: *Mmuhlwa.* [Termite.]

- Question: *Ngesitimela sami asikhambi esiporweni?* [By my train that does not go on the railway track?]
  Answer: *Lisongololo.* [Millipede.]

The following are examples of possible cross-curricular activities:

1. Tell students the Sphinx riddle and together talk through how and why it is considered a "riddle."
2. Have students create their own riddles. Share student creations with one another.
3. Have students critique the riddles based on whether they are funny, clever, annoying, or complex.

The following is an example of a riddle to help students with their own creations:

Question: What always ends everything?
Answer: The letter "g."

The following are examples of language arts activities:

1. During writing class, have students create their own riddles. Share student creations with one another. Have students serve as "riddle critics" and categorize the riddles based on whether they are funny, insightful, challenging, or complex.
2. Have students make a "top 10" riddle box for your class, one that can be shared with other classes, friends, or peers. This can also be converted into a bulletin board or even included in the school announcements.
3. Much like *Jeopardy*, initiate a riddle performance or a "riddle game" to see who can out-riddle the other team.

The following are examples of social studies activities:

1. Using a map of Africa, ask students to locate the countries of origin of the riddles.
2. Have students conduct interviews with local African citizens or immigrants online, by phone, or in person. Guide students in preparing questions to find out about the culture and traditions of Africa as well as about the individual's favorite African riddle. Also, teachers should consider contacting university students and professors in the departments of African studies for more information on riddles and their role within different ethnic groups in Africa.
3. Similar to a poetry anthology, students can collect riddles and establish an anthology of riddles from around the world to share.

REFERENCES

Beyer, B. K. (1995). *Critical thinking*. Bloomington, IN: Phi Delta Kappa Educational Foundation.

Chatton, B. (2010). *Using poetry across the curriculum*. Oxford, UK: ABC-CLIO.

Cole-Beuchat, P.-D. (1957). Riddles in Bantu. *African Studies 16*(3): 133–149.

Delpit, L. (1995). *Other people's children: Cultural conflict in the classroom*. New York, NY: The New Press.

Fafunwa, B. A. (1974). *A history of education in Nigeria*. London: Allen & Unwin.

Finnegan, R. (1970). *Oral African literature*. Oxford, UK: Clarendon Press.

Freire, P., & Macedo, D. (1987). *Literacy: Reading the word and the world*. Westport, CT: Bergin & Garvey.

Gay, G. (2000). *Culturally responsive teaching: Theory, research, & practice*. New York, NY: Teachers College Press.

Grant, R., & Asimeng-Boahene, L. (2006). Culturally responsive pedagogy in citizenship education: Using African proverbs as tools for teaching in urban schools. *Multicultural Perspectives, 8*(4), 17–24.

Gwaravanda, E. T., & Masaka, D. (2008). Shona reasoning skills in Zimbabwe: The importance of riddles. *The Journal of Pan African Studies, 2*(5), 193–208.

Harries, L. (1971). The riddle in Africa. *Journal of American folklore, 84,* 377–393.

Howard, T. C. (2003). Culturally relevant pedagogy: Ingredients for critical teacher reflection. *Theory Into Practice, 42*(3), 195–202.

Ishumi, A. (1980). *Kiziba: The cultural heritage of an old African kingdom.* Syracuse, NY: Syracuse University.

Jones, A. (1995). *Larousse dictionary of world folklore.* New York, NY: Larousse.

Ladson-Billings, G. (1995). But that's just good teaching! *Theory Into Practice, 34,* 159–165.

Leach, M. (Ed.). (1950). *The standard dictionary of folklore, mythology and legends* (Volume Two: J-Z). New York, NY: Funk & Wagnalls.

Lee, C. D. (2000). Signifying in the zone of proximal development. In C. D. Lee & P. Smagorinsky (Eds.), *Vygotsky perspectives on literacy research: Constructing meaning through collaborative inquiry* (pp. 191–224). Cambridge, UK: Cambridge University Press.

Lynch, K., & Baker, J. (2005). Equality in education: An equality of condition Perspective. *Theory and Research in Education, 3,* 131–164.

Maxim, G. W. (2010). *Dynamic social studies for constructivist classrooms: Inspiring tomorrow's social scientists.* Boston, MA: Allyn & Bacon.

Meacham, S. (2000). Literacy at the crossroads: Movement, connection, and communication within the research literature and cultural diversity. *Review of Educational Research, 25,* 181–208.

Moll, L. C. (1990). *Vygotsky and education: Instructional implications and application of sociohistorical psychology.* Cambridge, UK: Cambridge University Press.

National Council for the Social Studies. (1994). *Curriculum standards for social studies: Expectations of excellence.* Washington, DC: National Council for the Social Studies.

National Council for the Social Studies Task Force on Early Childhood/Elementary Social Studies. (1989). Social studies for early childhood and elementary school children preparing for the 21st century. *Social Education, 53,* 16.

Nieto, S. (1999). *The light in their eyes: Creating multicultural learning communities.* New York, NY: Teachers College Press.

Nosich, G. M. (2009). *Learning to think things through: A guide to critical thinking across the curriculum* (3rd ed.). Columbus, OH: Pearson/Prentice Hall.

Oakes, J., & Lipton, M. (1999). *Teaching to change the world.* New York, NY: McGraw-Hill.

Paul, R., & Elder, L. (2010). *The miniature guide to critical thinking: Concepts and tools.* Dillon Beach, CA: Foundation for Critical Thinking Press.

Reagan, T. (2005). *Non-Western educational traditions: Indigenous approaches to educational thought and practice* (3rd ed.). Mahwah, NJ: Lawrence Erlbaum.

Riddles. (1967). In *Chamber's encyclopedia: New revised edition* (Vol. XI). New York, NY: Pergamon.

Riddles. (2005). In *Encyclopedia Americana: International edition* (Vol. 23). Danbury, CT: Scholastic Library Publishing.

Semali, L., & Kincheloe, J. (Eds.). (1999). *What is indigenous knowledge? Voices from the academy.* New York, NY: Falmer.

Waxman, H., & Padron, Y. (1995). Improving the quality of classroom instruction for students at risk of failure in urban schools. *Peabody Journal of Education, 70*(2), 44–65.

SECTION III

BLACK MULTICULTURAL LITERATURE THAT TARGETS HIGH SCHOOL GRADES: 9–12

Reading "Black" Poverty in Postcolonial Anglophone Caribbean Young Adult Fiction

Michael Anthony's *The Year in San Fernando* and Cyril Everard Palmer's *The Cloud with the Silver Lining*

Denise Jarrett

Young adult literature based on different African diaspora experiences has become relevant in a global environment. As diasporic nations, Caribbean peoples have immigrated to diverse parts of the world. Therefore, introducing young adults from other regions to young adult Caribbean literature gives nonnatives a chance to experience the Caribbean culture vicariously through these novels. In *Against Borders: Promoting Books for a Multicultural World* (1993), Hazel Rochman agrees that "[r]eading makes immigrants of us all . . . it takes us away from home, but, most important, it finds homes for us everywhere" (p. 15). It is hoped that in teaching and studying young adult Caribbean novels, many stereotypes of Caribbean peoples will be debunked and a positive and well-defined Caribbean culture will emerge in the minds of readers.

Caribbean culture is closely affected by its history. Since Africans are scattered throughout the world, their experiences are told through the eyes of adolescents who have only heard about the stories of their ancestors. Of course, these African descendants are not the first, second, or third generation migrants who still have very close ties to Africa. Thus, the young adolescents who narrate their stories in the novels are descendants from Africans who were connected to the greatest migration of Africans who were forcefully transported to the Americas by the institution of slavery. Slavery has long been abolished in the region, and many of these nations are now independent from their colonial rulers. Like the lives of the people who once lived under colonial rule and have practiced colonial lifestyles, colonial literatures presented young adults of African descents as subjects without an identity and voice because these literatures mimicked colonial lifestyles and cultures.

Additionally, these young adults are void of their histories and their cultures because their histories and cultures are projected as backward and unacceptable. The adolescents are educated in colonial schools with colonial curriculums that emphasize knowledge which allows these young adults to remain loyal to their colonizers. Religion plays the same role as education. The traditional African religions such as voodoo and obeah are seen as evil, while the Eurocentric religions are promoted as pure and true. Cultural celebrations are often banned or scorned by the elitists—whites and blacks—in the society. Moreover, language was a great force for the colonized. Therefore, the lingua franca of the colonized was rejected and disapproved of by the ruling class. All these objections to the African descendants' lifestyles, languages, and cultural practices are direct results of their colonization, leading to their position as the underclass in the society.

Furthermore, the stereotypes that have guided colonial writers in presenting blacks in roles such as Josephine, the mammy in Jean Rhys' *Wide Sargasso Sea* (1966), and Gip in the same role in Geoffrey Drayton's *Christopher* (1972), have transcended decades of casting black women as mammy figures in writings. Likewise, black males, young or old, are stereotyped as subservient as depicted in Daniel Defoe's *Robinson Crusoe* (2001). The protagonist saves the life of a man, Friday, from savages on an island, and Friday becomes his slave. Friday is assimilated into European culture and serves his master willingly. Additionally, Joseph Conrad's *Heart of Darkness* (1990) is perhaps the most studied colonial novel about blacks and one that presents blacks most negatively as savages, almost subhumans. Since blacks are stereotyped in colonial literatures, a rewriting of the roles of blacks in postcolonial writings becomes a need, and in rewriting Caribbean people in novels, many Caribbean writers have presented black characters, including young adult males, who are affected by colonialism, but these folk characters are not stereotyped using characteristics that are ascribed by the colonized.

CARIBBEAN YOUNG ADOLESCENT LITERATURE

All young adult diasporic literatures are relatively new. In the Caribbean, young adult literature has grown out of the need to rewrite literatures that will help Caribbean adolescents develop an identity based on their Caribbean cultures and experiences.

It is within this framework that Caribbean writers have decided to erase the legacies of white colonial writers that infiltrated the literary world in the Caribbean. For colonial writers, children and/or adolescent literatures are undefined. Children were microcosms of adults, so literatures did not seek to meet children and adolescents' physical, emotional, psychological, and social needs. The main quest in colonial literatures was to teach children the political, social, and even economic implications of colonization. Thus, the protagonist of Jonathan Swift's *Gulliver's Travels* (1983) visits diverse lands and claims them for England. Even after Charles Dickens, William Golding, Thomas Hardy, Emily Bronte, Charlotte Bronte, Mary Shelley, and American Mark Twain, to name a few, and the advent of new writers and new series such as *Hardy Boys* and *Nancy Drew*, initially with many racist stereotypes which are ostensibly tampered today, adolescents' lives, as presented, are far removed from Caribbean cultures and experiences.

In developing a new paradigm, Caribbean writers from Anglophone, Francophone, and Hispanophone Caribbean countries created their own literatures, rewriting their images and "writing back" to their colonizers, creating literatures for all ages, races, ethnicities, and genders. In focusing on young adult Caribbean literature, I conceptualize these works in the broader nexus of Caribbean literature, before showing how one novel by Michael Anthony and one novel by C. Everard Palmer follow the tradition to present cultural bildungsroman of males and the effects of cultural, social, educational, and economical colonial Caribbean societies on their socioeconomic status. Consequently, one of the main focuses of Caribbean literature is "pulling down colonial mythic walls of Caribbean culture and rebuilding Caribbean reality" (Deena, 2009, p. 8). It is through this rebuilding that Caribbean adolescents are made aware of the uniqueness of their landscapes, languages, cultures, roots, and also the origin and perpetuation of many blacks in improvised socioeconomic states. It is also in rebuilding Caribbean literature that characterization in Caribbean writings has fast outgrown the criticism that "white American reviewers of the fifties and sixties showed a tendency to regard West Indian [Caribbean writers] as naïve and incapable of grasping the significance of the subject matter" (Deena, 2009, p. 8), because Caribbean writers have written the lives and experiences of the Caribbean folk in their text. Based on this and other subjective world literary views that have placed Caribbean writers on the periphery, Caribbean writers have rewritten novels, depicting the differences between classes, races, ethnicities, genders, and generations. However, despite the positive attempts to rid Caribbean writings of colonial legacies, the legacy of poverty faced by the Caribbean peoples is still inscribed in the plots of these novels. Thus, poverty is a central theme in novels for young adults, such as those by Trinidadian Michael Anthony in the *The Year in San Fernando* originally published in 1965 and a similar novel by Jamaican Cyril Everard Palmer, *The Cloud with the Silver Lining* originally published in 1966. Poverty affects the lives of the young male protagonists in each of these novels, propelling them prematurely to manhood.

An examination of poverty in the Caribbean will give credence to poverty in the novels. The Anglophone Caribbean societies have struggled with poverty after their prosperous days as rich sugar and rice plantation economies. Although the colonies were used to produce the products which gave Great Britain dominance socially, economically, and politically, the colonies were not entitled to this wealth. Rex Nettleford in *Caribbean Cultural Identity* (1978), contends that "[p]ersistent poverty among the Black mass serves further to entrench the European cultural hegemony" (p. 53); thus, Nettleford blames blacks' poverty in the Caribbean on their colonial heritage. Today, many former British colonies border on poverty because they are dependent on institutions such as the International Monetary Fund (IMF) and the World Bank to maintain their economies, causing these countries to remain indebted to countries like the United States, which has become one of the most dominant neo-colonial powers of the world.

Additionally, in the Caribbean, unemployment is very high, especially for youth. According to the International Labor Organization (ILO), the urban youth unemployment rate is at 16.3 percent in seven Caribbean countries surveyed in 2010. Moreover, if employed, the uneducated are resigned to low-paying jobs. Males are also endowed with the task of taking care of their families, or if they are not able to be, they should at least be independent. Bridget Brereton explains that "[t]here was a general assumption that the male ex-slaves were to assume responsibilities of heads of families, once the apprenticeship came to an end. . . . They had the obligation to support their aged parents" (1999, p. 103). In *The Year in San Fernando* (Anderson, 1965), the young male protagonist has to support himself, and in *The Cloud with the Silver Lining* (Palmer, 1966), the young male protagonist supports his younger brother and his grandfather. Poverty in the Caribbean has propelled young males, before manhood, to become breadwinners or self-supporters, thrusting them into manhood prematurely.

In presenting "black" poverty in postcolonial Anglophone Caribbean young adult fictions by Anthony and Palmer a study of young adult males in these Caribbean novels posits that (a) lack of economical support and educational opportunities drive male adolescents to apprehend hybridized roles in the society, (b) the role of breadwinner or self-supporter forces acceptance of adult responsibility at an early age, (c) colonial rule and influences foster a dependency syndrome or independence, and (d) young adult males make moral choices based on their economic situations. The writer also examines the historiographical and sociological positions of the young male protagonists; thus, a brief biography of each author is given, and theories of moral, social, and economic developments are incorporated in examining the characters.

MICHAEL ANTHONY'S SEMIAUTOBIOGRAPHICAL NOVEL

Michael Anthony was born in Mayaro, Trinidad, in 1932. He was educated in Mayaro Roman Catholic School, but because of poverty, at ages 11–12, he spent a year with relatives in San Fernando, Trinidad, where he attended school. Anthony's *The Year in San Fernando* (1965) is prompted by his experiences in that city. In addition, Anthony's father died when he was young, and he states that the relationship between his protagonist and the protagonist's father in *Green Days by the River* (1982) reflects his relationship with his father. Although Anthony lived in England from 1954 to 1968, none of his novels is set in England. The setting for most of his novels, and surely all his young adult novels, is in his homeland, southern Trinidad. Anthony writes about the folk experiences, incorporating some of his experiences in his stories. In his work, *The Year in San Fernando* (1965), Anthony uses his memories, class, and race relations in Trinidad, and his socioeconomic conditions, to depict the values of lives for his young black male protagonist, who is affected by poverty.

Poverty in *The Year in San Fernando*

A familiar trope in Anglophone postcolonial Caribbean young adult literature is presenting young characters that reflect the social and economic state of the country. In *The Year in San Fernando*, Anthony does not deviate from this trend as he presents poverty mainly through his characters and settings. While poverty still persists as a serious problem in all nations, poverty was written about as a major problem in colonial Trinidad. Brereton (1989) states that "[w]hen Trinidad and Tobago entered the era of independence, the national economy was considerably stronger than that of most developing countries, but there were fundamental weaknesses that hindered economic growth and better living standards for the people" (p. 222). Anthony presents an authentic young Anglophone Caribbean male protagonist whom he patterns from his life experiences as a young adult. Anthony, like his protagonist, lost his father at an early age and was from the country and was sent to live with a family in the city. The theme of poverty propels the actions in *The Year in San Fernando* and is examined through characterization, setting, and events.

Anthony's protagonist, Francis, is a poor, twelve-year-old Trinidadian boy who tells his story. Francis narrates his mother's description of her family's economic position: "Then she changed to the subject of our own father, and how he died out and left her with four starving children and how God alone knew how hard she was fighting to raise us" (Anthony, 1978, pp. 4–5). Francis' decision to accept his mother's proposal to go to San Fernando to live with Mrs. Chandles is based on his recognition of his family's poverty and his mother's hard work to maintain her household:

> Mrs. Samuels was very kind but nobody would believe it if you said how much she was pay-
> ing Ma to do almost everything in that big house. . . . But her money was keeping us from
> starvation. No one knew about the pay but people could not help seeing how Ma slaved. They
> said she would run her blood to water. Hearing this so often I seriously feared it would hap-
> pen. I always thought, if it *could* happen, would it happen on [one] of these days? (Anthony,
> 1978, p. 5).

It is therefore obvious that Francis' basic needs, food, shelter, and clothing, are barely met, since his mother is underpaid.

Thus, from Mayaro, a country town, Francis is sent to live with an old woman, Mrs. Chandles, as a companion and helper in San Fernando, a major city. Francis' mother hopes that in his transition from country to city, Francis will receive an excellent education that will help him to gain upward social mobility. In fact, she hopes that one day, her children will become financially successful, and she plots their future as Francis explains when his mother visits him in San Fernando that "she always counted on things far away. She counted on Anna getting married, and on Sil taking up teaching, and she counted on having life easy one of these days. This gave her much strength" (Anthony, 1978, p. 62). Although Francis' mother dreams of a better life for her son in San Fernando, Francis' journey from country to city does not afford Francis the comfort, love, and care that he receives from his poor mother, but he matures emotionally, achieving a high level of moral development.

Francis moves to San Fernando for a better life, but he is not given the comforts of a better economic life, fulfilling his mother's vision; however, he matures emotionally. Francis enters Mrs. Chandles' home, but there is no preparation for his accommodation. On his first night, Mrs. Chandles tells Francis, "'You'll have to sleep here. . . . Mr. Chandles ain't fix up anywhere for you yet. You'll have to make it out here for the time being'" (Anthony, 1978, p. 14); however, this arrangement becomes permanent, only with fewer clothes and added newspaper for his bed. Although Francis is physically sheltered from the natural elements because he lives in a house, he is not given the comforts that are fit for human beings. Because of this lack of comfort, Francis' shelter does not fulfill Abraham Maslow's concept of safety and security, since Francis is not in the safety and security of his own room and does not sleep in a comfortable bed. Furthermore, it can be posited that the Chandles do not take more care in accommodating Francis because they are aware of his poor background, and they assume that he is not accustomed to a better lifestyle.

In contrast, the Chandles are obviously from a higher class based on Francis' description of their house, when he states that "[e]ven I, now so well used to it, was always impressed whenever I looked upon it from the street. There was no deny-ing but that it was one of the finest houses of the town" (Anthony, 1978, p. 59). In placing the Chandles in a higher class than Francis, the novel depicts the disparity between the different classes in the society and the persistent classism problem that faces many Anglophone Caribbean nations. The division in social classes is described by Vladimir Lenin as "large groups of people differing from each other by the place they occupy in a historically determined system of social production" (1971, p. 486). Francis is from the class that is at the lowest level of production: his mother is a maid in Mrs. Samuels' household; whereas, the Chandles are at a higher level of produc-tion, since Mr. Chandles has "a big job at the Great Asphalt Company in La Brea" (Anthony, 1978, p. 4). An examination of Francis and the Chandles in two differ-ent social strata suggests that Anthony is making readers aware of the existence of the exploited and downtrodden poor in Trinidad.

This social class structure also reflects the colonial structure, a structure in which the working class is ruled, controlled, and exploited by the other classes, especially the upper class. Francis' position in the society is then one of subservience—a colonial subject. Because he is poor, he has to accept the treatments that are meted out to him to fulfill his basic needs, even if these needs are just partially met. When Anthony positions Francis in a subservient role, Anthony gives the reader an understanding of Francis' mindset. Francis tells his mother that he is comfort-able when she comes to visit him (Anthony, 1978, p. 64), even when he is free from Mrs. Chandles' eavesdropping on his conversation with his mother.

Hence, Francis acts maturely when he does not admit to his mother that he is being ill-treated, resulting in an act of high moral development. The Chandles com-mit many immoral acts against Francis, but he decides not to tell his mother of their unkind treatment, because he still wants to relieve his mother from the responsi-bility of caring for him. Moreover, Francis does not tell his mother about all the events that are taking place, such as the relationship between Mrs. Chandles and her estranged son, Linden; her favoritism toward another son, Edwin; the malice between the two Chandles brothers; and the womanizer, Mr. Chandles, who allows everyone in Mayaro to believe that he is going to marry Marva Samuels, his mother's employer's daughter, but he has a relationship with Julia when he is in San Fernando. He also does not reveal to his mother that Mr. Chandles is a liar because he has not bought him any new clothes (Anthony, 1978, p. 64) and that Mrs. Chandles has even forgotten to feed him. In projecting an image that he is treated well, Francis is at Stage 6: The Universal Ethical-Principle Orientation of Lawrence Kohlberg's (1971) Stages of Moral Development, because he defines his rights based on his conscience and his ethical principles, not on societal morals or principles, which is logical to his particular situation to maintain dignity and to help his mother, because he has allowed her to have one less child to take care of. Basically, he does not contribute to his mother's reasons to worry about him. This high level of moral thinking shows Francis' emotional growth.

Although Francis is from a poor family, his mother shows her children love when talking to them. Francis' move to the city removes him from his mother's presence; thus, he does not hear her loving words. He is placed in an environment where love is lacking. If love is lacking, Maslow's need for love and belonging will not be met. Unfortunately, Francis is not shown love or given a sense of belonging in the Chandles household. It can be argued that Mrs. Chandles does not show her son, Linden, any love and neither does Linden show any love to his mother. From Francis' entrance in the household, he realizes that the mother-son relationship is strained:

> "'Linden?'"
> "'Mother.'"
> "'Oh. It's you.'"
> "'Who you thought it was!'"
> "'Well I only said that. You bring the little boy?'"
> "I said I was going to." (Anthony, 1978, p. 12)

Francis notices that Mr. Chandles "seemed to be bristling" (Anthony, 1978, p. 12), and Mr. Chandles was still looking irritated (Anthony, 1978, p. 12). Throughout the year, he witnesses several arguments between the two over every subject that they try to converse about. Francis then lives in fear of both Mr. Chandles and his mother. Mrs. Chandles only shows pleasure when Francis does all that she asks without care for his well-being, leaving Francis with a great need to please her in order to appease her bad temper. Additionally, Mr. Chandles' first visit, after taking Francis to San Fernando, leaves Francis with a feeling of rejection. Mrs. Chandles sends Francis to help her son with his luggage on his return from his job in La Brea, but Mr. Chandles coldly remarks, "'Look at your condition. What you doing out here at the front?'" (Anthony, 1978, p. 29). Francis' ragged pants that he inherited from his brother and the dirt that had built up on his clothes because Mrs. Chandles prohibited him from changing his clothing offend Mr. Chandles, but he never buys Francis any new clothes. Francis echoes his feelings when Mr. Chandles insults him, trying "to overcome my dejection. . . . I supposed I had expected some friendship from Mr. Chandles" (Anthony, 1978, p. 31). However, the Chandles only recognize Francis as a helping hand and not as a growing boy who needs love and a sense of belonging to develop emotionally.

Although Francis is not given any love from the Chandles, the Chandles project different types of love to different people. Francis is exposed to sexual intimacy between Julia and Mr. Chandles. This is the only form of love that Mr. Chandles demonstrates in the novel. Francis has also heard stories of Mr. Chandles and Marva in Mayaro, as he refers to "the whispers about Mr. Chandles and Marva" (Anthony, 1978, p. 1). In trying to evade contact with the Chandles because he fears their rage, he witnesses Mr. Chandles and Julia making love beneath the house: "Mr. Chandles' voice rose, and it was appealing and caressing and tender. I heard him saying, 'Jule, Jule,' many times" (Anthony, 1978, pp. 38–39). Since Francis is also aware of the relationship between Mr. Chandles and Marva, he is left to further question Mr. Chandles' integrity. Yet, Francis considers Julia his friend. Julia feeds him with information about Mr. Chandles that helps him avoid Mr. Chandles' harsh treatments, and she provides him with his own sexual awakening. Francis confesses that he loves Julia whom he sees as a mere girl, but Julia's intent is to force him into a relationship with her sister, Enid. Francis admires Enid and thinks about her "half buttoned bodice" (Anthony, 1978, p. 107), a sure sign that his sexuality is being awakened. Likewise, Mrs. Chandles shows love to Edwin who reciprocates her love. When Edwin visits his mother on Holy Thursday, he ignores his brother. Although his visit is brief, his presence causes a huge quarrel between Mr. Chandles and his mother. Francis is then convinced that having money and belonging to a higher social class has nothing to do with one's integrity; thus, he compares his family with the Chandles: "And now I thought of our own poverty and of my mother sending me here because she could not feed us all. Yet no such row could take place in Ma's house. And we weren't refined or anything. And we had not been to the big college" (Anthony, 1978, p. 46).

Francis shows further emotional growth, as he is still at Stage 6 of Kohlberg's moral development state. He has to break conventions to take care of himself. Because of Mrs. Chandles' anger, she does not feed Francis; however, Francis realizes that his hunger need has to be met, so he steals some biscuits to stop his hunger. Emotionally he accepts his seemingly adverse action because he has rationalized his deed as morally correct, since Mrs. Chandles eats in his presence and retires without offering him food (Anthony, 1978, p. 46). Francis is perplexed and angered, uttering, "I wondered to myself what sort of human being this old lady could be. She hadn't cooked. She couldn't expect that I had eaten. She had left me to starve and like Mr. Chandles she did not care a damn" (Anthony, 1978, p. 47). He also decides that in order to survive, if Mr. Chandles asks him about the biscuits, he would say, "I didn't know anything about it. I'd swear to God I didn't" (Anthony, 1978, p. 47) because earlier Mr. Chandles had threatened to put him out of the house after accusing Francis of not working and eating his food (Anthony, 1978, p. 33). Francis has learned to survive even if he has to break the moral codes that he is taught and which society upholds. Francis learns about self-preservation firsthand, but he is forewarned by Brinetta, Mrs. Chandles' helper whom he replaced, that "it was proper to stand on your own two feet and to be good for yourself" (Anthony, 1978, p. 31), a saying that convinces him to take care of himself.

Additionally, Francis learns to care of himself with the greatest economic tool, money. Since Francis shops for Mrs. Chandles, he has access to money. To supplement his meager diet, Francis learns the art of being thrifty, using the excess change to buy food. After Brinetta leaves, Francis goes to the market to shop for fresh produce for Mrs. Chandles. He explains, "I was beginning to learn the ways of the market and most times I bought things cheaply and had money left. I sampled watermelons or pomerac or balata. Sometimes I bought barah and channa from the Indian women" (Anthony, 1978, p. 26). Becoming familiar with the market and its produce, Francis learns the skill of spending money economically and getting the best quality goods for his money. This is one area in which Francis' year in San Fernando has helped his development. Coming from a poverty-stricken home, Francis would not have easily learned to budget money, since money was very scarce in his home in Mayaro. While money is presented as a positive force that helps Francis to survive, it is mostly presented as an evil that causes division and unkindness when accessible and suffering and subservience when absent.

Francis moves from country to town in search of a better economic life. Although his physical environment is more affluent than his mother's humble house, he is not afforded love, comfort, and care. Francis stays in town hybdrizing his lifestyle to fit into the mode of his new accommodation. He becomes thrifty and saves money from shopping to supplement the meager food supply that is given to him by Mrs. Chandles. Francis does not experience love, but his sexuality is awakened when he is teased by Enid. There is also the need to fulfill his mother's wishes, so he stays in San Fernando, living with the memory of her voice telling him to "[s]tay and take in education, boy. Take it in. That's the main thing" (Anthony, 1978, p. 67). His mother believes, like many Caribbean mothers, that education will result in upward social mobility. In serving in the Chandles household, Francis had to use higher order moral judgment where he chooses to defy societal laws that dictate right or wrong, so he steals and lies in order to survive. Although his stay abruptly ends at the end of a year because Mrs. Chandles dies, Francis has learned how to control his emotions, using this control as a survival tool.

CYRIL EVERARD PALMER'S SEMIAUTOBIOGRAPHICAL NOVELS

Cyril Everard Palmer was born in 1930 in the parish of Hanover in a rural district, Kendal, Jamaica. At age 25, he graduated from Mico Training College, Jamaica, with a teaching diploma. Palmer then migrated to Canada in 1975, where he still lives. Recognized as one of Jamaica's pioneer adolescent authors, writing ten novels addressing male *bildungsroman* in Jamaica, Palmer, like Anthony, focuses on the same issues in the same setting in his writings about young black males in Jamaica. In describing three of his novels, *A Cow Called Boy* originally published in 1972, *My Father Sun-Sun Johnson* originally published in 1974, and *The Cloud with the Silver Lining* originally published in 1966, Palmer reveals to Glenda Anderson, *Jamaica Gleaner* reporter, that his novels are "stories of young boyish exploits, simple childhood fears, and the dreams of a village or its heroes." He also describes the setting in his novels as "smokey hillsides set in acres and acres of dew covered vegetation, and generously dotted with fruit trees and loveable farm animals [as] the backdrop for many of [his] stories about rural life." Thus, Palmer gives the common experience of young males, nothing unusual, in most rural postcolonial Jamaica. With humor and bitter satire at times, he presents stories that are bound to shift the outlook and behavior of young Jamaican adolescents throughout life. Palmer draws on all aspects of Jamaican culture, providing a conduit for Jamaican adolescent males to build their identities even when they are faced with poverty.

Poverty in *The Cloud with the Silver Lining*

Before independence and even after independence in 1962, many Jamaicans battled dire poverty without any social structure to aid individuals who were once self-supportive but have lost their ability to fend for their families. Like Trinidad and its booming asphalt industry economy shortly before independence (Brereton, 1989, p. 222), Jamaica had its aluminum industry, which was responsible for sustaining its economy (Black, 1994, p. 160), but the wealth did not stretch to the colonists, so social infrastructures to better the lives of the people were never implemented.

Told from the point of view of the younger grandson, *The Cloud with the Silver Lining* (Palmer, 1966) depicts a Jamaican Grandpa or Mr. Licorice, who has lost his power to support his household, forcing his two grandsons, Milton and Timmy, to support the household. Palmer continues in the same vein as Anthony, presenting a young male protagonist, Milton, who has to become self-supportive, but on the contrary, Palmer's character also takes on the responsibility as breadwinner in order to ensure that his family survives. Unlike *The Year in San Fernando*, the story takes place in rural Jamaica, Boswell District, without any movement to the metropolis, and the young adult is not suppressed by the upper class in his society, although the two novels are set in the same colonial era. The period is more specific in *The Cloud with the Silver Lining*, where it is stated that the actions take place before 1959, the year when Grandpa died (Palmer, 1987, p. 157). However, Milton must become innovative to survive and help his grandfather regain his daily activities after he loses his leg in an accident. Palmer does not include the ages of Milton, who is assumed to be about fifteen, and Timmy, who is assumed to be about nine years old, but both young males are adults at the beginning of the text, so early events are recalled. Similar to *The Year in San Fernando*, the events in the text take place within the same year.

Timmy, now an adult, becomes retrospective about the events that take place in Boswell after he describes, "its paved roads and a new school and its many beautiful houses that have spouted erect and solid out of concrete and lit with electricity passing on poles" (Palmer, 1987, p. 11), current developments in the district. Conversely, although these developments underscore the former poverty in the community, adult Timmy concludes that Boswell "has lost something" (Palmer, 1987, p. 10). He goes on to describe the woodlands with the birds and the river that are used for bathing and fishing, but he also creates a contrast by describing the poverty of the old Boswell: "We lived in one, two-, and three-room houses, and our kitchen was always separate shacks with wattle-and-daub and roofed with thatch. They were dirt floored" (Palmer, 1987, p. 10). What Timmy suggests is missing is the communal support and love in the old Boswell when people were poor. Milton could not have helped his grandfather regain his position in society after he lost his leg in the accident without the communal spirit. Poverty in *The Cloud with the Silver Lining* is conceptualized as a tool that fosters community spirit and creativity in young minds and cultivates a survival mode in colonial times.

Community spirit is the major characterizing factor of the villagers in Boswell. After the accident occurs and Grandpa is hospitalized, the young males are left to fend for themselves, since there is no mention of any other family member. They sold surplus food "at home in Boswell, since there was always a grocer willing to buy a bunch of bananas, or the postmistress needing a dozen eggs" (Palmer, 1987, pp. 12–13). Unlike Francis, Milton and Timmy are able to fulfill their basic needs because they live in an agrarian society, and they provide most of the food that they need, selling the surplus to buy what they do not produce. Furthermore, their neighbors, Allen Bent and his wife, Ethel, help the boys, becoming their surrogate parents in their grandfather's absence. Allen helps "in the field with the crops and with the animals we had left" (Palmer, 1987, p. 12), and his wife "kept an eye on what [they] were cooking" (Palmer, 1987, p. 12). In addition, Ethel, who was paid to wash their clothes, continued doing so without any payment (Palmer, 1987, p. 12). The boys are guided by community support, making their transition from being dependent on their grandfather to self-dependence more tolerable, even if they are forced to become men at an early age. Fortunately, the boys were able to support themselves, since the colonial society did not have social services that would aid the boys with food or other amenities that would make their lives more comfortable.

Subsequently, when their grandfather comes home from the hospital, Milton becomes more proactive in maintaining his family. After his grandfather's plot to sell their cow, Red Gal, to get additional income, is foiled, much to the delight of Milton, because she is his calf, Milton makes plans for his family's survival. First, he restores order to the house, creating a timetable listing the daily duties for Timmy and himself. These duties include house and farm chores as well as time for school, homework, church, and fun (Palmer, 1987, pp. 33–34). At an early age, Milton considers the holistic development of young adults as he includes time for social, economical, spiritual, and educational developments. Despite his attempts to fulfill all the needs in his family, Milton's and Timmy's emotional needs are not met because they still suffer from feeling inadequate in helping their grandfather who is now inactive and sad, and Milton realizes that his grandfather is suffering emotionally because he is unable to continue his normal activities at home, at the market, and at church.

However, Milton does not give up. He plots for his grandfather to become active once again by inveigling Grandpa to make a fish pot, a needed tool that would be used to catch fish to supplement the protein in their meals. Timmy states that "Grandpa was the maker of fish pots, so he made ours for us; and the other boys obtained theirs, also manufactured by grandpa of course, but through their parents who had to pay for them" (Palmer, 1987, p. 35), while others were given as gifts to friends who could not afford to pay. Nonetheless, Grandpa's "craft had been shelved. I could only hope that that he would indeed slip out of his melancholy and make us that fish pot" (Palmer, 1987, p. 36). Milton and Timmy get the materials before asking Grandpa to make the fish pot, forcing him to notice by throwing down the bamboo within his sight and hearing. Having recognized the materials to make the fish pot, he consents after a little fuss (Palmer, 1987, p. 38). In honing his skills to make the fish pot, Milton is helping Grandpa to realize that he is not useless because he has lost a limb, an aid in building Grandpa's self-esteem, a high stage on Maslow's Hierarchy of Needs. It is important that Grandpa move to this level, since his physiological, safety, love, and belonging needs are already met with the help of his grandsons and the community.

Milton, like Grandpa, will not feel accomplished until he feels a sense of achievement. Milton's achievement is juxtaposed with Grandpa's achievement because his aim is to find a way for Grandpa to resume his normal activities. Milton's quest to achieve this feat is dampened by his family's lack of financial resources, so he has to think of ways to supplement the family's budget. Milton moves from meeting the basic needs of his family to self=achievement. He decides to become an entrepreneur, operating a food stand at the annual Christmas fair. It is at this point the colonial interjection is made in the novel, since Milton seeks help from Margaret Chaney and her mother. Margaret is the only child of the Chaneys, who own the Great Plantation in Boswell. Palmer's inclusion of the colonial powers as a matriarchal figure is not parallel to postcolonial disdain of the patriarchal and matriarchal roles of the colonizers. The Chaneys are presented as helpful and sensitive to the plights of the poor, as Milton explains,

> I talked it over with Margaret and told her how Grandpa had become grumpy and sad and was not really alive. I told her what I'd like to do for him and she talked it over with her mother. Her mother went to Mr. Chaney with it and then both of them, the elder Chaneys, wanted to give Grandpa a buggy for Christmas, but I would have none of it. And you know very well, too, that Grandpa would have none of that. (Palmer, 1987, p. 70)

In refusing this offer, Milton devises a plan to purchase a buggy for his grandfather.

Milton had become "the man of the house and he controlled the money that came in from the scanty produce that we sold, and also what went out to buy the necessities. Of course he talked things over with Grandpa, who only gave his consent in the form of a grunted Uh-huh but offered no criticisms" (Palmer, 1987, p. 50). Therefore, Milton has become an accountant and economist, since he has to plan, spend, and balance the family's budget. With a deep knowledge of his family's finances, Milton knows that he needs credit to have a stall at the Christmas fair, a plan that he hopes will yield enough profit to buy the buggy for Grandpa. The benevolence of the colonizers is welcomed. Milton gets a loan from Mrs. Chaney along with her baking services to supply pastries for the stall. The stall, named *The Cloud* by Margaret, is a big success, and Milton is able to buy the buggy for Grandpa. His last challenge is to purchase a horse for the buggy, but innovative Milton solves the problem by training Pal Joe, the offspring of the donkey who caused his grandfather's accident. Grandpa proudly rides in his buggy, also named *The Cloud*, to church on Christmas Sunday.

The Cloud becomes a symbol of self-actualization for Milton and Grandpa. Milton wins the admiration of all the villagers who helped him achieve his dream for his grandfather. Furthermore, he shows expertise in problem solving as he tackles each challenge, finding apt solutions for each. It is because of his resilience that Margaret is attracted to him, forging a friendship between them that later leads to marriage. He courts Margaret throughout the novel, and she works side by side with him at the stall during the Christmas fair. Hence, Milton reaches the apex of Maslow's Hierarchy of Needs. With use of indigenous materials by Milton in the building of the fish pot to the materials and pastries for his stall, Milton shows how a colonial subject becomes independent by being creative in using the natural products of the land, since money is never readily available to buy foreign products. It is therefore plausible that the Great Plantation owner would allow his daughter to marry a poor young man, since the Chaneys are conversant with the brilliance of Milton. In marrying Margaret, he also becomes partial owner of the plantation. Giving a twist to the usual marriage of a female into a rich family, allowing her to experience upward social mobility, Palmer affords his male protagonist that luxury. Milton's brother describes his continuous innovations as he expands the plantation, making it more financially viable, and his general development: "In time he left school and went to work for Mr. Chaney on his plantation, starting as a book-keeper. . . . He courted and married Margaret, the only daughter and heiress [of the plantation]. . . . Milton put into effect new ideas on the running of it, and the result is a first-class farm on scientific lines" (Palmer, 1987, p. 157). Milton experiences social uplift because of his creativity and innovativeness.

While Milton achieves self-actualization, Grandpa also reaches his zenith of achievement. According to Maslow, one can reach self-actualization when that person accepts his or her position in life. Grandpa's life changes after he receives the buggy. He accepts his limbless self and once again becomes productive. "The coming of the buggy had indeed wrought a miracle, injecting new life into him, and once again my grandpappy was a man on the go. It was pretty to see him on a Saturday morning setting out to market, baskets and fish pots filling the buggy and hanging from the sides as well" (Palmer, 1987, pp. 156–157). Because Grandpa regains his self-worth, he is able to become, once again, a productive member of society.

Although the colonial society does not provide social services for its poor and handicapped, the people use their agency to create opportunities that supplement their needs. In supplementing their needs, young male adults are forced into manhood, reflected in a statement made by Timmy about Milton: "By the time he was sixteen he had developed a man's awareness of responsibility" (Palmer, 1987, p. 157). The people also survive by their communal spirit, where they share food, labor, and love. Although Palmer introduces the patriarchal role of the colonizer, he reverses this role, giving the colonizer a positive role as an economic source independent from the colonial government. Thus, Palmer presents the Great Plantation owners as caring, sharing, and loving members of society. Palmer's presentation then differs from Anthony's because Anthony shows the divide between two classes while Palmer demonstrates unity despite one's class.

TEXT RELATED ACTIVITIES

These activities focus on presenting awareness of Caribbean young adult identity development and poverty in the texts discussed, focusing on their settings, history, cultures, and the literary components of the novels.

Activities Goals

- Recognize the historic, social, political, and linguistic traditions that are represented in young adult Anglophone Caribbean literature
- Appreciate the variety of cultural influences that inform young adult Anglophone Caribbean literature
- Identify and describe literary forms, such as plot, characterization, setting, and point of view in young adult Anglophone Caribbean literature
- Appreciate the written literatures for young adult Anglophone Caribbean literature
- Understand how to identify development of young adult Anglophone Caribbean literature

Activity 1: Locating the Caribbean

Have students identify Anglophone Caribbean countries on a map of the Caribbean.

Activity 2: Researching Specific Countries Such as Jamaica and Trinidad

Place students in groups of three or four to research each area. Have them research the following: history, population, political parties, languages, foods, cultures, music, education, government, and religion.

Activity 3: Interviewing Young Adults From Anglophone Caribbean Islands

Have pairs of students interview their peers in Anglo Caribbean countries. This could be a Facebook or Internet interview.
Recommended questions:

1. Which country are you from?
2. How old are you?
3. What is your country like?
4. What are some favorite activities for young adults in your country?
5. What languages do you speak?
6. Can you greet me in your native language?

7. Do you have any experiences with prejudice or hostility because of your race?
8. What was the most difficult part of growing up in your country?
9. Do you live in the country or town?
10. What are some cultural practices that you observe?
11. Can you describe your experiences in school from sixth through ninth grade?
12. Can you tell me something about your family?
13. What are some of the foods from your country that you enjoy?

Activity 4: Character Sketch

The writing process will be emphasized as students write a character sketch of the person they interviewed. Character sketches will be shared. Discuss stereotypes. Students will then make a comparison between the character sketch of the person they interviewed and the characters in the text. The same questions will apply to the characters studied.

Activity 5: Plot Development—Role-Play

Students can recreate selected incidents that the protagonists experience, making the experiences relevant to their culture.

REFERENCES

Anderson, G. (2003, November 30). New challenges for C. Everard Palmer. *Jamaican Gleaner.* Retrieved from http://jamaica-gleaner.com/gleaner/20031130/arts/arts.html

Anthony, M. (1978). *The year in San Fernando.* London: Heinemann. (Original work published 1965).

Anthony, M. (1982). *Green days by the river.* London: Heinemann. (Original work published 1967).

Ashcroft, W. D., Griffith, G., & Tiffin, H. (Eds.). (1989). *The empire writes back: Theory and practice in post-colonial literatures.* London: Routledge.

Black, C. V. (1994). *The history of Jamaica.* San Juan, Trinidad: Longman.

Brereton, B. (1989). *A history of modern Trinidad: 1783–1992.* Oxford, UK: Heinemann.

Brereton, B. (1999). Family strategies, gender and the shift to wage labour in the British Caribbean. In B. Brereton & K. A. Yelvington (Eds.), *The colonial Caribbean in transition: Essays on postemancipation social and cultural history* (pp. 77–107). Gainesville: University of Florida.

Conrad, J. (1990). *Heart of darkness.* New York, NY: Dover.

Deena, S. F. H. (2009). *Situating Caribbean literature and criticism in multicultural and postcolonial studies.* New York, NY: Peter Lang.

Defoe, D. (2001). *Robinson Crusoe.*

Drayton, G. (1972). *Christopher.* London: Heinemann.

Kohlberg, L. (1971). Stages of moral development. Retrieved from http://faculty.plts.edu/gpence/htlm/Kohlberg.htm

Lenin, V. I. *(1971). Selected Works.* Moscow: Progress Publisher, 486.

Maslow, A. Maslow Hierarchy of Needs. Retrieved from http://netmba.com/mgmt/ob/motivation/maslow/

Nettleford, R. (1978). *Caribbean cultural identity: The case of Jamaica: An essay on cultural dynamics.* Los Angeles, CA: Center for Afro-American Studies.

Palmer, C. (1972). *A cow called boy.* London: Andre Deutsch.

Palmer, C. (1987). *The cloud with the silver lining.* Oxford, UK: Macmillan. (Originally published 1966).

Palmer, C. (1992). *Baba and Mr. Big.* London: Macmillan.

Rhys, J. (1966). *Wide Sargasso Sea.* Middlesex, UK: Penguin.

Rochman, H. (1993). *Against borders: Promoting books for a multicultural world.* Chicago, IL: American Library Association.

Swift, J. (1983). *Gulliver's travels.* Mahwah, NJ: Watermill.

CHAPTER 13

Alternative Families in Young Adult Novels

Disrupting the Status Quo

CORINNA CRAFTON

Family: Unity formed by those who are nearly connected by blood or affinity.
—OXFORD ENGLISH DICTIONARY

This chapter explores richly woven stories that offer teachers and students provoking ways to reconsider family. While stereotypical notions of family abound and have permeated our bookshelves for generations, many of today's writers of young adult African American fiction feature families that more accurately resemble the reality of family for millions of our students. If we fail to recognize that family can take many forms, we impart subtle yet powerful judgments about what constitutes "real" family. If we do not include among the books we choose to read with our students those that offer a variety of family forms, we shortchange our students and devalue real families.

Barbara Kingsolver, author and advocate for families of all sorts, has written that "Divorce, remarriage, single parenthood, gay parents, and blended families simply are. They're facts of our time" (Kingsolver, 2003, p. 140). Yet, family structures that depart from a dual heterosexual parent household are often considered failures. What messages about tolerance, love, and inclusion do we send to our students, for whom alternative family structures are the norm?

Historically, characters of color included in American fiction have been placed in texts written for a white readership to support the activities of a white protagonist. The nonwhite voices in texts of the nineteenth and early twentieth centuries were silenced or subsumed by the interpretive lens of whiteness: "Blacks in those early materials were presented as plantation stereotypes, objects of ridicule or laughter, or faithful and comical servants to White children and their families" (Bishop, 2007, p. 24). We have moved far from that place, but we still have work to do. In her guide to critical literary theory, Lois Tyson writes that "most of us are also familiar with the continuing problem of exposing children and young people to racially unbalanced curriculum materials based too much (and sometimes exclusively) on white experience as well as the continuing problem of white teachers who respond to black students as if those students 'spoke for,' or represented, their entire race." (Tyson, 2006, p. 370). No one book, of course, can speak to all readers; however, we must acknowledge that variety and choice among the book titles we provide to our students increase the odds that a child will develop a love of reading.

Many of our students do not live the nuclear family model that is the norm to which we compare other family structures. Therefore, realistic fiction, complete with imperfect family members, nonblood relatives, shifting living arrangements, and difficult secrets, must be featured as valid and representative of the real lives of our students. In fact, over 25 percent of Americans live in nontraditional families (United States Census, 2000). In many parts of the country, the percentage is considerably higher. Single parent (male or female head of household), multigenerational, and nonrelated persons living together as a family unit represent over one quarter of all American households. Yet, images and assumptions of *normal* or *ideal* family permeate the pages of many books we place in the hands of our students.

There is no *normal, ideal,* or *real* family structure that supersedes any other, as Stephanie Coontz (1992) has argued in *The Way We Never Were:*

> Whenever people propose that we go back to the traditional family, I always suggest that they pick a ballpark date for the family they have in mind. Colonial families were tidily disciplined, but their members (meaning everyone but infants) labored incessantly and died young. Then the Victorian family adopted a new division of labor, in which women's role was domestic and allowed time for study and play, but this was an upper-class construct supported by myriad slaves. For every nineteenth-century middle-class family that protected its wife and child within the family circle, there was an Irish or German girl scrubbing floors . . . a Welsh boy mining coal to keep the home-baked goodies warm, a black girl doing the family laundry, a black mother and child picking cotton to be made into clothes for the family, and a Jewish or an Italian daughter in a sweatshop making "ladies" dresses or artificial flowers for the family to purchase. (Coontz, cited in Kingsolver, 2003, pp. 141–142)

Essential to understanding our students is developing an understanding of their lives outside of the classroom. As educators, we bring to our classrooms our own assumptions about family, values, and traditions. We can choose to read books with our students that reflect our own assumptions and stereotypes or work to broaden perceptions of family and belonging. A commitment to addressing the issues and realities confronting our students is necessary to fully embrace the potential we have to positively influence young lives. Young adult fiction is a powerful tool to use in helping students to answer their own questions about family, belonging, and identity. This chapter provides teachers with information about three African American young adult novels which may be used as a part of an enriching and diverse language arts curriculum. The varied representations of family portrayed in each novel can help us to develop a better understanding of damage wrought by stereotypes and misunderstanding, broaden our own conception of community, improve our ability as teachers to facilitate learning about African American culture, and address issues of voice, agency, and otherness present for members of many cultures and groups.

ESCAPE AND EMANCIPATION

Why focus on family? As teachers, we know that many students gravitate toward books that feature characters that are in some way similar to the reader. With the right book in her hands, a student may go beyond simply identifying with a character to achieve a measure of emancipation from oppression. Jean-Paul Sartre has argued that "each book proposes a concrete liberation on the basis of a particular alienation" (cited in Galbraith, 2001, p. 1). African American young adult fiction offers liberation from the predominantly Eurocentric perspective that has filled the American literary canon. Reflective of the real diversity that is America, African American young adult fiction presents characters, settings, and conflicts that may be more in line with the very real experiences of many of your students. In other words, reader identification is key to engagement with the emancipatory value of a given text. When we fail to provide texts that reflect something of our students' own family struggles and confusion, we discredit their experiences in favor of fictional representations that may bear little resemblance to anything they have experienced. Rudine Sims Bishop has argued that a liberatory text "not only frees the subject of record and evidence but the witness as well, who is also the reader, who then becomes part of the struggle" (Bishop, 2007, p. 198). And no struggle is as personal as that of the family in turmoil.

Family struggles and stories of young people transcending the limitations of problematic family relations abound in the books selected for this chapter. Readers can be helped along the path to developing internal emotional resources by such books. An ability "to maintain an internal resilience to temporarily bad experiences through memory of the good, is crucial to development, and depends in part on power of language, play, and imagination" (Rustin & Rustin, 1987, p. 11). Indeed, student readers may grow stronger and more resilient to some of the struggles in their own families.

The three books briefly examined in this chapter offer a glimpse at the intersection of important themes and motifs historically present in African and African American literature and how alternative family structures are built and maintained. I've chosen these three because they represent three reading levels within the young adult range; however, there are many equally compelling titles included at the end of this chapter. Key concepts and themes ripe for discussion and activity from these books include the following: *the power of memory, orality and the oral tradition, otherness, the supernatural, and forgiveness.* To embrace the potential of these three novels, one must also move away from the subtle yet ever-present white perspective in critical theory: "After all . . . most contemporary mainstream critical theories . . . have European roots" (Tyson, 2006, p. 365). An integral component to broadening the scope of the literature we offer our students to include works by and about African Americans is a deliberate choice also to honor a variety of forms of English. There is currently little in most English curriculums to reflect any understanding or need to study forms of English other than Standard English. The Black Vernacular has been utterly disregarded as a legitimate form of English by most in academia and the lesson that it is inferior to Standard American English is not lost on anyone who has spent time in an English classroom.[1]

OF GHOSTS, MEMORY, AND MOTHERS

Sweet Whispers, Brother Rush by Virginia Hamilton (1982)

Sweet Theresa Pratt, called Tree throughout the book, is, at the age of fourteen, the default matriarch of her two-person family. While their mother works and lives most of the week away from home, Tree and Dab are on their own. When the ghost of a long dead uncle, Brother Rush, starts visiting, Tree begins to question what it means to be a family. In the process, she learns about troubling family secrets and the power to forgive and heal. By the end of the novel, Tree is a member of an eclectic blended family, several of whom are not blood relatives. (Young Adult, Grade 9+, third person/semiomniscient)

Memory is power. This novel presents teachers with an opportunity to explore the pivotal role of the supernatural and memory in the African and African American storytelling tradition. Tree's mystical journeys through place and time, led by a trusted family member, become her only means of gaining access to family history. Introduced to generational legacy by her ghostly uncle, Tree learns to confront many obstacles in order to repair damaged relationships. Through active control of her own future, Tree rejects a passive role in her relations with adults, demanding finally a full accounting of her mother's past and her own place within the family.

This novel provides teachers with a vehicle for introducing and exploring the power of memory as shared communal and familial knowledge. Silversmith, who becomes Tree's stepfather, says it best: "Folks stay with us whether dead or alive . . . to keep time from wearin' out" (Hamilton, 1982, p. 132). As members of a community, we share in all that has come before. We enjoy eternal membership in the community with those who have come before. The strength displayed by the protagonist as she navigates a world of hardship and loneliness is inspiring to students of many backgrounds and experiences. Indeed, the ending of the novel—at once tragic yet hopeful—provides an excellent point for broaching difficult discussions on the value of working to repair the most important relationships of our lives. The family cobbled together by the conclusion of this novel includes a stepfather figure, Silversmith, whose dealings with Tree are forthright and mature. He speaks to her as the young adult she is becoming and exhibits a patience and kindness that she has never known. He is a gentle counterbalance to M'Vy's brusque, aloofness. Ms. Pritcherd, once the object of Tree's derision and hatred, becomes a stand-in grandmother.

Of particular importance in reading this book with students is to pay careful attention to Hamilton's use of language. The use of Black Vernacular in this novel is further affirmation of its value as a form of expression equally as valid as Standard English. Judith Baker, English teacher and author, asserts that we all master three forms of English: that spoken at home, formal as taught in school, and professional language we use in our careers. She sees "no reason why students have to be convinced that the way they talk is wrong in order to master formal English grammar and speech" (cited in Delpit, 2002, p. 52). Hamilton's characters illustrate this ability we have to alternate between forms of English. They operate within two language cultures: the Black Vernacular spoken in the home and immediate community and the formal English of the white world. Tree's English teacher sees great promise in her young student's written work and urges her to participate in testing for the Black Achievement program for gifted students. At the same time, Tree masters the use of Standard American English used in the school setting, and she is capable of code switching, or moving between two forms of spoken English depending on her needs. Tree can use the language of white America in school and easily switch to Black Vernacular when home. In both instances, Tree understands and is understood. Indeed, Hamilton makes a strong point in favor of non-Standard English with the character of Mrs. Cerise Noirrette, the English teacher "from the islands" who tells Tree, "Yah could be getting full scholarship monies for deh entire college program when you graduate" (Hamilton, 1982, p. 21). An English teacher's use of an alternative form of English gives to that form legitimacy and authenticity. Myriad forms of English are equally valid and expressive. Why should we not accept this fact as teachers? Accepting and embracing many forms of English expression in the classroom empowers children and builds an environment of acceptance and affirmation.

Suggestions for Teaching Sweet Whispers, Brother Rush

INTRODUCTION

- Begin by introducing the oral tradition and vernacular English. By using Black Vernacular English, Hamilton captures the nuance and rhythm that give this novel its read-aloud quality. I have found that reading the first ten pages (or even more) aloud with students is necessary to understanding the power of the oral tradition and to their understanding the cadence and rhythm of the dialogue in this story.

- As a book of its place and time, the idiomatic language used can be challenging for today's young reader. It is worth exploring regionalism and dialect as you begin the novel with your students.

- Additionally, it is important to discuss with students the power of nicknames. The act of naming itself is interesting to explore here, for "emphasizing the importance of naming, including pet names, nicknames, and being called out of one's name (being called a derogatory name)" has a unique place within the history of many African American communities (Tyson, 2006, p. 386). A fun introductory activity is to have students think of two or three adjectives they can use to describe themselves and then creating a unique nickname using a hybrid of several adjectives (i.e., Catherine is creative and silly = Cresilly).

READING ACTIVITIES

- Class discussions about parenthood and the requisite attributes for becoming a parent are often extremely productive in terms of students articulating their own connections to Tree and Dab. M'Vy represents a very real type of parent, one who is complicated, flawed, and falls far short of the ideal image of a caring mother. In a supportive environment, student readers display eagerness to dissect her flaws and grapple with their own experiences of disappointment in unsatisfactory relationships with their own parents.

- Kinesthetic Learning: For some struggling readers, it is helpful to use a physical approach to unwrapping the difficult idiomatic language used by the Pratt community. "Branch hopping" allows students to position themselves physically on a branch of the Pratt family tree and retell a piece of Tree's family history from the point of view of a family member. Using a tree made of brown poster board cut into large segments approximating branches, students can select which branch of the family tree they would like to explore and then work in small groups to analyze a brief passage of text, rewrite that passage into their own words, and share with the class the perspective of this relation. For example, students may take on the point of view of M'Vy, examining the reasons why she is distant, why she must work so much, how she became abusive toward Dab, and how she feels about her own past. This activity is an excellent way to build empathy and help students to become close, critical readers.

WRITING ACTIVITIES

- Reflective journal writing allows a space for readers to explore their own reactions to Tree's story as they learn of her isolation and deprivation. It is not uncommon for my students to experience myriad reactions including anger, frustration, confusion, and disappointment as they learn that Tree and her brother are profoundly neglected both physically and emotionally by a mother that is present only on the periphery of the narration for the first half of the novel. As they read and continue journaling, frustration often gives way to recognition of Tree's strength and resilience in the face of challenge and loss.

- Essay Questions: It is through M'Vy's poor parenting that Tree is able to learn so much about her family, for it, when she has been left on her own without a mother's care that the ghost of her dead uncle appears. It is due to M'Vy's continued absence that Tree develops a relationship with this apparition and begins to learn about her family's true history. Would the ghost of her dead uncle have ever appeared if M'Vy had been an ever present figure in the household?

FATHERS

The First Part Last by Angela Johnson (2003).

Bobby is an introspective teenage boy who becomes a single parent to his infant daughter after his girlfriend suffers near fatal complications during childbirth. The split narrative, alternating sequences told by Bobby before, during, and after the birth of his daughter, reveals a boy who is grappling with more than the challenge of single fatherhood. (Young Adult, High School, Grade 11+ [mild sexual language], first person)

A departure from the stereotypical image of single mothers raising children, this novel features a single teenage father. Bobby becomes a single father suddenly, after preeclampsia places his girlfriend in a coma. This novel challenges a multitude of stereotypes and expectations in terms of family structure and power relations within families. Bobby presents an alternative father figure and may speak to students for whom a father has not been present and those who themselves are parents. The parents of Bobby and his girlfriend Nia are also featured as complex and flawed individuals for whom teen pregnancy brings out the best and worst of their own parenting skills. Bobby's close friends, K-Boy and J. L., are not sure how Bobby's new fatherhood will change their friendship. The messiness of relationships is investigated candidly in this book of a mere 131 pages. As readers, we are made to share in some of the confusion and helplessness Bobby feels as we travel back and forth in time as he recounts his relationship with his daughter's mother before and during her pregnancy. Chapters titled "Then" are juxtaposed with chapters titled "Now," as Bobby works to mature quickly into being "a man . . . a good man" (Johnson, 2003, p. 8). Bobby's self-reflection, offered continuously throughout the novel, allows young adult readers to learn with Bobby as he works to figure out how his concept of family is changing. As he sleeps with his infant daughter, he thinks deeply about the bonds between parents and their children and how "if the world were really right, humans would live life backward and do the first part last. They'd be all-knowing in the beginning and innocent in the end" (Johnson, 2003, p. 4). His own family fractured prior to his becoming a father, Bobby has good reason to dream of an ideal world. This novel presents teachers with a valuable tool for reading and discussing what it means to be a family and how our daily decisions impact our lives and our families. A controversial decision to leave the only community he has ever known, the only family he has ever had, and to venture West to begin a new life with the support of an older brother leaves the ending ambiguous and rich for discussions about growing up and into parenthood.

Suggestions for Teaching *The First Part Last*

INTRODUCTION

- Begin with a brief journaling assignment: "What makes a good parent?"

- Share journals and include a discussion of single parenthood. Discussions of single parenthood generally assume a female head of household and absent father. Many students are able to add their own experiences to the discussion, making it quite personal and immediate.

- Read aloud the first two pages and return to the original discussion question positing a single father instead of a single mother.

READING ACTIVITIES

- Keeping a reading journal, which traces Bobby's progression from a teenage boy who loves to hang with friends, tag graffiti, eat tacos with his girlfriend, and visit the arcade to a very young father with profound and solitary responsibility for another life. An interesting twist on journal writing is to have students imagine they are Bobby's daughter, Feather, who is now their current age (usually around fourteen to sixteen at reading this novel). What questions do they have about their father's younger life? Their mother who lies comatose in a nursing home at the end of the novel?

- The book's short length and easy, direct prose make it a very suitable text for struggling readers. Bobby's choice at the novel's end to move far from home is often met with some skepticism by young adult readers. He leaves the supportive home of his father in Brooklyn for the remote unknown of a small Ohio town where his brother lives.

- An inter-disciplinary activity is to research daily life and the resources available for families in cities and in small towns.

- Build the American Dream. The novel concludes with Bobby moving west toward an American Dream of his own. Students feel compelled to discuss the merits of his choice. Is it worth leaving the majority of his family behind? Will he have enough support to raise his daughter in an unfamiliar place? What resources will be available to Bobby away from the city? Would you make the same choice?

WRITING ACTIVITIES

- Culminating writing questions may include all of those listed above as reading discussion activities.

- Revisit the introductory journal question: What makes a good parent? Have any of your assumptions about parenthood changed as a result of reading this book?

- What stereotypes are disrupted, which remain? Is this book a positive model for teens?

BROTHERS... AND OTHERS

Autobiography of My Dead Brother by Walter Dean Myers (2005)

Visually compelling, Myers' novel is written as a hybrid graphic/traditional prose novel that tells the story of two best friends who live in a section of the city that is increasingly beset by gang violence. Told in the first person, the protagonist, Jesse, lives in a traditional nuclear family and struggles to avoid the dangers of teen life in his community, while his "blood brother," Rise, a boy living in a multigenerational home without a father, falls into a life of crime. (Young Adult, Grade 7+ [very mild sexual reference], first person)

Myers' novels posit hope and compassion against tragedy and struggle. By endowing his child and adolescent characters with "great sympathy and great compassion" (Bishop, 2007, p. 208), he empowers them, giving them agency in the course of their own lives. This novel offers our students the opportunity to journey with two boys as they make choices that will put them on very different courses. It is a particularly effective novel to use as a tool with reluctant readers and adolescent boys. The illustrations are large, dynamic, and rendered in a style that approaches tagging or graffiti. The two main characters, Jesse and Rise, are not related by blood but consider each other blood brothers nonetheless. On the cusp of late adolescence, something changes in Rise, which challenges his family relationships and his relationship with Jesse. Two divergent paths taken by these blood brothers call into question much of what we think we know about family. Profound questions of belonging, responsibility, and forgiveness challenge the reader to consider stereotypes, including some stereotypes that may be reinforced by the text. The direct, first-person narration helps readers identify early on with Jesse as he struggles to understand profound changes in his friend's personality and behavior. A loaded question for discussion revolves around the families of each boy. Jesse comes from a traditional nuclear family, with basically stable relationships, and he steers clear of serious trouble in his life. Rise, on the other hand, lives with extended family but no father, a point which is restated on several occasions. It is he who falls in with a gang and begins to descend into a life of crime and danger. Does Rise's fatherless childhood explain his descent into a life of depression and crime? Older students especially explore this question with passion. How critical is a father in the life of a young man? Does his absence result in anger? If so, can this anger be to blame for Rise's deliberate choices to adopt a gang as family? In her book *Six Myths of Our Time*, Marina Warner argues that "monsters are made, not given. And if monsters are made, not given, they can be unmade too" (Warner, 1994, p. 42). Indeed, Jesse works hard to save Rise from the consequences of his poor choices and from the angry, violent man he is becoming. Jesse struggles to repair his relationship with Rise and to save Rise from his most monstrous enemy—himself.

Myers' use of "speakerly text" (Gates, cited in Bishop, 2007, p. 208) gives an oral quality to the story, for we feel as if we are taking part in a conversation rather than reading a book. This oral quality is achieved through the use of a first-person narration that intimately allows access to the protagonist's deepest thoughts combined with powerful illustrations. The most poignant turns in the plot occur when the protagonist Jesse is reflecting on his "blood brother" Rise's rapidly changing personality and behavior. His reflections *rise* off the page, echoed by carefully placed black and white sketches depicting Jesse's frustration: "As I washed up, I thought about Rise and what he had said. He looked the same, but the way he was acting, even the way his voice sounded it wasn't the same Rise I had in my head. I wasn't sure whether he was only acting different or if he was different, but I didn't know how a person could be different. Not so suddenly anyway" (Myers, 2005, p. 108). Opposite this passage is an illustration of Rise as three slightly different people: three faces are shown, each a strikingly altered aspect of one individual.

By novel's end, one blood brother has died and one remains to pick up the pieces of a shattered family. Honoring the memory of the dead and treasuring the gift of the living, the remaining boy speaks to his lost brother, "telling him that I would finish his life story, and I would make it as good as I could" (Myers, 2005, p. 212). Similar to Hamilton's *Brother Rush*, Myers posits family to include anyone for whom we share a special bond, blood related or no, as well as those who have died, for in memory they continue to teach and to comfort the living.

SUGGESTIONS FOR TEACHING *AUTOBIOGRAPHY OF MY DEAD BROTHER*

INTRODUCTION

- A picture can paint a thousand words. Have students search magazines or online photo databases for images that depict the following themes, motifs, and symbols: family, gangs, friends, fear, hope, obstacle, power, freedom, knowledge, blood, hate, honor, misunderstanding, bravery, opportunity.

- Working in groups or independently, have students share their pictures and explain to the class how an image can capture an emotion, symbol, idea, or event.

- Begin by sharing with students the opening illustration from the novel (an image of Bobby Green in death). Ask students to predict the situation of the first few pages of the novel.

READING ACTIVITIES

- An interesting interdisciplinary activity is to pair sequences of the novel with music. Students can create a soundtrack to go with the narrative or one that simply captures a range of emotions that the student experiences while reading the story. One might consider Jesse's changing feelings about Rise and his own life and pair up samplings of instrumental or lyrical songs to match with the feeling.

- Hip Hopping: A kinesthetic activity done near the end of reading involves investigating our abilities as readers to shift perspective and to view the narrative from several viewpoints. Using colorful duct tape, I make a series of concentric circles on the floor of the classroom. Each circle represents a perspective from the novel (Jesse, Rise, Jesse's parents, Rise's mother, etc.). Students select a scene or passage from the novel to explore. As a class, we reach consensus on the details of the scene. I then have volunteers take on different roles and move to the ring on our circle of the person they have chosen. More than one person at a time can stand in any ring (I've had four people representing Rise at one time with great results). Students must retell the scene as that character. A recent adaptation to this activity is using rap poetry to retell a scene with a call-and-response audience component bringing the entire class into the activity.

WRITING ACTIVITIES

- The highly visual nature of this text creates a plethora of equally interesting visual possibilities when thinking of lesson activities to pair with reading. Artists especially enjoy this novel and gravitate toward activities involving the merging of text with picture. An interdisciplinary project is for students to choose a scene from the novel, alter the setting to their own town or city, and retell the scene from the perspective of Rise using Manga style artwork.

- A culminating writing assignment asks students to choose one or two themes, motifs, or symbols from the introductory activity, i.e., blood and family, and show how each is used within the novel. A pictorial essay that is modeled on the style of this graphic novel is especially powerful.

RESOURCES, RECOMMENDATIONS, AND CONCLUSIONS

Ultimately, the young adult fiction discussed in this chapter highlights one quality of young people more than any other: resilience. Through struggle and setback, often many times over, the protagonists in each of these texts must work to build functioning families. Tree fights herself and her mother before finally settling in to a close family made up of blood and nonblood relations. Bobby must meet the new obligation before him as a single parent and somehow weave his newfound fatherhood into his concept of family. Jesse learns the value of family when he loses someone who has been like a brother to him. In each case, the readers of these books are witnesses to what Rudine Sims Bishop has termed "the oppressive conditions that affect young people growing up," particularly when those young people are also "disenfranchised" by race, ethnicity, or language (Bishop, 2007, p. 208). Read and discuss these books with your students, for many of you have among your class rosters a Theresa "Tree" Pratt, young single father Bobby, or blood brothers Jesse and Rise.

There are a number of worthy young adult titles that grapple with family issues and offer a plethora of family structures and possibilities. The list that follows includes works of fiction and nonfiction and features male and female African American protagonists and the common thread of the formation of an alternative family structure as salient text features.

What makes a family?

non-fiction and historical fiction

- *Over 1,000 Hills I Walk With You* by Hanna Jansen
- *Mare's War* by Tanita S. Davis
- *Damn Near White: An African American Family's Rise from Slavery to Bittersweet Success* by Carolyn Marie Wilkins

middle grades and up

- *Heaven* by Angela Johnson
- *Jaded* by Kimani Tru
- *Tutored* by Allison Whittenberg
- *The Soul Brothers and Sister Lou* by Kristin Lattany
- *Justice Trilogy* by Virginia Hamilton
- *Sister* by Eloise Greenfield
- *It Ain't All for Nothin'* by Walter Dean Myers & Joel Peter Johnson III.
- *Chevrolet Saturdays* by Candy Dawson Boyd
- *Somewhere in the Darkness* by Walter Dean Myers
- *Higgins the Great* by Virginia Hamilton

high school

- *The Color Purple* by Alice Walker
- *Song of Solomon* by Toni Morrison
- *Beloved* by Toni Morrison

- *I Know Why the Caged Bird Sings* by Maya Angelou
- *I Hadn't Meant to Tell You* by Jacqueline Woodson
- *Fire Trilogy* by Joyce Carol Thomas

for teachers

- *African Images in Juvenile Literature: Commentaries on Neocolonialist Fiction* by Yulisa Amadu Maddy and Donnarae MacCann
- *Drinking Coffee Elsewhere* by Z.Z. Packer
- *The All White World of Children's Books & African American Children's Literature* by Osa Osayimwense
- *Virginia Hamilton: Speeches, Essays, and Conversations*

SUGGESTED READING

YULISA AMADU MADDY (AUTHOR)
- Visit Amazon's Yulisa Amadu Maddy page.
- Find all the books, read about the author, and more.
- See Search Resluts for this author.
- Are you an author? Learn about Author Central.

GUIDING QUESTIONS FOR ENRICHMENT

The following guiding questions support deeper reading. Several of these questions assume that a political or ideological framework is used while reading a text and are based on Lois Tyson's (XXXX) *Critical Theory Today: A User-Friendly Guide.*

ADDITIONAL TEACHING STRATEGIES AND DEEPER READING QUESTIONS

RACE AND POLITICS

- What are the racial politics presented in the text?
- Does the text work to correct or reinforce stereotypes of African Americans within society?
- What ideological agendas are at work in the text?
- How is white privilege evident in the novel?
- Marxism assumes raceless, sexless workers and "ignores real conflict of

interest between these workers and so fails to articulate the true situation of black women" (Tyson 19). How does this novel work toward or fail to work to disrupt Tyson's criticism of a Marxist worldview

HISTORY AND CULTURE

- Does the text correctly represent African American history?
- Does the text celebrate African American culture?
- What economic, social, or psychological effects of racism are presented by the character struggles in the text?

LANGUAGE AND LITERACY

- Examine the use of Black Vernacular in the text. How does vernacular work as a literary device in the text?
- Does the text draw on African or African American myth, folktale, or motif?
- What imagery in this novel depicts traditional African American female domestic space?

HELPFUL WEBSITES

- On the historical underpinnings of stereotypes of the African American in literature, visit http://www.pbs.org/teachers/connect/resources/1392/preview/
- On an inspiring project to broaden access to the diversity of African American writing, visit The Givens Foundation at http://www.givens.org
- The de Grummond collection of African American children's literature contains over 3,000 titles. Visit http://www.lib.usm.edu/~degrum to start browsing.

NOTE

1. For an excellent discussion of the merits and value of including a variety of forms of English, including Black Vernacular, read Lisa Delpit's *The Skin That We Speak* (2002, New York, NY: New Press).

WORKS CITED

Bishop, R. S. (2007). *Free within ourselves: The development of African American children's literature.* Portsmouth, NH: Heinemann.

Coontz, S. (1992). *The way we never were: American families and the nostalgia trap.* New York, NY: Basic Books.

Delpit, L. (Ed.). (2002). *The skin that we speak: Thoughts on language and culture in the classroom.* New York, NY: The New Press.

Galbraith, M. (2001). Hear my cry: A manifesto for an emancipatory childhood studies approach to children's literature. *The Lion and the Unicorn, 25*(2), 187–205.

Hamilton, V. (1982). *Sweet whispers, Brother Rush.* New York, NY: Avon Books.

Johnson, A. (2003). *The first part last.* New York, NY: Simon & Schuster.

Kingsolver, B. (2003). *High tide in Tucson: Essays from now or never.* New York, NY: Harper Perennial.

Myers, W. (2005). *Autobiography of my dead brother.* New York, NY: HarperCollins.

Oxford University Press. (2010). *Oxford English dictionary.* Retrieved from http://www.oed.com/

Rustin, M., & Rustin, M. (1987). *Deep structures in children's fiction. Narratives of love and loss: Studies in modern children's fiction.* New York, NY: Verso.

Tyson, L. (2006). African-American criticism. In *Critical theory today: A User-Friendly Guide* (pp. 359–415). New York, NY: Routledge.

United States Census. (2000). *Demographic household data narrative.* Retrieved from http://www.census.gov/prod/2001pubs/

Warner, M. (1994). *Six myths of our time.* New York, NY: Vintage Books.

WORKS CONSULTED

Brooks, R. (2006). Reading representations of themselves: Urban youth use culture and African American text features to develop literary understanding. *Reading Resources Quarterly, 41*(3), 372–392.

Chambers, A. (1996). *Tell me: Children, reading, and talk.* London: Stenhouse Publishers.

Crago, H. (2005). Healing texts: Bibliotherapy and psychology. Peter Hunt (Ed.), *Understanding children's literature* (2nd ed., pp. 180–189). New York, NY: Routledge.

Davis, A. (1971, December). Reflections of the black woman's role in the community of slaves. *The Black Scholar, 12*(6), 3–15.

Friedman, S. S. (1995). "Beyond" white and other: Narratives of race in feminist discourse. *Signs, 21*(1), 1–49.

Hade, D. (1988, October). Children, stories, and narrative transformations. *Research in the Teaching of English, 22*(3), 310–325.

Hade, D. (2002). Living well in a time of terror and tests: A meditation on teaching and learning with literature. *The New Advocate, 15*(4), 293–303.

Harding, S. (1991). Reinventing ourselves as other: More new agents of history and knowledge. In X. XXXX (Ed.), *Whose science? Whose knowledge? Thinking from women's lives* (pp. 268–295). Ithaca, NY: Cornell University.

hooks, b. (1989). Racism & feminism: The issue of accountability. In G. Columbo, R. Cullen, & B. Lisle (Eds.), *Rereading America* (pp. 110–119). New York, NY: St. Martin's Press.

Hunt, P. (2005). *Understanding children's literature* (2nd ed.). New York, NY: Routledge.

Lorde, A. (1980, April). *Age, race, class, and sex: Women redefining difference.* Paper presented at the Copeland Colloquium, Amherst College, Amherst, MA.

Lorde, A. (1984). *Sister outsider: Essays and speeches by Audre Lorde.* Trumensburg, NY: Crossing Press.

Meek, M. (1982). What counts as evidence in theories of children's literature? *Theory into Practice: Children's Literature, 21*(4), 284–292.

Obourn, M. (2005). Audre Lorde: Trauma theory and liberal multiculturalism. *MELUS: Personal and Political, 30*(3), 219–245.

Paul, L. (2005). Feminism revisited. In Peter Hunt (Ed.), *Understanding children's literature* (2nd ed., pp. 114–127). New York, NY: Routledge.

CHAPTER 14

Disability in Africana Adolescent Literature

VIVIAN YENIKA-AGBAW

INTRODUCTION

"What does it mean to teach literature to adolescents?" This is how Richard Beach, Deborah Appleman, Susan Hynds, and Jeffrey Wilhelm (2006) open their book on the same subject. In so doing, they address head-on key variables such as the students in one's classroom, theories that inform one's practice, and pedagogy that makes such practice visible. They draw attention to the different purposes for teaching literature, urging teachers to understand how their "teaching techniques" serve their "larger purposes and goals" (Beach et al., 2006, p. 10). As a teacher of literature, one of my larger goals has always been to enable my pre-service teachers to construct "text worlds as social worlds" (Beach et al., 2006, p. 12). To me, this seems like a logical way for them to forge connections amongst and across texts and cultures, as they also attempt to make sense of their multiple realities and worlds they experience. Literature, therefore, can be a powerful teaching and learning tool to further enhance our understanding of culture and society.

One "culture" that I believe has been consistently left out in many of our schools' "literary" curriculum and/or "literary book clubs" (Edelsky, Smith, & Wolfe, 2002) within school settings is disability. Without conducting formal research it is hard for me to explain why this is so. However, I know that disability, considered a culture (Smetana, Odelson, Burns, & Grisham, 2009) and a "condition" (Siebers,

2008) is constructed stereotypically in both the classics and contemporary literature for children and young adults (Blaszk, 2007; Little, 1986; Rubin & Watson, 1987; Yenika-Agbaw, 2011). Understanding full well that these scholars are referring to studies done on literature about white characters with disability, my chapter strives to fill a cultural gap by answering the following question: How is disability represented in Africana (African and African diaspora) adolescent novels?

I begin by presenting briefly the dominant models of disability as constructed in society. I then proceed with discussing the representations of black characters with disability that prevail in seven randomly selected adolescent novels set in Africa and in the United States, while arguing that race as a signifier in and of itself marginalizes an entire cultural group in our global community. Therefore being black and disabled may predispose one to double marginalization in society; however if educators socialize children on the principles of equity, then these future leaders of our global community may be more prone to respecting our collective humanity regardless of our varied racial and bodily forms. I conclude with some ideas for classroom practice.

DISABILITY AS A CONDITION/CONSTRUCT

Whilst the subject of disability may be relatively new to literary scholars and educators, disability theorists have been working hard to sensitize the reading public about the significance of multiple bodily forms and societal perceptions of these forms (Garland-Thomson, 2002; Siebers, 2008; Snyder, Brueggeman, & Garland-Thomson, 2002). One of their goals is to draw attention to the different models of disability that exist in the minds of the average person, as they interrogate deficit models of disability such as the medical model that presents "disability as an individual defect lodged in the person, a defect that must be cured or eliminated if the person is to achieve full capacity as a human being" (Siebers, 2008, p. 3). Siebers (2008) presents the social model of disability as an alternative, noting that this model "challenges the idea of defective citizenship by situating disability in the environment, not in the body. Disability seen from this point of view requires not individual medical treatment but changes in society" (p. 73). This framework informs my analysis of representations of disability in literature about Africans and African Americans. Thus, while it has already been established that stereotypes exist in the constructions of disability in literature with white characters, it is also necessary to understand how cultural nuances factor in the different constructions of black characters with disability. And since Ladson-Billings and Tate (1995) attest that race is always culturally situated, I am also interested to see how these constructions differ in Africans and African American novels.[1]

REPRESENTATIONS OF DISABILITY IN AFRICANA NOVELS

Like representations of disability in literature about nonethnic cultures in the West, Africana adolescent novels display two models of disability: disability as a medical condition and disability as a social construct.

Disability in Novels Set in Africa or About Africans

The four novels vary in publication dates and settings, with the oldest published in 1963 and 1966 and the most recent in 2009. Disability, according to these novels, is a consequence of parental neglect, as Ekwensi (1966) infers in *The Drummer Boy*; it is rooted in superstition and mythical traditions as in the case of Sunjata, and/or a result of war as is evident in Cooney's (2007) *Diamonds in the Shadow* and Combres' (2009) *Broken Memory: A Story of Rwanda*. The implication, therefore, is that disability is an unnatural phenomenon, since it is partly because of some kind of negligence, is steeped in mythical traditions, and is imposed on individuals through unnecessary warfare. Ironically, as communicated in these novels, it is difficult to reverse this "unnatural" phenomenon unless one relies on the paranormal.

In Justine and Ron Fontes' (2008) *Sunjata, Warrior King of Mali: A West African Legend*, disability is constructed as a temporal situation that can be transcended at will. Fontes and Fontes' (2008) graphic novel on how Mali kingdom came to be evokes Mande mythical traditions that demand a suspension of disbelief. This is because readers follow Sunjata's transformation from a crippled bodily form to able-bodiedness, and eventually this enabled him to become a legend. The irony is that while he is able to transcend his disability, his mother, who is a hunchback, remains deformed throughout. This construction, while driven by Mande mythology, can be problematic; however, in understanding that folklore is not meant to be real, readers can indeed suspend their disbelief for one brief moment. People with disabilities as depicted here are in a sense human with supernatural capabilities to transcend any physical deformity, if they put their minds to it.

Ekwensi's (1966) *The Drummer Boy* brings a different dimension to how disability is perceived within a fictional Nigerian community. The story follows a medical model of disability depicting Akin's loss of sight as a major medical defect, which predisposes the protagonist to exploitation by seeing humans. He is a talented musician who is vulnerable and susceptible to abuse by his able-bodied companions and friends. The bulk of the story revolves around characters trying to plan his life for him or making decisions about his career path without consulting with him. He ends up in a rehabilitation center sponsored by a rich woman who hopes he will learn or hone practical skills that would make him more independent instead of living on the streets. Thus, if his eyesight cannot be restored, as the medical model typically sees this as a defect that needs to be fixed, then he may at least be rehabilitated in some form to gain respectability in society. The Nigerian society of the 1960s depicted here is hostile toward him and thus he needs to be protected.

Amongst the novels about Africa two focus on disability that is incurred as a result of war in Rwanda and Sierra Leone. These novels explore physical and mental disabilities that exist as by-products of war. In Elisabeth Combres' (2009) *Broken Memory,* readers witness Emma's struggle to adjust in postwar Rwanda. While physically she is able-bodied, her psychological state is problematic. When the novel begins, she is awoken by a nightmare. Readers find out later that she had witnessed her mother and other relatives being killed and had barely escaped the same fate that befell all Tutsi. She remains fragile, though, in the care of a loving Hutu woman who had hidden her from the assailants. Ndoli is another character who suffers this same plight; however, he is physically disabled as well. Known to the townspeople simply as "dented head" (p. 31), he remains a "spectacle" wherever he goes (Garland-Thomson, 1996). The two characters share a common bond as outsiders in this postwar Rwandan setting. Combres' construction reveals the pain—physical and psychological—that these characters endure. And to alleviate the psychological trauma that continues to compromise the overall quality of life for these youths, therapy is encouraged. She presents Ndoli's physical disability as a manifestation of Rwanda's violent past that cannot be fixed or ignored and so is acknowledged as a spectacle by both the perpetrators and victims of the war. Thus, while mental disability may be soothed or even remedied by therapy, characters with physical disability must learn to live with this new bodily form for the rest of their lives. By approaching the subject in this manner, Combres communicates that at times, the medical and social models of disability may overlap.

Caroline Cooney's (2007) *Diamonds in the Shadow,* another novel that links disability with war, constructs African disability in a complex manner. First, the story straddles two continents, with the bulk of it taking place in the United States. Her narrative style reflects the cultural reality of both settings, as readers closely follow the lives of five African refugees, expecting the two worlds to collide at some point. Cooney sets up the story in such a way that the reader is as shocked and confused as the Connecticut Refugee committee when Mr. Amabo's bodily form is revealed. He is handless; Mattu, the "son," has a scar; and Alake, the "daughter," "trudged along as if she were only half there or just half a person" (p. 16). As constructed, Cooney emphasizes disability as a social construct with the host characters unable to repress their emotions once they realize they are now saddled with African refugees who may become a burden to the American taxpayer. Because they are so consumed with emotions and feelings of betrayal, they are unable to sense that something is indeed amiss. This draws attention to our collective humanity and raises ethical questions on how well-intentioned members of charitable organizations should act. Should these refugees be deported to the camps in Africa where they risk dying because of Mr. Amabo's deformity or should they be given an opportunity to establish a new home for themselves in the United States?

The four novels are very clear on their stances on disability as their titles insinuate. *The Drummer Boy* (Ekwensi, 1963/6) pitches the blind character as a talented musician. In spite of this, readers are later led to believe that there is something "wrong" with him from the way the other characters either talk about him or interact with him. He needs to be saved from himself, the characters' actions communicate. *Sunjata* (Fontes & Fontes, 2008), on the other hand, conjures an image of a grand leader only for readers to learn later in the novel that he was once a cripple, and for this reason we should admire him even more. *Broken Memory* (Combres, 2009) and *Diamonds in the Shadow* (Cooney, 2007) also send out hints as to the real focus of the novels. Whereas Combres (2009) prepares readers for an exploration of another form of disability that is not talked much about in schools—psychological disability—Cooney (2007) discloses the sociopolitical causes of physical and psychological disability as integrally a side effect of greed. These four titles therefore reinforce themes of disability within African settings or amongst Africans as an unnatural phenomenon, a phenomenon that should be accepted as is or be alleviated through therapy or by supernatural means.

Disability in African American Adolescent Novels

Like in the African novels, disability in the three African American novels discussed in this chapter reflects the two models identified earlier. This is more evident in Paul Griffin's (2009) *The Orange Houses* and Sharon Draper's (2010) *Out of My Mind*. In Woodson's (2007) *Feathers*, although there's a hint at the medical model, the focus is mainly on societal attitudes. Griffin's *The Orange Houses*, set in an urban housing project, opens in a dramatic manner. Jimmi Sixes, an unstable veteran, is hung by a gang. The plot from then on is a countdown to when the vigilantes actually get hold of Jimmi. This shocking opening, while disturbing, becomes a cautionary tale on how innocent characters are marginalized in the novel. Griffin's novel inadvertently invites readers to participate in a larger dialogue around issues of social justice and otherness. Interestingly, the novel is not really about Jimmi. The author simply uses him to introduce us to Tamika, the protagonist. It is Tamika's story and the marginalized characters who give her strength, one of whom is James Semprevivo (AKA Jimmi). Constructed as a fifteen-year-old girl who is hard of hearing because of a bout with meningitis, Griffin exposes the injustices that permeate this urban setting. He does not glorify the disabled experience. Rather, he provides the sordid details that come along with being different. Tamika, like Jimmi and their mutual friend, Fatima, a refugee, live in constant pain, be it emotional or physical. While there is really very little Tamika can do to alleviate the pain that comes with her semi-deafness, Griffin communicates that what aggravates her situation most is her immediate (the people and the institutions that serve the community) society. Tamika's peers shove her into the bathroom: "The bell stabbed her ears" (p. 45); the vigilantes assault her friends who are already scarred from wars.

Griffin (2009) combines both models of disability eloquently in this novel with a gentle tone of disapproval of the dominant hurtful, nonchalant, and insensitive attitudes from the immediate community. When the vigilantes attack Jimmi, "Their hatred stunned him. He knew these men; their brothers, mothers, sisters, daughters, helloed them daily in these streets" (p. 128). They would not listen to the screams of the almost deaf girl in her desperate attempt to stop the assault. Griffin seems to communicate that the actions of the able-bodied people are not humane.

Draper's (2010) *Out of My Mind*, similar to Griffin's (2009) novel, takes a socio-political approach to her subject. The subject of disability is not broached aside. On the contrary, readers are made to understand that the narrator has a problem with words. "I have never spoken one single word. I am almost eleven years old" (p. 2). This is reinforced on page 3: "I can't talk. I can't walk. I can't feed myself or take myself to the bathroom." In Chapter 4, Melody finally names her disability: she has cerebral palsy. But then she describes societal attitudes toward her, noting that when people look at her all they see is

> a girl with dark brown eyes that are full of curiosity. But one of them is slightly out of whack. Her head wobbles a little. Sometimes she drools . . . her legs are very thin . . . [and] her body tends to move on its own agenda, with feet sometimes kicking out unexpectedly and arms occasionally flailing, connecting with whatever is close by . . . (p. 3)

This visual image is so powerful that it is hard for readers to ignore the otherness inscribed in the works. We learn her name only after she has acquainted us with her disability. Perhaps in approaching the subject in this manner, Draper is reminding readers of the way society continuously objectifies persons with disability.

The fascinating aspect of this novel is that Melody tells her own story sharing her joys, challenges, and sorrows, most of which stem directly from who she is. Disability as a medical condition is reinforced heavily. Melody and her family are constantly visiting the hospitals in search of one form of remedy or advice on how to handle her condition. By the middle of the novel her communication problems are partially resolved with the assistance of the technology Meditalker. Her narrative voice is strong and commands our attention in this same manner that she overwhelms her peers via the electronic communicator. Unlike Tamika, who sometimes chooses to retreat into her silent world by simply taking off her hearing aids, Melody prefers to be part of the talking world. With her new communication device, she comes across as arrogant at times, alienating some of her closest allies at school. In the end, there is not much she can do besides continue to fight to be seen, heard, and treated with respect.

Woodson's (2007) *Feathers,* as mentioned earlier, differs in style, tone, and construction of disability from the first two novels. Sean, who is the character with disability, is not the protagonist. Instead, readers hear about his deafness from his younger sister, Frannie. The plot, while not as engaging as the other two, revolves around the daily experiences of Frannie. In typical Woodson fashion, the novel touches on several issues, with disability being one more. She constructs it as an integral part of a family's daily reality. There is nothing really special about the fact that Sean communicates by signing. Her use of sign language as an alternative and acceptable form of communication is apt. Unlike Griffin's (2009) and Draper's (2010) novels, we learn very little about deaf culture. While it remains a story of hope with Frannie looking forward always, as advised by her mother and teacher, Woodson introduces us to the social problems that prevail in her preadolescent world. There is no attempt to cure Sean of his deafness or to objectify him. However, his biggest concern is his inability to date a hearing girl. As he explains to his sister, while he likes hanging out with people like him, he would prefer a world that is not so segregated. This way his options are limitless.

The three African American novels, unlike those about Africans, construct disability as a natural part of life. Whilst Woodson (2007) does not give the cause of Sean's deafness, Tamika's is caused by meningitis, and Melody is born with disability. Consistent with the authors' constructions, there are visible markers of disability in these novels. Characters who are hard of hearing use hearing aids and/or sign language to communicate. These hearing aids become symbols of their otherness in that while they enable these characters to function in a hearing world, they also set them apart as different. Additionally, they cause discomfort, as we notice with Tamika. The wheelchair, already a universal symbol for people with disability, serves as an effective image in Draper's (2010) novel. Melody is wheelchair-bound. While the chair provides her the mobility she needs, it also stigmatizes her as helpless. All these characters would want to communicate with loved ones and sign language facilitates this process in both Griffin's (2009) and Woodson's (2007) novels. Draper's (2010) novel introduces a high-tech communication tool to serve this purpose. These cultural markers are visibly absent in the novels set in Africa or about Africans. But on the whole, the images of disability constructed by all seven authors reflect the basic models of disability that disability theorists often wrestle with, for as Pothier and Devlin (2006) noted, the objective is to create a system whereby everyone is able to participate as full citizens. Some of these authors attempt to do this.

CONCLUSION

Even as the details may vary from author to author and are shaped by cultural nuances depending on whether the story is set in Africa or in the United States, it is imperative that educators ponder why African novels construct disability as "unnatural" and African American novels as "natural." This may be as a result of cultural differences that are shaped by environmental factors. For instance, while African characters are shown to exhibit belief systems that are closely tied to the natural environment, African American characters are constructed with a consciousness that is informed by a more scientific environment. So at once they are similar in terms of skin tone that establishes their otherness in a racialized society; but at the same time, they are different somewhat culturally. Educators need to be aware of this.

Additionally, it is important to be familiar with the constructions of disability that dominate literary texts for youth. Some critical disability theorists would argue that as a minority group that has been ignored in the curriculum, there is the danger of rendering people with disability invisible and voiceless. To be proactive then, educators should make every effort to include diverse literature into their curriculum, for too long we have sat on the fence watching how different groups are marginalized by mainstream dominant cultural practices. It becomes even more pressing to include literature about black characters with disability to begin to understand how these children who are twice marginalized fare in their fictional communities. I now share some ideas for classroom implementation to enable us to create possibilities for all children to participate as contributing citizens in their respective communities.

TEACHING SUGGESTIONS

Critical Thinking, Research, and Writing

- Have students in groups of four research current policies toward people of disabilities. While two perform library and archival research, the other two should interview members of their community on their views of existing policies. After this preliminary research, have groups of students now propose in writing major changes to policies they deem may continue to marginalize people with disabilities.

- Have students become characters in any of the novels. As these characters, they should keep an ongoing log that contains their emotions, questions, and thoughts about the experience. What questions do they have for medical personnel, parents, teachers, and politicians?
- Since disability tends to affect the entire family, students could keep an interactive blog of the experience from a sibling's perspective. What unfair social patterns would they draw attention to? What key ideas would each include in the blog as discussion prompts?

Vocabulary Log

Have students keep a vocabulary log of key terminology associated with disability as is evident in the different novels. Furthermore, students can research synonyms and antonyms of these words.

NOTE

1. Because most are written by an outsider, I refer to this category as novels set in Africa or about Africa instead of as African novels.

CHILDREN/ADOLESCENT BOOKS

Combres, E. (2009). *Broken memory: A story of Rwanda*. Translator: Shelley Tanaka. Toronto, Ontario, Canada: Groundwood.

Cooney, C. B. (2007). *Diamonds in the shadow*. New York, NY: Delacorte Books for Young Readers.

Draper, S. (2010). *Out of my mind*. New York, NY: Atheneum.

Ekwensi, C. (1966). *The drummer boy*. Cambridge, UK: Cambridge University Press.

Fontes, J., & Fontes, R. (2008). *Sunjata, warrior king of Mali: A West African legend*. Illustrated by Sandy Carruthers. Minneapolis, MN: Graphic Universe, Lerner Publishing Group.

Griffin, P. (2009). *The orange houses*. New York, NY: Dial.

REFERENCES

Beach, R., Appleman, D., Hynds, S., & Wilhelm, J. (2006). *Teaching literature to adolescents*. New York, NY: Routledge.

Blaszk, M. (2007). Children's literature needs to portray disability: Three novels and how they show disability. *Humanising Language Teaching, 9*(5), unpaged. Retrieved from http://hltmag.co.uk/

sep07/mart01.htm. This article was originally published in "Problemy Wczesnej Edukacji" Rok II 2006, Numer 2(4), ISSN 1734–1582, Polskie Towarzystwo Pedagogiczne.

Edelsky, C., Smith, K., & Wolfe, P. (2002). A discourse on academic discourse. *Linguistics and Education. 13*(1), 1–38.

Garland-Thomson, R. (Ed.). (1996). *Freakery: Cultural spectacles of the extraordinary body*. New York, NY: New York University Press.

Garland-Thomson, R. (2002). Integrating disability, transforming feminist theory. *NWSA Journal, 4*(3), 1–29. Retrieved from http://www.iupress.indiana.edu/journals/nwsa/nws14–3.html

Ladson-Billings, G., & William, T., IV (1995). Toward a critical race theory of education. *Teachers College Record, 97*(1), 47–68.

Little, G. D. (1986). Handicapped characters in children's literature: Yesterday and today. *Children's Literature Association Quarterly.,10*(4), 18–184. Retrieved from http://muse.jhu.edu/journals/childrens_literature_association_quarterly

Rubin, E., & Watson, E. (1987). Disability bias in children's literature. *The Lion and the Unicorn. 11*(1), 60–67.

Siebers, T. (2008). *Disability theory*. Ann Arbor: University of Michigan.

Snyder, S., Brueggeman, B., & Garland-Thompson, R. (Eds.). (2002). *Disability studies: Enabling the humanities*. New York, NY: Modern Language Association Press.

Smetana, L., Odelson, D., Burns, H., & Grisham, D. L. (2009). Using graphic novels in the high school classroom: Engaging deaf students with a new genre. *Journal of Adolescent and Adult Literacy, 53*(3.4), 228–240.

Yenika-Agbaw, V. (2011). Reading disability in children's literature: Hans Christian Andersen's tales. *Journal of Literary and Cultural Disability, 5*(1), 91–108.

Woodson, J. (2007). *Feathers*. New York, NY: Putnam Juvenile.

CHAPTER 15

Lessons on Discrimination

Historical Fiction and the Culture of Struggle

LAUREN LEWIS

INTRODUCTION

When a teacher begins to examine the African American influence in literature and the arts, he or she may consider writers such as Richard Wright, Anne Moody, Langston Hughes, Alice Walker, and Ralph Ellison. The teacher will quickly notice that most of these writers approached the theme of struggle and discrimination through a personal reflection, forming a nonfictional account of these obstacles.

In the past few decades, it has been fascinating to watch how literature has evolved as new writers have begun to return to the struggles of their ancestors and created a work of *fiction* based on historical events. Writers such as Sharon Draper, the granddaughter of a slave, have created fictional accounts of the slave trade and the struggles during the civil rights movement.

As I began to stumble upon these works, I started to ask myself how I could integrate them into the classroom and how I could use these texts as windows into the historical events that are documented in American literature. These works offer an examination of slavery, civil rights, segregation and discrimination in the South, and a longing to find justice in a society that is anything but equitable.

This historical approach to fiction allows the teacher to access the literature in a whole new way. Students reading the text become engrossed with the dialogue and stylistic structure of the writing, while simultaneously examining and understanding the historical context of it.

These works give teachers license and latitude to bring in comparative pieces of literature for cross-examination as well as provide material for powerful discussions about moral, social, and personal reactions to the writing.

In this chapter, I attempt to share works that I teach in my courses as well as works that I have read and feel could smoothly be integrated in any literary curriculum. I share strategies to implement these works as well as suggestions for comparative study, in which I have included autobiographical works, speeches, and poetry, in order to provide various genres that could be examined alongside a more modern historical novel. In addition, such strategies would enable students to better understand and empathize with African American struggles for equality.

THEORETICAL FRAMEWORK

As I have evolved in my teaching career and immersed myself in the field of literacy education, I have realized the necessity of assessing students' prior knowledge, previewing text, modeling reading strategies, and the importance of integrating highly engaging, authentic literature in order to motivate readers.

Undoubtedly, students' motivation to read increases when the student feels an investment in the unit of study and when it applies to an interest he or she may have. Including historical fiction in the classroom provides students with an opportunity to examine history in a different light. Through these accounts they are able to step into the world of a character, imagining what their life might have been like, the struggles they faced, and how they overcame the obstacles that impeded them. Harper and Brand (2010) write about using literature as a "window" into a previous time or different culture as well as using the writing as a "mirror" to how the themes and conflicts expressed in the writing may mirror our students' own circumstances. They state, "Books can make a difference in dispelling prejudice and building community: not with role models and literal recipes, not with noble messages about the human family, but with enthralling stories that make us imagine the lives of others. . ." (p. 224).

However, I have found African American historical fiction, and fiction in general, lacking in the anthologies that many schools use to teach American literature, which is the focus of my teaching. When I peruse through the table of contents of my college preparatory literature anthology, I find a plethora of nonfictional accounts from Equiano to Wheatley to Douglas as well as poetry from the Harlem Renaissance. However, when I look to implement a fictional text, I am left to choose between a short story by Eudora Welty or Alice Walker. Likewise, in my technical preparatory anthology, I have only the choice of Welty, as hers is the only short story about African American characters included within the work.

While I do not dispute the power of the nonfictional accounts of our early African American writers and the impact these reflections can have on young adults, I also stop to consider students who, like Sharon Draper, are motivated to learn more about the historical anecdotes after being immersed in a fictional account where she could "learn about events from long ago through the eyes of the characters who explained the historical information and made the history come alive… the fiction led me to the facts" ("*Copper Sun*," n.d., para 10).

Therefore, I personally feel that it is of the essence to offer our students historical fiction as a way to understand and reflect upon our past as well as a means of comparative study to the nonfictional accounts that are part of our curriculum and required text.

HISTORICAL FICTION FOR YOUNG ADULTS

Eudora Welty's "A Worn Path"

> . . . it is the journey, the going of the errand, that is the story. (Welty, 1998, p. 815)

This work is one that is included at each of my levels of American literature as we examine modern fiction. The story is set in the Deep South of Mississippi and examines the theme of sacrifice and the importance of family as well as a theme of race and the struggle of the African American, particularly in the South. In his critical essay of this work, Greg Barnhisel (1997) writes that "Her [Welty's] stories deal with race relations on a personal level" (p. 320) and that some critics argue that "Welty's portrayal of the black race through her main character, Phoenix Jackson, is eminently sympathetic" (p. 320).

The story is centered upon protagonist Phoenix Jackson, who makes the arduous trip to town in order to obtain medicine for her grandson, who has an obstinate case after swallowing lye a few years before. Throughout her journey, Phoenix must overcome many obstacles, yet she remains indestructible.

I like to use this story to examine several concepts: the theme of race, the importance of family, as well as the idea of sacrifice. I begin the lesson by giving my students the definition of "sacrifice" as defined in the *Merriam-Webster's Dictionary*. The definition reads as follows: "Destruction or surrender of something given for the sake of something else." I ask students to identity sacrifices that they have made for someone else or that someone has made for them. My goal is to have students develop text-to-self connections, which, according to Rosenblatt (1978), " . . . results when the reader focuses on an awareness on the very personal meaning that he or she is shaping" (as cited in Hancock, 2008, p. 6).

We read the story together as a class, and as we do so, I have students list all of the obstacles that Phoenix has to overcome; these obstacles are a result of her age and her race. As a woman who is speculated to be one hundred years old, Phoenix finds herself exhausted at several points during her journey, having to stop and take a rest or encourage herself to press onward. Once we conclude our reading, I then show students several video clips from YouTube that illustrate family members making sacrifices for one another. The first clip I show is a video created by ESPN about Tim Thomas, a prominent NHL player. His family made sacrifices for him to play the sport that he loves—this included his parents pawning their wedding rings to help offset the cost of his hockey equipment and tournaments. Students relate this sacrifice to Phoenix's act of sacrifice as she journeys to town to get her grandson's medicine.

The second clip that I show is another video created by ESPN about a father, Dick Hoyt, who, like Phoenix, makes a physical sacrifice for his son, as he trains rigorously to compete in triathlons, marathons, and Iron Man challenges with and for his son, Rick, who suffers from cerebral palsy and is confined to a wheelchair. This video is set to a song sung by Christian band Mercy Me titled "I Can Only Imagine." With the use of audio to enhance the powerful image of sacrifice, students are often moved as they watch this.

After we watch these video clips, I ask students to revisit "A Worn Path" and the sacrifice that Phoenix makes. We are able to examine this work for the struggle of Phoenix, but also, as Barnhisel (1997) indicates, "the race relations on a personal level" (p. 321). This story transcends race, as the idea of sacrifice is universal. Welty herself comments, "There are relationships of blood, of the passions and affections, of thought and spirit and deed. This is the relationship between the races. How can one kind of relationship be set apart from others? Like a great root system of an old and long-established growing plant, they are all tangled up together; to separate them you would have to cleave the plant itself from top to bottom" (as quoted in Barnhisel, 1997, p. 321).

Sharon Draper's *Fire from the Rock*

I was a little girl in 1957, and I watched the events in Little Rock unfold at home on our fuzzy little black and white television. Somehow the combination of horror at what I saw, and the courage of those nine students, who were just teenagers, stuck with me (Draper, "*Fire from the Rock*," n.d., para 8).

This novel is a fictional account that centers on the segregation that existed in Little Rock, Arkansas. This work is told through the voice of young Sylvia Patterson, who finds herself in the middle of "the fire" that exists in the South during the 1930s. Sylvia recounts many of the obstacles she and her family have had to overcome—from family disputes regarding how to respond to the racism that the family faces to the possibility of Sylvia being chosen as one of the students to integrate Central High School. The work is filled with poignant reflection and a voice that truly separates Draper as an author. Her ability to convey the struggle felt by a fourteen-year-old girl pulls readers in and leaves them hanging on Sylvia's every word—sympathizing with her and encouraging her forward.

What this work offers is also an examination of the treatment of Sylvia's friend Rachel, whose family is Jewish. Sylvia is able to tell both her own story and Rachel's as well, as both families face discrimination and struggle to press onward, despite their mistreatment. Sylvia finds herself caught in between a rock and a hard stone—wanting to have the courage to take a stand and be one of the ones chosen to integrate Central High School, while also fearing for her life and the lives of her family members, who have been threatened and harassed as a result of the possibility that she may be attending Central High School the following academic year.

This work could certainly be read on its own as a historical examination of the struggle of African Americans to obtain equal rights. While the work is fictional, in that Sylvia's family is fictitious, the description of brutality and the process of integrating Central High School is established based upon documents and images that were taken during this time in our nation's history. However, I would suggest doing a comparative study with this work.

As I was reading this work by Draper, I thought it would pair nicely with Anne Moody's (1968/1992) *Coming of Age in Mississippi*. Moody's work is one of non-fiction, but it offers a perspective that enhances Sylvia's voice in the work by Draper. Moody's account is one that is currently included in my technical preparatory American literature curriculum. In this nonfictional account, Moody provides a detailed description of a sit-in at Woolworth's in Jackson, Mississippi, during the civil rights movement.

The imagery is horrific, as Moody retells how the angry white men and women who were in the store verbally and physically assaulted her and her fellow classmates. Moody also provides a background of her struggle, expressing a desire to win the respect of her family, who do not support her actions of protest. The excerpt ends with a statement about the foreseeable future in which her family member(s) will be killed for her actions and involvement in the demonstration.

There is so much controversy in this excerpt and so much that is left unsaid. Using Paul Fleischman's (1988) *Joyful Noise: Poems for Two Voices* as a model, I have students create their own two-voice poems based on this account by Moody. I ask students to work in pairs and to choose one of the following scenarios for their poem:

1. Depict a conversation between Anne and her mother, who disapproves of her being involved in the protests.
2. Depict a conversation between John Salter and Anne Moody. What advice do you think Moody and the other protestors received before the sit-in? Consider the conversation the two would have with Salter, and provide a list of instructions or encouragement.
3. Write from the police officers and Anne Moody's perspectives about their roles and responsibilities during the sit-in.
4. Write the dialogue that may have occurred between Martin Luther King, Jr., and Anne Moody after he picks up Moody and the other protesters after the sit-in.
5. Imagine you are the hairdresser who has chosen to help Anne; consider the conversation that may have taken place between the two as she helps Anne get cleaned up.

Students work with partners to complete their poems and then read them aloud to the class. We end with a culminating discussion of the perseverance, dedication, and courage exemplified by Moody as she fights for this cause. The decision that Moody is forced to make mirrors the dilemma that Sylvia faces in Draper's work. Both females must choose if they are willing and have the courage to do something that will require extreme bravery and may ultimately cost them their lives or (and perhaps worse) the life of one of their family members. Sylvia vacillates between participating in the integration of Central High School and does in fact want to make a difference. Her family struggles with this choice, as they fear for Sylvia's life, her safety, and her education. They have seen their own son beaten and bruised and left on their doorstep, and they do not want to think about what could happen to their little girl. However, the Pattersons overcome this fear and encourage Sylvia to do what she feels is right, and they offer support for whatever decision that may be.

In Moody's case, her family shares some of the same initial feelings of the Patterson family—why do you have to be involved? Change will come, but let someone else test the waters, so to speak. The Pattersons transcend these thoughts, but in Moody's case, her mother does not. In the excerpt, her mother makes clear that she does not want Anne participating in the sit-ins and protests taking place in Mississippi. Moody cannot accept her mother's argument and feels very passionately that she should do something, anything, to guarantee equal rights for every human being. If you chose to incorporate this account, you could certainly change the options of the two-voice poem and include the following options for students:

1. Depict a conversation between Moody and Sylvia, where Moody encourages Sylvia to be one of the integrators.
2. Depict a conversation where both Moody and Sylvia share their fears about being part of these demonstrations.
3. Depict a conversation between the Pattersons and Moody's mother, offering their different viewpoints and reasons for wanting or not wanting their child to be involved in the demonstrations.

Examining these texts side by side would allow students to further analyze the style and structure of Draper's work in comparison to Moody's. The imagery in both accounts is extremely powerful, as is the voice of the protagonist who must make a difficult decision. Students can also evaluate and research the historical significance and accuracy that is presented in Draper's fictional work to Moody's autobiographical account. The written response of the two-voice poem also "encourages the reader to capture and record her or his personal transaction with literature" (Hancock, 2008, p. 21) and forces students to consider a perspective beyond the text, as they have to infer and empathize, placing themselves in Sylvia's and Moody's position.

Sharon Draper's Slave Narrative: *Copper Sun*

> When I visited the slave castles, where millions of Africans were housed like cattle before being shipped as cargo and sold as slaves, I felt their spirits crying out to me. When I crawled on my hands and knees through the "door of no return," which led from the darkness of the prison to the incomprehensible vastness of a beach, I knew I had to tell the story of just one of those who had passed that way. (Draper, "My Spirit Speaks," n.d.)

In the opening of *Copper Sun* (2006), Draper establishes a context for the reader, as she writes, "I am the granddaughter of a slave" (Author's Note, para. 1). She continues to discuss briefly the story of her grandfather and ends this Author's Note with praise for the novel's main character, Amari, who "carries their spirit. She carries mine [Draper's] as well" (Author's Note, para. 6). Though this work is one of fiction, Draper's voice rings through and tells the horrific, yet optimistic account of a fourteen-year-old slave girl, named Amari, who lives a seemingly "normal" life filled with adventure, curiosity, and the love she has for a village boy, Besa. This happy life is quickly transformed to something grotesque as Amari watches each member of her family die and as she herself struggles to survive. The novel models Oloudah Equiano's voyage on a slave ship, his capture, and ultimately his freedom.

I read the opening pages of this novel aloud to the class, as these pages illustrate Amari's comfortable village life before the arrival of her white captors. I ask students to compare and contrast this account to Equiano's. We generate a list of similarities and differences and discuss the viewpoints of the narrator.

As students read from *The Personal Narrative of Oloudah Equiano* (1789/2004), they learn that Equiano was captured at the age of eleven from his native village in Africa. In the following paragraphs, students are overcome with the graphic imagery that Equiano includes of his time aboard the slave ship. Students are asked to pay particular attention to the sensory images that he describes so prolifically. I also ask students to describe the emotional distress he must have felt, based on the details he chooses to include in this excerpt. Students are quick to notice the number of times Equiano writes, "I now wished for the last friend, Death, to relieve me" (p. 35). As a class, we discuss the implications of such a statement, especially that spoken by an eleven-year-old boy. We conjure images of the pictures painted by Equiano, and as a class, we discuss similar stories of oppression and struggle. At this point in the lesson, I ask students to reflect back upon the introductory passage from Sharon Draper's (2006) fictional account, *Copper Sun*. As a class, we come up with a list of similarities and differences, and I ask students to pay particular attention to the voice of each of the protagonists. I ask students questions such as these: Which is stronger or more compelling and why? What sensory details are used? What pictures came to mind during your reading as a result of these details? I then have students follow up with a piece of creative writing in which they try to mimic the writing style of Draper and Equiano by including images that "show" rather than "tell" a story. I use think-alouds and model such writing strategies as students use their journals to begin their own descriptive passages.

Harper Lee's Portrayal of Racial Injustice: *To Kill a Mockingbird*

> Atticus was right. One time he said you never really know a man until you stand in his shoes and walk around in them. (Lee, 1960, p. 279)

To Kill a Mockingbird (Lee, 1960) is one classic that I cannot imagine *not* teaching in my classroom. Set in the fictional town of Maycomb, Alabama, Lee loosely bases this work upon the Scottsboro Trials, which took place in Scottsboro, Alabama, in the 1930s. In this highly controversial case, nine young African American boys were accused of raping two white women aboard a train. The older female, known for her reputation as a prostitute, was most likely taking this younger girl with her across state lines for the intended purpose of prostitution, an act that was illegal at the time. The nine boys were tried by an all-white jury, found guilty, and after many appeals, many were later released.

Using this historical context, Lee creates a similar scenario of a man wrongly accused. Tom Robinson is to be commissioned to court on charges of allegedly raping Mayella Ewell, an impoverished, unfortunate youth who fuels society's prejudice rather than taking responsibility for her actions, which many believe resulted in an attempt to seduce the young Robinson. Told from the perspective of a young girl, Jean Louise "Scout" Finch, the novel is a classic in that it allows the reader to examine the questions of a naïve child who does not fully understand the injustice that exists during the time in the Jim Crow South. Scout, instead, becomes the target of her classmates' bullying and insults, as her father has agreed to defend this African American man, Tom Robinson. The novel is intertwined with stories of childhood games, mischief, and curiosity, but the focus repeatedly comes back to the town of Maycomb, its prejudice toward African Americans, and how Atticus Finch tries to instill a sense of morality and acceptance in his children.

John Grisham's *A Time to Kill*

I would like to preface this selection by commenting that the opening of this novel is extremely graphic. For that reason, I would suggest incorporating this text only with a mature audience of students. The following pages in which the court trial takes place become less explicit than the opening and the details of the rape are restated by the victim; however, the opening may be difficult for some students to read.

This work takes place in Clanton, Mississippi, and tells the story of the brutality that innocent ten-year-old Tonya faced walking home one day. She is sexually and physically assaulted by two white brothers who are referred to as the "Cobb boys" by the townspeople and who are known for their drunken tirades. Tonya is found and brought home to her family after her attack and therein the investigation begins. Tonya is able to remember the truck that she was taken in, and it is obvious that the Cobb boys are responsible for her assault. Given that the novel takes place in the segregated South, the plot quickly thickens as the reader begins to realize that for all intents and purposes, justice will not be properly served. A lawyer by the name of Jake Brigance takes on the case; however, after facing obstacles in the courtroom as well as at the hands of the police department, Brigance begins to somewhat predict the horrific events as they begin to unfold—an enraged father (Carl Lee) who is unwilling to sit back yet again and watch a member of his community exploited by the very offices that are supposed to offer protection. Tonya's father enters the courtroom armed with a gun and takes justice into his own hands, executing the Cobb boys.

Brigance's job then becomes defending Carl Lee and trying to argue that his actions were not premeditated but extemporaneous. Through this novel, Grisham's craft for explaining the due process of law and the rhetoric of the courtroom allows this novel to read like an episode of the highly praised *Law and Order,* captivating readers and drawing them into this story, demanding one to examine this question: What would you do? In comparing and contrasting *To Kill a Mockingbird* and *A Time to Kill,* I think that you could have very powerful discussions and debates within the classroom. In one text we have an innocent black man accused by a white woman and thereby sentenced to death as soon as the alleged rape was reported. Robinson, like Carl Lee, takes matters into his own hands and tries to escape from prison. As Atticus states when referring to Tom's attempted escape, "I guess Tom was tired of taking white men's chances and preferred to take his own" (Lee, 1960, p. 236).

In contrast, in *A Time to Kill,* a young black girl is brutalized, and the likelihood of the two men who assaulted her, since they are white, receiving a severe sentence is low. Her father decides to deal with the matter as he feels he ought to, and he kills her two assailants. This provides a great counterdiscussion wherein one can juxtapose these two cases that take place in the segregated South. Teachers could pose the following questions to students:

- What is society's role in both of these cases?
- What is the court's role?
- How can the integrity of the court be upheld when its jurors and/or judge are/is prejudiced?
- Whose job is it to intervene when it appears that one will not receive a fair trial?
- Are there other historical trials where similar instances have occurred?

These questions provide a text-to-self, text-to-text, and text-to-world connection, as well as thoughts for discussion and reflection in allowing students to examine the struggles of the individual to transcend society's prejudice and the difficulty of doing so.

Langston Hughes' Theme of Individuality

"Theme for English B," composed by Hughes (1994), is one that he completed in response to an assignment he received in his college English class. In this poem, the reader learns of Hughes' upbringing and his passion for life. Hughes also touches upon the theme of race, as he lives during a time when African Americans were not guaranteed equal rights. In this work, Hughes illustrates how he loves to dance, listen to music, and how he is black, and his professor white—yet they share something in common, as they are connected to one another by the very nature of the class. The struggle that Hughes poses in this work is the difficulty in understanding others—their point of view and their circumstance.

I use this poem to illustrate the perception one can project through verse. Students are asked to compose a self-portrait poem in which they include details of their own life and struggles they may have encountered and overcome. Students are given license to write free verse and can choose how they wish to structure their self-portrait poem, which must consist of at least twenty lines. Students then share their poems aloud with the class. To encourage the focus of the theme of struggle, I ask students to consider one personal challenge that they have had to face or overcome, much as Hughes did in his work.

CONCLUSION

The works that I have provided in the preceding pages are poignant accounts of the theme of struggle and the historical fiction that details these injustices and, in some cases, the triumph over adverse conditions. Each account relates an emotional and personal story that captivates the reader and allows teachers and students alike to respond at a deeper level. I believe these works can be interwoven into any curriculum in which the focus is to explore individual struggle, conflict, and the appreciation and empathy for the situations others have had to face.

It is certainly a challenge to examine our own curriculums and seek to add diversity, a relevant perspective, and to consider the factual and emotional responses students have to text. Engaging students in the reading process can be facilitated with the use of powerful literature, social learning opportunities, written and oral response, and certainly in asking students to make connections to their own lives by stepping into the roles of the characters, seeking to understand their struggles and how these may mirror situations in which they have found themselves. I have ended this chapter with other suggestions for both fictional and nonfictional accounts that you could use as a piece of comparison or that can be taught on its own. I hope that you examine the roles that these works can have in the classroom and upon the individuals who read them.

CONTEMPORARY AFRICAN AMERICAN TEXTS

The Color Purple by Alice Walker (1982), Grades 10–12

This work by Walker follows the life of Celie, who is abused by her father and then forced to marry an older man, who she refers to as Mister, who also abuses her. The novel contains many letters that Celie writes to her sister Nettie, a missionary, of the trauma that she faces. As the novel progresses, Celie is able to find her voice and becomes a strong independent woman who is beholden to no one and who has finally mustered the strength to stand on her own.

The Bluest Eye by Toni Morrison (1993), Grades 10–12

This is Morrison's first novel, and it tells the story of Pecola Breedlove, who is an eleven-year-old African American. Pecola longs for her eyes to be blue—the color she associates with beauty. This fictional account tells more than just the story of a child wanting to "fit in" but also the story of understanding and appreciating one's background, denouncing the prejudices of society, and the struggle for acceptance, which transcends race.

"Ain't I a Woman?" by Sojourner Truth (1994), Grades 7–12

Sojourner Truth delivered this extemporaneous speech in May 1851 at a Woman's Rights Convention in Akron, Ohio. After listening to several men discuss the reasons why women should not be permitted to vote, Truth made her way to the podium to state her views to the contrary, in which she expressed the struggles she, as a woman, has had to overcome and the struggle for women to obtain voting rights.

Sojourner Truth's "Step-Stomp-Stride" by Andrea Davis Pinkney and Brian Pinkney (2009), Grades 7–12

In this work, students learn more about Sojourner Truth—that her name had been Isabella Baumfree and she was always very motivated and sought to do more with her life. She ran away from her master, John Dumont, and was taken in by a Quaker couple, who were abolitionists. They offered her a place of safety and then purchased her freedom. Baumfree then went to New York, where she changed her name to Sojourner Truth. The book ends with her famous speech, "Ain't I a Woman?" which provides a great way to study the speech in the context of understanding more about Truth herself.

Black Boy by Richard Wright (1945), Grades 10–12

Many American literature anthologies include excerpts of this autobiographical work by Wright. In my honors level anthology, the excerpt included is from Chapter 11, where Wright is persuaded to participate in a "Five Dollar Fight" against a fellow African American as a mode of entertainment for the white coworkers. This example is one of the many in his work in which he examines the prejudice he faced in the South and the behavior that he succumbed to as a way of coping with the injustices he faced. You could integrate the entire work in your curriculum or include an excerpt for close examination, as many textbooks do.

The Negro Speaks of Rivers by Langston Hughes, illustrated by E. B. Lewis (2009), Grades 7–12

This picture book was released in 2009 and includes the full texts of Hughes' powerful poem "The Negro Speaks of Rivers." The poem points to the struggles of African Americans through the centuries while also highlighting many of the civilizations of which they have been a part. Hughes references the Euphrates, the Congo, the Pyramids by the Nile, and the Mississippi, chronicling the voyage of the African American from Egypt to the New World. The illustrations by Lewis enhance the powerful words and tone of the poem, enabling students to better appreciate the significance of the struggle of many African Americans.

REFERENCES

Barnhisel, G. (1997). A worn path. In K. Wilson (Ed.), *Short stories for students* (Vol. 2, pp. 320–322). Detroit: Gale.

Draper, S. (2006). *Copper sun.* New York, NY: Atheneum.

Draper, S. (2007). *Fire from the rock.* New York, NY: Dutton Children's Books.

Draper, S. (n.d.). My spirit speaks. Retrieved from http://sharondraper.com/

Draper, S. (n.d.). *Copper sun:* Intro, summary, and general questions. Retrieved from http://sharondraper.com/

Draper, S. (n.d.). *Fire from the rock:* Intro, summary, and general questions. Retrieved from http://sharondraper.com/

Equiano, O. (2004). *The interesting narrative of the life of Olaudah Equiano or, Gustavas Vassa, the African.* New York, NY: The Modern Library.

Fleischman, P. (1988). *Joyful noise: Poems for two voices.* New York, NY: HarperTrophy.

Grisham, J. (1989). *A time to kill.* New York, NY: Island Books.

Hancock, M. R. (2008). *A celebration of literature and response: Children, books, and teachers in k–8 classrooms.* Upper Saddle River, NJ: Pearson Education.

Harper, L. J., & Brand, S. T. (2010, Summer). More alike than different: Promoting respect through multicultural books and literacy strategies. *Childhood Education, 86*(4), 224–233.

Hughes, L. (1994). "Theme for English B." In *Selected poems.* (Original work published 1959) Retrieved from http://www.poetryfoundation.org/archive/poem.html?id=177397

Hughes, L. (2009). *The negro speaks of rivers.* New York, NY: Hyperion.

Lee, H. (1960). *To kill a mockingbird.* New York, NY: Warner Books.

Moody, A. (1992). *Coming of age in Mississippi.* New York, NY: Bantam Dell.

Morrison, T. (1993). *The bluest eye.* New York, NY: Plume Printing.

Pinkney, A. D., & Pinkney, B. (2009). *Sojourner truth's "step-stomp-stride."* New York, NY: Disney Jump at the Sun Books.

Rosenblatt, L. M. (1978). *The reader, the text, the poem: The transactional theory of literacy work.* Carbondale: Southern Illinois University Press.

Truth, S. (1851, 1994). "Ain't I a woman?" In A.N. Applebee et al. *Literature and language: American literature* (pp. 348–349). Evanston, IL: McDougal Littell.

Walker, A. (1982). *The color purple*. New York, NY: Pocket Books.

Welty, E. (1998). *Stories, essays, & memoir*. New York, NY: Literary Classics of the United States.

Wright, R. (1945). *Black boy*. New York, NY: Harper & Row.

CHAPTER 16

Keeping Hope Alive

Reading and Discussing Adolescent Novels and Modern-Day Miracles

BARBARA A. WARD & DEANNA DAY

Hope is the thing with feathers
That perches in the soul,
And sings the tune—without the words,
And never stops at all.

> —EMILY DICKINSON (1924, P. 116).

If, as poet Emily Dickinson (Johnson, 1890) would have it, hope is, indeed, "the thing with feathers," it is somehow hard to see how that hope flutters on, even against the harshest winds. Hope may well be the most precious commodity that friendship, education, or literature can provide to a child or a teen faced with bleak surroundings. It can counterbalance the hopelessness often fostered by the nightly news and daily newspapers that so frequently focus on heart-rending stories of lives gone wrong.

Here are items from recent headlines:

- In Chicago, 2009, teens savagely beat one high school student to death with railroad ties as he walks home.
- Another teen microwaves her baby to punish the child's father.
- Yet another young teen father burns his own baby in the microwave.

But it isn't just the reports of violence, early death, and anger that fuel the hopelessness. Often, it is the lives that most live, the environment through which they are forced to navigate, even the lowering of expectations on the part of their teachers that alienate many of today's youth. The numbers of black male teens who are incarcerated and who die at the hands of others continue to rise, and generations speak of an entire age group that has been lost. Many of today's teens struggle with poverty, abuse, and neglect, often being forced to' shoulder familial, financial, and emotional responsibilities long before they are ready to do so.

While some classrooms and schools rely on stale, scripted curriculum in order to raise test scores, others turn to authentic literature and trusted authors whose books talk to young adolescents. Jacqueline Woodson's picture books and novels speak powerfully to young readers on many levels. Her characters face issues with which student readers are familiar, yet her books consistently offer hope and examples of strong family units. Education and self-expression—whether it be in the poems written in *Locomotion* (2003) or the songs written and sung in *After Tupac and D Foster* (2008)—offer readers a way to soothe their souls and endure challenges. These creative efforts also offer solutions to situations that seem almost overwhelming. In a world where hope is a scarce commodity, Woodson's books somehow distill hope, spreading its message ever outward. While most of her novels seem to take place in New York City, the picture books seem to evoke the Deep South and certainly remind readers of rural areas.

In this chapter, we describe how we critically read and discussed some of Jacqueline Woodson's novels with eighth graders who live in a small northeastern town in Louisiana. We wondered what middle school students would think about exploring an African American author who writes books about characters who are experiencing similar, yet different circumstances that they themselves face. Would students recognize that there is hope for everyone, including themselves?

AUTHOR STUDIES

Jacqueline Woodson is a highly acclaimed author of children's and young adult literature. In 2006 she won the Margaret A. Edwards Award honoring an author, as well as a specific body of work, for significant and lasting contribution to young adult literature. It also recognizes an author's work in helping adolescents become aware of themselves and addressing questions about their role and importance in relationships, society, and in the world.

Woodson's writing spans 20 years, having garnered much attention and many awards. *Coming on Home Soon* (2007) was a Caldecott Honor Medalist, *Feathers*

(2007) and *Show Way* (2005) both won the Newbery Honor Medal, and *Locomotion* (2003) and *Miracle's Boys* (2000) received Coretta Scott King Honor and Medalist distinction, respectively. *After Tupac and D Foster* (2008) also was named a Newbery Honor winner as well as one of five finalists for the Amelia Elizabeth Walden Award, whose criteria includes a positive approach to life as well as high literary quality and widespread teen appeal.

Young readers can come to understand Jacqueline Woodson's books by reading her speeches or interviews in which she has participated. For example, Caswell (2005) interviewed Woodson and found that she thinks about her audience: "For young people, adolescence is the greatest tragedy, so seeing some of themselves reflected in the lives of others gives their own lives some sort of value and truth" (p. 10). Casement (2003) inquired about Woodson's writing process. Woodson explained that she takes one sentence at a time, which eventually leads her to somewhere. She admitted that writing is hard work, but the difficulty makes it rewarding. Woodson (2007) explained in a speech, "I think about the people in the story constantly—what's going to happen to them? I never outline, never know where a story is going, never know how it's going to get there" (p. 123).

Woodson's culturally rich stories with believable characters are widely read and often taught in classrooms at various levels. For example, Napoli and Ritholz (2009) used Woodson's book *Locomotion* (2003) to motivate a small group of middle school students. These authors found that this verse novel piqued their readers' curiosities toward poetry and inspired them to use different poetry forms such as haiku and epistle. This exploration stimulated the young adolescents in reading and writing. Regarding this current research, Barbara hoped that reading Jacqueline Woodson's books would do the same thing—stimulate reading, writing, and thinking—with her eighth graders.

The majority of Woodson's books are contemporary realistic fiction. Brooks, Browne, and Hampton (2008) note that African American youth gain self-affirmation and identify from stories about others who look like them racially because they are able to see and understand themselves. These authors conducted an afterschool book club to enhance critical thinking skills with some adolescent black girls. They found that the study participants engaged in discussions about colorism, body image, status, and identity—topics that helped the young girls understand a novel and position themselves as readers.

Author studies are a great way to expose students to a variety of books written by the same author. Readers are given the opportunity to get to know an author intimately by exploring their website for biographical information and facts, helping students view the author as a person. For middle level readers, author studies open the door to understanding an author's craft and writing. Students can identify and categorize the variety of elements of style within the author's books. For students who struggle with reading and writing, they may not perceive the classroom to be personally relevant to their needs. Author studies could provide students the opportunity to read books by the same author, providing common discussion topics where they can make personal connections, have real-world interactions, and make personal reading preferences (Day, 2004). Reading, talking, and exploring about an author typically spark an interest in reading more books and exploring other authors.

Daniels' (2006) work with literature circles reinforces the importance of implementing discussion in our classrooms, which is perhaps the most essential ingredient for igniting the interest of young adolescent readers. Hill, Noe, and King (2003) suggest that literature circles are formed on the basis of students' selections. Teachers provide four or five copies of several novels, and students choose the book they want to read and begin preparing for the discussion that is guided by students' insights, observations, and questions. Through this dialogue, different interpretations and understandings are constructed and multiple meanings are made (Rosenblatt, 1995).

Reader response theorist Louise Rosenblatt (2005) sees reading instruction as necessitating connection. Reading involves growth, a process that occurs only when readers find books that evoke personal responses based on their own experiences. She writes, "Without this, literature remains something inert, to be studied in school and henceforth avoided. But when books arouse an intimate personal response, the developmental process can be fostered" (Rosenblatt, 2005, p. 67). Consequently, Rosenblatt urges teachers to help their students find connections to their own lives in books. By finding connections, perhaps they will find hope and alternate solutions to the challenges in their lives.

SCHOOL CONTEXT

Barbara taught in a state-mandated and test-driven middle school in its fifth year of academic probation. Located in Louisiana, this middle school was considered an academically unacceptable school (AUS) due to students' test scores on the annual Louisiana Educational Assessment Program, and because of its designation, it required its English language arts teachers to follow basal texts that are heavily prescribed, using literature anthologies consisting primarily of excerpts from longer pieces of literature. Schools are placed on AUS status after several years of low performance scores, provided support in the form of a distinguished educator in order for them to reach state testing standards, and given five years to reach their goals. Schools failing to reach the goals are taken over by the state, and the school staff is replaced. The curriculum and the teaching methods are disheartening and unappealing to students. Students have come to consider the only purpose for reading to be finding the answers for questions or in order to pass the state-mandated standardized test.

The town in which the students reside stretches along a bayou, with white and black segregated neighborhoods. With little industry and a seemingly bleak economic future, many older teens often become affiliated with gangs and the violence and cynicism often associated with them. Many middle grade students see no way out of their present circumstances, and school has little relevance. The parish in which the school is situated has only 11,385 residents, and its revenue comes primarily from agriculture. The town itself has only 9,000 residents, 74.8 percent of whom are black and 22.5 percent white. The median household income in the town is $22,603, almost half of the typical household income in the state. The school itself served 425 students during the 2009–2010 academic year; 93 percent of the students were African American, and 96 percent received free lunch.

SEARCHING FOR HOPE

Since students were becoming increasingly disenchanted with school, Barbara turned in desperation to picture books because they are short and often capture students' attention in a way that longer texts fail to do. Subsequently, she read aloud and facilitated whole class discussions on the following picture books by Jacqueline Woodson: *Coming on Home Soon* (2004), *The Other Side* (2001), *Show Way* (2005), *Sweet, Sweet Memory* (2000), and *Visiting Day* (2002). These books provided background information on Woodson's books and themes (see Figure 1 on p. 249).

After this introduction, students were invited to participate in a voluntary lunchtime book club to explore Jacqueline Woodson and a couple of her novels: *Miracle's Boys* (2000), *If You Come Softly* (1998), *Locomotion* (2003), *After Tupac and D Foster* (2008), and *Peace, Locomotion* (2009). Barbara was unable to use classroom time for the novel discussions because of the AUS status.

The students quickly ate their lunch in the cafeteria and then came to the classroom to read and talk. Often, they simply took their lunch trays and dumped the contents in the trash can, and when they ate the meals, they only stayed in the cafeteria for five to ten minutes. Typically, the discussion began with a recap of what had been discussed the prior day. When a new book was being introduced, students examined the book cover for clues about the book's content. The discussions lasted for 30 minutes every day for five weeks. The students often read the books before coming to the lunchtime discussions, but at other times, they relied on the lunchtime for reading. As students read the novels, they marked areas they wanted to talk about with sticky notes. Students had response journals in which they wrote their thoughts and connections to the books. Artistic and musical responses were encouraged as well.

THE LUNCHTIME GROUP

The six members of the lunchtime group (all pseudonyms) came from three different eighth-grade classes. While two of them typically made the honor roll, the other four earned grades that put them on academic probation. All of them liked to read aloud, but none considered themselves to be readers or "schoolboys" or "schoolgirls," a term of derision used for those who followed all the school rules and completed all their assignments diligently. All of them had school suspensions on their records.

Ashley, 14, was more interested in spreading the latest news than school, and her already tenuous hold on an academic future seemed to wane after a life-changing event occurred. She became pregnant during the school year and was forced by her mother to have an abortion. This depressed her since she and the baby's father had made plans for their young family. Ashley's mother had given birth to Ashley when she herself was a teen, and she was determined that the same fate would not happen to Ashley. In order to keep tabs on her daughter, she required Ashley to call her whenever she was moving from point to point.

Bridney, 14, had given birth to a son at the end of the year and was balancing school and home responsibilities since she did not live with the baby's father, who was still in high school. She often came to class tired since the baby kept her awake at night, and she stayed to herself most of the time. It had been a tough year for Bridney, whose brother was shot two days before the academic year began, allegedly the victim of drug lords who had infiltrated the area.

Katie, 13, had moved back into the area to stay with her grandmother while her mother was incarcerated for a felony. Because of her record and work history, her mother cleaned the rooms in a local motel despite the fact that she had been trained as an accountant. Her mother had just reentered Katie's life to take over her upbringing from her grandmother. Katie had artistic talents and was usually called upon when the others lacked creative inspiration. When she first began eighth grade, she spent the class periods hiding behind other students and sleeping. But she had opinions on the stories being read and liked to share her thoughts. She was the only white student in the group.

Kemberly, 14, was well-liked by her classmates. After spending much of seventh grade and the beginning of eighth grade fighting with others, including boys, often in order to protect her younger sisters or to defend her mother's reputation, Kemberly had turned completely around and was focused on school. Although she still flirted with the boys in the class and could quickly fling back an insult to anyone who bothered her, she had learned to channel her energies in a positive direction. She lived with her grandmother, who had taken in Kemberly and her two younger sisters when her mother's boyfriend was unable to tolerate them and had beaten Kemberly severely.

Michael, 17, had been retained several times, and this was his second time in eighth grade. His academic performance was spotty, varying from an A in English language arts one semester to a D in another. Claiming that he had had a rough night, he often came to class, closed his eyes, and tried to rest. He had a longtime girlfriend who broke up with him after 15 months of monogamy because she "wanted to be a free spirit." To Michael's surprise, her need to be free expressed itself in her having sex with not one, but three, different boys less than a week after their breakup. Michael turned to poetry, reading, writing, and singing to express his anguish and disappointment.

Princess, 17, was also a teen mother, raising a daughter while still living with her mother and younger brother. She had been retained several times due to excess absences. Her relationship with her mother was fraught with complications, epitomized by her refusal to call her mother by that moniker, choosing to call her by her name, denoting the more equal relationship they had. Her mother often expected Princess to take care of her little brother while she was occupied with other tasks.

KEEPING HOPE ALIVE

The lunchtime discussion group was familiar with reading material aloud, stopping ever so often to react to what students had just read, talking about it, and then writing about it, since Barbara often conducted the eighth-grade English language arts class in the same way. At first, when she stopped her students and asked them to think about what they had just read and what it meant, they were puzzled, annoyed, and even angry. They just wanted to finish the assignment and get done. One student, D. J., even said, "If you'd quit stopping us when we're reading, we could get this stuff done and move on to what matters. This is just school, you know. We've got more important stuff in our lives." The more important stuff to which he referred was secretly texting others on cell phones they weren't allowed to have in school, rehashing the weekend's social events, and planning for the next weekend's events. School seemed of little relevance, and the students apparently had never been encouraged to question what they were reading or make connections to the text.

Over time, they grew accustomed to large group discussions about the stories in the literature anthology and being encouraged to express their thoughts. By the time the handful of students joined the lunchtime discussions, they were familiar with this practice and utterly comfortable in saying the most personal things. They would knowingly smile when they finished an especially memorable passage, expecting to be asked to record their thoughts before speaking them. The students were given the books and told to read a certain number of pages, usually a chapter, each night. Some read the assigned reading and more while others forgot and relied on the lunchtime discussions to fill in any blanks in their knowledge about the story.

After settling in their seats in a circle, Barbara would ask for a volunteer to read or share a passage from the book that spoke to them. At first hesitantly and then with growing confidence, the students began to share their thoughts and to choose passages they liked. They noted how Woodson used certain words over and over for effect, and they also made note of her use of names to reveal personal characteristics or to illustrate how others regarded the character. They were intrigued, for instance, with the name of the Jesus-boy in *Feathers* and New Charlie in *Miracle's Boys*. Kemberly was quick to pick up on the fact that New Charlie wasn't the same brother who left for the boys' home. By having Lafe call him New Charlie, she explained, Woodson was allowing Lafe to distance himself emotionally from New Charlie, just as his brother had already done to him, even pretending that he didn't hear anyone talking when Lafe tried to speak to him. Although they are brothers still, she said, they really aren't close any more.

Finding Hope by Understanding Texts

The students reacted particularly strongly to *After Tupac and D Foster* and *Miracle's Boys*. *After Tupac and D Foster* is the story of three preteen girls living in New York City. D Foster is a girl who steps off the bus in Queens one day, drawn by the trees in the neighborhood, and starts a friendship that extends to music. Many teens spend hours listening to the music of Tupac Shakur. His lyrics speak to them in powerful ways, and they are convinced that he sees them, sees into their hearts in a way that their family members are unable to do. Life isn't easy for the three friends. Neeka has a mother who keeps a close watch on her and plenty of family responsibilities. The narrator—who is never named—is trying to survive. D Foster herself lives with a foster mother until the time her own mother can reclaim her. All three have secrets, but they have coping mechanisms as well. In fact, it is D's contention that each of us has a purpose, and throughout the book the girls try to find their own purposes. The narrator wants more for herself than what has been put on her shoulders, and she reads and studies.

As soon as the lunchtime group began reading the book, several wondered who Tupac was and why the book was about him. Kemberly asked, "Who is that guy? Is he famous or something? What'd he do? I've heard his name before."

Michael was glad to provide insider information, quickly googling "Tupac" and begging to play "Brenda's Got a Baby" for the group. Michael listened to the music and lyrics, shook his head sadly, and remarked, "That's deep, man, that's deep."

The other students gathered around the computer where Michael was sitting and watched the video again. "Naw, that's not just deep," said Kemberly. "That's real. That kind of stuff happens all the time around here." She proceeded to describe some of the messed up relationships in her own neighborhood.

Fame and attractiveness appealed to the students as they all remarked on how handsome the Tupac depicted on the book's cover was. Some were puzzled about why he was on the book's cover and part of its title when he wasn't even a character in the book. "But he is in the book," Michael explained impatiently. "His music's all in the book. Look? It's like this: When I'm chilling in my crib, I just have to have my music. It makes the bad stuff go away."

The others nodded in recognition, agreeing that music can have a calming effect at times while at other times incite action. "This video makes me wanna go slap somebody," Kemberly said. "It makes me want to tell everybody—all the young girls—to watch out for him [the sexual predator] because he takes advantage of young girls. They don't know better, and I gotta warn them."

Not surprisingly, music was important to the students; in fact, the music of Tupac drew the discussion participants deeper into *After Tupac and D Foster*, and all of them shared their newfound respect for this musical artist with other classmates, showing them YouTube videos and discussing his lyrics with siblings. Michael, for instance, returned to the lunch group after talking about Brenda's situation with his older brother and proudly told them, "He knew all about Tupac." His brother had proceeded to share additional songs by Tupac and pointed out how his music lived long after he had been killed.

When the lunchtime group read and discussed *Miracle's Boys*, one passage about New Charlie's fondness for strays, especially the stray dogs he saw along the streets of their New York neighborhood, evoked much response and showed the students' ability to empathize with others. Lafe reflects on the brother New Charlie before spending time in the boys' home, and he remembers how upset New Charlie was when he saw that a stray dog had been hit by a car and he tried but failed to save it. The students began discussing the strays that eke out an existence on their own town's streets.

Ashley: I see stray dogs and cats out on the street near where I live
           all the time. They just walk the street 'cause they have
           nowhere else to go and they have nothing to eat.

Katie: It makes me feel bad because I know they be needing

	somewhere to go and something to eat. They need some-thing. They look so hungry.
Bridney:	Yeah, they're all skin and bones, and you can see their ribs and everything.
Kemberly:	Strays don't have any family or friends or a home or even a place to lay their head down in or clean clothes to wear. I think they're lonely. It's hard not to have a home.
Bridney:	You talking about people who are strays?
Kemberly:	Yeah, I think there are people who are strays who don't have anywhere to go or can't find a place to stay.
Princess:	Huh! There are a lot of strays down the block. These men I know hang out on the street, just walking from block to block. They don't have any home, and they stay in that old house, that one that nobody has stayed in for awhile. I wonder where they belong.
Michael:	I wonder how they got to be strays.
Bridney:	What do you mean?
Michael:	I just wonder. I mean, I wonder where they come from and who they left behind. I wonder who loved them. Didn't somebody once love them?
Katie:	Are you talking about the animals or the people?
Michael:	Both. Nobody is born a stray so I wonder how they got that way.
Bridney:	I wish they could have a home where they are warm and safe and be taken care of.
Katie:	If I had a bunch of money, I'd make a shelter where all these strays, all these cats and dogs, could have a home and somebody to love. Everybody needs to have somebody to love.
Kemberly:	Everybody needs somebody to love them too. I'm glad I have my grandma.

During the lunchtime discussions, these adolescents tried to understand portions of the different novels together. Students retold parts of the books, their favorite scenes or events that were meaningful. Vygotsky's (1978) concept of zone of proximal development was evidenced as the students helped each other understand the books they were reading. Further, the transcripts testify as to how the eighth graders grew in their understandings of the texts as they conversed. Together, this lunchtime group made sense of the books and had what Rosenblatt (1995) called a "lived through experience."

Finding Hope by Making Connections

Miracle's Boys touched the students deeply since the events at its heart mirrored their own life experiences. The novel revolves around three boys whose parents have both died unexpectedly, the father as the result of hypothermia after saving a white woman and her dog, the mother through the consequences of diabetes. A case could be made for good health care since both die as the result of neglect in some respects. The oldest brother has given up his career and education in order to keep the family together while the middle brother, New Charlie, has just returned from detention after a robbery and seems headed down a dangerous path. The youngest brother, Lafe, is filled with guilt over the loss of their mother and the sacrifices his oldest brother has made to take care of him.

In one particular discussion after reading a passage in which Tyree spends time with Lafe and tells him he loves him, Bridney shared her thoughts on how difficult it is to share emotions with others, especially parents. Expressing honest emotion, especially positive feelings of love, to parents somehow seems awkward. Her comment leads the other teens to discuss their experiences with expressing their feelings to the adults in their lives. The discussion segues into an assessment of the students' own mothers and their sometimes strife-ridden relationships with the women in their lives. A couple of girls even noted that they became the moms in their families, taking care of siblings while their mothers were in prison, messed up on drugs, or running around the countryside having fun.

Bridney: I think sometimes it's hard to say "I love you" to your parents. You can say it easier to your boyfriend and stuff.

Princess: Yeah. I don't say I love you or whatever to Kitty or Harriet or Mom or whatever I call her because there's so much that has gone between the two of us, that I just can't.

Katie: I don't know how you can say that. Your mom is your MOM.

Princess: Yeah, but we've been through some stuff, and she just wasn't always there for me.

Katie: I've only had my mom for one year. This is the first year I've had my mom. She's trying so hard right now. This is the first year that I've been with her. She was always gone with her drugs or guys or whatever, and then when she was in prison, I went to see her, and I told her I loved her, but I

	don't know. I don't think I loved her then because I really didn't know her, but I still said it. I guess I think you should love whoever is your mom no matter what.
Kemberly:	My mom was the same way too. She was always traveling and running around and messed up on drugs or men. She was all the time leaving us alone, and I had to take care of everything. I had to take care of my sisters and get them up and make breakfast and get them off to school and clean up and everything. I felt like I was their mom. I've been a mom for a long time. I had to do everything and make sure everything was under control. There was just so much that I had to do. That's why I missed so much school that year. Then when we came to live with my grandma, I still felt like I had to control everything and do everything. I had to learn that I don't have to do everything.
Princess:	She was always leaving me and doing stuff. And I had to take care of all the kids. Finally, I got tired of it, and I said, "I'm not doing this. I'm not these kids' mom."
Bridney:	Yeah! Yeah! My mom left me one time for five months, and I had to be in charge. I didn't even know where she was. But she only did that once, and when she came back, she took over again.

In another discussion inspired by Woodson's description of the death of Milagro, the boys' mother, and her subsequent funeral, the students reacted passionately and angrily. The passage in which New Charlie attends the funeral with guards while wearing the orange prison suit, struck a nerve for several students who saw that treatment of New Charlie as embarrassing and unnecessary.

Kemberly:	That's just shameful. It's just a shame.
Michael:	Awww! They didn't need to do him that way. Uh huh! They wrong for that!
Ashley:	Man! His mama is dead, and they got him all tied up and guarded like he's gonna do something crazy. That's just stupid. All he did was rob a candy store. It just don't make no sense. They just don't make no sense.
Bridney:	When my brother's [funeral] service was held, the same thing happened. I had this other brother, and he was in prison, and they let him out. I was crying in the front of the room, and I looked up, and I saw him, and I wanted to go

	give him a hug. But there was two guards with him. They wouldn't let me near him. My mama was so mad, and I was just so hurt.
Katie:	What'd you do?
Bridney:	I just smiled at him and waved at him, and after he left, we went home and ate. Everybody in the neighborhood had brought us all these good things to eat. That was some good food too.
Princess:	Yeah, we still can get some good times rolling and eating and hanging out with folks even when bad stuff happens.
Michael:	Maybe folks know that food, good food, heals your soul.
Princess:	Well, it sure do make your tummy feel better. [Laughter]

The students were keenly aware of the fleeting quality of life and of the losses in their young lives as well as the individuals such as grandparents and kindly neighbors whose rock solid support made it possible to endure the inevitable hard times. Even during the loss of beloved grandparents and siblings, they were able to find ways to endure, savoring the comfort of southern home cooking:

Bridney:	I remember when my brother died. Ooh, wee! I just went crazy. They kept telling me he wasn't dead, but I knew he was. I mean, he was shot several times. We knew he was shot in the back, and there was a big old hole there.
Katie:	How'd you find out?
Bridney:	People kept calling us, telling us that they heard he was dead over there. So my mama went over there and found him. The police was there, and they took him to the hospital. I went too, but he was gone. I just didn't want to believe it. I still can't believe he's not around anymore.
Princess:	I remember when my grandmother died, I wanted to spend the night in the hospital with her, but my mama said no. She told me I had to get on home and take care of the kids. She said I'd see her tomorrow. But I didn't. That hurt me, and I'm still upset about it. I wanted to say goodbye, and I didn't get a chance to.
Ashley:	It hurts so bad when somebody goes, and you won't ever see them again. Makes me want to be nice to my folks right now just in case I lose them. I mean, you never know when something bad might happen.
Princess:	Yeah, and you might never get to say goodbye. That hurts.

That's not right. I was so angry with my mama. Really I'm still angry with her about that. I loved my grandma, and she kept me from telling her goodbye. She was alone when she went.

Bridney: I didn't care about nothing after I lost my brother. I had my boyfriend, but I didn't have him anymore. I just didn't care what happened to me. I'd get drunk, and he and I would fight with knives, and I'd fall down on the ground and just cry. I couldn't think about nothing but him and why he had to die. I still had to go to school, but I didn't want to. Who cares about some stupid test when you lost your brother, and he ain't coming back?

For these six teens, life and happiness were often fleeting. They had lost parents and grandparents, and they worried about the health of their sometimes elderly caregivers. Unlike some of the adults in their lives, they recognized the need to say goodbye to someone who was dying as well as the need to celebrate and remember the good times.

The student readers also recognized the power of connections, whether they come in the form of a connection to another person or a connection to a loved one. The students' personal stories of pain and standing against all odds made it clear how relevant to their lives Woodson's stories were. Because her characters suffered losses that mirrored their own and somehow found a way to endure and thrive, they also drew on their own resiliency and hoped for something better.

In Woodson's Zena Sutherland Lecture (2007), she tells the audience that as a third grader, books became real to her and she was in the "dream of fiction." Just like Woodson, these eighth graders were living in the dream. Although painful and devastating at times, reading and discussing books with characters they recognized helped them make sense of the world around them and understand themselves better. These students were indeed in the "dream of fiction" and thinking about their own power inside those dreams.

CONCLUSION

Although we recognize that merely selecting books written by an African American author or books featuring African American characters is not enough to entice students to read, Barbara became convinced that the book selection, coupled with how the books were approached, instilled interest to read in the students. There is no monolithic African American and no book that speaks to all African Americans or to all southerners or to all Westerners, but Woodson's books spoke to these eighth graders. Although the settings of the novels they read were urban areas while they lived in a tiny town few outside of the area have ever heard of, they recognized the struggles Woodson's teens faced as being universal, and more importantly for them, to be like their own. Just as they and their families did, Woodson's characters struggled to pay the bills, faced the death of parents, and recognized themselves in books and the community they created. Most importantly of all, they never lost sight of hope.

Author Mike Rose (2009) reminds us that there is "no ready match-up to writers from these backgrounds. Black kids won't automatically respond to Alice Walker. How a story of hers is taught becomes a key variable" (p. 112). Rose contends that the subject matter does matter, reaching back to the words of John Dewey for support. It is clear, Dewey wrote, that "the teacher should be occupied not with subject matter in itself but in its interaction with pupils' present needs and capabilities" (Dewey, 1966, pp. 182–183). Rose maintains that what Dewey called "the intimate and powerful relationship" between a subject and human development should interrelate with teaching, acting as the mediating force.

For Rose (2009), choices about school and curriculum matter and reveal our purpose for schooling: "It affects what we put in or take out of the curriculum and how we teach the curriculum. It affects the way we think about students—all students—about intelligence, achievement, human development, teaching and learning, opportunity and obligation. And all of this affects the way we think about each other and who we are as a nation" (pp. 168–169).

The students in this lunchtime discussion group found "the thing with feathers" in the books of Woodson, in their conversations with one another, and in the supportive community created in the safe spaces of the book club. Although it may not have shown on the test scores, there was clearly a difference between the students who entered eighth grade in August and those who left the school in June. The discussion group participants became more sophisticated and thoughtful as they read. Not only are they making connections to the books they read, they are learning to honor the connections of others and to recognize that the stories other classmates have to share are as poignantly relevant in their own ways as the published stories of authors.

All six lunchtime participants faced challenges in their lives, but they found ways to endure the trials, never giving up, and as Bridney says, "Keep on keeping on. I just believe it has to get better." Whether it was the books Woodson wrote or the community that formed during those lunchtime discussions, small seeds of hope began to grow in those six students. As Kaywell's book *Dear Author: Letters of Hope* (2007) demonstrates, teen readers identify strongly with the characters in their favorite books by their favorite authors, even writing the authors for advice or to thank them for helping them navigate treacherous waters. For these teens, on the verge of important life decisions, Woodson's books offered hope.

The right books will speak to today's students, and used carefully, with only a little guidance and a lot of trust, they will provide a forum through which students can express their feelings about a wide variety of issues, issues that matter to them. What do they care about? Over and over, throughout the book discussions, conversations revolved around a need to belong or to fit in, the roles of mothers and family in their lives, and of a resilience that might surprise others. Death and the high price of making mistakes or being in the wrong place at the wrong time also were topics that came up in just about every discussion, in part because those are aspects in many of Woodson's books, but also because the students are mindful of those issues in their own lives.

As we were coming to the end of our discussion groups in May, torrential rains and winds began to whip the school and pound against the windows. We raced from the cafeteria in order to talk about our books. But before we entered the classroom, the students stood under the arch of the breezeway adjoining the hall that led to the room. The students were exhausted from all the stress surrounding standardized tests and a recent bout of fighting among groups of overage girls in the school. As they stood, weary but resolute, determined to continue to talk about the books and characters they had somehow come to love, Michael looked up and pointed at the sky. "Look! See the bird!" he shouted at all of us. "It's just like that poem says, just like that book says." As we raised our eyes to see what he was talking about, suddenly it was clear. There was a tiny brown bird, its wings fluttering for all it was worth, struggling—and succeeding—to stay in the air while the wind and rain assaulted it. There was the hope, the thing with feathers, that incontrovertible desire to survive on the part of the bird. How could we be less filled with determination than that bird?

(1990). *Last summer with Maizon*. New York, NY: Dell.

(1991). *The dear one*. New York, NY: Delacorte.

(1992). *Maizon at blue hill*. New York, NY: Putnam.

(1993). *Between Madison and Palmetto*. New York, NY: Putnam.

(1994). *I hadn't meant to tell you this*. New York, NY: Bantam Doubleday.

(1995). *From the notebooks of Melanin Sun*. New York, NY: Scholastic.

(1997). *The house you pass on the way*. New York, NY: Delacorte.

(1997). *We had a picnic this Sunday past*. Illus. D. Greenseid. New York, NY: Hyperion.

(1998). *If you come softly*. New York, NY: Putnam.

(2000). *Miracle's boys*. New York, NY: Putnam.

(2000). *Lena*. New York, NY: Bantam.

(2000). *Sweet, sweet memory*. Illus. F. Cooper. New York, NY: Hyperion.

(2001). *The other side*. Illus. E. B. Lewis. New York, NY: Putnam.

(2002). *Hush*. New York, NY: Putnam.

(2002). *Our Gracie aunt*. Illus. J. J. Muth. New York, NY: Hyperion.

(2002). *Visiting day*. Illus. J. Ransome. New York, NY: Scholastic.

(2003). *Locomotion*. New York, NY: Putnam.

(2004). *Coming on home soon*. Illus. E. B. Lewis. New York, NY: Putnam.

(2004). *Behind you*. New York, NY: Putnam.

(2005). *Show way*. Illus. H. Talbott. New York, NY: Putnam.

(2007). *Feathers*. New York, NY: Putnam.

(2008). *After Tupac and D Foster*. New York, NY: Putnam.

(2009). *Peace, Locomotion*. New York, NY: Putnam.

(2010). *Pecan pie baby*. Illus. S. Blackall. New York, NY: Putnam.

FIGURE 1. Children's and young adult books by Jacqueline Woodson (http://jacquelinewoodson.com/).

REFERENCES

Brooks, W., Browne, S., & Hampton, G. (2008). "There ain't no accounting for what folks see in their own mirrors": Considering colorism within a Sharon Flake narrative. *Journal of Adolescent & Adult Literacy, 51*(8), 660–669.

Casement, R. (2003). Jacqueline Woodson: Real characters, real voices. *Language Arts, 81*(1), 80–83.

Caswell, R. (2005). "A voice, a power, a space in the world": 2004 ALAN award winner Jacqueline Woodson talks about her works. *The ALAN Review, 32*(3), 9–11.

Daniels, H. (2006). What's the next big thing with literature circles? *Voices from the Middle, 13*(4), 10–15.

Day, D. (2004). Amazing Aliki. *Journal of Children's Literature, 30*(1), 19–25.

Dewey, J. (1966). *Democracy and education.* New York, NY: The Free Press.

Hill, B. C., Noe, K. L., & King, J. A. (2003). *Literature circles in middle school: One teacher's journey.* Norwood, MA: Christopher-Gordon.

Johnson, T. H. (Ed.). (1890). *The complete poems of Emily Dickinson.* Little, Brown.

Kaywell, J. (2007). *Dear author: Letters of hope.* New York, NY: Philomel.

Napoli, M., & Ritholz, E. R. (2009). Using Jacqueline Woodson's *Locomotion* with middle school readers. *Voices from the Middle, 16*(3), 31–39.

Rose, M. (2009). *Why school? Reclaiming education for all of us.* New York, NY: The New Press.

Rosenblatt, L. (1995). *Literature as exploration* (5th ed.). New York, NY: Modern Language Association of America.

Rosenblatt, L. (2005). *Making meaning with texts: Selected essays.* Portsmouth, NH: Heinemann.

Vygotsky, L. S. (1978). *Mind in society: The development of higher psychological processes.* Cambridge, MA: Harvard University Press.

Woodson, J. (2007). How do I come home again? *The Horn Book, 83*(2), 119–125.

CHAPTER 17

The Exoticizing of African American Children and of Children of Color

Care Work and Critical Literacy

TAMARA LINDSEY

Exoticism presupposes a deliberate opposition of what is alien to what is one's own, the otherness of what is foreign is emphasized, savored, as it were, and elaborately depicted against an implied background of one's own ordinary and familiar world.

(BAKHTIN, 1981, P. 101).

... exoticism implies a constant measurement against a native standard, which is therefore an active and evaluating force. To describe something as exotic, something else must be ordinary and familiar, at least by implication.

(MORSON & EMERSON, 1990, P. 379)

The words of Morson and Emerson (1990) describe Bakhtin's notion of the exotic as it is relates to studying the Greek novel. However, these ideas lend clarity to our understandings of how issues of difference and diversity are often made exotic in our teaching lives with all ages of students. In schools of education across this nation, there is much talk about caring for all children given into the hands of specific teachers. However, we know that only those children most like the "native standard" of the school community are cared for with attention and instruction designed for academic success. What commonly occurs is that children coming to school without the normative skills of schooling receive less nurturing care, less instruction, and reduced expectations for achievement. (For the purposes of this chapter,

Bakhtin's term *native standard* will refer to the white, middle-class, status quo and not to any native culture of people.) Our caring responses, then, are not caring at all, unless we examine our own tendencies to exoticize those different from white, middle-class norms.

Notions of a "native standard" can be interrupted by initiating the use of book discussions with young children that involve a critical examination of the status quo—multicultural literature which "has the potential to help us understand ourselves and others, to change our attitudes and embrace cultures different from our own, and to gain insights into social cultural conflicts" (Cai, 2008, p. 214). Topics such as race, class, gender, ableness, and sexuality have come to be identified as adult issues, and therefore, unsuitable for child consumption. As a result, refusing to discuss the social implications of such topics with young children, and older learners as well, is a way of refusing to acknowledge biased traits in teachers. Thus, the silence that supports oppression in our homes and schools is maintained, and consequently, we as teachers often fail to allow terms of "antiracist practice—whether to emphasize racial identities or to highlight human similarities—be jointly determined by adults and children" (Chang & Conrad, 2008, p. 38). By incorporating mutual literacy mediations with students, we can begin to make our classroom communities sites for addressing social justice issues.

As teachers, we enact our personal "native standards" as we respond to our students and our notions of them when we care for them and design pedagogy for them. This pedagogy is too often planned for students who are white and middle-class. Those whose cultural scripts are different from the status quo are often treated as foreign and exotic. It is important to examine what we make exotic in our teaching lives and how those constructions limit our abilities to care effectively for all children. This study examines how we respond to the exotic by glorifying or fearing it; I have stories for each.

PERSONAL EXPERIENCE STORIES

These personal experience studies (Clandinin & Connelly, 2000) focused on two different sets of classes. The first study focused on my teaching of reading and language arts to two different groups of second-year, early childhood majors at a midwestern university. The other study was done with two different sections of language arts classes. For the first set of literacy classes, I gathered data representing a wide range of narratives in the form of various written and spoken dialogic texts—interviews with students, class evaluations, and my own journals. For the second set of literacy classes, I administered a questionnaire which elicited responses to two read-alouds that could be used with young children. With both sets of students, I wanted to try to interpret how we all came to think about ourselves as caring teachers and learners with all children and their learning lives.

My curriculum design for both sets of preservice teachers played a crucial role in what happened to us each day as we met together as a community of learners and teachers. Implementing different types of pedagogical strategies to help my students learn how to become effective literacy teachers was fundamental to my role as their teacher. My understandings of caring for preservice teachers are shaped by my concern for the kinds of teachers they will become for all young children. So, my goal was to keep all of our voices "tethered to the social, cultural, historical, and the political contexts that comprise language" (Graue & Smith, 1995, p. 26) and literacy pedagogy that deals with issues of race, class gender, and sexuality. My expectation was that we would explore how those concerns affect our beliefs about teaching. I further expected that how my students perceived this instructional design and how we responded and reacted to one another as a result of it would play a significant part in our communal understandings of caring as well as of culturally relevant literacy pedagogy (Ladson-Billings, 1994).

I wanted to establish notions of caring that would move us beyond simplistic and sentimental representations of caring behavior in a classroom. I wanted us all to use our time together to take an unrelenting look at how our many privileges restrict our capacity to care for and teach all children. For the purposes of this chapter then, the term *care work* (Lindsey, 2000) refers to teaching practices characterized by a close scrutiny of the privileges which surround our lived experiences as teachers—a constant measurement of ourselves and holding those selves to close scrutiny. The words of Bakhtin and Morson and Emerson cited in the opening epigraph highlight the tensions encountered when privileged teachers attempt to offer care in an equitable manner to all children. Bakhtin's powerful notions implore us to look inward toward ourselves in order to move beyond those privileges which cause us to exoticize so many students and the pedagogy we design for them.

> . . . exoticism implies a constant measurement
> against a native standard,
> which is there and active and evaluation force . . .

It is important to examine our perceptions of teaching and learning and how those ideas guide our thinking—how our thoughts are always serving as an "evaluative force" behind how we "evaluate" our students, ourselves, and our pedagogy. Bakhtin's (1994, 1990a, 1990b, 1986) ideas on excess of sight gave me the theoretical tools to interpret the dialogue that drove the students' and my social interactions. According to him, words are "borderzones" between participants in shared living. These zones of human interaction are filled with communication in the present, which is infused with the life patterns of our past (Bakhtin, 1994). The extra vision, or "excess of seeing," is closely linked to the ways in which caring is enacted between and among those same individuals—words and actions of care, which are oriented by expressed speech and behavior as well as by the historical inheritances which undergird them. Examining these zones of communicative interaction requires that we interrogate both what and why specific events occur within a learning community.

However, what tends to prevail in the classroom space is our preconceived notions of who children are and should be. Since we seldom examine the role our perceptions play in constructing certain children as lesser, we dysconsciously[1] regard those children as finalized in negative ways. Those initial perceptions often begin and end the process of the evaluation of children, including the need to look inward at the sources of our responses and the impact those responses have on the finalized child. Bakhtin (1990b) notes that when we verbally give our extra vision to another person, "it does not provide him with an intuitable image of his inner body's *outer* value, it does make him the possessor of that body's potential value— a value capable of being actualized only by another human being" (p. 51). The words of caring we offer our children will not serve as possessions from which personal value can be obtained, unless we are willing to examine our motives for extending them.

> . . . the otherness of what is foreign is
> emphasized, savored, as it were
> and elaborately depicted . . .

One of the threats to extending extra sight, which is *life affirming* rather than *life diminishing*, is the way in which we exoticize concepts of difference from the "native standard." The first story in this chapter exemplifies how I "emphasized" and "savored" a student's sharing of a personal story. It reveals how difficult it is to struggle against assumptions that do not require us to examine our intentions for caring.

Since we had spent the entire academic year discussing children's books, on the last day of class I had asked each person to bring and share her/his favorite book. As different people told why the books they had brought were their favorites, others took notes. Then about halfway around the room, Xiou, a student from the Hmong culture, began by saying that she had never been a big reader because there were never many books in her home. She added, however, that what had always been present in her home were folktales and she wanted to share her favorite with us. As we continued going around the room, two students shared, both in an apologetic manner, that they had never read much until they came to college.

After we had gone around the group, I told everyone how embarrassed I was that I had even made the assignment in the manner I did in the first place. I was the one who wanted to help them broaden their concepts of literacy, and yet when I asked them to share theirs, I assumed that to do so would mean to participate by selecting a professionally published text. I had not asked for personal or family stories, much less cultural tales. I had not considered that I would make uncomfortable those students who did not have a long history of reading print upon which they could call. I relied entirely on a conventional construction of literate knowledge and then designed an equally prejudicial class activity.

The students I addressed when I made that assignment were exactly like me—they had grown up with books and were adept at reading, interpreting, and discussing them. Certainly, we should expect our university students and our young children to be able to demonstrate these important reading skills. However, this specific activity, conducted on the final day of class, was supposed to celebrate the literacy of the participants in that class in an informal way by a sharing of favorites. Although I had spent two semesters preaching to my students to try to shed their privileged views of teaching and learning, I had not heeded my own words when I made that assignment. Had those students not served as an example for me, I probably would never have been aware of how privileged my teaching had been on that last day.

When Xiou told her Hmong creation story, we all clapped because it was an enchanting tale. However, when the white, middle-class students shared their favorite books, the rest of us did not respond with applause and we did not cheer the courageous admissions made by the other two women. With these actions, we exoticized Xiou's sharing by constructing it as more charming than the rest. We had constructed her life as more colorful based on her difference from the status quo. Our response continued to set her apart by her difference rather than fold her story into a blended narrative with the other sharings. The goal in addressing all students within a specific learning community is to search for methods of response which "neither glorif[y] nor dismiss" the participation of all of its members (Fisher, 1990, p. 109). Caring for children who are different from the middle-class norm involves not only honoring their stories but also ensuring that their stories and lived experiences become part of the fabric of the total community.

My care work in this situation was stunted by my inability to extend extra vision of promise to all students because of the ways I exoticized my students' differences and failed even to consider that there might be experiences of literacy very different from my own. Both the exercise I planned and my response to it set students apart from the rest of the class and constructed them as Others in that classroom space. As teachers, we exoticize students by our responses to them with our interactions in classrooms, and we exclude students by the pedagogy we design carelessly for them.

There are other ways in which I think we exoticize difference as we tend to tip-toe around open discussions about race, class, gender, and sexuality with preservice teachers and young children. The next set of stories reveal how my students tended to exoticize notions of difference by constructing young children as being unable to be serious enough to participate in dramas and discussions which dealt with social justice issues. Many of the preservice teachers also described such activities as too negative for young children. In both instances, difference was made exotic as it was perceived as a topic that was negative and to be avoided.

> . . . against an implied background
> of one's own ordinary
> and familiar world.

The following pair of stories, one based on drama activities and the other on read-aloud sessions, both with two different language arts classes of preservice teachers, describes how what is familiar can often define the unfamiliar as exotic and something to be excluded from the teaching/learning lives of young children. The first set of stories is based on two distinctly different drama activities. One drama was whimsical, based on familiar fairy tales, and apparently devoid of potential for critical commentary; the other was somber and dealt with obvious critical social issues. Many of my students sanctioned the laughter and fun that were generated by the lighthearted drama and were eager to try it with young children. On the other hand, many judged the second drama as negative and too weighty to use with young students. However, both laughter and seriousness generate important elements of relational care work in the classroom.

The first improvisational drama was based on a response to a picture book, *The Jolly Postman or Other People's Letters*, by Ahlberg and Ahlberg (1986). The title character delivers mail to a community of fairy tale and Mother Goose characters; one of those pieces of mail is an invitation to a birthday party for Goldilocks. After reading the book aloud to the class, I asked students to imagine that they are to plan a birthday party for Goldilocks with nothing but tape, glue, construction paper, and markers. They create invitations, refreshments, presents, and games, and once Goldilocks arrives, they are also forced to think of activities to provide entertainment because the magician who is supposed to perform at the party is unavoidably detained elsewhere.

Everyone had a part and although we knew that it was all pretend, the personal accents the students placed on the creation of the props and the play of the drama itself were generated by their personal histories. One student reported that the cookies she drew while making the refreshments for the party represented actual ones made by her Swedish grandmother. Some students planned a game of musical chairs for the party during which they proceeded to sing tunes from the 1960s! Others made grass skirts and taught Goldilocks how to hula. All of these were personal signatures given to a community drama project.

The next improvisational drama we did was in response to a piece of adolescent literature, Crew's *Children of the River* (1991). The novel is about a young teenage Cambodian girl and her experiences as a new immigrant to America. Although it won an International Reading Association Children's Book Award, it is a problematic text since it is written from a white perspective. Nonetheless, I chose this text because there are not many young adult novels representing characters from Southeast Asia. I divided the students into groups of four or five; each group selected a different main character in the text, and then students had about fifteen minutes to design a living statue representation of the chosen character. One person narrated the meaning of the statue for the rest of the class.

As students completed their performances, I asked that they freeze in place while the rest of the class walked by, one by one, responding to the statues with comments as if they knew the character personally. Adding the immediate response to the statues transformed a pure performance situation into yet another dramatic portrayal of the book, one in which everyone in the group responded interchangeably as statue and respondent. Participants were no longer responding to a distant text, as they were given the opportunity to become the text and respond to one another through that dramatization.

Once we began speaking to the statues, one student spoke about feeling almost frightened by how "quiet and tense the room got." This person also commented that, "walking by the statues made me feel like I was walking by a casket at a funeral." This comment captured the intensity we all felt as we enacted the statues and responded to them. Although all of us knew that we were in character during the drama, there was also some uncertainty as to what was genuinely expressed from personal perceptions and what was not. One of the students noticed the following:

> . . . some people took on other characters while other people, most people, seemed to be themselves. I was one of the people who remained myself because I felt that I was expressing to the character or statue how I felt about them and that could only come from me as myself.

This student recognized that even during the drama, she could not avoid being herself. She could not separate her self in the drama from her self outside the play.

A student who had portrayed the main character Sundara, reported the following:

> . . . playing the role of Sundara and listening to what everyone had to say to her/me was an unusual feeling. I really felt like I was her and that they were speaking directly to me. It forced us to open our minds and really question what we thought about the characters.

Another student commented that she was

> . . . surprised to see how strong the comments to the characters were. For me, it was hard to act. I had to say comments to the characters that pertained to my real feelings while reading the novel. Then I began to wonder if the comments other people were saying came from them as readers, or if they were acting. Some of the comments were so shocking that I can't believe they were actually said and I wondered where they came from.

Both of these students found it impossible not to be themselves. The second student's dismay seemed to come not from how surprised that she was herself even during the drama, but from the sense that perhaps others did the same and still made what she considered to be negative remarks.

Not everyone thought that the harsh comments made during the drama constituted a negative experience. In the discussion afterward, several students expressed an appreciation that the activity was not a sugar-coated affair. A few others also thought that "just because there were negative comments doesn't mean the experience wasn't valuable or even positive." Creating action as participants and observers allowed us to recreate some of the tensions that we experienced as we argued about the rights and privileges of white authorship and readership during our initial discussion of the text. Yet, during the dramas, we became the characters and those who knew them; we were actors and spectators all within the same activity. Rather than freezing a moment in time, we froze a "problem in time" (Heathcote, 1980, p. 115) and were able to take yet another critical look at the feelings and emotions involved in reading and responding to a highly racialized text as a community of learners.

One student had a particularly interesting response to what many in both groups considered to be negative when she said:

> I loved with when you [Lindsey] same up to our statue of Sundara and said, "Go back to where you came from." Everyone was saying nice and encouraging stuff which does not represent everyone. I've gotten a lot of "go back to where you came from" when I was little because we lived in an all white town at the time. It brought a smile to me, thought I did not show it because I was just thinking about it when you said it. You read my mind.

I certainly did not read her mind. I made that intentionally provocative comment to her statue because it does represent a common reaction to an immigrant who is new to the U.S. soil and in our very community. She knew that the nurturing remarks did not represent what all people really feel.

The student, the only person of color in the room, smiled when a racial slur was verbalized, while many of the white students were appalled that such a comment would be spoken. Those same preservice teachers talked about caring for young children by shielding them from such comments. Yet the student of color obviously felt cared for by the acknowledgment of the existence of racism. Even so, many of the white students wanted to retreat into a provocative silence when overt racism was voiced. This uncommunicative stance is damaging to the lives of everyone in our classrooms since it squelches any genuine dialogue that could work to dispel negative notions of social justice topics. Crafton, Brennan, and Silvers (2007) remind us that " . . . communicating only a slice of how events and people are perceived shapes thinking and action in ways that can be damaging to others: uncovering messages that effectively oppress people or position them as 'less than' is at the heart of critical literacy" (p. 513). Care work must acknowledge race and racism in the classroom, especially with white students, because it begins to break the silence, which allows us to maintain the status quo of privilege.

> . . . at least by implication . . .

The most troubling aspect of the students' responses to the statue activity was not their conclusion about how to deal with what they termed negative responses to racism white readership and authorship, but that many expressed belief that children need to be protected from participation in similar activities. These responses suggest that young children are unable to think about such concepts in a critical manner and also that such ideas are somehow too exotic for them as well. For example, one student was shocked by the comments but still thought it was a great way for adult learners to respond to a novel. However, she expressed doubt that it would work well with young children because she did not "know if they'd take it seriously."

I fear that this notion of seriousness is linked to a refusal to regard young children as "equally worthy, complicated, and capable" (Pollack, 2008, p. xx) of perceiving how their own lives are critically tied to social issues that relate to the larger world context. It is interesting to note that no such concern for the seriousness of the activity was expressed about the Goldilocks drama, despite its being a Eurocentric tale that not all children in a specific classroom might have had access to as part of their cultural lives. Difficult, critical issues are rarely explored in the elementary classroom, although young children are already aware of notions concerning privilege by the time they begin school. Au (2009) reminds us of the following:

> Between the ages of 2 and 5, children not only become aware of racial differences, but begin to make judgments based on that awareness. They do this even though they may not be able to understand in an intellectual way, the complexities of race and bias as issues. Teachers have a responsibility to recognize the influence of racism on themselves and their students. And we can help children learn the skills and strategies they will need to counteract it in their lives. (p. 256)

By refusing to engage children in critical dialogue, teachers perpetuate the silences that keep the power of privilege in place. They also underestimate children's ability to become actively involved in exercising "their rights and responsibilities as good, caring citizens" (Crafton et al., 2007, p. 516).

Another student said that, at first, she too was doubtful that young children would participate as her classmates had. Then after she reflected upon the drama, she "realized that it was really all about feelings and [she] knew that, of course, [she] could do this with her kids." Children do know how they feel, especially when they are given a space to share those feelings and hear how others respond to them. Several of these preservice teachers saw children as being limited in their abilities to respond with solemn respect to an activity that would require them to look critically into their own lives to search for meanings in a text. By constructing young children as deficient in their ability to grasp ideas soberly, those preservice teachers denied the possibility of their young students being "open to the living event" (Morson & Emerson, 1990, p. 76) of critical response to their own learning.

This is one of the reasons why critical literacy work is so important—it offers privileged teachers a variety of ways to initiate conversations which begin with those privileges by designing lessons based on a published text. It also provides us with the opportunity to remove the veil of the exotic, which leads us to dismiss these serious life issues as being inappropriate topics of exploration with young children.

> . . . what is alien to one's own . . .

A study I recently conducted with two classes of language arts students revealed similar attitudes about young children, that young children would find serious issues "alien" and would, hence, be unable to deal with them. I asked that these two classes, fifty-five in all, provide me with their impressions of the read-alouds of two picture books. The texts I used were both written by Jacqueline Woodson (2002, 2004). The first, titled *Visiting Day*, is illustrated by James E. Ransome and tells the story of a young girl, Maya, who is eagerly anticipating a visit with her father, who is in prison. She and her grandmother fix his favorite foods to pack into a picnic for them to share when they see him. The second book, illustrated by E. B. Lewis, is titled *Coming on Home Soon*. This story, set during World War II, is also about a young girl, Ada Ruth, who has a parent absent from the home. Her mother has gone to Chicago to work, leaving Ada Ruth to stay on the family farm with her grandmother. I paired these two texts since both are uplifting tales of loving parents, hope, and reunion. However, although both of the picture books are positive representations of two African American families, the first book could be seen as less positive than the second, since it deals with a father who is incarcerated.

When examining *Visiting Day,* I asked the students to describe the age group that would be most appropriate for a read-aloud of this text. Of the fifty-five pre-service teachers, nineteen stated that the topic would be more suitable for older learners, and seventeen stated that young children would simply be unable to deal with such a sensitive issue as a parent being imprisoned. The following responses are representative of many who wrote that the book would be effective only with upper elementary students:

> Intermediate-age children will be better able to identify emotions and realize thoughts and responses to issues addressed in the book.

> As children are older, the teacher would be able to talk about the book more in depth.

> They would be able to talk about the book in a more meaningful way than younger age groups. This age would be more open to the situation in the story.

These responses exoticize young children and portray them as incapable of understanding a text written specifically for them and one which so lovingly illustrates a constructive response to a serious family situation.

A dozen students provided positive responses to the book, noting that young children are in need of stories that "are not always picture-perfect" and that "families are not bad if they have a few problems." However, it was troubling that thirty-five of the preservice teachers expressed the opinion that this text would be most suitable for children with "low socioeconomic status," even describing such children as being more capable of providing feedback for other, more economically fortunate classmates. One student acknowledged the perception that "Children in inner cities have more problems with the law and they would benefit more from this book." Another student noted that the picture book would be "most appropriately used in a predominantly African American classroom, particularly in the inner city." Other terms used to portray target populations closely aligned with this text were children from "high crime areas," "disruptive city life," and "lower income areas."

My students exoticized all of the young children as being unable to understand complex social issues. Although they identified older learners as possessing the ability to grapple with serious issues, they still exoticized even those children as well by assuming that they would be of poverty or of color. They further assumed that such children would be the only ones uniquely qualified to understand issues such as the incarceration of a parent. They made broad generalizations about all African American children, portraying them all to be from dysfunctional families and homes—continuing to set them apart from children of the middle class and viewing their lives as alien. While there are poor whites who also may encounter incarceration, they would not face racial stereotyping connected to their poverty. The confluence of race, poverty, and imprisonment were all highly exoticized by my students. In particular, African American children were "blackened" as Collins (2009) tells us—"pushed down a social scale of some kind" (p. 42). These children were portrayed as lesser humans who were already so harmed by life that shielding them from difficult lived experiences was not even a consideration.

The second text, *Coming on Home Soon*, was much more positively received by the students. All of the preservice teachers thought that it should be used as a read-aloud for all grade levels. Not one student commented that it would be inappropriate for younger learners. Since the book was set in the 1940s, the word *colored* is used to refer to African Americans, and several students noted that this term should be explained in light of its unsuitability in the modern day. During conversational moments in the text, Woodson uses African American Vernacular English. Two students noted that this dialect could be hard for "children to understand." This is yet another form of exoticizing African American children, deciding that their home language is incomprehensible and cannot be viewed as a fully formed system of effective cultural communication.

In both sets of activities, the dramas and the read-alouds, the preservice teachers were most comfortable with those that did not deal with any serious topics. If we only extend extra vision to children that involves laughter and joy, then we have, to use Bakhtin's terms, "finalized" or "completed" those children as incapable of being addressed as persons who possess the ability to respond with critical thought and understanding. Moreover, we have assumed that such intellectual undertakings are negative and foreign activities for children. When Bakhtin (in Morson & Emerson, 1990) discusses notions about laughter and seriousness, he describes both as being significant tools of "fearlessness: 'True seriousness fears neither parody or irony. . .for it is aware of its attachment to an uncompleted whole'" (Morson & Emerson, 1990, p. 454). With this quote, Bakhtin links the act of being serious to his notion of extending extra sight to one another. If seriousness is approached with a sense of fearlessness that refuses to set rigid limitations on those being addressed, then their responses are seen to possess potential rather than deficiency. Using these dramas and read-alouds with young children would address them as capable of understanding how to deal with critical issues surrounding social justice and view them as "uncompleted" or prepared to open themselves to look critically on their world.

CONCLUSION

Just as I kept Xiou wedded to her cultural historical tale, so many of my students kept their notions of pedagogy also wedded to their privileged positions of silence. As a community, even though we had experienced how difficult it is to give voice to privilege and unjust social structures as we lived within dramas, it felt very familiar to retreat back into privilege and refuse to acknowledge what we had all just experienced together. In doing so, these dramas and selections of children's literature and the topics they explored were made exotic—too foreign from the "native standards" of what should occur with young children.

The novelist Peter Smith (2001) wrote an article revealing how, as a father, he tends to make "others" of his daughters and not his son in whom he is able to see himself:

> We fetishize the "otherness" of women. I'd spent a lifetime under the mistaken impression that I really knew women when in fact my knowledge was based largely on fantasy and projection. Otherness was staring me right in the face, but it was actually me in disguise. (p. 181)

When we exoticize people and situations, we are, as Smith writes, staring at our own privileged, biased selves. However, rather than take a closer look at how our privileges implicate us all in maintaining unjust social structures, we endorse the silence that allows them to go unchallenged. Unless we utilize our pedagogy of critical literacy to provide opportunities to explore the "workings of social power" (Collins, 2009, p. 15), then African American children and other children of color will continue to be exoticized in our schools and our care for them will serve primarily to perpetuate the status quo.

NOTE

1. King (1991) uses this word to refer to an "uncritical habit of mind (including perceptions, attitudes, assumptions, and beliefs) that justifies inequity and exploitation by accepting the existing order of things as given" (p. 338).

REFERENCES

Ahlberg, J., & Ahlberg, A. (1986). *The jolly postman or other people's letters*. Boston, MA: Little, Brown.

Au, W. (2009). Decolonizing the classroom: Lesson in multicultural education. In W. Au (Ed.), *Rethinking multicultural education: Teaching for racial and cultural justice*. Milwaukee, WI: Rethinking Schools Publication.

Bakhtin, M. M. (1981). In M. Holquist (Ed.), *The dialogic imagination: Four essays by M. M. Bakhtin*. Austin: University of Texas Press.

Bakhtin, M. M. (1986). In C. Emerson & M. Holquist (Eds.), *Speech genres & other late essays*. Austin: University of Texas Press.

Bakhtin, M. M. (1990a). In G. Morson & C. Emerson (Eds.), *Mikhael Bakhtin: Creation of prosaic*. Stanford, CA: Stanford University Press.

Bakhtin, M. M. (1990b). In M. Holquist & V. Liapunov (Eds.), *Art and answerability: Early philosophical essays by M. M. Bakhtin*. Austin: University of Texas Press.

Bakhtin, M. M. (1994). In P. Morris (Ed.), *Bakhtin reader: Selected writing of Bakhtin, Medvedev, and Voloshinov*. London: Edward Arnold.

Cai, M. (2008). Transactional theory and the study of multicultural literature. *Language Arts, 85*(3), 212–220.

Chang, K., & Conrad, R. (2008). Following children's leads in conversations about race. In M. Pollack (Ed.), *Everyday antiracism: Getting real about race in school*. New York, NY: The New Press.

Clandinin, D. J., & Connelly, F. M. (2000). *Narrative inquiry: Experience and story in qualitative research*. San Francisco, CA: Jossey-Bass.

Collins, P. H. (2009). *Another kind of public education: Race, school, the media, and democratic possibilities*. Boston, MA: Beacon Press.

Crafton, L. K., Brennan, M., & Silvers, P. (2007). Critical inquiry and multiliteracies in a first-grade classroom. *Language Arts, 84*(6), 510–518.

Crew, L. (1991). *Children of the river*. New York, NY: Laurel Leaf.

Fisher, B. (1990). Alice in the human services: A feminist analysis of women in the caring professions. In E. K. Abel & M. K. Nelson (Eds.), *Circles of care: Work and identity in the women's lives*. Albany: State University of New York Press.

Graue, M. E., & Smith, S. (1995). *Ventriloquating the meanings of mathematics*. Unpublished manuscript. Madison, WI: University of Wisconsin-Madison.

Heathcote, D. (1980). Material for significance. In L. Johnson & C. O'Neill (Eds.), *Dorothy Heathcote: Collected writings on education and drama*. Evanston, IL: Northwestern University Press.

Holquist, M. (Ed.). (1981). *The dialogic imagination: Four essays by M. M. Bakhtin*. Austin, TX: University of Texas Press.

King, J. (1991). Dysconscious racism: Ideology, identity, and the miseducation of teachers. *Journal of Negro Education, 60*(2), 336–348.

Ladson-Billings, G. (1994). *The dreamkeepers: Successful teachers of African-American children*. San Francisco, CA: Jossey-Bass.

Lindsey, T. (2000). Responding to the call to care with pre-service teachers. *Reflective Practice, 1*(2), 269–282.

Morson, G. S., & Emerson, C. (Eds.). (1990). *Mikhail Bakhtin: Creation of a Prosaics*. Stanford, CA: Stanford University Press.

Pollack, M. (2008). Introduction. In M. Pollack (Ed.), *Everyday antiracism: Getting real about race in school*. New York, NY: The New Press.

Smith, P. (2001). Girls in the house. *O, The Oprah* Magazine, 180–181.

Woodson, J. (2002). *Visiting day*. New York, NY: Scholastic.

Woodson, J. (2004). *Coming on home soon*. New York, NY: Puffin.

Global Literacy

Implications for the Classroom

MARY NAPOLI & VIVIAN YENIKA-AGBAW

At a time when K–12 public school educators are experiencing significant mandates related to high-stakes testing and the related pressures that accompany such mandates (Darling-Hammond, 2000; Greene, 1988), it is even more critical to integrate high-quality African and African American literature selections to empower students. The integration of multimodal strategies, response activities, and the arts offers teachers meaningful ways to intellectually stimulate and instill a sense of identity and hope in their students' lives.

In a seminal essay, Greene (1988) wrote the following:

> We do not know how many educators see present demands and prescriptions as obstacles to their own development, or how many find it difficult to breathe . . . a teacher in search of his/her freedom may be the only kind of teacher who can arouse young persons to go in search of their own. It will be argued as well that children who have been provoked to reach beyond themselves, to wonder, to imagine, to pose their own questions are the ones most likely to learn. (p. 14)

Greene's observation is pertinent for today's global classrooms, especially as a means to empower teachers to use high-quality literature selections, to problematize these texts, and to invite students to wonder and to imagine.

We certainly believe that the variety of outstanding literature coupled with sound pedagogical implications included in this text will launch your own literary journeys. With the ever-changing trends in our population and global events, the need to infuse African and African American literature in K–12 classrooms is paramount. Through the use of African American children's literature, teachers can provide African American children with opportunities to discover their own cultural identities. By using African and African American literature, teachers can help students form a strong identity and deconstruct society's views that are often negative and forced upon them. Therefore, in the preceding chapters of this collection, we have tried to include varying perspectives about the importance of integrating a variety of high-quality literature within the classroom. The contributing authors have touched upon theories, strategies, and models to use with our youngest to adolescent learners. As we look forward to the future, we can find wisdom from Marantz and Marantz (1994), who wrote the following:

> Teachers should connect literature to the goals of multicultural education: content integration, knowledge construction, prejudice reduction, equity pedagogy, and empowering school culture and social structure. Because of this, we need to choose multicultural literature that will enhance "the self-esteem of children of all cultures and respect the culture of others, while expanding aesthetics as well as their horizons. (p. 1)

Moreover, the chapters provide information about how to find, select, and evaluate African and African American literature for children. Bieger (1996) encourages teachers to use multicultural literature:

> What cannot be taught through facts may be taught through the heart. Literature can help effect multicultural understandings. Through reading, we briefly share in the lives and feelings of the characters rather than dealing with facts. Literature provides food for both the head and the heart. Books may be used as agents for change, vehicles for introducing concepts, and catalysts for activities. (p. 309)

When teachers make the decision to use books that expose children to other cultures, they tell students that it is important to know about others. "By involving the children with characters and situations that they can identify with, books increase children's appreciation of other ways of life and help them see unfamiliar people as individuals" (Ramsey, 1987, p. 69). Books have the power to create a common shared experience that can facilitate dialogue. Rochman (1993) asserts that the best books "break down borders. They surprise us—whether they are set close to home or abroad. They

> change our view of ourselves; they intend the phrase 'like me' to include what we thought was foreign and strange" (p. 9). As the authors in this collection have cited, it is not enough to just expose children to multicultural literature. Readers need to be helped to identify issues, question ideologies that make up the story, and understand how the aforementioned affects the lives of the readers. (Yenika-Agbaw, 1997)

Choice is both desirable and empowering (Iyengar & Lepper, 1999). As tomorrow's teachers make good choices, they must do so with the knowledge of their local community and their world. An essential ingredient in making choices is "care" (Gaudelli, 2003). Yokota (1993) maintains that multicultural literature allows

> children to take part in experiences from cultures other than their own; and these experiences help them understand different backgrounds, thereby influencing their decisions about how they will live in this culturally pluralistic world. As we encourage teachers to choose books from other languages and cultures with guided discussions to help children develop an understanding of other people and their customs, we can provide a transformative effect in our curriculum.

For those of you who want to transform your students' understanding of their world across local, national, and global contexts, take inspiration from the practical strategies that the authors have included and begin a collection of high-quality books to share with your students. As we share quality books with our students, we will become co-participants in the process of reflecting upon our own beliefs, attitudes, and practices relating to diversity in the classroom and beyond. The authors of the collection have presented powerful arguments for weaving African and African American selections to gain broader understandings about the world. Sleeter and Grant (1999) argue that while teachers should strive to help students develop appreciation and respect for other cultures, they should also help them understand sociopolitical factors surrounding cultural groups. In other words, as Bishop (1994) explains, multicultural literature "offer(s) opportunities to examine critically the society in which we live, and the values and assumptions that underlie conflicts, events, and behaviors" (p. xvi). By infusing critical race theory and culturally grounded frameworks when reading literature about African Americans, teachers can guide students to think critically about themselves and the world in which they live. Though there are some adolescent novels, with an emphasis on tenets related to individual or cultural identity (i.e., multiple oppressions of race, class, and gender in the lives of young African American or African individuals), there is still a silence surrounding issues of sexuality. For this reason we have provided some possible titles pertaining to black sexuality. These include *Orphea Proud* (2004) by Sharon Dennis Whyeth, *From the Notebooks of Melanin Sun* (1995) by Jacqueline Woodson, and *Love Rules* (2001) by Marilyn Reynolds. Issues of sexuality continue to remain silent despite the tragic events that have plagued society in recent years. There are some professional resources for teachers to refer to as they guide readers to selections that connect to lived experiences in order to reach the goals of the multicultural education movement, particularly self-analysis, critical thinking, and social action. These resources include the following: *The Heart Has Its Reasons: Young Adult Literature with Gay/Lesbian/Queer Content, 1969–2004*

(2006), by Michael Cart and Christine Jenkins; *Voices Rising: Celebrating 20 Years of Black Lesbian, Gay, Bisexual & Transgender Writing* (2007), edited by G. Winston James; and *Lesbian and Gay Voices: An Annotated Bibliography and Guide to Literature for Children and Young Adults* (2000), by Frances Ann Day.

Topics such as teenage mothers and fathers, rape, incest, and so forth, in young adult literature pertaining to African and African American culture, are also available for readers. It is important to note that these topics are pervasive in the lives of all cultures; however, there are limited research articles featuring adolescent responses to these novels in classroom settings (Brooks, Sekayi, Savage, Waller, & Picot, 2010). These themes form the nexus in the lives of African American and African children and adolescents, and, yet, there is more that teachers can do pedagogically in the classroom to promote positive attitudes and social justice. A few titles that can be shared with adolescent readers about real issues include *The First Part Last* (2003), by Angela Johnson, which explores the challenges of becoming a teenage father, or *Tyrell* (2006), by Coe Booth, which introduces readers to fifteen-year-old Tyrell, who is living in a homeless shelter with his younger brother and mother. Some books from the continent that address difficult issues appear in graphic novel format. These include *Deogratia or a Tale of Rwanda* (2006), which addresses rape and genocide. Other novels, such as *Chanda's Secrets* (2004) by Allan Stratton, unmask the stigma of AIDS and the struggles of one young woman faced with its presence in her village.

We realize that it is sometimes challenging to locate outstanding titles for the classroom. In the appendix, we include a list of awards and book publishers that offer outstanding works for children. We also recommend that teachers and professionals support various organizations which devote their time to promoting global literature, including the American Library Association (ALA, http://www.ala.org/), the United States Board on Books for Young People (USBBY, http://www.usbby.org), the Notable Books for Global Society (NBGS, http://mysite.verizon.net/vzeeioxu/), and Africa Access, an organization that works with the Outreach Council of the African Studies Association (ASA) to distribute information about books on Africa and those that are affiliated with the Children's Africana Book Awards (CABA). The Outreach Council annually honors outstanding authors and illustrators of children's books about Africa published in the United States (http://www.africaaccessreview.org/aar/index.html). It is our responsibility as educators to make conscious choices about text selection for our curriculum. With the increasing demands on teachers, it becomes very challenging to find the time to stay abreast of the latest releases of children's or adolescent books that would promote diversity. Yet, we must work together to carve out space and to form book clubs, read and create blogs, or attend seminars to read and discuss critical works of outstanding global titles to reach the needs of our changing society. As Jonda McNair (2008) states, "[B]ecause much of African American children's literature has a strong social justice component, using books written by and about African Americans offers increased opportunities to raise students' consciousness and engage them in discussions of equity and fairness in regards to issues surrounding race, class and gender" (p. 21). In our school communities, we must foster critical conversations through the use of literature to provide opportunities for our students to make connections between learning and life. As Brooks (2006) noted, "The more we know about the ways students from different ethnic backgrounds respond to texts, the better informed our curricula and instruction can become. Teachers have at their disposal cultural knowledge and experiences to rely and build upon during instruction" (pp. 389–390).

So, as we consider how to help our students understand their ever-changing world, their culture, and their multiple identities and realities, we can begin by listening to their stories and by sharing the best possible literature for our students to identify. It is this oral and literary journey that will help affirm our students' cultural experiences, which will in turn reflect upon their educational and personal success. It is a journey that may also offer students an opportunity to take a peek at the multiple perspectives of what is considered to be black in Africa, the Americas, and other African diasporic communities. It may also enable them to rethink the stereotypical views they hold about these cultures and to cultivate a new sense of appreciation and understanding for their complex diversity. In this collection, the authors hope that you have been given the tools and inspiration necessary to take the journey with us and to help your students build hope and new discoveries.

REFERENCES

Banks, C. A., & Banks, J. A. (1995). Equity pedagogy: An essential component of multicultural education. *Theory Into Practice, 34*(3), 152–158.

Bieger, E. M. (1996). Promoting multicultural education through a literature based approach. *The Reading Teacher, 49*(4), 308–311.

Bishop, R. S. (Ed.). (1994). *Kaleidoscope: A multicultural booklist for grades K–8*. Illinois: NCTE.

Brooks, W. (2006). Reading representations of themselves: Urban youth use culture and African American textual features to develop literary understanding. *Reading Research Quarterly, 41*(3), 372–392.

Brooks, W., Sekayi, D., Savage, L., Waller, E., & Picot, I. (2010). Narrative significations of contemporary black girlhood. *Research in the Teaching of English, 45*(1), 7–35.

Darling-Hammond, L. (2000, Dec. 7–8). *Transforming urban public schools: The role of standards and accountability*. Paper presented at the Creating Change in Public Education seminar, John F. Kennedy School of Government, Harvard University, Cambridge, MA. Retrieved from http://www.ksg.harvard.edu/urbanpoverty/Urban%20Seminars/December2000/hammond.pdf

Gaudelli, W. (2003). *World class: Teaching and learning in global times*. Mahwah, NJ: Lawrence Erlbaum.

Greene, M. (1988). *The dialectic of freedom*. New York: Teachers College Press.

Iyengar, S. S., & Lepper, M. R. (1999). Rethinking the value of choice: A cultural perspective on intrinsic motivation. *Journal of Personality and Social Psychology, 76,* 349–366.

Marantz, S. S., & Marantz, K. (1994). *Multicultural picture books: Art for understanding others*. Worthington, OH: Linworth.

McNair, J. C. (2008). A comparative analysis of The Brownies' book and contemporary African American children's literature written by Patricia C. McKissack. In W. Brooks & J. C. McNair (Eds.), *Embracing, evaluating, and examining African American children's & young adult literature* (pp. 3–29). Lanham, MD: Scarecrow.

Ramsey, P.G. (1987). *Teaching and learning in a diverse world*. New York: Teachers College Press.

Rochman, H. (1993). *Against borders: Promoting books for a multicultural world*. Chicago, IL: American Library Association.

Sleeter, C. E., & Grant, C. A. (1999). *Making choices for multicultural education: Five approaches to race, class, and gender*. Upper Saddle River, New Jersey: Merrill.

Yenika-Agbaw, V. (1997). Taking children's literature seriously: Reading for pleasure and social change. *Language Arts, 74*(6), 446–452.

Yokota, J. (1993). Issues in selecting multicultural children's literature. *Language Arts, 70*(3), 156–166.

Listing of African American and Small Multicultural Children's Book Publishers

AFRICAN AMERICAN IMAGES
P.O. Box 1799
Sauk Village, IL 60412
http://www.africanamericanimages.com/

AFRICA WORLD PRESS
541 West Ingham Avenue, Suite B
Trenton, NJ 08607
http://www.africaworldpressbooks.com/servlet/StoreFront

CHILDREN'S BOOK PRESS
965 Mission Street, Suite 425
San Francisco, CA 94103
http://www.childrensbookpress.org/

DARE BOOKS
33 Lafayette Avenue
Brooklyn, NY 11217
http://www.darebooks.com/

ESCHAR PUBLICATIONS
P. O. Box 1194
Mount Dora, FL 32756
http://www.escharpublications.com/

JUST US BOOKS
356 Glenwood Ave., 3rd Floor
East Orange, NJ 07017
http://www.justusbooks.com/?id=220

LEE & LOW BOOKS
95 Madison Ave., Suite 1205
New York, NY 10016
http://www.leeandlow.com/

OPEN HAND PUBLISHING
P.O. Box 20207
Greensboro, NC 27420
http://www.openhand.com/

THIRD WORLD PRESS
P.O. Box 19730
7822 S. Dobson Ave.
Chicago, Illinois 60619
http://www.thirdworldpressinc.com/

Contributors

DR. LEWIS ASIMENG-BOAHENE is currently an associate professor at The Pennsylvania State University–Harrisburg. He is a teacher educator and researcher who teaches social studies education, world regional geography, and comparative education. He is an author of several journal articles and book chapters in his field. His research interests include African oral traditional literature as pedagogical tools in content area classrooms, social studies education, multicultural education, and international comparative education. Dr. Asimeng-Boahene has led workshops and presentations both at U.S. and international schools and conferences.

APRIL WHATLEY BEDFORD is a professor and the interim dean of the College of Education and Human Development at the University of New Orleans. She is the upcoming Chair of the Notable Children's Books in the Language Arts award committee, editor of the Children's Books review column of *Childhood Education*, and a former editor of the *Journal of Children's Literature*. Dr. Bedford is an active member of the Children's Literature Assembly of the National Council of Teachers of English, the Children's Literature and Reading Special Interest Group of the International Reading Association, and the Publications Committee of the Association of Childhood Education International. She and her coauthor, Renée Casbergue, are codirectors of Project Recovery, an Early Reading First grant-sponsored preschool initiative in New Orleans.

ANN BERGER-KNORR, PhD, is an assistant professor of Education at The Pennsylvania State University–Harrisburg where she teaches both undergraduate and graduate courses in elementary education and literacy education. Prior to teaching at The Pennsylvania State University–Harrisburg, Ann was employed at Shippensburg University, Temple University, Harrisburg, and Wilson College. Ann brings to her work over twenty-five years of teaching experience at the preschool, kindergarten, elementary, middle school, and college levels across private, public, clinical, and independent settings. In her research, she attempts to bridge teacher education, literacy education, and multicultural education. Ann lives in Carlisle, Pennsylvania, with her two daughters, Taylor and Abbey.

RENÉE CASBERGUE holds the Vira Franklin and James R. Eagle professorship at Louisiana State University, where she serves as interim associate dean for Graduate Studies and Research. She has authored or coauthored numerous publications that address a variety of aspects of early literacy development, including *Writing in Preschool: Learning to Orchestrate Meaning and Marks,* published by the International Reading Association. She is a past president of the Literacy Development in Young Children IRA Special Interest Group, and she serves on the *Reading Teacher* editorial board. She coedits the *Focus on Pre-K* newsletter of the Association for Childhood Education while also serving on the ACEI publications committee. With coauthor April Bedford, she directs an Early Reading First project in New Orleans preschools.

MICHELE D. CASTLEMAN is a PhD candidate, studying young adult and children's literature in The Ohio State University's (OSU) College of Education and Human Ecology. She teaches an introductory children's literature course to OSU undergraduate students. The focus of her dissertation research is to examine the ways figures from myth are represented in children's novels set in contemporary America. She has an MFA in writing for children from Chatham University. She can be contacted at castleman.8@buckeyelink.osu.edu.

SHANETIA P. CLARK, PhD, is an assistant professor of education at The Pennsylvania State University–Harrisburg. She is also the site director of the Capital Area Writing Project, a regional site of the National Writing Project. She currently serves on the board of the Special Interest Group Network on Adolescent Literature (SIGNAL) for the International Reading Association. Dr. Clark teaches courses in adolescent literacy, secondary English methods, and writing pedagogy. Her research focuses on teachers' pedagogical decisions that support and integrate authentic and aesthetic experiences with adolescent literature in the classroom.

CORINNA CRAFTON is a language arts teacher at the Wardlaw–Hartridge School in Edison, New Jersey. She has a great deal of experience working with students of many backgrounds at the secondary and college levels, and she specializes in finding creative ways to kindle students' love of reading and writing. She is also the founder and director of the Shakespeare theater program at Wardlaw–Hartridge School. Ms. Crafton holds degrees from Rutgers and The Pennsylvania State University.

PATRICIA A. CRAWFORD is an associate professor at the University of Pittsburgh, with appointments in the Early Childhood Education and Language, Literacy, and Culture programs. A former teacher of children in kindergarten and the primary grades, she now works with prospective and practicing teachers, as well as aspiring researchers and teacher educators. Her research situates literacy learning as a form of social practice and focuses on the dual areas of professional development of and early childhood literacy experiences. Her current work explores the ways in which authentic literature both addresses and problematizes the social issues that surround the lives and learning of young children. Her work has appeared in a variety of journals including the *Journal of Research in Childhood Education, Early Childhood Education Journal, Childhood Education, Young Children*, and the *Journal of Reading Education*, among others.

DEANNA DAY teaches undergraduate and graduate literacy courses for Washington State University, Vancouver. Previously she was a classroom teacher in Arizona for fifteen years. One of her goals as an elementary teacher was to help students become lifelong readers and to critically think about what they were reading. She has continued this goal as a professor, helping teachers become readers and to pass their love of literacy into their classrooms. Her scholarly interests have centered around children's literature, including interviewing authors and illustrators, critically examining books, and researching literature circles in different settings. Her professional work has appeared in several literacy journals, including *The Dragon Lode, Journal of Children's Literature, Language Arts*, and *Reading Horizons*.

RACHEL A. GRANT is an associate professor of Multilingual/Multicultural Education and director of the Center for Language and Culture at George Mason University. Her research interests include application of critical pedagogies focusing on intersections of race, class, and gender in first and second language literacies, literacy teacher education, and urban education.

KIMETTA R. HAIRSTON, PhD, is the sole proprietor of Critical Diverse Interventions. She received her degree from the University of Hawaii at Manao, with a focus on qualitative research design, diversity, and disability studies. Her twelve years of teaching experience ranges from public school to higher education. She has conducted over one hundred diversity training sessions in American Samoa, Hawaii, New Orleans, North Carolina, Nevada, Pennsylvania, Virginia, and Washington, DC. Her coauthored books include *They Followed the Trade Winds—African-American Experiences in Hawaii* and two encyclopedia entries in the *Encyclopedia of Race and Crime*. Currently her research interests are critical race theory and urban education.

JANET HELMBERGER has worked as a classroom or substitute teacher with students in kindergarten through fourth grade in Washington, DC, public schools since May 2009. She retired from Minneapolis Public Schools in 2008 after teaching in dual-immersion and F.L.E.S. programs in grades 1 through 8. She also taught in bilingual programs in south Texas. She earned her PhD in bilingual/multicultural education from The Pennsylvania State University in 2004. Her dissertation focused on how choices and decisions are made in the publication and distribution of multicultural children's books. Her article "Language and Ethnicity in Multiple Languages and Cultures" appeared in *Bilingual Research Journal* in spring 2006. In 1988, she earned an MA from the University of Minnesota in Teaching Second Languages and Cultures. Her research interests include children's literature in both Spanish and English, literacy and language acquisition in first and second languages, and biliteracy programs in the United States and abroad.

DENISE JARRETT is a PhD candidate in English at Morgan State University. She is from Ocho Rios, Jamaica, West Indies. Jarrett gained her first BA degree in English from the University of the West Indies, Mona. She teaches college composition courses at Morgan State University and Community College of Baltimore County, Baltimore, Maryland. Jarrett started her teaching career as a middle and high school English teacher, where she taught English language and literature for over ten years. Her special interest is in postcolonial Caribbean children's literature. Jarrett is also an editorial assistant for *Sankofa: A Journal of African Children's and Young Adult Literature*.

LAUREN LEWIS is currently an eleventh-grade English teacher at Hempfield High School in Landisville, Pennsylvania. Lauren obtained her BS in Education from Millersville University and is currently pursuing her MA in Literacy Education through The Pennsylvania State University. Lauren has been teaching American Literature, and this year she began teaching a new elective course, 20th-Century Multicultural Literature, which she created to expose students to a wider diversity of literature. Her research interests center on increasing students' motivation and the role of multicultural literature to develop empathy and a larger worldview. Lauren can be contacted at Lauren_lewis@hempfieldsd.org.

TAMARA P. LINDSEY is a professor of education studies at the University of Wisconsin–Eau Claire. Her areas of research interest are care work, multicultural children's and young adult literacy, and social justice issues. Prior to earning her PhD at the University of Wisconsin–Madison, she taught in elementary classrooms for over twenty years in Texas, West Virginia, and Indiana. She has taught graduate and undergraduate classes in reading, language arts, and children's literature.

RUTH MCKOY LOWERY is associate professor in language, literacy, and culture in the College of Education at the University of Florida. She teaches courses in children's and adolescent literature and multicultural education. Her research incorporates students' responses to literature, multicultural literature in schools' curricula, immigrant populations, and teaching diverse student populations. Her work has been published in various journals, including the *Journal of Children's Literature*, *Multicultural Education*, *Multicultural Perspective*, *ALAN Review*, and *Dragon Lode*. She is the author of *Immigrants in Children's Literature* (Lang, 2000).

BARBARA A. MARINAK, PhD, is an Associate Professor of Education in the School of Education & Human Services at Mount St. Mary's University. Prior to joining the faculty at Mount St. Mary's, Dr. Marinak taught at Penn State Harrisburg and Millersville University. Dr. Marinak received a Ph.D. in literacy from the University of Maryland, College Park. Her dissertation was awarded the 2005 J. Estill Alexander Future Leaders in Literacy Dissertation Award from the Association of Literacy Educators and Researchers. Prior to her career in higher education, Dr. Marinak spent more than two decades in public education. She held a variety of leadership positions including reading supervisor, elementary curriculum supervisor, and acting superintendent. Dr. Marinak co-chairs the Response to Intervention (RTI) Task Force of the International Reading Association. Along with colleagues Karen Costello, Marjorie Lipson, and Mary Zolman, Dr. Marinak co-authored a chapter on starting and sustaining a systemic approach to RTI in *Successful Approaches to RTI: Collaborative Practices for Improving K–12 Literacy*. She is also the co-editor, along with Jacquelynn Malloy and Linda Gambrell, of *Essential Readings on Motivation*. Dr. Marinak's research interests include reading motivation, intervention practices, and the use of informational text. Her work can be found in *The Reading Teacher, Literacy Research and Instruction, and Young Children.*

MARY NAPOLI is an assistant professor of reading and children's literature at The Pennsylvania State University–Harrisburg, where she teaches both undergraduate and graduate courses in children's and adolescent literature, language arts, and children's literature and writing. Prior to working at the university level, Dr.

Napoli taught kindergarten and first grade in the Pocono Mountain School District. Her research interests include the integration of multicultural literature across the curriculum and girls' responses to popular cultural texts. She currently serves on the Notable Children's Books in the Language Arts Committee and the National Council of Teachers of English Excellence in Poetry for Children Committee.

LINDA T. PARSONS is an assistant professor at The Ohio State University at Marion in the College of Education and Human Ecology, School of Teaching and Learning, where she teaches courses in middle childhood literacy and children's and young adult literature. Her research interests include the analysis of children's and young adult literature, interrogating single novels and text sets as repositories that reinforce and/or challenge established cultural norms. She also explores children's and adolescents' engagement with and response to literature. She is an active member of the National Council of Teachers of English, the International Reading Association, and the American Library Association.

BARBARA A. WARD spent twenty-five years teaching English language arts in the public schools of New Orleans, primarily in grades 7–12. She has taught at every grade level, K–12, and has worked with students with different ability levels ranging from nonreaders to gifted students. Currently a visiting literacy assistant professor at Washington State University–Pullman, she is an avid reader and loves sharing her passion for literacy with her own students. Barbara has served on several book award committees, including the Notable Books for a Global Society (chair), the International Reading Association's Children's and Young Adult Book Awards, the National Council of Teachers of English Award for Excellence in Poetry for Children Committee (chair), the American Library Association's Amelia Bloomer Project, and the Amelia Elizabeth Walden Award Committee for outstanding young adult literature. She was proud to receive the State Literacy Award in 2009 from the Washington Organization for Reading Development as well as the Celebrate Literacy Award from the Benton/Franklin Council of the IRA. Her professional work has appeared in several literacy journals, including *Book Links*, *Dragon Lode*, *Journal of Children's Literature*, *Language Arts*, *The New England Reading Association Journal*, and *Reading Horizons*.

DR. VIVIAN YENIKA-AGBAW, associate professor of literacy at The Pennsylvania State University–University Park, has published articles in *Children's Literature Association Quarterly*, *The New Advocate*, *Journal of Literary and Cultural Disability Studies*, *International Review of Education*, and *Bookbird: A Journal of International Children's Literature*, among others. She has also presented papers on children's and young adult literature at major conferences, including the Modern Language

Association (MLA), the International Research Society for Children's Literature (IRSCL), and the National Council of Teachers of English (NCTE). Her most recent book is *Representing Africa in Children's Literature: Old and New Ways of Seeing*. In addition, she is an assistant editor of *Sankofa: Journal of African Children's and Young Adult Literature*, and she is currently serving on the editorial boards of *Journal of Adolescent and Adult Literacy* (JAAL) and *Language Arts*. Her research interests include West African children's and young adult literature, literature and critical literacy, cultural studies, and postcolonial theory.

Index

A is for Africa (Onyefulu), 152

"A Worn Path" (Welty), 221–222

AAFL. see African American female literacies (AAFL)

Aaron, Hammerin' Hank (Henry)
Henry Aaron's Dream, 144
A Negro League Scrapbook, 143
We Are the Ship: The Story of Negro League Baseball, 143

academically unacceptable school (AUS) status, 236

accuracy
of excellent informational text, 140
multicultural children's books and cultural, 40–41

active listening, 56

ADDL (American Double Dutch League), 97

adolescent literature
alternative families. see alternative families, young adult novels
building literacy through, 99
Caribbean black poverty. see Caribbean postcolonial fiction
disability in. see disability, in Africana adolescent literature
exoticizing children in. see exoticizing of African American and colored children
grief in. see grief, adolescents reading through
Jacqueline Woodson author study and, 66–68, 234–236
keeping hope alive in. see hope, and modern-day miracles
racial discrimination in. see racial discrimination

adventures, fathers for pre-K-3 and, 11–12

affirmation, through poetry, 20

Africa is Not a Country (Knight & Melnicove), 27

African American female literacies (AAFL)
activities for building and honoring, 99–100
activities for discussion and writing, 100–103
children's literature, 103
double dutch, 97–98
Double Dutch (Draper), 98–99
girls, 95–96
history of children's literature, 92–94

history of literature reflecting racism, 91
multicultural movement in U.S education, 90–91
overview of, 94–95
references, 103–105
white teachers with students of African ancestry, 90–91
African American literature
created by non-African Americans, 70
disability as natural phenomenon in, 213–216
exoticizing children. *see* exoticizing of African American and colored children
in global literacy, 265–269
list of children's book publishers, 271–272
poetry for young children, 23–25
raising awareness of race and racial relations, 107
scholarly definition of children's literature, 60
African Holocaust of Enslavement, 95
Africans
disability as unnatural in novels, 211–213, 216
oral tradition of. *see* riddles, as critical thinking tools
poetry for young children. *see* poetry for young children, Africans
After Tupac and D Foster (Woodson)
award-winning, 234–235
in family book club, 66–67
inspiring hope, 237, 240–241
Against Borders: Promoting Books for a Multicultural World (Rochman), 173
AIDS, 268
"Ain't I a Woman?" (Truth), 230
alternative families, young adult novels
Autobiography of My Dead Brother, 200–203
escape and emancipation of, 193–194
The First Part Last, 198–200
helpful websites, 206
overview of, 191–193
questions for enrichment, 205–206
resources, recommendations and conclusions, 203–204
suggested reading, 204–205

Sweet Whispers, Brother Rush, 194–198
works cited, 207
works consulted, 207–208
American Double Dutch League (ADDL), 97
American dream
appendix, 134–137
Billie Holliday in *Becoming Billie Holliday*, 128–129
children's books cited, 137–138
discovering the dreams, 123–126
interpretations of, 122–123
Leah Hopper in *The Red Rose Box*, 127–128
November Nelson in *November Blues*, 129–131
overview of, 122–123
references, 138
Steve Harmon in *Monster*, 131–132
teachers and students considering, 132–134
anchors, representations of pre-k-3 authors as, 12–13
Anderson, Marian, 147–149
anger
hopelessness fueled by, 234
as manifestation of grief, 54, 76–77, 79–82
racism requiring more than, 113
responding to discrimination with, 115
writing letters to and from absent mother, 87
animals, African poetry and, 27
Anthony, Michael
about the author, 177
about the novel, 175
The Year in San Fernando, 177–182
antiliteracy campaigns, 95
appropriation issues, in black fiction, 140
aristocratic construct of American dream, 123
Aristotle, on value of riddles, 160
art
adolescent interpretation of grief through, 86–87
Autobiography of My Dead Brother teaching suggestions, 202
pairing African poetry with, 28
riddles as element of critical thinking in, 161
spiritual exploration through, 56

students bringing in family stories through, 42

in "This Little Light of Mine" books, 50

Asimeng-Boahene, Dr. Lewis, 273

assertive language, African American female literacy, 95

Associated Publishers, 93

Association for the Study of Negro Life and History, 93

AUS (academically unacceptable school) status, 236

authenticity, books in classroom of cultural, 37–38

authors

African American books by non-African American, 70

of African American children's literature, 60

Coretta Scott King Award for African-American, 122

history of African American children's literature, 92–94

Jacqueline Woodson, 66–68, 234–236

Jerry Pinkney, 64–66

Autobiography of My Dead Brother (Myers), 200–203

bargaining stage of grief

demonstrated by students, 85

in *Everett Anderson's Goodbye*, 54

overview of, 79–82

writing letters to and from absent mother, 87

baseball desegregation. *see* Negro League Baseball, nonfiction

Baseball Hall of Fame, players from Negro Leagues in, 143

Baumfree, Isabella, 230

Beautiful Ballerina (Nelson), 62

Becoming Billie Holliday (Weatherford), 128–129

Bedford, April Whatley, 273

beginning period (1890–1900), of African American children's literature, 92

Berger-Knorr, Ann, PhD, 274

bias, in multicultural nonfiction, 141

Bippity Bop Barbershop (Tarpley), 10, 15, 61

Black Boy (Wright), 230

black experiences. *see* nonfiction about black experiences

Black Vernacular English

English curriculums disregarding, 194

in *Sweet Whispers, Brother Rush*, 195–196

blacks toward blacks, identifying discrimination of, 111–112

blacks toward whites, identifying discrimination of, 111–113

Bleich's Response Hueristic, 149–150

The Bluest Eye (Morrison), 230

Board of Education v. Brown, 95

Bontemps, Arna, 93–94

book club. *see* Family Book Club

border-crossing, with books, 34–36, 266

boundary-crossing relationships, books demonstrating spirit of, 54–55

breaking down borders, with books, 34–36, 266

Broken Memory: A Story of Rwanda (Combre)

addressing rape and genocide, 268

disability as result of war in, 211–212

stance on disability in, 213

Brown v. Board of Education, 95

Bud, Not Buddy (Curtis)

adjusting to life without mother, 80

anger stage of grief, 80

depression, reflection and loneliness stage, 83

the upward turn stage of grief, 84

captains, representations of pre-K-3 fathers as, 8–11

care work. *see also* exoticizing of African American and colored children

children most like native standard and, 251–252

definition for teaching practices, 253–256

Caribbean Cultural Identity (Nettleford), 176

Caribbean postcolonial fiction

Cyril Everard Palmer's novels, 182–187

Michael Anthony's novel. *see The Year in San Fernando* (Anthony)

overview of, 173–174

references, 189–190

text related activities, 187–189

young adolescent literature on, 174–176

Casbergue, Renée, 274

Castleman, Michele D., 274

CDs, of poets reading for young children, 23–24

Chandra's Secrets (Stratton), 268

character portrayal
    of American dream. *see* American dream
    analysis of multicultural children's books, 40–41
    black poverty in *The Year in San Fernando,* 177–182
    Mr. George Baker (Hest), 54
    supporting spiritual wonderings and concerns, 49

Children of the River (Crew), 257–259

Christopher (Drayton), 174

Civil Rights Act of 1964, 146

civil rights movement
    from 1955–1965, 146
    in dugouts. *see* Negro League Baseball, nonfiction
    in *Fire from the Rock,* 222–225
    performances from the stage and, 146–150
    spiritual component of, 51–52

Clark, Shanetia, PhD, 274

classroom libraries, spiritual literature in, 56

The Cloud with the Silver Lining (Palmer), 175–176, 183–187

The Color Purple (Walker), 229

Coming of Age in Mississippi (Moody), 223–225

Coming on Home Soon (Woodson)
    award-winning, 234
    exoticizing of children and, 260, 262

Coming Out the Door for the Ninth Ward (Nine Times Social and Pleasure Club), 63–64

Community Book Clubs, 63

community spirit, in *The Cloud with the Silver Lining,* 184–187

comprehension, picture books promoting, 62–63

connections, power of, 243–246

conservative construct of American dream, 123

conundrums, riddles as, 161

coping skills
    in challenges of daily life, 53–55

spirituality and. *see* spirituality and young children

Copper Sun (Draper), 225–226

Coretta Scott King (CSK) Award. *see* American dream

A Cow Called Boy (Palmer), 183

Crafton, Corinna, 275

Crawford, Patricia A., 275

CRF (critical race feminism), 100–101

crime
    in *Autobiography of My Dead Brother,* 201
    in current African American children's literature, 94
    Visiting Day and children's understanding of, 261

critical race feminism (CRF), 100–101

critical race theory (CRT)
    critical thinking and, 267
    of education, 100

Critical Theory Today: A User-Friendly Guide (Tyson), 205–206

critical thinking
    activities using African riddles, 166–168
    characteristics and functions of riddles, 162–164
    conceptual framework about riddles, 160–161
    definitions of, 159
    perspectives of riddles in Africa, 162
    references, 168–169
    riddles as tools for, 157–158, 164–168
    in social studies, 159–160
    what riddles have in common with, 164–166

cross-cultural literature
    Double Dutch, 98–99
    within multicultural literature, 140–141
    reading about differences and similarities in, 35, 38–39
    The Soul of Baseball as, 145, 154
    using African riddles, 166
    The Voice That Challenged a Nation as, 148–150, 154

cross-cultural schools, in urban setting, 90

culturally conscious literature (1980s-present), African American children, 94

culturally relevant literature, sharing with families
  children's books cited, 71
  enriching literacy environment, 60–61
  Family Book Club model. *see* Family Book Club
  instruction, 62–63
  overview of, 59
  picture books for classrooms, 70–71
  references, 72
  reflecting on experiences, 68–70
  supplementing curriculum, 61–62
  theoretical foundation of, 59–60
  where we go from here, 70
culture
  book clubs focusing on local, 63–64
  Caribbean. *see* Caribbean postcolonial fiction
  exploring in African poetry, 20, 25–26, 28
  Harlem Renaissance influence on, 93
  literature as conduit for formation of, 96
  multicultural literature understanding, 267
  oral art within. *see* riddles, as critical thinking tools
  representing identity. *see* identity

Daddy Goes to Work (Asim), 11–12, 15
daily life
  books exploring on relationship between sacred and, 51
  books on challenges of, 53–55
DAR (Daughters of the American Revolution), 147
Daughters of the American Revolution (DAR), 147
Day, Deanna, 275
death
  in *Autobiography of My Dead Brother*, 201
  books demonstrating challenges of, 54–55
  in Everett Anderson's *Goodbye*, 54
  reading through grief. see grief, adolescents reading through
Declaration of Independence, 123
dedications, book, 64, 66
democratic ideals, American dream, 123
depression stage of grief, 82–83

dialogue journals, 41
Diamonds in the Shadow (Cooney), 211–213
disability, in Africana adolescent literature
  books, 217
  left out in school curriculums, 209–210
  in novels of African Americans, 213–216
  in novels set in Africa, 211–213
  references, 217–218
  social model of, 210
  summary conclusion, 216
  teaching suggestions, 216–217
  vocabulary log, 217
discourses, primary, 34
discrimination. *see* racial discrimination
The Distant Talking Drum: Poems from Nigeria (Olaleye), 26
diversity
  across cultural groups, 35
  adding to curriculums, 69–70, 229
  African American children's literature reflecting, 94
  African American young adult fiction reflecting, 193
  Africana poetry celebrating cultural, 18–19
  exoticizing. *see* exoticizing of African American and colored children
  global vs. domestic, xiii
  social studies of cultural, 160
  stories representing cultural, 37–38
  understanding Africa's geographical, 27
  in U.S. schools, 90
Dodgers, baseball desegregation and, 142–143
domination, discrimination through, 114
double dutch, African Americans and, 97–98
Double Dutch (Draper), 99–103
Down the Winding Road (Johnson), 12
dramatization
  exoticizing notion of difference through, 256–259
  interpreting grief through, 86–87
  of poetry, 24–25
Draper, Sharon, 219, 221
dreaming the dream. *see* American dream
The Drummer Boy (Ekwensi), 211–213

Early Reading First (ERF) projects

enriching literacy environment, 60–61
Family Book Club model. *see* Family Book Club
overview of, 59
reflecting on our experiences, 68–69
supplementing literary-focused curriculum, 61–62
economic achievement, in American dream
Becoming Billie Holliday, 128–129
security and personal satisfaction of, 132
economic conditions. *see also* poverty
black poverty in Jamaica, 183–188
black poverty in postcolonial Caribbean, 176–182
in Caribbean colonial societies, 174–175
in current African American children's literature, 94
in early African American children's books, 35
and hope. *see* hope, and modern-day miracles
The Mis-Education of the Negro on, 93
overview of, 125
portraying in children's literature, 35
unfair economic control of blacks, 109, 111, 116–118
in *The Year in San Fernando*, 177–182
economic control, racial discrimination
identifying, 111
overview of, 109
understanding, 117–118
emancipatory value, of African American fiction, 192
Emeka's Gift: An African Counting Story (Onyefulu), 152
emergent tradition period (1900–1920s), African American children's literature, 92–93
emotions
affirming through poetry. *see* poetry for young children
evoked in *The Soul of Baseball*, 145
reading through grief. *see* grief, adolescents reading through
spirituality offering solace to. *see* spirituality and young children

empathy
building through kinesthetic learning, 197
developing in non-Afro-American readers, 94
evoking in *Roll of Thunder, Hear My Cry*, 115
evoking in *Yesterday I Had the Blues*, 13
Miracle's Boys evoking, 241–242
responding to discrimination with, 115
Enigma of an Autumn Afternoon (Riddles), 161
Enigma Variations (Elgar), 161
enigmas, riddles as, 161–162
ERF projects. *see* Early Reading First (ERF) projects
event maps, and discrimination, 113–116
Everett Anderson's Goodbye (Clifton), 53–54
exotic, notion of, 251
exoticizing of African American and colored children
attitudes about serious issues, 259–261
definition of care work, 253–256
notions of difference through drama, 256–259
overview of, 251–252
personal experience stories, 252–253

fables, as earliest type of created thought, 161
faith-based schools
pedagogical considerations for spiritual explorations, 55–56
spiritual support in, 47–48
family
in "A Worn Path," 221–222
alternative. *see* alternative families, young adult novels
involving in spiritual exploration and discussions, 56
sharing literature with. *see* culturally relevant literature, sharing with families
family, dream of
Becoming Billie Holliday, 128–129
in *November Blues*, 129–131
overview of, 125–126
in *The Red Rose Box*, 127–128
teachers and students considering, 132–134
Family Book Club

concept of, 63
experiences with, 69–70
Jacqueline Woodson author study, 66–68
Jerry Pinkney author and illustrator study,
    64–66
local culture focus, 63–64
Faraway Home (Kurtz), 10
"Father knows best" stories, 3–4, 8–11
fatherhood, single, 198–200
fathers, representations for pre-K-3
    adventuring with dad, 11–12
    analyzing roles of, 3–4
    as anchors (always my daddy), 12–13
    books cited, 15
    as captains (daddy knows best), 8–11
    list of literature portraying, 9
    in picture books, 6–7
    references, 16–17
    research on, 5–6
    review summary, 14–15
    in stories, 7–8
Feathers (Woodson), 215, 235
female literacies. *see* African American female
    literacies (AAFL)
Fire from the Rock (Draper), 222–225
The First Part Last (Johnson), 198–200, 268
Fitzgerald, Ella, 142
folktales
    African riddles rooted in, 162
    as earliest type of created thought, 161
    importance in Africa, 163
    pairing poetry with African, 28–29
Fortune (the slave), legacy of, 150–152
Fortune's Bones: The Manumission Requiem
    (Nelson), 150–152
Foster, Rube, 142
friendships, nature of, 53
From the Notebooks of Melanin Sun (Woodson),
    267
Full, Full, Full of Love (Cooke), 61

geographical exploration, African poetry,
    27–28
girls, African American
    activities for building female literacies,
        99–100

double dutch and, 97–98
oppression of, 103
poor quality of education of, 95–96
global literacy
    African/African American literature in
        schools for, 265–266
    on black sexuality, 267–268
    list of children's book publishers, 271–272
    organizations promoting, 268
    outstanding titles for classroom, 268–269
    on teenage mothers and fathers, rape and
        incest, 268
    understanding other cultures, 266–267
    understanding sociopolitical factors in the
        world, 267
God's Dream (Tutu), 51
*God's Photo Album: How We Looked for God and
    Saved Our School* (Mecum), 48
Grant, Rachel A., 275
"Great Migration" of blacks, and Harlem
    Renaissance, 93
Green Days by the River (Anthony), 177
grief, adolescents reading through
    anger and bargaining, 80–82
    artistic interpretations, 86–87
    depression, reflection and loneliness, 82–83
    grieving absent mother, 79–80
    hiccups, 75–79
    inviting students to select texts, 85–86
    letters to and from the absent mother, 87
    references, 88–89
    seven stages of grief, 79
    summary review, 87–88
    upward turn, 84–85
    writing and, 85–86
grief, *Everett Anderson's Goodbye* (Clifton),
    53–54
Gulliver's Travels (Swift), 175

Hairston, Kimetta, PhD, 275–276
Hardy Boys, 175
Harlem Renaissance (1920–1930), 93
Harmon, Steve, 131–132
*The Hatseller and the Monkeys: A West African
    Fairytale* (Diakité), 28
The Heart Has Its Reasons: Young Adult

Literature with Gay/Lesbian/Queer Content (Cart and Jenkins), 267–268
Heart of Darkness (Conrad), 174
The Hello, Goodbye Window (Juster), 53
Helmberger, Janet, 276
Henry Aaron's Dream (Tavares), 144
Here Comes Our Bride! (Onyefulu), 152
"Hiccups," 75–79
high school literature
    alternative families. *see* alternative families, young adult novels
    building literacy with, 99
    Caribbean fiction. *see* Caribbean postcolonial fiction
    disability in. *see* disability, in Africana adolescent literature
    exoticizing children. *see* exoticizing of African American and colored children
    Jacqueline Woodson author study and, 66–68, 234–236
    keeping hope alive. *see* hope, and modern-day miracles
    passing through grief. *see* grief, adolescents reading through
    racial discrimination. *see* racial discrimination
    After Tupac and D Foster (Woodson), 66–67
Hip Hop Speaks to Children: A Celebration of Poetry with a Beat (Giovanni), 24
hip hop, teaching suggestions, 203
historical fiction, and culture of struggle
    "A Worn Path," 221–222
    "Ain't I a Woman?," 230
    Black Boy, 230
    The Bluest Eye, 230
    The Color Purple, 229
    Copper Sun, 225–226
    Fire from the Rock, 222–225
    To Kill a Mockingbird, 226–227
    Langston's Hughes Theme of individuality, 228–229
    overview of, 219–220
    references, 231–232
    "Step-Stomp-Stride," 230
    summary conclusion, 229
    "The Negro Speaks of Rivers," 231

theoretical framework, 220–221
    A Time to Kill, 227–228
Holliday, Billy, 128–129
homelessness, 268
Honey, I Love and Other Love Poems (Greenfield), 19
hope, and modern-day miracles
    author studies, 234–236
    book list, 249
    conclusion, 246–248
    counterbalancing hopelessness with, 233–234
    finding by making connections, 243–246
    finding by understanding texts, 240–243
    keeping alive, 239–240
    lunchtime group, 238–239
    references, 250
    school context, 236–237
    searching for, 237–238
hopelessness, 233–234
Hopper, Leah, 127–128
Hughes, Langston, 228–229
Hugo, Victor, 166

I

identity
    in African/African American literature, 235, 266
    Caribbean literature and, 174–176
    double dutch fostering African American, 97–98
    evoking through poetry. *see* poetry for young children
    Harlem Renaissance fostering new, 93
    importance of books mirroring own racial, 68
identity, representing in children's literature
    border crossing and, 34–36
    choosing books in classroom, 37–39
    cultural awareness and knowledge, 39–42
    overview of, 33–34
    primary discourses, 34
    references, 43–44
    selection of stories and their settings, 36–37
    suggested children's books, 42–43
If You Come Softly (Woodson), 237
Ikenna Goes to Nigeria (Onyefulu), 27, 152

illustrations
    God's Dream (Tutu), 51
    The Hello, Goodbye Window (Juster), 53
    Jerry Pinkney author and illustrator study,
        64–66
    Martin's Big Words (Rappaport), 51
    My Best Friend (Rodman), 53
    The Other Side (Woodson), 67
    of spiritual exploration, 56
    Virgie Goes to School With Us Boys
        (Howard), 52
    Visiting Day (Woodson), 55
illustrators
    African American children's literature, 60
    Jerry Pinkney, 64–66
    non-African American, 70
incarceration, in Visiting Day, 55, 260–261
individual racial discrimination, 108, 118
institutional discrimination, 108, 111
intellectual audacity, riddling developing, 164
internal pressure, racial discrimination, 109,
    117–119
International Sweethearts of Rhythm, 65
I-Search (Short et al.), 142–143

Jamaica, black poverty in, 183–187
Jarrett, Denise, 276
Jazz (Myers), 63–64
The Jolly Postman or Other People's Letters
    (Ahlberg and Ahlberg), 256–257, 259
Joyful Noise: Poems for Two Voices (Fleischman),
    223–224

Keep on Singing: A Ballad of Marian Anderson
    (Livingston), 147–148
kinetic orality, and double dutch, 97
King, Martin Luther, 51
Kingsolver, Barbara, 191
Kubler-Ross, Elizabeth, 79

language
    activities using African riddles, 168
    representing cultural identity, 36
    in Sweet Whispers, Brother Rush, 195–196
Law and Order, 227
leaders, pre-K-3 fathers as, 8–11

Lesbian and Gay Voices: An Annotated
    Bibliography and Guide to Literature for
    Children and Young Adults (Day), 268
letter writing, to absent mother, 87
Lewis, Lauren, 276
Lily Brown's Paintings (Johnson), 13
Lincoln Memorial, Marian Anderson concert,
    147–149
Lindsey, Tamara P., 277
The Lion and the Mouse (Pinkney), 65–66
literacy development
    pairing African poetry with, 28
    reading and writing through grief, 84–85
literary merit, analysis of multicultural chil-
    dren's books, 40
literature discussion groups, 41
literature discussion sessions, 39–41
local culture focus, of Family Book Club
    model, 63–64
Locomotion (Woodson), 67, 234–235, 237
logical thinking. see critical thinking
Lola Loves Stories (McQuinn), 11–12
loneliness stage of grief, 82–83
love
    as common theme in African American lit-
        erature, 19
    The Year in San Fernando and lack of, 178,
        180–181
Love Rules (Reynolds), 267
Lowery, Ruth McKoy, 277
low-self esteem, and absent mothers, 80
lunchtime group
    finding hope by understanding texts,
        240–241
    keeping hope alive, 239–240
    searching for hope, 237–238
    students in, 238–239
    summary conclusion, 247–248

Major League Baseball, Jackie Robinson
    crossover to, 142–144
males, young adult, 176
manumission, defined, 150–152
Marinak, Barbara A., PhD, 277
married couples, fathers with children in, 5–6
Martin's Big Words (Rappaport), 51

Maslow, Abraham, 178

math, pairing African poetry with, 28

Mattatuck Museum in Waterbury, CT, 150–152

Mays, Willie, 145

medical condition, disability as result of, 214–215

Meditalker, 214

memory, in *Sweet Whispers*, 194–198

metaphors, riddles as, 160–161

military, female literacy on blacks in, 95

The Miniature Guide to Critical Thinking (Paul and Elder), 159

Miracle's Boys (Woodson)
  adjusting to life without mother, 80
  anger and bargaining over loss of mother, 80–81
  award-winning, 235
  finding hope, 240–241, 243–246
  inspiring hope in middle school children, 237
  upward turn stage of grief in, 84

The Mis-Education of the Negro (Woodson), 93

Miz Berlin Walks (Yolen), 54–55

mobility, dream of
  in *Monster*, 131–132
  overview of, 125
  in *The Red Rose Box*, 127
  teachers and students considering, 132–134

money. *see* economic conditions

Monster (Myers), 131–132

moral development, in *The Year in San Fernando*, 179–182

mother
  connected to how her child will thrive, 79–80
  presence and impact throughout child's life, 79
  The Year in San Fernando and love of, 177–182

mothers, absent
  adolescents in classroom grieving over, 75–79
  anger and bargaining stage of grief, 80–82
  depression, reflection and loneliness stage of grief, 82–83
  grieving, 79–80
  inviting students to select texts, 85–86
  reading and writing through grief, 84–85
  upward turn stage of grief, 83–84
  writing a letter to and from, 87

Mr. George Baker (Hest), 54

multicultural children's literature
  analysis of, 39–41
  awareness of race and racial relations in, 107
  cross-cultural literature in, 141–142
  definition of, 140
  global literacy using, 265–269
  parallel cultural literature in, 141
  world literature in, 140–141

multicultural movement, in U.S education, 91

multimedia presentations, 87

music
  accompanying African poetry with, 26–27
  adolescent interpretation of grief through, 86–87
  Autobiography of My Dead Brother teaching suggestions, 202–203
  Harlem Renaissance influence on, 93
  Marian Anderson, 147–149
  study of *After Tupac and D Foster* and, 241
  "This Little Light of Mine," 50

My Best Friend (Rodman), 53

My Father Sun—Sun Johnson (Palmer), 183

naming, exploring act of, 196–197

Nancy Drew, 175

Napoli, Mary, 277–278

National Council for Social Studies (NCSS), 159

National Council of Teachers of English Award for Excellence in Poetry for Children, 21

National Geographic website, Sherpa of Mount Everest, 153

native standard
  care work in teaching and, 253–256
  definition of, 251–252

NCSS (National Council for Social Studies), 159

Negro history week, 93

Negro League Baseball, nonfiction

beginning of civil rights movement, 141–142

Henry Aaron's Dream, 144

A Negro League Scrapbook, 142–143

Negro Leagues Baseball Museum, 144–145

Our Children Can Soar, 142

The Soul of Baseball: A Road Trip Through Buck O'Neil's America, 145

story of, 142

using I-Search matrix to study, 142–143

We Are the Ship: The Story of Negro League Baseball, 143

A Negro League Scrapbook (Weatherford), 142–143

Negro National League, 142–143

The Neighborhood Mother Goose (Crews), 62

Neighborhood Story Project, 63–64

Nelson, Marilyn, 65–66

Nelson, November, 129–131

Newberry Award, 106

nicknames

    Jacqueline Woodson's use of, 240

    power of, 196–197

Ninth Ward (Rhodes), 80–81

No Child Left Behind legislation, 39, 59

nonfiction about black experiences

    around the world, 152–154

    framework for selecting excellent, 140–141, 154–155

    methods for engaging children about, 141

    overview of, 139–140

    performances from the stage, 146–150

    players on the diamond. *see* Negro League Baseball, nonfiction

    references, 155–156

    a requiem for bones, 150–152

    summary conclusion, 154–155

November Blues (Draper), 129–131

nuclear family model, 191–192

Obama, President Barack, 3

Off to the Sweet Shores of Africa and Other Talking Drum Rhymes (Grimes), 29–30

One Big Family: Sharing Life in an African Village (Onyefulu), 152

One Child, One Seed: A South African Counting Book (Cave), 28

One Death and Dying (Kubler-Ross), 79

O'Neil, Buck

    A Negro League Scrapbook, 142

    The Soul of Baseball: A Road Trip Through Buck O'Neil's America, 145

    We Are the Ship: The Story of Negro League Baseball, 143

online references

    African poetry for children, 26

    alternative families, 222

    list of children's book publishers, 271–272

    Mattack Museum, 152

    organizations promoting global literacy, 268

    selecting quality poetry, 21

Onyefulu, Ifeoma, 152

Opening the World of Learning (OWL) curriculum, 61–62

open-mindedness of young readers, 155

oppression

    ignoring in Black girls, 103

    stories telling how people have withstood, 35

oral traditions. *see* riddles, as critical thinking tools

The Orange Houses (Griffin), 213–214

Orangeburg Massacre, 140

organizational racial discrimination, 108–109, 118

Orphea Proud (Whyeth), 267

The Other Side (Woodson), 66–68

Our Children Can Soar (Cook), 142

Out of My Mind (Draper), 214–215

overt discrimination, 108, 111

OWL (Opening the World of Learning) curriculum, 61–62

ownership issue, black fiction, 140

Paige, Satchel, 145

Palmer, Cyril Everard, 175, 182–183

parallel cultural literature, 141, 154

parental neglect, as result of, 211

parenthood, single, 198–200, 268

Parks, Rosa, 142

Parsons, Linda T., 278

Peace, Locomotion (Woodson), 67, 237

Peekaboo Morning (Isadora), 62
peer relationships, building in primary years, 53
performative silence, African American female literacy, 95
personal growth, and grief, 84–85
physical intimidation, racial discrimination
    identifying, 111
    overview of, 109
    understanding, 117–118
physical symptoms, of grief, 79, 84
picture books
    cultural authenticity in, 38–39
    cultural identity in, 36
    Emeka's Gift: An African Counting Story, 152
    exoticizing notion of difference, 256–259
    Family Book Club model, 64, 69–70
    fathers in, 6–7
    Henry Aaron's Dream, 144
    inspiring hope in middle school using, 237
    A is for Africa, 152
    Keep on Singing: A Ballad of Marian Anderson (Livingston), 147–148
    The Lion and the Mouse (Pinkney), 65
    literacy development using, 62
    My Best Friend (Rodman), 53
    The Other Side (Woodson), 67
    for pre-K classrooms, 70–71
    spiritual wonderings and concerns in, 49
    When Marian Sang, 147–148
Pinkney, Jerry, 64–66
Pinkney family, 65–66
players on the diamond. *see* Negro League Baseball, nonfiction
poetry
    Joyful Noise: Poems for Two Voices (Fleischman), 223–224
    Locomotion (Woodson), 234
    "Theme for English B," 228–229
poetry for young children
    African American, 23–25
    benefits of, 18–19
    cited works, 29–31
    Jazz, 63
    learning riddles similar to learning, 162–163
    list of literature, 22–23
    references, 31–32

    selecting and using, 19–21
    Sweethearts of Rhythm, 65
poetry for young children, Africans
    art and culture, 29
    generating interest, 27
    geographical exploration, 27–28
    overview of, 25–26
    pairing with folktales, 28–29
polite language, African American female literacy, 95
poverty. *see also* economic conditions
    African American female literacy on high rate of, 95
    of blacks in postcolonial Caribbean, 175–176
    in *The Cloud with the Silver Lining,* 183–187
    in current African American children's literature, 94
    struggle of black teens with, 234
    in *The Year in San Fernando,* 177–182
power, discrimination through, 114
preaching, in African American female literacy, 95
prejudice
    Black Boy, 230
    Copper Sun, 225–226
    racial discrimination vs. racial, 108
prejudice-causes-discrimination-model, 108
primary discourses, framing core identity, 34
prison
    African American female literacy on blacks in, 95
    spirit of resilience in, 55
    Visiting Day, 55, 260–262
privileges. *see* exoticizing of African American and colored children
proverbs, as earliest type of created thought, 161
Psalm Twenty-three (Ladwig), 49–50
psychological disability, in novels of Africa, 213
psychological power, racial discrimination
    identifying, 111
    overview of, 109
    understanding, 117–118
publishers, African/African American book,

271–272

quilts, family stories through, 42

racial discrimination
    children between ages 2 and 5 aware of, 259
    lessons on. *see* historical fiction, and culture
        of struggle
racial discrimination (and adolescents)
    African American literature reflecting, 91,
        94
    of blacks toward blacks, 112
    of blacks toward whites, 112–113
    conversing with students about, 119–120
    defining, 107–108
    examining and explaining, 113–116
    identifying, 110–113
    levels of, 108
    naming, 116–120
    overt vs. institutional, 108
    racial prejudice vs., 108
    raising awareness of, 106–107
    references, 120–121
    social control through, 109–110
    studying *Roll of Thunder, Hear My Cry,*
        106–107
    of whites toward blacks, 110–111, 114–115
    of whites toward whites, 112
racial prejudice. *see* prejudice
Radcliff, Ted "Double Duty"
    A Negro League Scrapbook, 142–143
    The Soul of Baseball, 145
    We Are the Ship, 143
rape
    addressing in African American literature,
        268
    Becoming Billie Holliday, 128
    A Time to Kill, 227–228
read-alouds, multicultural children's books,
    40–41
reading centers, Early Reading First projects,
    61
reasoning, developing through reasoning, 164
The Red Rose Box (Woods), 127–128
reflection stage of grief, 82–83
relationships, messiness of, 198–200

religion
    parent involvement and, 5
    in postcolonial Caribbean, 174
    When Daddy Prays (Grimes), 9–10
requiem for bones, 150–152
research, African American father involvement,
    5–6
resilience
    demonstrating spirituality of, 54–55
    fostering in black girls, 96, 100
    literature modeling wide range of circum-
        stances, 56
    in novels about alternative families,
        203–204
responsiveness, spiritual development through,
    56
rhymes
    in African American female literacy, 95
    promoting with picture books, 62
rhythm, African American poetry and, 24
riddles, as critical thinking tools
    African oral tradition of, 157
    conceptual framework about, 160–161
    critical thinking in social studies using,
        159–160
    definition of critical thinking, 159
    failure to use in education, 157–158
    overview of, 164–168
    perspectives in Africa on, 162–164
    references, 168–169
Robinson, Jackie
    beginning of civil rights movement,
        142–143
    Henry Aaron's Dream, 144
    integration of pro baseball, 142
Robinson Crusoe (Defoe), 174
Roll of Thunder, Hear My Cry (Taylor)
    awareness of race and racial relations,
        106–107
    examining and explaining discrimination,
        113–116
    identifying discrimination, 110–113
    naming discrimination, 116–120
Roosevelt, First Lady Eleanor, 147, 149
Rose, Mike, 247
Rosenblatt, Louise, 236

Rwanda
    addressing rape and genocide in, 268
    disability as result of war, 211–212

Sacred Mountain Everest (Taylor-Butler),
    152–154
sacrifice
    in "A Worn Path," 221–222
    of players in Negro League Baseball, 142
Scottsboro Trials, 226
segregation. *see also* racial discrimination
    creating Negro League Baseball. *see* Negro
        League Baseball, nonfiction
    Fire from the Rock (Draper), 222–225
    Marian Anderson and, 146–149
    Orangeburg Massacre and, 139–140
self-actualization, The Cloud with the Silver
    Lining, 186–187
selfhood, dream of
    overview of, 125–126
    in *The Red Rose Box,* 127–128
    teachers and students considering, 132–134
self-selected texts, 85–86
serious topics
    approaching with sense of fearlessness, 262
    exoticizing young children from, 256–262
sexuality
    books on issues of black, 267–268
    in *The Year in San Fernando,* 181–182
Shakur, Tupac, 66–67, 240–241. *see also After
    Tupac and D Foster* (Woodson)
sharing literature. *see* culturally relevant litera-
    ture, sharing with families
shift to assimilation period, African American
    children's literature, 93–94
Sierra Leone, disability as result of war in,
    211–212
Sing to the Sun (Grimes, Thomas, and Bryan),
    19
Sister Anne's Hands (Lorbiecki), 52
slavery
    African American female literacy and, 95
    Caribbean. *see* Caribbean postcolonial fic-
        tion
    in *Copper Sun,* 225–226
    nonfiction books on, 150–152

Smith Hammond Middleton Memorial
    Center, 140
social class, in *The Year in San Fernando,* 179
social conscience literature, 94
social control
    discrimination and forms of, 116–120
    racial discrimination as, 109–111, 114
social issues
    African/African American literature and,
        265–269
    disability in African American novels,
        213–216
    evoking through poetry. *see* poetry for young
        children
    exoticizing young children as not under-
        standing, 259–262
    racial discrimination. *see* racial discrimina-
        tion
social justice, dream of
    Becoming Billie Holliday, 129
    overview of, 125–126
    teachers and students considering, 132–134
social studies
    critical thinking activities, 168
    critical thinking in, 159–160
    poetry in, 24–25
socialization, with double dutch, 97–98
Socratic discussion, 151–152
The Soul of Baseball (Posnanski), 145
speakerly text, *Autobiography of My Dead
    Brother,* 201–202
Sphinx (Chatton), riddle of the, 160
spiritual leaders, writings and works of, 51
spirituality, definitions of, 47
spirituality and young children
    in challenges of life, 53–55
    children's books cited, 56–57
    discomfort of teachers in dealing with,
        45–46
    exploring differences and similarities, 48
    exploring faith and the sacred, 49–52
    pedagogical considerations, 55–56
    references, 57–58
    role in cultures with religious traditions,
        46–47
    role in nurturing, 46–47

role of literature in, 48–49
search for explanations, 48
task of guiding, 47
stage performances
contributions to racial equality, 146
singing of Marian Anderson, 147–149
stepping, in African American female literacy, 95
"Step-Stomp-Stride" (Truth), 230
stereotyping
of blacks in books for whites, 192
of blacks in colonial literatures, 174
history of African American children's literature, 92
of nuclear families in books, 191
The Story of Ruby Bridges (Coles), 52
storytelling
in African American female literacy, 95
exploring supernatural and memory in, 195
pairing African poetry with folktales, 28
strengthening of the tradition period (1930–1940), African American children's literature, 93
structural racial discrimination, 109, 118
style shifting, African American female literacy, 95
Sunjata, Warrior King of Mali: A West African Legend (Fontes), 211, 213
supernatural, in *Sweet Whispers, Brother Rush*, 194–198
Sweet Whispers, Brother Rush (Hamilton), 194–198
Sweethearts of Rhythm (Nelson), 65

Talking Drums: A Selection of Poems from Africa South of the Sahara, 26
Teaching Black Girls: Resiliency in Urban Classrooms (Evans-Winters), 96
tensions, books giving pleasure through, 39
Text Impression study, Sacred Mountain Everest (Taylor-Butler), 153
"The Negro Speaks of Rivers," 231
"The Untitled Story" (Stimpson)
adjusting to life without mother, 80
anger and bargaining over loss of mother, 81
the upward turn stage of grief, 84

"Theme for English B" (Hughes), 228–229
"This Little Light of Mine" (Lewis), 50–51
A Time to Kill (Grisham), 227–228
timelessness, of excellent informational text, 140
To Kill a Mockingbird (Lee), 226–228
traditional African American family, 4
traditional father, 4
transcendence, of disability, 211
Trinidad, poverty in, 177–182
Truth, Sojourner, 230
Tuft's University laboratory school, 48
Tyrell (Booth), 268

unemployment, postcolonial Caribbean youth, 176
unfair treatment
discrimination at organizational level, 118
of whites towards blacks, 114–115
upward turn stage of grief, 83–84

Violet's Music (Johnson), 61
Virgie Goes to School With Us Boys (Howard), 52
Visiting Day (Woodson), 55, 260–262
vocabulary
promoting with picture books, 62
wordless books developing, 66
The Voice That Challenged a Nation: Marion Anderson and the Struggle for Equal Rights (Freedman), 148–150
Voices Rising: Celebrating 20 Years of Black Lesbian, Gay. Bisexual & Transgender Writing (James), 268
Voting Rights Act of 1965, 146

war, disability as result of, 211–212
Ward, Barbara A., 278
The Way We Never Were (Coontz), 192
We Are the Ship: The Story of Negro League Baseball (Nelson), 143
Welcome, Precious (Grimes), 10
What Mama Left Me (Watson)
adjusting to life without mother, 80
anger over loss of mother, 81
depression, reflection and loneliness stage of grief, 83

upward turn stage of grief, 84
wheelchairs, as symbol of disability, 215
When Daddy Prays (Grimes), 9–10
When Marian Sang (Ryan), 147–148
whites toward blacks, discrimination of,
    110–112, 114–115
Who Will I Be, Lord? (Nelson), 13
Wide Sargasso Sea (Rhys), 174
Woodson, Carter G., 93 ·
Woodson, Jacqueline
    author study, 66–68, 234–235
    children's and young adult books by, 249
    inspiring hope in middle school, 237–238
world literature, 140–141, 152–154

writers' workshops, critical literacy through,
    41–42
writing activities
    African American female literacy, 102
    using poetry as model for, 25

The Year in San Fernando (Anthony), 175–182
Yenika-Agbaw, Dr. Vivian, 278–279
Yesterday I Had the Blues (Frame), 12–13
You Can Do It (Dungy), 8–9
young adult literature. see high school literature

Zena Sutherland lecture, Woodson, 246
zone of proximal development, 242

ROCHELLE BROCK &
RICHARD GREGGORY JOHNSON III,
Executive Editors

Black Studies and Critical Thinking is an interdisciplinary series which examines the intellectual traditions of and cultural contributions made by people of African descent throughout the world. Whether it is in literature, art, music, science, or academics, these contributions are vast and far-reaching. As we work to stretch the boundaries of knowledge and understanding of issues critical to the Black experience, this series offers a unique opportunity to study the social, economic, and political forces that have shaped the historic experience of Black America, and that continue to determine our future. Black Studies and Critical Thinking is positioned at the forefront of research on the Black experience, and is the source for dynamic, innovative, and creative exploration of the most vital issues facing African Americans. The series invites contributions from all disciplines but is specially suited for cultural studies, anthropology, history, sociology, literature, art, and music.

Subjects of interest include (but are not limited to):

- EDUCATION
- SOCIOLOGY
- HISTORY
- MEDIA/COMMUNICATION
- RELIGION/THEOLOGY
- WOMEN'S STUDIES

- POLICY STUDIES
- ADVERTISING
- AFRICAN AMERICAN STUDIES
- POLITICAL SCIENCE
- LGBT STUDIES

For additional information about this series or for the submission of manuscripts, please contact Dr. Brock (Indiana University Northwest) at brock2@iun.edu or Dr. Johnson (University of Vermont) at richard.johnson-III@uvm.edu.

To order other books in this series, please contact our Customer Service Department:

(800) 770-LANG (within the U.S.)
(212) 647-7706 (outside the U.S.)
(212) 647-7707 FAX

Or browse online by series at www.peterlang.com.